CW00972437

ESRC Innogen Centre
Technology Faculty
Development Policy and Practice
The Open University
Walton Hall
MILTON KEYNES, MK7 6AA

GENETIC PRIVACY

A Challenge to Medico-Legal Norms

The phenomenon of the New Genetics raises complex
lems, particularly those relating to privacy. This book
and legal perspectives on the questions of a right to kn
know genetic information from the standpoint of indi
relatives, employers, insurers and the state.

Graeme Laurie provides a unique definition of priva
a concept of property rights in the person, and argues
legal protection of privacy in the shadow of developi
man genetics. He challenges the role and the limits c
principles in medical law and ethics, including respec
autonomy and confidentiality.

This book will interest lawyers, philosophers and
cerned with both genetic information and issues of priva
be of interest to genetic counsellors, researchers and p
worldwide for its practical stance on dilemmas in mc
medicine.

GRAEME LAURIE is senior lecturer in law at the I
Edinburgh. His research interests include the role of th
moting and protecting science, medicine and technol
co-director of the Arts and Humanities Research Boar
Studies in Intellectual Property and Technology Law – a
as an adviser and rapporteur on genetic databases to the V
Organisation.

GENETIC PRIVACY

A Challenge to Medico-Legal Norms

GRAEME LAURIE

CAMBRIDGE
UNIVERSITY PRESS

PUBLISHED BY THE PRESS SYNDICATE OF THE UNIVERSITY OF CAMBRIDGE
The Pitt Building, Trumpington Street, Cambridge, United Kingdom

CAMBRIDGE UNIVERSITY PRESS
The Edinburgh Building, Cambridge CB2 2RU, UK
40 West 20th Street, New York, NY 10011-4211, USA
477 Williamstown Road, Port Melbourne, VIC 3207, Australia
Ruiz de Alarcón 13, 28014 Madrid, Spain
Dock House, The Waterfront, Cape Town 8001, South Africa

http://www.cambridge.org

First published 2002

Printed in the United Kingdom at the University Press, Cambridge

Typeface Adobe Minion 10.5/14 pt.   *System* LaTeX 2_ε [TB]

A catalogue record for this book is available from the British Library

Library of Congress Cataloguing in Publication data
Laurie, G. T. (Graeme T.)
Genetic privacy : a challenge to medico-legal norms / Graeme Laurie.
p.   cm.
Includes bibliographical references and index.
ISBN 0 521 66027 0 (hardback)
1. Genetic engineering – Law and legislation.   2. Genetic screening – Moral and ethical
aspects.   3. Privacy, Right of.   I. Title.
K3611.G46L38   2002
344'.04196 – dc21   2001052683

ISBN 0 521 66027 0 hardback

To those who know who they are

CONTENTS

PREFACE

This book was written in three institutions, each of which has an international reputation in the field of medical law. These are the universities of Glasgow, Edinburgh and Boston. I am extremely privileged to have worked in all of these with colleagues whose scholarship and enthusiasm for their subject has inspired me greatly in my own work. The focus of much of that work – from my undergraduate days and throughout my professional career – has been the troublesome concept of privacy. I confess to a degree of obsession about my own personal privacy, and a scholarly interest in the subject has always felt like a natural corollary to the rest of my life. But the breadth and depth of privacy analysis is overwhelming, and little headway can be made unless one's attention is focused on a relatively narrow area of debate. It is primarily for this reason that I have written this book about *genetic* privacy.

Advances in genetics pose some of the most intractable problems that medical lawyers and bioethicists have faced since the emergence of their disciplines only a few decades ago. These problems are often hailed as being unique and therefore deserving of special attention. I disagree that they are unique. I do believe, however, that these problems are presented in a more acute form in the realm of genetics, and accordingly this exemplar provides an excellent vehicle to examine broader matters that impact on these disciplines as a whole. What, for example, is the role of privacy in protecting individual and familial interests surrounding genetic information and its uses? How does a privacy analysis fare against a confidentiality model? These concepts are often erroneously treated as being synonymous, leaving much doubt about their respective roles in the health care setting. Elsewhere, the principle of respect for individual autonomy has emerged triumphant from the ethical principles that inform medical law, such that the search for patient consent now seems to be the sole legitimating factor in all dealings with patients. I argue that this is a flawed approach for a number of reasons, not least because it ignores the limitations of consent as a means of respecting and empowering individuals, and because it tends to prefer individualistic interests over crucial public interests, such as the pursuit of genetic and other medical research. Each of these issues is examined in this book from the perspective of an original analysis of the value and function of privacy. This novel conception of privacy is proposed as a necessary adjunct to existing paradigms in the medico-legal sphere, and not as an alternative to them. This places it as a vital element in the broader enterprise of protecting rights of *personality* – an area that has hitherto received short shrift.

The book is divided into three parts. 'Privacy: the general part' considers historical, philosophical and legal treatments of privacy and explains why it is often thought of as a poor cousin in the family of values that lie at the heart of many cultures, and particularly Western cultures. A new definition of privacy is offered that is theoretically sound but also sufficiently robust to be of practical utility. The second part, 'Genetic knowledge: the existing models', examines current responses to genetic advances in light of the interests of the parties who might stake a claim to genetic information or material. These include individuals, their families, employers, insurers, researchers and the state. The relative merits of these claims are considered, as is the utility of an appeal to autonomy and confidentiality to resolve the dilemmas that emerge. These existing norms are found wanting in a number of respects, including their failure to protect the interest in not knowing information about oneself, and the problems they cause for the furtherance of public interests in research. Finally, 'A new privacy paradigm' argues for a greater role for privacy in guiding our ethical and legal responses to these issues. At the same time, the limits of privacy and the law must be recognised. It is acknowledged, for example, that greater legal protection is not always the answer; nor does privacy complete the picture on its own. Rather, privacy forms but one piece in the puzzle, and – as a primer for further debate – the book concludes with a consideration of how this new view of privacy as an aspect of personality should lead us to recognise yet other personality rights, most notably those of property rights in the person.

I have drawn from a number of my publications in writing this book. These are: 'Challenging Medical–legal Norms: The Role of Autonomy, Confidentiality and Privacy in Protecting Individual and Familial Group

Rights in Genetic Information' (2001) 22 *Journal of Legal Medicine* 1;
'Consent or Property? Dealing with the Body and its Parts in the Shadow
of Bristol and Alder Hey' (2001) 64 *Modern Law Review* 710 (with J. K.
Mason); 'Susceptibility Genes and Neurological Disorders: Learning the
Right Lessons from the Human Genome Project' (2000) 57 *Archives of
Neurology* 1569 (with M. A. Grodin); 'Genetics and Patients' Rights:
Where are the Limits?' (2000) 5 *Medical Law International* 25; 'Protect-
ing and Promoting Privacy in an Uncertain World: Further Defences of
Ignorance and the Right Not to Know' (2000) 7 *European Journal of
Health Law* 185; and 'In Defence of Ignorance: Genetic Information and
the Right Not to Know' (1999) 6 *European Journal of Health Law* 119. I
am grateful for permission to reproduce elements of these works here.

So many people have contributed to this book in myriad ways that it
would be impossible to name them all. They know who they are. I only
hope that they also know how appreciative I am of their efforts. Two
people from my professional life do, however, require special mention.
Sheila McLean has supported me throughout my academic existence,
including two degrees. She is the person to whom I am most grateful for
kindling and helping to sustain my enthusiasm for medical law. Kenyon
Mason has inspired me from the day I met him. I am indebted to him
beyond measure for what he has taught me about my discipline and the
true meaning of being a scholar.

For reasons I prefer to keep private, I have attempted to state the law
as at 19 June 2001.

GTL

Old College, Edinburgh
August 2001

TABLE OF CASES

United States

TABLE OF LEGISLATION

Germany

Iceland

Ireland

Israel

Netherlands

United Kingdom

United States

INTERNATIONAL INSTRUMENTS

MISCELLANEOUS DOCUMENTS

United States

Other

1

Health care, patient rights and privacy

Privacy as a problem

Privacy is a problem. Or rather, privacy causes problems. It causes problems for sociologists,[1] psychologists,[2] anthropologists,[3] philosophers,[4]
politicians,[5] doctors,[6] lawyers,[7] governments,[8] states,[9] communities,[10]
groups[11] and individuals.[12] The problems that it causes relate to its
definition,[13] its function,[14] its nature,[15] its utility,[16] its value[17] and its
protection.[18] The sheer extent of the difficulties is revealed by the length
of the first few notes to this text.

---

[1] S. I. Benn and G. F. Gaus (eds.), *Public and Private in Social Life* (London, Croom Helm;
New York, St. Martin's Press, 1983).

[2] See E. Goffman, *The Presentation of Self in Everyday Life* (London, Pelican Books, 1971),
R. Ingham, 'Privacy and Psychology', in Y. D. Young (ed.), *Privacy* (Chichester, Wiley &
Sons, 1979), ch. 2, S. M. Jouard, 'Some Psychological Aspects of Privacy' (1966) 31 *Law
and Contemporary Problems* 307, P. A. Kelvin, 'Social Psychological Examination of Privacy'
(1973) 12 *British Journal of Social and Clinical Psychology* 248, S. T. Margulis (ed.), 'Privacy
as a Behavioural Phenomenon' (1977) 33 *Journal of Social Issues*, Issue No. 3.

[3] See B. Moore, *Privacy: Studies in Social and Cultural History* (New York, M. E. Sharpe Inc.,
1984), R. F. Murphy, 'Social Distance and the Veil' (1964) 6(1) *American Anthropologist*
1257, and A. Westin, 'The Origins of Modern Claims to Privacy', in F. D. Schoeman (ed.),
Philosophical Dimensions of Privacy (Cambridge, Cambridge University Press, 1984), at
56–74, H. Arendt, *The Human Condition* (Chicago, University of Chicago Press, 1958).

[4] J. Kupfer, 'Privacy, Autonomy and Self Concept' (1987) 24 *American Philosophical Quarterly*
81, G. Negley, 'Philosophical Views on the Value of Privacy' (1966) 31 *Law and Contemporary
Problems* 319, J. H. Reiman, 'Privacy, Intimacy and Personhood' (1976) 6 *Philosophy and Public
Affairs* 26, and generally, F. Schoeman (ed.), *Philosophical Dimensions of Privacy: An Anthology*
(Cambridge, Cambridge University Press, 1984).

[5] See J. Ames, 'Privacy Law Forced Back on the Agenda' (1992) 89(6) *Law Society's Gazette* 8.

[6] K. Berg, 'Confidentiality Issues in Medical Genetics: The Need for Laws, Rules and Good
Practices to Secure Optimal Disease Control', Second Symposium of the Council of Europe
on Bioethics, Strasbourg, 30 November–2 December 1993, CDBI-SY-SP (93) 3, D. C. Wertz
and J. C. Fletcher, 'Privacy and Disclosure in Medical Genetics Examined in an Ethics of Care'
(1991) 5 *Bioethics* 212, G. Dworkin, 'Access to Medical Records: Discovery, Confidentiality
and Privacy' (1979) 42 *Modern Law Review* 88, and T. Cantrell, 'Privacy: The Medical
Problems', in Young, *Privacy*, ch. 9.

[7] For example, G. Dworkin, 'Privacy and the Law', in Young, *Privacy*, ch. 5, R. Gavison,
'Privacy and the Limits of the Law' (1980) 89 *Yale Law Review* 421, B. S. Markesinis, 'Our
Patchy Law of Privacy – Time to do Something about it' (1990) 53 *Modern Law Review* 802,

One might wonder, as a result, what another text on privacy could meaningfully contribute to the debate. A first step to answering this question is to realise that the scope of privacy is so wide-ranging that no reasonable attempt can be made to analyse the concept in all of its facets and guises. This book examines the role of privacy in a health care setting. It considers patient privacy and the interface between medicine and law in the protection of individual rights as regards the provision of health care. In particular, the contribution of this work to the general debate about privacy lies in an examination of the privacy issues raised by what has been termed the New Genetics.

W. A. Parent, 'A New Definition for Privacy for the Law' (1983) 2 *Law and Philosophy* 305, W. L. Prosser, 'Privacy: A Legal Analysis' (1960) 48 *California Law Review* 338, R. Wacks, *Personal Information, Privacy and the Law* (Oxford, Clarendon Press, 1989), and S. D. Warren and L. D. Brandeis, 'The Right to Privacy' (1890–91) 4 *Harvard Law Review* 193.

[8] See R. F. Hixson, *Privacy in a Public Society* (New York, Oxford University Press, 1987), J. P. Gould, 'Privacy and the Economics of Information' (1980) 9 *Journal of Legal Studies* 827, C. Mellors, 'Governments and the Individual: Their Secrecy and His Privacy', in Young, *Privacy*, p. 87, J. F. Handler and M. K. Rosenheim, 'Privacy in Welfare: Public Assistance and Juvenile Justice' (1966) 31 *Law and Contemporary Problems* 377, and W. A. Creech, 'The Privacy of Government Employees' (1966) 31 *Law and Contemporary Problems* 413.

[9] See, for example, Article 8 of the European Convention for the Protection of Human Rights and Article 12 of the Universal Declaration of Human Rights, both of which provide for the protection of personal privacy. For comment on the former see L. G. Loucaides, 'Personality and Privacy Under the European Convention on Human Rights' (1990) 61 *British Yearbook of International Law* 175.

[10] As Westin has commented, 'Needs for individual and group privacy and resulting social norms are present in virtually every society. Encompassing a vast range of activities, these needs affect basic areas of life for the individual, the intimate family group, and the community as a whole', A. Westin, *Privacy and Freedom* (London, Bodley Head, 1967), p. 13.

[11] F. D. Schoeman, 'Adolescent Confidentiality and Family Privacy', in G. Graham and H. LaFollette (eds.), *Person to Person* (Philadelphia, Temple University Press, 1989), pp. 213–34, I. N. Walden and R. N. Savage, 'Data Protection and Privacy Laws: Should Organisations Be Protected?' (1988) 37 *International and Comparative Law Quarterly* 337.

[12] L. Blom-Cooper, 'The Right to be Let Alone' (1989) 10 *Journal of Media Law and Practice* 53, J. Kupfer, 'Privacy, Autonomy and Self Concept' (1987) 24 *American Philosophical Quarterly* 81, S. I. Benn, 'Privacy, Freedom and Respect for Persons', in Schoeman, *Philosophical Dimensions of Privacy*, Gavison, 'Privacy and the Limits of Law', H. Gross, 'Privacy and Autonomy', in J. Feinberg and H. Gross, *Philosophy of Law* (2nd edn, Wadsworth Inc., USA, 1980), L. Henkin, 'Privacy and Autonomy' (1974) 74 *Columbia Law Review* 1410, C. Fried, 'Privacy' (1968) 77 *Yale Law Journal* 475.

[13] W. A. Parent, 'A New Definition for Privacy for the Law' (1983) 2 *Law and Philosophy* 305, W. A. Parent, 'Recent Work on the Concept of Privacy' (1993) 20 *American Philosophical Quarterly* 341, Gavison, 'Privacy and the Limits of Law', R. A. Posner, 'The Right to Privacy' (1978) 12 *Georgia Law Review* 393, D. N. McCormick, 'Privacy: A Problem of Definition' (1974) 1 *British Journal of Law and Society* 75, Fried, 'Privacy'.

[14] J. C. Innes, *Privacy, Intimacy and Isolation* (New York, Oxford University Press, 1992), S. I. Benn, 'Privacy, Freedom and Respect for Persons', in Schoeman, *Philosophical Dimensions of Privacy*, Gavison, 'Privacy and the Limits of Law', Fried, 'Privacy', and Murphy, 'Social Distance and the Veil'.

The advent of modern genetic science and genetic testing has given rise to acute problems in the health care context, some real and others imaginary. For example, the discovery of a predisposition to a genetic condition in one individual often also reveals potential risks to the blood relatives of that individual. Thus, individual genetic information can unlock many secrets within the wider genetic family. There is, therefore, potential for conflict over access to, and control of, such information. Traditionally, the duty of confidentiality owed by a health care professional to a patient has provided an appropriate means by which personal health information has been kept secure. There are serious doubts, however, whether the issues that surround genetic information in the familial milieu can be adequately dealt with within the envelope of confidentiality. This is an amorphous and ill-defined duty that is compromised by its twin roles of protecting both the confidential relationship and the confidential information which arises from that relationship. Moreover, to the extent that the duty of confidentiality is solely concerned with keeping confidential information out of the public sphere, it says nothing about the duties that might be owed within the confidential relationship towards the subjects of the information so as to ensure, inter alia, that the personal interests of these individuals are not treated with a lack of respect by unwarranted uses of information with regard to the subjects themselves.

[15] Much debate centres on the philosophical nature of privacy. Is it a right, a claim, an interest, an issue of control or a state of being? For a discussion of the possibilities and a review of the literature, see Schoeman, *Philosophical Dimensions of Privacy: An Anthology*, ch. 1.

[16] J. H. Reiman, 'Privacy, Intimacy and Personhood' (1976) 6 *Philosophy and Public Affairs* 26, J. Rachels, 'Why Privacy Is Important' (1975) 4 *Philosophy and Public Affairs* 323, J. J. Thomson, 'The Right to Privacy' (1975) 4 *Philosophy and Public Affairs* 295, T. Scanlon, 'Thomson on Privacy' (1975) 4 *Philosophy and Public Affairs* 315.

[17] Wacks, *Personal Information, Privacy and the Law*, Hixson, *Privacy in a Public Society*, Thomson, 'The Right to Privacy', Scanlon, 'Thomson on Privacy', and Negley, 'Philosophical Views on the Value of Privacy'.

[18] Historically, this issue has given rise to much concern, but little productive action, in the United Kingdom. In the latter part of the twentieth century numerous attempts were made to pass some form of legislation to protect privacy. None succeeded. Several committees were established to examine the matter and report, such as the Younger Committee, Report of the Committee on Privacy, Cmnd 5012 (1972), and the Calcutt Committee, Report of the Committee on Privacy and Related Matters, Cm 1102 (1990), and in 1993 Calcutt re-examined the question of privacy legislation and recommended Parliamentary intervention (Review of Press Regulation, Cm 2135 (1993)). No direct legal protection resulted. It was not until the passing of the Data Protection Act 1998 in March 2000 and the Human Rights Act 1998 in October 2000 that anything approximating proper recognition and protection of privacy in the United Kingdom was realised.

The principle of respect for patient autonomy – which has been described as the guiding ethical principle in health care and which has received unprecedented recognition by the laws of most Western states – is similarly ill-equipped to provide a comprehensive solution to the problems posed by familial genetic information. This is because the focus of an autonomy-based argument is largely on the individual and her ability to control aspects of her life. The 'group' nature of claims concerning family information poses a serious conceptual threat to this paradigm. Moreover, health care professionals frequently confuse the desire to respect autonomous patient choices with a desire to facilitate those choices and, as a result, patients are often placed in the invidious position of having to make choices that they might otherwise have avoided.

This book examines these, and other, problems and argues for the value of an appeal to privacy in seeking to resolve some of the more intractable issues. A unique definition of privacy is offered by which to address these dilemmas. The construct is also intended to enrich the discourse on the role and the limits of established principles in medical law and ethics, such as respect for patient autonomy and confidentiality. The work advocates a greater role for privacy in the health care setting; more specifically, it examines the need for stronger legal protection of privacy in the shadow of new challenges arising from advances in human genetics.

Establishing parameters

The quest for the essential character of the concept of privacy centres on the search for a means to establish an identifiable and sustainable interface between the public and private spheres of human life.[19] Furthermore, because human lives are not passed in a social vacuum, privacy is also concerned with the regulation of the relationship between an individual and the society in which she lives.[20] Indeed, the two concepts of individual and society are inextricably linked – the definition of one provides, almost by analogy, the definition of the other. For example, Giddens defines *society* as 'a cluster, or system, of institutionalised modes of conduct. To speak of "institutionalised" forms of social conduct is to refer to modes of belief and behaviour that occur and recur – or, as

---

[19] See generally Benn and Gaus, *Public and Private in Social Life.*
[20] See Wacks, *Personal Information, Privacy and the Law,* p. 7, and J. P. Tomlinson, 'Privacy and Law Enforcement', in Young, *Privacy,* ch. 6.

the terminology of modern social theory would have it, are socially *reproduced* – across long spans of time and space.'[21] Yet, as he states, 'societies only exist in so far as they are created and re-created in our actions as human beings. In social theory we cannot treat human activities as though they were determined by causes in the same way as natural events are. We have to grasp what I would call the *double involvement* of individuals and institutions: we create society as we are created by it.'[22]

For the purposes of this book, privacy will be treated in the context of the relationship between the individual and Western liberal society, with its central tenets of democracy and commitment to individualism, and its concern for personal privacy. A specific context for privacy has to be supplied, because as a purely abstract concept it can only be defined meaningfully in terms of the cultural norms of a particular society and the position of the individual within that society. As Benn has stated, 'The judgements we make about our privacy arrangements must take the rest of our cultural ideals largely as we find them. Individuals like ourselves in our kind of culture, then, do have an interest in privacy in the management of the internal economy of their own personalities and of their personal relations with others.'[23]

In a developed, technologically advanced society information can be disseminated with great rapidity. People share their lives not only with family and friends but also with many other persons who live or work in the same places, who frequent the same establishments or who communicate over the internet. Strangers become pseudo-intimates, and vast tracts of a person's life can be shared with people for whom she may feel very little, yet about whom she may know a great deal. But because individuals often do not choose these pseudo-intimates, and because they cannot necessarily control the flow of information about themselves between such persons and others, they can experience an increasing sense of loss in relation to a side of their lives that has come to epitomise the private sphere, namely, the realm of personal information.[24] At the same time, the physical division between the workplace and the

---

[21] A. Giddens, *Sociology: A Brief But Critical Introduction*, 2nd edn (London, Macmillan, 1986), p. 8. Social systems he defines as: '[involving] patterns of relationships among individuals and groups', p. 12.

[22] *Ibid.*, p. 11.

[23] S. I. Benn, *A Theory of Freedom* (Cambridge University Press, New York, 1988), p. 287.

[24] See A. Charlesworth, 'Data Privacy in Cyberspace: Not National vs. International but Commercial vs. Individual', in L. Edwards and C. Waelde (eds.), *Law and the Internet: A Framework for Electronic Commerce* (Oxford, Hart Publishing, 2000), pp. 79–122.

home has led to a greater separation between the two environments in people's minds,[25] with an increased reluctance to allow one to encroach on the other. Indeed, Prost has documented the spread of privacy concerns through all strata of society in the twentieth century. As he says, 'the twentieth century may be seen as a period during which the differentiation of public and private, at first limited to the bourgeoisie, slowly spread throughout the population. Thus, in one sense the history of private life is a history of democratization.'[26]

Privacy: a definition

The notions of privacy considered above embody two conceptions of privacy. First, it can be viewed as a state of non-access to the individual's physical or psychological self – what can be called *spatial privacy*. Second, privacy can be seen as a state in which personal information about an individual is in a state of non-access from others – *informational privacy*.[27] One unifying definition can be deduced from these two concepts: privacy is a state of separateness from others. This is the definition of privacy that is adopted in this book and the reasons for this choice will be more fully considered and justified in chapter 2. For the moment, privacy should be taken to refer to a state in which an individual is apart from others, either in a bodily or psychological sense or by reference to the inaccessibility of certain intimate adjuncts to their individuality, such as personal information.

Why protect privacy?

Private interests

It has been posited that a need for individual privacy arose in tandem with the evolution of Western liberal democracy. It has also been suggested that the privacy interests of individuals are of two distinct kinds.

---

[25] See A. Prost, 'Public and Private Spheres in France', in A. Prost and G. Vincent (eds.), *A History of Private Life* (London, Belknap Press, 1991), V, pp. 9–49.

[26] A. Prost, 'Introduction', in Prost and Vincent, *A History of Private Life*, p. 7.

[27] This view of privacy corresponds largely with a layman's view of the concept. The Younger Committee on privacy found that the responses of individuals to questions in a commissioned survey about what constituted invasions of privacy tended to place the notion of privacy into one or both of two groups: freedom from intrusion or privacy of information, see Younger Committee, *Report of the Committee on Privacy*, Cmnd 5012 (1972), p. 32.

What has not been explained is why individuals need privacy. Several arguments can be made.

First, a state of physical separateness from others is necessary in order to allow personal relationships to begin and to grow. The levels of intimacy that typify the modern personal relationship can only be achieved by ensuring and securing separateness from others. Trust – which is essential to the establishment and maintenance of all relationships – requires not only a degree of intimacy to develop but also a currency in which to deal. An important part of that currency is personal information. Individuals trade private information both as a sign of trust and on the basis of trust. The security of the information is guaranteed by the tacit undertaking that it will not be noised abroad. In this way personal and professional relationships flourish and an important part of the fabric of society is woven more tightly.[28] As Fried has said,

> Love and friendship ... involve the initial respect for the rights of others which morality requires of everyone. They further involve the voluntary and spontaneous relinquishment of something between friend and friend, lover and lover. The title to information about oneself conferred by privacy provides the necessary something. To be friends or lovers persons must be intimate to some degree with each other. Intimacy is the sharing of information about one's actions, beliefs, or emotions which one does not share with all, and which one has the right not to share with anyone.[29]

Second, a degree of separateness allows the individual personality to reflect on experiences and to learn from them. Constant company requires unceasing interaction and this in turn deprives the individual of time to assimilate life experiences and to identify her own individuality.[30]

Third, it has been said that the modern psychological make-up of individuals is such that a degree of separateness is required to ensure that individuals retain a degree of mental stability. Jouard has put a forceful argument that (Western) public life puts considerable strain on individuals, who must assume personae in order to integrate successfully with others.[31] These personae, being designed to conceal the true

---

[28] See Fried, 'Privacy'.
[29] C. Fried, *An Anatomy of Values: Problems of Personal and Social Choice* (Cambridge, MA, Harvard University Press, 1970), p. 142.
[30] M. Van Manen and B. Levering, *Childhood's Secrets: Intimacy, Privacy and the Self Reconsidered* (Williston, VT, Teachers College Press, 1996).
[31] Jouard, 'Some Psychological Aspects of Privacy', and see generally n. 2 above.

personality of the individual, cannot be maintained indefinitely without serious psychological consequences. A state of privacy allows the masks to be dropped and a degree of release to be obtained.

Fourth, tangible harm can come to an individual who is not granted a degree of privacy. Concerning spatial privacy, unauthorised invasion of the body is disrespectful of the individual and may cause physical harm. The criminal and civil laws of assault recognise and protect the inviolability of the physical self in this regard. Perhaps less obvious but no less valid, however, is the psychological harm that can arise if spatial privacy is not respected. For example, clandestine observation can produce profound feelings of violation in individuals even when no actual physical contact occurs.[32] Similarly, even within a paradigm of the private sphere such as the family home, an individual's psychological spatial privacy can be invaded if she is subjected to imposed stimuli, such as another family member's choice of music. Considerable mental anguish can occur as a result.[33]

Beyond spatial privacy concerns, the invasion of one's *informational* privacy can also lead to harm to individuals. Information about one's personal condition, behaviour or habits that others find distasteful can lead to individuals being ostracised by communities or becoming the object of violence and discrimination. As Greenawalt puts it, 'One reason why information control seems so important is precisely because society is as intolerant as it is, precisely because there are so many kinds of activity that are subject to overt government regulation or to the informal sanctions of loss of job or reputation.'[34]

Public interests

One final argument in support of protection of privacy can be offered. The above points concentrate on individual private interests. But there are also public interests in privacy protection. It can be argued, for example, that it is in the public (societal) interest to have a community inhabited by rounded individuals as opposed to two-dimensional

---

[32] See Benn, 'Privacy, Freedom and Respect for Persons', 230–1, and this is equally true when no personal information is gathered.

[33] C. M. Gurney, 'Transgressing Private–Public Boundaries in the Home: A Sociological Analysis of the Coital Noise Taboo' (2000) 13 *Venereology – The Interdisciplinary International Journal of Sexual Health* 39.

[34] K. Greenawalt, 'Privacy and its Legal Protections' (1974) 2 *Hastings Center Studies* 45, 53.

characters.[35] Similarly, it is clearly in the interests of a society which holds the individual in esteem to reduce all potential harm to individuals to a minimum.

Paradoxically, however, it is the development of a public interest in the welfare of individuals that has proved to be one of the greatest threats to individual privacy in the last century. This might be termed the phenomenon of the interventionist state, and it is a trend that has emerged as a central tenet of the Western liberal tradition. It is born out of democratic developments in the twentieth century that heralded an expanding role for the state and a marked increase in the interest which states show in the lives of their citizens. For example, most Western states have assumed a degree of responsibility for the provision of basic services such as housing and utilities, subsistence benefits, education and child welfare. The provision of health care is of primary importance among these; indeed, with the notable exception of the United States, a national health service is a key feature of many Western democracies. On another level, Western societies are typified by a glut of legislation stemming from paternalistic attitudes of the state towards its citizens. Thus, we find legislation prohibiting or severely restricting sales of alcohol and other drugs, limiting the purchase of lottery tickets, and requiring the wearing of seat belts or safety helmets when using motor vehicles. Such legislation comes in a variety of forms ranging from prohibition with the threat of criminal sanction, through civil liability, to the use of fiscal means to control citizens' behaviour. Strömholm explains this in part when he writes:

> prevailing democratic ideologies stress the need for continuous debate on matters of public interest ... the complexity of modern society and the subtle interwovenness of facts and interests within its framework have led to the feeling that almost everything concerns everyone in one sense or another. Thus, any unimportant event may touch upon matters in which the public may claim a legitimate interest.[36]

[35] Benn notes that 'the children of the kibbutz have been found by some observers defective as persons, precisely because their emotional stability has been purchased at the cost of an incapacity to establish deep personal relations. Perhaps we have to choose between the sensitive, human understanding that we achieve only by the cultivation of our relations within a confined circle and the extrovert assurance and adjustment that a *Gemeinschaft* can offer. However this may be, to the extent that we value the former, we shall be committed to valuing the right of privacy', in 'Privacy, Freedom and Respect for Persons', p. 237.
[36] S. Strömholm, *Rights of Privacy and Rights of the Personality: A Comparative Study* (P. A. Norstedt and Söners Forlag, Stockholm, 1967), p. 17.

Hence, while individual interests are given more importance in democratic communities, public interests are, at the same time, afforded greater weight. This increases tension at the interface between the public and private areas of life and requires that we define as clearly as possible where the boundaries of the two spheres lie. It is a function of privacy to provide a mechanism to ensure that such boundaries are well constituted. Privacy also forces recognition of the fact that at times certain areas of life can, and should, be kept separate. As Schoeman states, 'respect for privacy signifies our recognition that not all dimensions of persons or relationships need to serve some independently valid social purpose'.[37]

Finally, it should not be overlooked that harm can come to society itself if privacy is not respected. Important and valuable information will not be communicated if the element of trust that is so crucial to the development of relationships is lost because individuals cannot be guaranteed security of information. This can render important social organs impotent. An apposite example of this can be seen in the medical confidentiality decision of *X* v. *Y*.[38] A newspaper gained access to the medical files of two doctors suffering from AIDS who were continuing to work in general practice. The newspaper sought to disclose this information and argued that it was justified in doing so because the public had a right to know the facts. The court, however, rejected this argument and, in issuing an injunction, held that there was an overriding public interest in respecting the confidences of people such as the two doctors. Rose J summed up his reasoning as follows: 'In the long run, preservation of confidentiality is the only way of securing public health; otherwise doctors will be discredited as a source of information, for future patients "will not come forward if doctors are going to squeal on them".'[39] Similarly, in *Jaffee* v. *Redmond*[40] the US Supreme Court opined that the public good would be best served by protecting the confidentiality of mental health records and so preserving the special relationship of trust between psychotherapist and patient.

As these sentiments indicate, just as there are public and private reasons to protect privacy, the effective protection of privacy can serve both public and private ends.

---

[37] See F. D. Schoeman, 'Privacy and Intimate Information', in Schoeman, *Philosophical Dimensions of Privacy*, ch. 17, p. 413.
[38] *X* v. *Y* [1988] 2 All ER 648.   [39] *Ibid.*, at 653.
[40] *Jaffee* v. *Redmond* 518 US 1; 116 S. Ct. 1923 (1996).

Privacy in context: the health care setting

Because there is a differing role for privacy in very many areas of life, it is necessary, in order to carry out a worthwhile study of it, to focus on a single area, that is, a single aspect of the relationship between the individual and society.

The need to choose a context at all is dictated by the nature of the concept of privacy. Privacy is exceptionally difficult to define. An extremely wide variety of definitions can be offered, some of which conflict and some of which are antithetical. Yet almost all are plausible and defensible on some level.[41] This book is not intended as a philosophical discussion of this range of possible meanings, nor is its aim to provide a definitive account of privacy. Rather, it offers a particular concept of privacy that will help us to understand the kinds of interests that are at stake in the health care context and to appreciate the role that the law might have in recognising and protecting such interests. To achieve this, we require a particular setting, the limits of which are relatively certain and within which the function of privacy is relatively clear.

Health promotion and the cult of the body

The reasons for choosing the health care setting as a context for this discussion of privacy mirror to a large extent the reasons for setting this entire work within the broad context of the Western liberal tradition. The rise of Western liberal democracy has spawned a very egocentric society and, for the majority, one's private life takes precedence over social or community matters. In particular, Prost has argued that 'There is no more telling sign of the primacy of individual life than the modern cult of the body.'[42]

This is a reference to the near-obsessional interest displayed by many individuals in the Western world concerning personal appearance and body management. Prost cites increases in concern with personal hygiene, physical fitness and healthy eating as evidence of the development of such a cult.[43] The consequence of all of this, he notes, is that the body

---

[41] This will be discussed further in ch. 2.
[42] A. Prost, 'The Family and the Individual', in Prost and Vincent, *The History of Private Life*, p. 93.
[43] *Ibid.*, pp. 87–101.

has become the focal point of personal identity: 'To be ashamed of one's body is to be ashamed of oneself.'[44]

Increased interest in the body leads to increased concern with threats to the body. Arguably, the most consistent and persistent of threats is illness. Not surprisingly, therefore, concerns about ill health have escalated in recent times,[45] to such an extent that the promotion of health and wellbeing has become of paramount importance. Of course, the health of individuals is of importance to all societies, but it is with unwavering conviction that Western states place the pursuit of health as primary among the prerequisites of a good life. Further, health has come to mean, not just the absence of illness, but the attainment of a state of wellbeing that includes an entire range of desirable features and characteristics, including physical fitness, attractiveness to others, correctness of proportions and psychological stability.[46] Technological advances have allowed the boundaries of medicine to be pushed ever further forward, making the treatment of actual ill health but one option in a range of possible options offered to patients. As more can be done for the health of the populace, so more interest is taken by the populace in its health.[47]

Body, self and privacy

Not only is the body seen to house the self and be governed by it, it is a tangible and real manifestation of the abstract that we call the self. Body and self are inextricably linked, and often the two are perceived as being one and the same. Protection of the body therefore becomes synonymous with protection of the self. Individuals can experience feelings of deep violation of their inner self when the body is under threat from disease or illness, and there is a corresponding sense of profound invasion of a sphere of their lives over which they thought they had exclusive control. As the Danish Council of Ethics has put it,

---

[44] *Ibid.*, p. 93.   [45] *Ibid.*, pp. 95–8.

[46] The World Health Organisation (WHO) defined 'health' in its Constitution of 1946 as a 'state of complete physical, mental and social well-being, and not merely the absence of disease or infirmity', World Health Organisation, *Constitution* (New York, WHO, 1946).

[47] The habit of turning to medicine for the promotion of health has been called the 'medicalisation of health' and it is not always perceived as appropriate or desirable, see, for example, R. S. Downie, C. Fyfe, and A. Tannahill, *Health Promotion: Models and Values* (Oxford, Oxford University Press, 1990), p. 1.

Disease – especially severe disease – is a personal matter in the sense that it concerns fundamental aspects of a human being's person: the potentiality for physical development, pain, suffering and, ultimately, death. A person's outlook on his own disease is therefore a decisive part of his relationship with himself. To a very great degree, this relationship is instrumental in determining an individual's personal sphere, that part of life which a person is entitled to keep to himself.[48]

Moreover, the process of subjecting themselves to health care may exacerbate any feelings of violation or invasion that have already been experienced. Intimate aspects of the self often have to be revealed to health care professionals (HCP). Thus, the body must be exposed to detailed examination, personal details must be disclosed, family histories must be recounted, and humiliating procedures must be braved. The end result of all of this may or may not be an improvement in health and the ultimate goal of health care may or may not be achieved. But, in the process, the individual has revealed her inner self to others, has given away personal information and knowledge, and has been exposed to incursions on her body. This is not to say that health care is necessarily a threat to the individual's private life, but it does highlight how the two are intimately connected and also how the health care system is itself a potential conduit for serious invasions of privacy.

Threats to patient privacy in the health care setting

There are many ways in which the provision of modern health care and the machine of modern medicine can invade privacy. The use of wards to care for patients provides an example. A system that places patients together in the same room with no separation between them save a flimsy curtain affords easy access to their persons, yet some of the most personal moments of one's life are experienced in hospitals. Conversations about diagnosis, prognosis and treatment can be overheard, notes are left at the end of patients' beds where they can easily be read, and generally, the practice of everyday medicine is conducted before an audience consisting not only of other patients, but also of their families and friends and other visitors to the institution. The position is not much

---

[48] See Danish Council of Ethics, *Ethics and Mapping the Human Genome* (Copenhagen, Notex, 1993), p. 52.

improved when patients have private rooms. Access to their person and information about their condition is freely available to a range of hospital staff, both clinical and ancillary. Doctors, nurses, auxiliaries, support staff, cleaners and administrators can all gain such access.[49] Even unauthorised visitors can easily breach the security of hospitals to invade the privacy of patients. One of the most celebrated privacy cases to be heard in the UK courts involved just such a scenario.

In *Kaye v. Robertson*[50] a British television actor, Gorden Kaye, had been seriously injured during the winter storms of 1990 and underwent brain surgery at Charing Cross Hospital in London. While he was recovering in a private room, two reporters from a tabloid newspaper gained access to the room, carried out an interview and took some photographs intended for publication. Kaye, however, had no recollection of the interview minutes after it had taken place and, in any event, was in no state to give valid consent to its use. Yet he was, in effect, unsuccessful in obtaining a remedy to prevent publication. In the absence of specific legal protection of privacy in the United Kingdom, Kaye relied on four different existing forms of action – libel, malicious falsehood, trespass to the person and passing off. Only malicious falsehood was considered to be of any relevance, but no damages were awarded and the injunction that was granted was limited to a prohibition on publishing anything which 'could be reasonably understood or convey to any person reading or looking at the Defendant's *Sunday Sport* newspaper that the Plaintiff had voluntarily permitted any photographs to be taken for publication in that newspaper or had voluntarily permitted representatives of the Defendants to interview him while a patient in the Charing Cross Hospital undergoing treatment'.[51] In other words, Kaye could not prevent publication of the story or photograph, merely publication of his consent. In his judgment Leggatt LJ made the following comments: '[the] right [of privacy] has so long been disregarded here that it can be recognised now only by the legislature... it is to be hoped that the making good of this signal shortcoming in our law will not be long delayed'.[52]

This case more than any other highlights the historically woeful inadequacy of English law in relation to the legal protection of personal

[49] N. Okino Sawada *et al.*, 'Personal and Territorial Space of the Patients: A Nursing Ethics Question' (1996) 15 *Medicine and Law* 261.
[50] *Kaye v. Robertson* [1991] FSR 62.   [51] *Ibid.*, at 66.   [52] *Ibid.*, at 71.

privacy, and no better protection has been accorded by the Scottish courts. It is significant that the circumstances which gave rise to this case took place in a health care setting. As Bingham LJ said, 'If ever a person has a right to be let alone by strangers with no public interest to pursue it must surely be when he lies in hospital recovering from brain surgery and in no more than partial command of his faculties.'[53]

The vulnerable position in which persons find themselves in the health care context makes all the more pressing the need for adequate and effective protection of their interests, including those of privacy. Moreover, the Kaye case provides a good example of how the privacy interests that patients have in the health care setting are of two distinct, yet related, kinds – both informational privacy and spatial privacy are at stake. The invasion of Gorden Kaye's privacy occurred at two levels: the invasion of personal space by uninvited parties and the invasion of his privacy interests in personal information by the publication of photographs of him and details about his condition. The plaintiff's failure to secure adequate legal protection of either of these interests is lamentable. And, while very recent judicial and legislative initiatives have now created express privacy protection in the United Kingdom,[54] the absence of a tradition of such protection will have ramifications for a significant time to come.[55]

More sensitivity to the vulnerable state of patients has been shown in the United States. In *Berthiaume* v. *Pratt* it was held to be a violation of a moribund patient's right to privacy when clinical staff took photographs of him without his consent.[56] In *Noble* v. *Sears, Roebuck & Co.*[57] the plaintiff was successful in convincing the court that she had 'an exclusive right of occupancy of her hospital room', at least as against an investigator who gained unauthorised access in order to obtain information pertaining to the plaintiff's suit against the defendant. Such

---

[53] *Ibid.*, at 70. In like manner, in *Barber* v. *Time*, 348 Mo. 1199; 159 S. W. 2d 291 (1942) the Supreme Court of Missouri confirmed that 'Certainly if there is any right of privacy at all, it should include the right to obtain medical treatment at home or in a hospital for an individual personal condition (at least if it is not contagious or dangerous to others) without personal publicity', at 1207; 295.

[54] A common law right of privacy was eventually recognised in 2000 by the Court of Appeal in *Douglas and Others* v. *Hello! Ltd.* [2001] 2 All ER 289. Moreover, in the course of the same year the Data Protection Act 1998 and the Human Rights Act 1998 came into force. These developments are discussed in ch. 5.

[55] See further ch. 5.   [56] *Berthiaume* v. *Pratt* 365 A 2d 792 (Me., 1976).

[57] *Noble* v. *Sears, Roebuck & Co.*, 33 Cal. App. 3d 654 109 Cal. Rptr. 269 (1973).

an unreasonably intrusive investigation was directly actionable as an invasion of privacy. Similarly, in *Shulman* v. *Group W. Productions Inc.*[58] the California Supreme Court upheld as triable the plaintiff's argument that she was entitled to a degree of privacy during the rescue of her and her son from the scene of a car accident. While the plaintiff could not legitimately expect to be free from intrusion by the media at the scene of the accident itself, she was entitled to a higher degree of protection once in the air ambulance, for this was clearly a zone of intimacy where her suffering and conversations could reasonably be considered as private. This can easily be seen as protection of a spatial privacy interest. However, the court was not willing to hold that the filming of the rescue and its subsequent broadcast on television was an actionable cause on the basis of publication of private facts (an informational privacy interest). In this regard the court was bound to balance the plaintiff's privacy interests with the strong public interest in press freedom and the publication of matters of legitimate public concern. After weighing the various arguments, the court found that the broadcast of the disputed material was 'newsworthy as a matter of law'.[59] Thus, while strong public interests might well support protection of privacy as has been argued above, so too can those interests be challenged by competing public interests of equal or greater weight. We shall return to this dilemma presently.

Privacy, state interest and health care provision

We have seen that one sign of a democratic system is the extent to which the state takes an interest in the lives of individuals, and it is clear that one of the primary ways in which this occurs is in relation to health care. As Prost comments, 'sickness, a central concern of private life, has become the focus of much public policy. Nothing is as private as health, yet nothing is so readily made the responsibility of the public authorities. Health is now a public as well as private affair.'[60]

The interest of the state in health matters has consequences for patient privacy in at least two ways. First, in those countries that provide state-run health care, the public nature of the enterprise takes away

---

[58] *Shulman* v. *Group W. Productions Inc.*, 18 Cal. 4th 200; 955 P. 2d 469 (1998).
[59] *Ibid.*, at 228; 488.   [60] Prost, 'The Family and the Individual', p. 98.

from the individual patient control of the environment. While such a system might facilitate the chances of every individual of gaining access to medical care, it does little to address concerns for individual privacy that flow from this. Second, states take it upon themselves to intervene in the lives of individuals in circumstances where interference is thought to be justified on public health grounds (usually invoking a best interests argument) or when the individual is perceived as a threat to the health of the community at large (usually invoking a public interest argument).[61]

Notifiable diseases

Consider the concept of notifiable disease as an example of state intervention on health grounds. All states pass legislation requiring the notification of cases of specified infectious and contagious diseases to public authorities,[62] it being argued that the threat to privacy that notification poses is justified by the (greater) threat of the spread of disease in the wider community. In many cases this is undoubtedly true. However, the choice of the diseases that are deemed to be notifiable is sometimes open to question. In some states AIDS has been made a notifiable disease.[63] Yet AIDS – or rather its causative virus HIV – cannot be transmitted by casual contact. Individuals must engage in high risk behaviour before transmission is possible.[64] In fact, this disease has been labelled by American clinicians as 'the least infectious disease we have

---

[61] See, for example, the US Supreme Court decision in *Jacobson* v. *Massachusetts,* 197 US 11 (1905), at 24–30 in which it was held that the court could balance the interests of the individual in refusing smallpox vaccine (protected under the Constitution) against the state's interest in preventing disease. The conclusion of the court was that the state interest was sufficiently compelling not to render unconstitutional a law requiring compulsory vaccination against smallpox save in circumstances where the individual could show significant disadvantage or threat to life.

[62] For a critical account of disease control legislation in England, Germany, the Netherlands, Sweden and Switzerland, see J. Dute, 'Affected By The Tooth of Time: Legislation on Infectious Diseases Control in Five European Countries' (1993) 12 *Medicine and Law* 101.

[63] For comment on this issue and various other legislative responses to HIV/AIDS, see J. Keown, 'AIDS: Should It Be Made a Notifiable Disease?' (1989) July/August *Professional Negligence* 121, and M. D. Kirby, 'AIDS Legislation – Turning Up the Heat?' (1986) 12 *Journal of Medical Ethics* 187. Places where AIDS is notifiable include Denmark, Norway, Sweden and most US states. Neither HIV nor AIDS is notifiable in the United Kingdom.

[64] There are only three methods of transmission of HIV, which were identified in 1982. They are: unprotected anal or vaginal sex, the mixing of infected bodily fluids with the bloodstream of another person, and the infection by a mother of her unborn child. No other verified method of transmission has been identified.

ever come across'.[65] While data collection is undoubtedly beneficial to epidemiological research, the significant risks of stigmatisation and/or ostracisation that are attendant on disclosure of HIV status suggest to some that the balance between public interests in public health and public and private interests in personal privacy is not being struck in an acceptable manner in those states requiring notification.[66]

Moreover, the continued existence of such legislation becomes questionable if it is not supported by additional provisions designed to ensure that individual rights are protected.[67] A survey of the legislative provisions of five European countries concluded:

> In many respects current legislation on infectious diseases control appears to be outdated. For at least two reasons legal provisions need modernization: First, there has been a considerable increase in medical knowledge of disease transmission and as a consequence the methods of interrupting the spread of disease are today much more refined than they were in the past; second, in current legal analysis greater emphasis is placed on the protection of individual rights, especially the right to privacy and the right to physical integrity.[68]

Other examples of state interest in health matters include the regulation of abortion,[69] compulsory vaccination programmes,[70] the denial

---

[65] D. Jeffries, 'AIDS – The New Black Death?' (1986) *Medico-Legal Journal* 158, 158.

[66] This is especially true given the consequences of making a disease notifiable. Not only does this mean that all clinicians are legally obliged to pass patient information onto authorities, but also it means that the same authorities have considerable powers to collect further information through compulsory examination and contact tracing. Furthermore, in the name of disease management, such authorities can exercise strong control powers over individuals, including quarantine and compulsory treatment, see Dute, 'Affected By the Tooth of Time', 101. See also S. Guttmacher, 'HIV Infection: Individual Rights v. Disease Control' (1990) 17 *Journal of Law and Society* 66.

[67] M. Brazier and J. Harris, 'Public Health and Private Lives' (1996) 4 *Medical Law Review* 171.

[68] Dute, 'Affected By the Tooth of Time', 107–8.

[69] In the United States the debate about the legality of abortion has largely been conducted in the context of the constitutionally protected right of privacy: see ch. 2.

[70] Most Western states require, or strongly encourage, parents to inoculate their children against a range of diseases including measles, polio, rubella, tuberculosis and whooping cough. This is not, however, a litigation-free zone. In 1973, in the United Kingdom, the Association for Vaccine Damaged Children was established to lobby for compensation for children harmed as a result of vaccination. A Royal Commission was established in 1978, leading to the Vaccine Damage Payments Act 1979, which provided for a no fault scheme for the compensation of vaccine damaged individuals. The no fault nature of the scheme directly reflects the public nature of the vaccination enterprise. Vaccination is encouraged as a public good and our participation is therefore required as a duty to the community,

of property rights in one's own body[71] and the prohibition of assisted suicide and euthanasia.[72]

It is not argued here that all of these examples necessarily relate exclusively to an invasion of personal privacy – for issues of personal liberty and autonomy also arise – but each instance does involves a blurring of the division between the public and private spheres of life. In this regard, it is important to recognise and understand the inevitable tension that exists between public and private interests in the health sphere and to ensure that the case for striking acceptable balances between the two is made as strongly and clearly as possible.

Current threats to patient privacy

The justification for examining privacy in the health care setting at the present time is found in the increased threat that technological medical advances pose to patient privacy. Just as it has been argued elsewhere that technological advances have given rise to more concerns about privacy generally,[73] so too it can be seen that medical advances have heightened patient concern for privacy in a clinical context.

but the few individuals who are harmed as a result should not be unduly burdened in the search for compensation by trying to prove fault on the part of a third party.

[71] See *Moore* v. *The Regents of the University of California* 793 P 2d 479 (1990). For comment, see Nuffield Council on Bioethics, *Human Tissue: Ethical and Legal Issues*, 1995, pp. 2, 5, 10–12, 55, 67, 72–3, 123, 139–40.

[72] Most Western states expressly forbid assistance in the taking of one's own life. Generally the criminal law acts as the sanction, as in the United Kingdom, *R* v. *Cox* (1992) 12 BMLR 38. In the United States the Supreme Court has expressly rejected argument on a constitutional 'right to die', *State of Washington* v. *Glucksberg et al.* 138 L. Ed. 2d. 777 (1997), and *Vacco et al.* v. *Quill et al.* 138 L. Ed. 2d. 834 (1997), although the Oregon Death with Dignity Act 1994 has withstood constitutional challenge and now permits physician-assisted suicide in that state. In the Northern Territory of Australia the Rights of the Terminally Ill Act was enacted in 1995. It allowed active euthanasia and physician-assisted suicide for certain classes of patient, and was the first piece of legislation anywhere in the world to do so. However, a Private Member's Bill introduced in 1996, which sought to relieve territories of any power to pass legislation of this kind, was successful in the federal legislature, and its passing effectively rendered the euthanasia legislation defunct. The Netherlands legalised euthanasia within strictly controlled limits in 2000. For general comment on this area, see M. Otlowski, *Voluntary Euthanasia and the Common Law* (Oxford, Oxford University Press, 2000 [1997]).

[73] For discussion of the general trends in concern for privacy in recent times see P. Birks (ed.), *Privacy and Loyalty* (Oxford, Clarendon Press, 1997), chs. 1–6, A. M. Froomkin, 'The Death of Privacy?' (2000) 52 *Stanford Law Review* 1461, B. S. Markesinis (ed.), *Protecting Privacy* (Oxford, Clarendon Press, 1999), and R. Wacks, *Privacy and Press Freedom* (London, Blackstone Press, 1995).

Advances in medical technology and the threat to patient informational and spatial privacy

As medical science pushes ever forward it reveals new and seemingly never-ending knowledge about homo sapiens. We understand better than ever before how we reproduce, grow, develop and die. In particular, the advent of modern genetic science has generally been heralded as one of the greatest advances in human history. Unfortunately, it is also perceived as one of the biggest threats to individual interests in the contemporary private sphere.

In the public realm, advances in genomic research are widely recognised as being in the interests of the collective good. The promise of considerable clinical benefit from genetics is a rarely-questioned given. The ability to gain knowledge about one's own genetic make-up can, however, be a frightening prospect for the individual. Such information might reveal an underlying disease or dysfunction, or indicate a predisposition to future ill health. It could also have implications for one's relatives, given the common genetic heritage that family members share. Moreover, once such information is discovered, a question arises over its use and possible misuse. Family members, the state, researchers, insurers and employers could all claim an interest in knowing the genetic information relating to individuals. The basis and legitimacy of such interests will be discussed in chapter 3. That such claims might be put, however, means that potential invasions of the informational privacy of the individuals to whom the data relate are very much more likely.

The profusion of electronic medical records serves only to exacerbate concerns, because these databases greatly facilitate the use and manipulation of personal health data. Such systems open up many potential uses of health data beyond the immediate care and treatment of the patient and facilitate their dissemination and use on a much wider scale than was possible previously. Databanks of health information have been proposed in various jurisdictions,[74] not least the United Kingdom, where a National Health Service super database of patient details offers multiple access points throughout the country.[75]

---

[74] See L. Gostin, 'Genetic Privacy' (1995) 23 *Journal of Law, Medicine and Ethics* 320.
[75] See A. Tonks, 'Information Management and Patient Privacy in the NHS' (1993) 307 *British Medical Journal* 1227. The handling and management of NHS data is governed by the NHS Information Authority, which sets standards and benchmarks for all users of NHS data.

In the United States the exceptionally ambitious National Health and Nutrition Examination Survey (NHANES) is a rolling programme of surveys designed to collect both genetic and non-genetic information from citizens so as to provide current statistical data on the nature, distribution and effects of illness and disability across the country. Each year, over 5,000 Americans are visited in multiple locations throughout the country. The data collected range over 500 separate issues concerning, inter alia, the individual's diet, bone density, blood pressure, risk status, drug use and history of sexually transmitted disease. NHANES also tests and stores biological samples for the purposes of long-term follow-up and statistical research.[76]

Most controversially, the Icelandic Health Sector Database was established after the Icelandic parliament adopted a law of 17 December 1998 that allows a private company, deCODE Genetics, to maintain and exploit a database of the population's health records.[77] One of the ultimate aims of this project is to tap the rich genetic resources of the Icelandic people as a unique genetically homogeneous population.[78] However, in order to provide the best epidemiological and statistical data possible, a high proportion of the population is required to participate. To facilitate this, the Icelandic law adopted an opt-out scheme for participation. That is, the presumption will be that every individual gives consent to the use of their records unless she or he indicates otherwise. This scheme has not been without its critics,[79] the main objection being that it does not pay sufficient respect to the autonomy of Icelandic citizens to choose freely whether or not to take part.[80] By the same token, this innovative approach seeks to protect the core personal interests at stake – namely those of privacy – while at the same time furthering the considerable public interests that can be served by the existence of such a resource. An adequate privacy protection mechanism is crucial to the success of the scheme. But more fundamentally, the Icelandic approach

[76] Gostin, 'Genetic Privacy', 322.
[77] O. M. Arnardóttir, D. T. Björgvinsson and V. M. Matthíasson, 'The Icelandic Health Sector Database' (1999) 6 *European Journal of Health Law* 307.
[78] H. T. Greely, 'Iceland's Plan for Genomic Research: Facts and Implications' (2000) 40 *Jurimetrics Journal* 153.
[79] R. Chadwick, 'The Icelandic Database – Do Modern Times Need Modern Sagas?' (1999) 319 *British Medical Journal* 441.
[80] H. Roscam Abbing, 'Central Health Database in Iceland and Patients' Rights' (1999) 6 *European Journal of Health Law* 363.

poses a challenge to the traditional method of protecting and promoting patient interests, which has been to focus on individual autonomy To the extent that this represents an exploration of the limits of autonomy and its social utility, this project serves as an apposite model for a correlative examination of the possible role of privacy as an alternative means to protect and further both private and public interests.[81] For these reasons we will return to consideration of this initiative in chapter 5.

Other avenues that have traditionally served to protect patient privacy have also been called into question in the face of the challenges posed by scientific and technological advances concerning patient records. Dierks, for example, has contended that medical confidentiality – the stalwart of bioethics – can no longer adequately protect patient rights.[82] He makes out a case for a greater role for data protection provisions both to protect patient rights and 'to let the enormous chances presented by new methods of data processing be fully exploited in research'.[83] Writing from within the German legal system, which has made 'informational self-determination' a constitutional right,[84] Dierks argues for an acceptable balance to be struck between 'optimized data exploitation and maximum protection of the individual's rights'.[85] However, to talk of balance within systems with a less developed sense of individual patient rights, such as that of the United Kingdom, is relatively meaningless. A balance cannot be struck if patients are denied recognition of the fundamental rights related to being a patient,[86] and, paramount among them, the right of privacy requires clear definition and recognition. Moreover, as will be shown in chapter 4, the law of confidentiality is often in an unsophisticated and confused state, and its precise parameters remain elusive in most jurisdictions. While it is not denied that confidentiality helps to

---

[81] Developments such as these have also provoked response at the international level. For example, in May 2000 the World Medical Association moved to develop ethical guidelines on centralised health databases as a direct result of the Icelandic initiative. See C. Kapp, 'WMA Drafts Guidelines on Genetic Databases' (2000) 355 *The Lancet* 1704.

[82] C. Dierks, 'Medical Confidentiality and Data Protection as Influenced by Modern Technology' (1993) 12 *Medicine and Law* 547.

[83] *Ibid.*, 550.   [84] *Ibid.*, 548.   [85] *Ibid.*, 549.

[86] The Information Commissioner has, for example, urged the British medical profession to adopt a 'culture of data privacy'. Speaking at a conference on health care computing in April 1997, Elizabeth France argued that the use of 'pseudonymised data' could go a long way to addressing the problems of privacy and confidentiality which surround the NHS's medical data networks; see D. Carnell, 'Data Protection Registrar Calls for Culture of Privacy' (1997) 314 *British Medical Journal* 922.

protect some privacy interests of medical patients, it is submitted that it cannot do so adequately when faced with new problems posed by medical advance.

None of this is to suggest that personal privacy has not received attention from legislators or other social institutions. Indeed, for many of the reasons outlined, the perception of an increased threat to privacy has resulted in a number of measures designed to assuage concerns about its protection. Thus, for example, the European Community (EC) Directive on the protection of individuals with regard to the processing of personal data and on the free movement of such data[87] required member states to implement compliant data protection legislation by 24 October 1998.[88] This legislation must lay down conditions under which all processing of personal data should be carried out, provide for the maintenance of quality data standards, and establish certain core rights for data subjects. 'Personal data' are defined as 'data which relate to a living individual who can be identified – (a) from those data, or (b) from those data and other information which is in the possession of, or is likely to come into the possession of, the data controller'.[89] A 'data controller' is 'a person who (either alone or jointly or in common with other persons) determines the purposes for which and the manner in which any personal data are, or are to be, processed'.[90] Personal health data, including genetic data, are clearly caught by the provisions of this legislation. Indeed, they qualify as 'sensitive personal data' and, as such, receive more stringent protection, permitting processing only in limited circumstances – for example, with the explicit consent of the data subject.[91] To the extent that these provisions are concerned with the security of personal data, they go a long way to providing strong protection for personal informational privacy interests. They do not, however, exhaust the limits of privacy as a means to protect individuals from all of the threats to their interests in respect of their genetic constitution.

---

[87] EC Directive 95/46/EC, OJ 1995 No. L281/31. On the same day and in the same document, the Commission also proposed a Council Directive on the protection of personal data and privacy in the context of public digital telecommunications networks, in particular the Integrated Services Digital Network (ISDN) and public digital mobile networks. It was felt that this second directive was necessary to supplement the general directive by applying the general principles of data protection to the specific requirements of new telecommunications networks.

[88] The UK legislation is contained in the Data Protection Act 1998, which came fully into force on 1 March 2000.

[89] See s. 1(1) of the Data Protection Act 1998.   [90] *Ibid.*   [91] *Ibid.*, s. 2.

The passing of the Human Rights Act 1998 in the United Kingdom has been proclaimed as a significant advance in the protection of individual rights.[92] Chief among these is the right to respect for private and family life, protected under Article 8(1) of the European Convention on Human Rights (ECHR), and now contained in Schedule 1 of the 1998 Act. For the moment, we must patiently await the British courts' attempts to put flesh on the bones of this new rights framework and to give meaning to the term 'private and family life'. If help is sought from European jurisprudence, as it undoubtedly will be, then it is worth noting that the European Court of Human Rights and its Commission have interpreted Article 8 very widely to include not only a right to control personal information, but also to the protection of interests in physical and moral integrity, the establishment and maintenance of personal relationships, and the development of personality more generally.[93] This leaves much scope for the British courts to grasp the nettle, should they choose to do so, and expand considerably the protection accorded to these kinds of individual interests in the United Kingdom.

These legislative initiatives reflect a healthy enthusiasm for the protection of personal privacy. It is not the aim of this work necessarily to call these measures into question, nor indeed to give an exhaustive account of the protection that they afford. Rather, they will be held up as examples of instances of protection that have arisen in response to particular problems or concerns but which do not reflect a common or coherent concept of privacy. The protection is piecemeal and without conceptual focus as to the nature of the enterprise at hand. Accordingly, one of the fundamental questions to be addressed in this work is: what are we protecting when we seek to protect privacy?

It is also a core aim to reassess privacy from its fundamentals towards its practical application. A conceptual framework must be established in order to achieve this. A definition of privacy has already been advanced which comprises the two elements of informational privacy and spatial privacy. Personal privacy interests in the health care setting relate to both of these. It has also been argued that medical advances heighten concerns about possible privacy invasions and reveal a need to ensure proper protection of the rights and interests of patients. We can find evidence of both forms of privacy interest being accommodated within

---

[92] This Act came into force fully in the United Kingdom on 2 October 2000.
[93] See further ch. 5.

the protection measures that have been outlined above. Data protection is almost exclusively concerned with the security of information, and as such is clearly designed to protect informational privacy interests. And, while the same class of interests might been protected under Article 8 of the ECHR, the European jurisprudence also reveals a much wider scope of protection that encompasses interests more akin to those described within the concept of spatial privacy. It is also important to note that Article 8 protects 'private life' and not simply privacy, and the former is accordingly a broader notion than the latter. None the less, it is not enough simply to find instances of privacy protection that accord with the definition of privacy offered in this work. What is lacking is a unifying and well justified view of privacy that can bring coherence to these instances of protection. This is necessary not only for the sake of conceptual clarity, but also for the protection of the concept itself. As we shall see in chapter 2, privacy has for a long time received short shrift and has often been regarded as a poor cousin to other related concepts such as autonomy, liberty and confidentiality. This book seeks to explore the nature of the interrelationships between these concepts and to argue for a clearer and more defensible role for privacy as an important and equally valid device to protect our personal and social values and interests.

Genetic privacy

There was no such concept as genetic privacy before scientific advances provided us with the means to gather and manipulate genetic information. Now, however, we must address directly the questions of privacy that arise from such work. This book focuses on the concept of genetic privacy as a contemporary exemplar of the crisis that has dogged the protection of personal privacy for many years. An examination of genetic privacy throws into sharp relief many of the concerns and problems surrounding the protection of privacy more generally. Not only do threats to genetic privacy typify the kinds of challenges that privacy has faced throughout its history, but the search for a definition of genetic privacy and an exploration of its limits can also say much about the role of the concept of privacy in our wider value system. Thus, while genetic privacy is an obvious focus for a book that seeks to examine new challenges in medical law and ethics, the body of this work does not exclude the possibility of a wider role for the view of privacy which is presented herein.

Privacy: a role for the law?

The public/private distinction is central to Western liberal society, arising from the pre-eminence within the latter of individualism. A private sphere embodies areas of life in which individuals are not subject to scrutiny, restraint or interference by society. The boundary between the public and private areas requires careful policing, for the division is in a constant state of flux. The law is crucial to this policing role and, also, to the very existence of the division itself.[94] Indeed, the question of the existence of the public/private distinction in Western life and the problem of the sustainability of a division between the two spheres is, in essence, a debate about the limits of law. The law has little part to play in the private sphere so long as it is characterised by non-interference, non-intrusion and non-action by others.[95] However, the law has a significant role as the prime motivator and regulator of human action in society in delimiting that sphere of life.

The history of privacy has been beleaguered by obscurantism and imprecision.[96] Clarity of function and scope are essential to the development of a workable concept that is designed to protect the interests with which it is concerned. This is all the more true if legal protection of privacy is envisaged, and if this is to become a viable option. The primacy of the role of the law in resolving disputes over matters of value to our society and the individuals in it cannot be disputed. But to date, at least in the United Kingdom, privacy has not received a clear commitment from either the courts or the legislature. While the introduction of the Human Rights Act 1998 and the Data Protection Act 1998 goes some way to redressing this, their passing does not foreclose the need for further examination of the possible protection of privacy by legal means. This book does not set out necessarily to champion this cause, but it is nevertheless founded on a belief that the law has an important role to play and that it is a role which has been ignored for too long.

[94] See O'Donovan, *Sexual Divisions in Law*, pp. 2–3.
[95] Cf. C. MacKinnon, *Towards a Feminist Theory of the State* (Cambridge, MA, Harvard University Press, 1989), p. 191.
[96] See generally ch. 2.

And a belief in the law in no way precludes acceptance of a role for other means of protecting privacy. Law has its limits, and an examination of these is as much a part of the search for an answer as is a thorough examination of any statute or body of case-law. This book offers a legal perspective on genetic privacy, but ultimately it is in the exploration of the limits of legal intervention that the symbiosis of privacy and law will be found.

2

Privacy: anti-social concept or fundamental right?

The public/private distinction

The distinction between public and private spheres of life has increased in importance in Western culture during the last few centuries along with the growing emphasis on individualism.[1] Its importance was concretised in American legal and political discourse in the nineteenth century. As Horowitz has noted, 'One of the central goals of nineteenth century legal thought was to create a clear separation between constitutional, criminal, and regulatory law – public law – and the law of private transactions – torts, contracts, property, and commercial law.'[2]

At much the same time in England, John Stuart Mill produced *On Liberty*, published in 1859, in which he defended the freedoms of the individual against social and political control: 'There is a limit to the legitimate interference of collective opinion with individual independence; and to find that limit, and maintain it against encroachment, is as indispensable to a good condition of human affairs as protection against political despotism.'[3]

As this suggests, the public/private distinction ensures that the legitimacy of interference with individual action is continually under scrutiny. This implies that individuals and individual action are of considerable importance in at least one sphere – the private sphere – and further, that it is a good thing that the boundary between the two spheres is maintained. Two points arise from this. First, it is not to be inferred that

---

[1] For a collection of views on the public/private distinction, see 'Symposium on the Public/Private Distinction' (1982) 130 *University of Pennsylvania Law Review* 1289.

[2] See M. J. Horowitz, 'The History of the Public/Private Distinction' (1982) 130 *University of Pennsylvania Law Review* 1423, 1424. Horowitz also links the development of the distinction with the rise of the sovereign nation state in the sixteenth and seventeenth centuries and the emergence of 'natural rights' theories in the seventeenth century: *ibid.*, 1423. This is also noted in R. Wacks, *Personal Information, Privacy and the Law* (Oxford, Clarendon Press, 1989), p. 8.

[3] J. S. Mill, *On Liberty* (Penguin Books, London, 1974 [1859]), p. 63.

placing conduct in the private sphere automatically precludes regulation of that conduct, indeed there might be strong and valid reasons to impose constraints. Most people would classify the decision to abort a genetically damaged foetus as a private matter, yet all Western governments require that abortions (if permissible at all) are carried out under medical supervision and duly reported. In this way the state seeks to prevent harm to women at the hands of unqualified individuals. Indeed, even in jurisdictions where abortion is accepted, women are frequently denied the procedure in the later stages of pregnancy because the state considers that, by that time, the potential child has a claim to an independent existence.

Nevertheless, there is considerable normative appeal in classifying conduct as private. Thus, although there is no absolute prohibition on regulation of conduct in the private sphere, there is a prima facie presumption that arbitrary interference is impermissible. The rebuttal of this presumption requires strong justification. The corollary is that conduct in the public sphere is not subject to such a presumption and that regulation in the public sphere is, therefore, both more commonplace and, a fortiori, permissible.

Second, it should not be thought that the importance attached to individuals and individual action in the private sphere dictates the location of all individual rights in that sphere. Many individual rights are found, and protected, in the public sphere. Obvious examples include civil liberties and equal protection laws. It follows that the division between the public and private spheres of life is by no means a clear-cut matter in either a literal, legal or metaphorical sense.

The value of the public/private distinction

Ruth Gavison provides valuable insight into the senses of public and private that are used in everyday life.[4] She notes that concern about being known or observed lies at the centre of the distinction. The private represents a sphere where it is possible to remain anonymous and unobserved; the public sphere offers no such guarantee. Similarly, as has already been noted, the private is seen to represent an aspect of freedom: freedom from interference and regulation. Finally, the division

[4] R. Gavison, 'Feminism and the Public/Private Distinction' (1992) 45 *Stanford Law Review* 1.

'polarises the unitary entity of the individual' with the collective sense of the group.[5] The private concerns individual action, the public regulates collectives such as the company, the village, the community or society generally.

These observations are premised on a view of the public/private distinction as an identifiable phenomenon. That is, it is presumed that such a distinction actually exists. This view, however, is by no means universally held. The above analysis might lead to a belief that the public and private spheres of life (if, indeed, they do exist) are clearly separate and independent states – and this may be a misleading conclusion. The reality is that the two spheres exist in very indeterminate states. A constant shifting of classification of conduct occurs between them, and their interface is persistently obfuscated. As a consequence, their limits are not easily determined and require frequent re-evaluation. This has important consequences. For example, if the private sphere is seen as the sphere of non-regulation or non-interference, then the main tool with which regulation and interference are legitimated, namely the law, has to be manipulated in many different ways in order to accommodate any changes. Thus, in a very real sense, the question of the boundaries between public and private becomes a question about the legitimacy of legal intervention and the limitations of law as a social expedient.

Proponents of the public/private distinction hold it out as a thing of value to society and the individual alike. Benn and Gaus argue that the concepts of publicness and privateness help to structure society.[6] Not only do these notions perform a descriptive function, but they also provide normative rules according to which our lives are organised. Thus, for example, to read correspondence without the permission of the addressee is within a Western culture normatively an invasion of privacy. Benn and Gaus argue further that the public/private distinction has a key role to play in a liberal conception of society and its relationship with the individual. As they state, '[The] idea of the "public" as the overwhelming mass is central to liberal theory. Liberalism is committed to the protection of the individual's conscience and projects; and when

---

[5] *Ibid.*, 7.
[6] S. I. Benn and G. F. Gaus, 'The Public and the Private: Concepts and Action', in S. I. Benn and G. F. Gaus (eds.), *Public and Private in Social Life* (London, Croom Helm; New York, St. Martin's Press, 1983) pp. 11ff.

his beliefs and plans are unpopular, this commitment translates into a defence of the individual from the pressure of public opinion.'[7]

Ryan has argued for the maintenance of the public/private distinction as a means of allowing individuals to escape the pressures and strains of everyday public life.[8] He sees a division between the natural persons that we are and the social roles that we are called upon to play. Sometimes society (the 'public') requires that we assume roles not in keeping with our natural character; and 'private' then provides us with an opportunity to step out of such roles and be ourselves. Similarly, the division between these spheres of life permits individuals to assume different personae in different situations as an elaborate coping mechanism. To remove this facility is to endanger the psychological security of the individual.[9]

By contrast, Sennett maintains that trends in Western civil society over the last two centuries have had profound effects on public life as a social institution. As a result this has blurred beyond recognition the divisions between the public and the private in social and political life.[10] He contends that the twin influences of secularisation and capitalism have orchestrated this phenomenon. Their development has brought about a shift in individual expectations. Bastions of the private sphere such as intimacy and the expression of personal feelings have broken free of their boundaries and assumed a role in the public sphere. Sennett regrets this. Not only does he acknowledge the existence of different spheres of life, but he calls for respect for their differences and a clear separation in their function.

A mistrust of the private sphere and what it represents runs through Sennett's work. He sees the concern of the Western state with individualism as a near-narcissistic obsession with the *self*, a condition that leads to the imposition of individual values on all aspects of life, public and private. This, he argues, results in the public sphere being regarded as an inferior state because it cannot provide the individual with self-affirming

---

[7] S. I. Benn and G. F. Gaus, 'The Liberal Conception of the Public and the Private', in Benn and Gaus, *Public and Private in Social Life*, p. 36.

[8] A. Ryan, 'Private Selves and Public Parts', in Benn and Gaus, *Public and Private in Social Life*, pp. 135–54.

[9] This has already been discussed in chapter 1. Additionally, and for an excellent discussion of this kind of theory from the perspective of anthropology/psychology, see E. Goffman, *The Presentation of Self in Everyday Life* (London, Penguin Books, 1969), and F. D. Schoeman, 'Social Freedom from the Perspective of Cognitive and Social Psychology', in F. D. Schoeman, *Privacy and Social Freedom* (Cambridge, Cambridge University Press, 1992).

[10] R. Sennett, *The Fall of Public Man* (London, Faber & Faber, 1986 [1977]).

affection and gratification through self-expression. This destroys the worth of both the public *and* the private. The public is reduced to a state entered under feelings of obligation rather than volition. Political life and city life are thereby rendered hollow experiences. By the same token, the private sphere ceases to serve a useful function since intimacy is sought everywhere and yet can be found nowhere. Moreover, for Sennett the public sphere has its own values which can be sought and enjoyed only if the public/private distinction is not blurred. As he puts it:

> How is society injured by the blanket measurement of social reality in psychological terms? It is robbed of its civility. How is the self injured by estrangement from a meaningful impersonal life? It is robbed of the expression of certain creative powers which all human beings possess potentially – the powers of play – but which require a milieu at a distance from the self for their realization. Thus the intimate society makes of the individual an actor deprived of an art.[11]

In essence Sennett argues for a clear division between public and private life, which he regards as having separate and distinct functions. For him, the two must work in tandem to produce a good society inhabited by rounded individuals, and his aim is to maintain the distinction between them. He does not, however, tell us how this is to be done.

The commentators cited above find common ground, even if they argue for different ends, because they perceive the public/private distinction to be of value. However, a considerable body of opinion would disagree and, as an example of the rejection of the public/private distinction, it is appropriate to examine the feminist perspective.[12]

Feminist views of the public/private distinction

The supposed existence of a public/private distinction in liberal society has concerned many feminists.[13] The main thrust of argument against its

---

[11] *Ibid.*, p. 264.   [12] I am grateful to Catriona Drew for introducing me to this literature.

[13] Consider the following works: M. Thornton (ed.), *Public and Private: Feminist Legal Debates* (Melbourne, Oxford University Press, 1994); K. O'Donovan, *Sexual Divisions in Law* (London, Weidenfeld & Nicolson, 1985), in particular Part One: 'Definition and History of Public and Private'; C. Pateman, 'Feminist Critiques of the Public/Private Dichotomy', in Benn and Gaus, *Public and Private in Social Life*; C. A. MacKinnon, *Feminism Unmodified: Discourses on Life and Law* (Cambridge, MA, Harvard University Press, 1987); and C. A. MacKinnon, *Towards a Feminist Theory of the State* (Cambridge, MA, Harvard University Press, 1989).

recognition or acceptance focuses on the exclusion of women from legal rights and legal protection through the classification of many areas of women's lives as private matters and therefore beyond the law. It is argued that this happens because the (male) organisation of (male) legal and social systems uses the public/private distinction to establish limits on the authority of law. That which is in the public sphere is open to scrutiny and can be regulated and controlled by law. By extension, that which is private is beyond significant outside interference. This can be liberating to some;[14] others, however, view it as an opportunity for abuse. Feminists who have criticised the public/private distinction have argued that divisions in society such as the State/Civil Society and the Market/Family dichotomies represent not only clear divisions between (respectively) public and private spheres, but also the division between (respectively) male and female worlds.[15] Men have constructed a social environment in which men inhabit the public worlds of state and the market and in which women occupy the private worlds of civil society and the home. Women then tend to spend their lives in a sphere that is beyond considered legal regulation and protection. This is not to say, of course, that the public and private enclaves are gender exclusive. Rather, it is suggested that women, as a group, are predominantly relegated to the private. The public/private distinction is then seen to be a gendered construct that can be used as an instrument to control the lives of women. As one commentator has put it, 'the non-regulation of the private realm legitimates self-regulation which translates ultimately into male dominance'.[16]

A good example of these arguments arises in the context of the protection afforded to women by international law. Burrows believes that there are several reasons why the question of women's rights has not been addressed with any particular vigour in the field of public international law.[17] First, international law has traditionally been concerned with the

---

[14] See Horowitz, 'The History of the Public/Private Distinction'.

[15] See, for example, F. E. Olsen, 'The Family and the Market: A Study of Ideology and Legal Reform' (1983) 96 *Harvard Law Review* 1497; K. E. Klare, 'The Public/Private Distinction in Labor Law' (1982) 130 *The University of Pennsylvania Law Review* 1358; and O'Donovan, *Sexual Divisions in Law*, ch. 1.

[16] See H. Charlesworth, 'Alienating Oscar? Feminist Analysis of International Law', in D. G. Dallmeyer (ed.), *Reconceiving Reality: Women and International Law* (Washington, DC, The American Society of International Law, 1993), pp. 10–11.

[17] N. Burrows, 'International Law and Human Rights: The Case of Women's Rights', in T. Campbell *et al.* (eds.), *Human Rights: From Rhetoric to Reality* (Oxford, Basil Blackwell, 1986).

relations between states and not between individuals or between states and individuals. Second, even when international law does so intervene, it does so in a limited fashion, bound by the principle of sovereignty. This dictates that states have exclusive control over those persons on or in its territory and that, therefore, there can be interference with the relationship between state and individual only in the most serious of circumstances.[18] This view is premised on a belief that international law should not interfere with state domestic affairs.[19] Looked at another way, it is an example of the operation of the public/private distinction at the international level. Legal intervention between state and state is a public matter between the states concerned; but the legitimacy of legal intervention in matters between state and individual is essentially a private matter.[20] This, Burrows suggests, is particularly problematic for women seeking international legal protection since they exist, in the main, in the private sphere of their state. Charlesworth puts it succinctly thus: 'The sovereign state is simply irrelevant to most women's experience.'[21]

Of course, the same can be true for men. The point, however, is that women are doubly disadvantaged. First, on an international level where, save in the event of gross violations of human rights, women are seen as an exclusively domestic (private) concern of the state. Compounding this is the treatment that women receive at the hands of the state. As we have seen, in the main they are relegated to the private sphere in family life and civil society where abuse can occur at the hands of private (male) individuals, yet where law rarely intervenes: 'If states sustain gendered hierarchies in national contexts, this is reinforced on the international plane.'[22]

Feminist response to this falls, generally, into one of two categories. Either it is argued that the predominant (male) view of the world as existing in two separate compartments stands in the way of protecting women and that, therefore, a reappraisal of the public/private distinction is required.[23] Alternatively, it is argued that the public/private

---

[18] *Ibid.*, p. 89.   [19] See Article 2(7) of the United Nations Charter (1945).

[20] Although, as Burrows points out, 'since 1945, it has come to be accepted that states may not use the argument of domestic jurisdiction to mask gross violations of human rights', 'International Law and Human Rights', pp. 89–90.

[21] Charlesworth, 'Alienating Oscar? Feminist Analysis of International Law', p. 9.

[22] *Ibid.*, p. 8. She later opines: '[the public/private distinction] . . . sustains women's oppression on a global level', p. 10.

[23] See, for example, K. Engel, 'After the Collapse of the Public/Private Distinction: Strategizing Women's Rights', in Dallmeyer, *Reconceiving Reality*, pp. 143–55.

distinction is a false construct that is used as an illegitimate tool to exclude women from the protection of law. On such a view the public/private distinction 'is both irrational and inconsistently applied'.[24] It is irrational because the distinction '[is] drawn for political reasons . . . it is not one which is inherent in the nature of society, neither is it natural, nor necessary'.[25] It is inconsistently applied because law *does* intervene in the private sphere to prohibit offensive acts such as slavery, violence and child abuse. Advocates of this second view maintain that the distinction should be 'collapsed' to allow the reach of law into the lives of women.[26] Each of these standpoints holds out that 'the private' is bad for women. However, even that view is not universally held among feminists.

Consider, for example, the writings of Karen Engel, who challenges the notion that 'private' is *necessarily* bad for women.[27] She argues that the private sphere can afford protection to women, primarily in the areas of reproduction and termination of pregnancy: 'The language of privacy, and sketching out zones of privacy, many would argue, is our best shot at legally theorizing women's sexuality. In the United States legal jurisprudence, the First Amendment has been used to a similar end, as often seen in the debates about pornography.'[28]

Engel also warns that by collapsing the public/private distinction one runs the risk of not paying due respect to the principle of cultural relativism: not all women in a particular culture who are happy to stay at home or wear certain items of clothing are 'replete with false consciousness'.[29] A further point concerns the frequently made assumption that the private sphere is a bad place for women to be because it is devoid of regulation. Engel challenges this: 'the private – or protection of the private – does not have to mean lack of interference'.[30] Her point is that interference can sometimes be welcome if it protects women from threats to their rights by others (men). The private sphere need not, therefore, be seen as an unregulated void and in particular, privacy can be used as a concept to further, rather than defeat, women's rights.[31]

---

[24] *Ibid.*, p. 144.   [25] Burrows, 'International Law and Human Rights', p. 82.

[26] See Engel, 'After the Collapse of the Public/Private Distinction', pp. 143–5.

[27] *Ibid.*   [28] *Ibid.*, p. 148.   [29] *Ibid.*, p. 149.   [30] *Ibid.*, p. 150.

[31] As Engel says, 'Privacy . . . is an indeterminate concept; in itself it neither creates nor requires a space outside of the state's protection or regulation', *ibid.* For a similar view and another defence of privacy against feminist arguments, see A. L. Allen, 'Taking Liberties: Privacy, Private Choice, and Social Contract Theory' (1987) 56 *Cincinnati Law Review* 461; and E. M. Schneider, 'The Violence of Privacy' (1991) 23 *Connecticut Law Review* 973.

A reluctance to accept privacy or 'the private' as undesirable notions is seen very clearly in the works of Ruth Gavison – doyenne of the privacy literature – and especially in her article 'Feminism and the Public/Private Distinction'.[32] In this work Gavison sets out to examine the nature of the arguments made by feminists who challenge the existence or worth of the public/private distinction. She identifies two forms of criticism that have been levelled at the distinction – internal and external: 'Internal challenges are criticisms of specific uses of terms like "public" and "private" or of specific arrangements designated by these labels. External challenges invite us to abolish or delegitimate such distinctions altogether.'[33]

These challenges correspond to the broad categories of argument that have been outlined above – either the public/private distinction serves the wrong purposes and should be reconceptualised (an *internal challenge* for Gavison), or the distinction is useless or harmful and should be collapsed altogether (an *external challenge*). In assessing the validity of such arguments, Gavison makes some distinctions of her own that are of fundamental importance to our understanding of the notions involved.

Gavison examines what she calls 'senses of public/private' to determine what, if any, differences exist between the two concepts, and what, if any, purpose the making of a distinction between them actually serves or could serve. This is an invaluable exercise because it reveals that often, if not always, feminists and others who criticise the public/private distinction use differing or inconsistent terminology. Axiomatically, this has profound consequences for the debate. Gavison identifies the following senses of public and private.

- *Accessible/inaccessible*: 'The private is that which is unknown and unobserved; the public is that which is known and observed, or at least is capable of being known and observed, because it occurs in a public place.'[34]
- *Freedom/interference*: 'Here, the "private" is "free", the sphere in which others do not interfere. The "public" will acquire a different meaning depending on the source of the interference.'[35] That is, state interference renders the 'public' political. Market influences and communitarian influences cast the 'public' as social.
- *Individuals/society (groups)*: 'the public/private distinction can highlight differences between individuals and various sorts of groups or collectives. The

---

[32] See n. 4 above.   [33] Gavison, 'Feminism and the Public/Private Distinction', 2.
[34] *Ibid.*, 6.   [35] *Id.*

distinction here is a matter of degree, with small voluntary groups existing somewhere in-between – labelled "private" when compared to larger, more anonymous "publics", but "public" when compared to individuals.'[36]

• *Complex meanings*: 'finally, all these senses may combine to create cluster-meanings'.[37]

This exercise greatly clarifies the issues. It shows how confusion is not easily avoided and it stresses the importance of conducting debate on a level playing field. However, the exercise also demonstrates that, although such different senses of public and private are used, they are not necessarily distinct from each other. One might legitimately talk of something as private in the normative sense of requiring not only non-interference but also inaccessibility, for example, a private room or a private meeting. Similarly, to use the expression 'private life' invokes normative feelings of non-interference, inaccessibility and individual, as opposed to societal, value. This complicates the task of ensuring that debate is indeed conducted on the same plane.

A main point made by Gavison is that the arguments of feminists are valuable and insightful because they call on us to question so-called social norms concerning women and to assess the ways in which women are treated at the hands of men. However, she defends the use of the public/private distinction and warns against the use of challenges that are misdirected: 'they become misleading and counterproductive and may actually facilitate the devaluation of important aspects of human life that are currently identified as "private" and "personal"'.[38]

Gavison clearly finds utility and protection for women (and others) in the private sphere. She argues for this on a variety of grounds. For example, the recognition by the Supreme Court of the United States of women's rights to abortion in *Roe* v. *Wade*,[39] using the concept of privacy, displays a commitment on the part of the United States to protect

[36] *Id.*
[37] *Ibid.*, 7. Here, Gavison offers the following example: 'we find such [complex] meaning in the idea of "private life" signifying that part of life which is often unknown and inaccessible, at least to the public at large. People often view the "private life" as a realm entitled to non-interference and freedom from accountability due to its basic self-regarding nature, connection to the intimate, and importance to one's self-identity and welfare.'
[38] *Ibid.*, 2.
[39] *Roe* v. *Wade* 410 US 113 (1973). Gavison mounts a strong argument against MacKinnon in this respect, 'Feminism and the Public/Private Distinction', 30–5. The latter has argued that the *Roe* decision does not guarantee women anything beyond that which they could receive from men in private; see C. A. MacKinnon, 'Privacy v. Equality: Beyond *Roe* v. *Wade*' in MacKinnon, *Feminism Unmodified: Discourses on Life and Law.*

individual private interests that are unique to women. Gavison also puts forward the powerful argument that the development of individual interests such as intimacy, the establishment of relationships and personality can only be achieved through the protection of a private sphere of life. Most significantly, she argues that such value in privacy or the private is recognised by most feminists:

> it is rare to find feminists who argue consistently either that everything should be regulated by the state, or that the family and all other forms of intimate relationships should disappear in favour of public communities ... When pushed feminists explicitly deny that this is their ideal. They advocate only local changes in the existing mix of private and public and in the existing institutionalization of both realms, with more equal access to the two main realms for both genders. They also want the freedom to explore these questions boldly and creatively.[40]

Gavison's response to those who mount external challenges to the public/private distinction focuses on their call for the terminology of public and private to be 'abandoned or delegitimated'.[41] This school holds that the language of privacy and of public and private spheres serves to create and maintain the marginalisation of women. Gavison denies this and warns against the sophistic attack on public and private as the progenitors of the evil that subjugates women. Her argument is three-fold. First, to attack the concepts per se does not necessarily address the true reasons why women are subjugated within society. Second, although 'private' and 'privacy' invoke normative responses of non-interference, the confusion that surrounds the meaning of these terms should not lead us to conclude that they are meaningless or that the confusion cannot be clarified. And, finally, clarification of what we mean may give us a better idea of which private acts legitimately invoke non-interference and which do not. Consider the case, as Gavison does, of domestic violence. It should not be argued that because domestic violence occurs primarily in the privacy of the home such behaviour should be accepted as lying outside the boundaries of legitimate legal regulation.[42] We may think that this is so because of normative confusion about what we mean by 'private', but if we were less confused about what is truly private – and therefore what is properly deserving of non-interference – then we should be

---

[40] Gavison, 'Feminism and the Public/Private Distinction', 28–9.
[41] *Ibid.*, 29.   [42] *Ibid.*, 35–8.

more willing to intervene and more likely to address the true causes of domestic violence. In particular, Gavison notes that the abandonment of language alone cannot help us to achieve such an end:

> Public treatment of domestic violence is plagued by dubious uses of the notion of privacy. The police are often extremely reluctant to interfere in domestic disputes, even when violence is alleged. Often, the reason offered for this reluctance is the private nature of the marital relationship. The potential for confusion generated by this variety of uses is not unique to the public/private distinction or to the feminist context. In fact, this kind of problem is pervasive in legal reasoning, especially when the conclusion must be justified in terms of interpretations of authoritative texts. Moreover, the confusion appears in many different fields of law. Although these mistakes should be avoided, a reform of the language and terminology is not necessarily the cure. Reforming the language by delegitimating the use of "private" and "privacy" will not clarify distinctions between descriptive and normative claims. The descriptive–normative ambiguity exists for all alternative candidates.[43]

Privacy, for Gavison, has valuable uses, and the abandonment of terminology that accurately reflects how we feel about private matters is lamentable, unnecessary and potentially harmful. She asserts that the private can be good for women just as it can be bad for women. It follows that what is required is a differentiation between the good and bad arguments in favour of privacy.[44] One way to do this is to determine the value of the conduct that occurs in the private sphere. Put simply, if privacy facilitates the development of personality and relationships it is good, but if it promotes domestic violence or other forms of exploitation of women it is bad. Gavison accepts this to a point but is quick to add a rider. The language of privacy should not be abandoned in favour of a value analysis of the behaviour concerned because (i) privacy provokes normative responses in us that can protect behaviour which many may find valueless but which those involved might find deeply satisfying (for example homosexual relations);[45] and (ii) respect for privacy as a social construct performs a valuable function in promoting

---

[43] *Ibid.*, 35.   [44] *Ibid.*, 37.

[45] As Gavison says: '... while privacy and intimacy should not provide blanket immunity from public interference, it does not follow that we *always* look at the substance of the activity rather than its context ... [w]e do *not* want to reduce the question to a debate about the morality of the conduct', *ibid.*, 37.

association between individuals and ensuring non-interference from the state. To examine the value of such association rather than respect its private nature would be detrimental in both social and personal terms.[46]

In sum, Gavison sees the feminist debate as revealing much about private and public and about the potential abuses of women that can result from such concepts. Her basic argument, however, is this: the abandonment of 'public' and 'private' as linguistic tools in describing our social order will not further the cause of women because it will not necessarily address the reasons why these tools have been used in the abuse of women. She expresses this in positive terms in arguing that 'public' and (particularly) 'private' do have value both for women and men and that their abandonment would be a loss.

This debate is important to the present work because it highlights many of the arguments that are made about privacy in general. Axiomatically, the role of privacy in the public/private distinction is crucial, but just as the function and parameters of the public/private distinction are by no means universally accepted, the same is true of those of the concept of privacy. This becomes apparent from even the briefest of forays into the literature on privacy. Moreover, it indicates a lack of consistency in attitudes that was long ago carried over from academic writings into the legal world where it has impacted greatly, and at times adversely, on the protection of privacy in many legal systems.

Privacy: anti-social concept or fundamental right?

Consider these two views of privacy:

> [Privacy] can be seen as the protector of reputations and sanities, a developer of intimate and personal relationships, and even a defender of hard-done-by individuals maltreated at the hands of overly bureaucratic government departments.[47]

> [Privacy] is seen as creating the context in which both deceit and hypocrisy may flourish: It provides cover under which most human wrongdoing

---

[46] *Ibid.*, 38.

[47] F. D. Schoeman, 'Privacy: Philosophical Dimensions of the Literature' in F. D. Schoeman (ed.), *Philosophical Dimensions of Privacy: An Anthology* (Cambridge, Cambridge University Press, 1984), p. 1.

takes place and then it protects the guilty from taking responsibility for their transgressions once committed... Concern for one's privacy may be regarded as a sign of moral cowardice, an excuse not to state clearly one's position and accept whatever unpopularity may ensue. Privacy may be seen as a culturally conditioned sensitivity that makes people more vulnerable than they would otherwise be to selective disclosures and to the sense of comparative inferiority and abject shame – a sense engendered by ignorance about the inner lives of others.[48]

To an extent these contrasting views of privacy mirror the arguments of Gavison and many feminists concerning the public/private distinction. They have been advanced, however, not in the context of that debate, but in the context of privacy *simpliciter*. And, just as the views of feminists and those who disagree with them reveal much about the public/private distinction, so too do these competing views reveal much about the nature of privacy. Furthermore, each view has much to support it, depending on one's perspective and theoretical standpoint. A communitarian, for example, would have no problem defending a negative view of privacy, for privacy seems to stand for many notions antithetical to that ethos, such as solitude, individuality and the furtherance of personal interests to the exclusion of other, less atomistic, values.[49] In contrast, anyone committed to a more individualistic approach to social relations would favour the first interpretation offered.[50] We have already seen that Ruth Gavison is such an individual, who has mounted a strong defence of the positive view of privacy.[51] Indeed, the arguments she puts so convincingly in defending the value of privacy for individuals, groups and society generally illustrate why many legal systems have chosen to protect the concept in law. By the same token, the indeterminate nature of privacy has caused problems of definition for the systems that have done so. Indeed, the definition of a concept that can be recognised as being fit for legal protection has been a recurring problem in this field. As one commentator has rightly observed, 'Privacy, like an elephant, is more readily

---

[48] *Id.*

[49] See, for example, A. Etzioni, *The Limits of Privacy* (New York, Basic Books, 1999).

[50] For a good account of both individualistic and communitarian (or republican) arguments in respect of privacy, see J. Rubenfeld, 'The Right of Privacy' (1989) 102 *Harvard Law Review* 737, 761–70.

[51] See, for example, R. Gavison, 'Privacy and the Limits of Law' (1980) 89 *Yale Law Journal* 421; 'Information Control: Availability and Exclusion', in Benn and Gaus, *Public and Private in Social Life*; pp. 223–45 and 'Feminism and the Public/Private Distinction'.

recognised than described.'[52] Such problems have led many writers to a conclusion similar to that of Walter Pratt: 'A concept flexible enough to comprise opposite ideals is not a likely subject for legislation.'[53]

These factors lead us to two important questions that face any writer or legislature examining privacy within a legal framework. First, is privacy of sufficient value to be deserving of protection? Second, even if the answer to this first question is given in the affirmative, is privacy sufficiently amenable to definition as to make legal protection viable and effective?

Examining privacy from its fundamentals

One need only look at the bibliography of any work on privacy to appreciate how many diverse and interconnecting definitions have been proposed over the years. These are almost as numerous as the number of works written on the subject itself. Nonetheless, valiant efforts have been made by Schoeman[54] and Parent[55] who have undertaken to categorise privacy writings according to the approach adopted. Three types of commentator can be identified from these and other works:

- Those who advance sceptical approaches to privacy and its value in society;
- Those who seek some fundamental core element that unites all privacy examples and explains the concept as a coherent whole; and
- Those who seek to define privacy in precise terms for application in specific areas only.

The sceptical approach

It has already been said that a problem for anyone interested in the study of privacy is the apparently indeterminate nature of the concept and its seemingly dubious functionality, sometimes promoting 'good', sometimes promoting 'bad' outcomes for individuals and society. Thus

---

[52] Taken from J. B. Young (ed.), *Privacy* (Chichester, John Wiley & Sons, 1979), p. 5.
[53] W. F. Pratt, *Privacy in Britain* (London, Associated University Presses, 1979), p. 63.
[54] See Schoeman, *Philosophical Dimensions of Privacy*, esp. ch. 1, and *idem*, *Privacy and Social Freedom*.
[55] W. A. Parent, 'Recent Work on the Concept of Privacy' (1983) 20 *American Philosophy Quarterly* 341; *idem*, 'A New Definition of Privacy for the Law' (1983) 2 *Law and Philosophy* 305; and *idem*, 'Privacy: A Brief Survey of the Conceptual Landscape' (1995) 11 *Computer and High Technology Law Journal* 21.

writers on privacy divide, in the first instance, into those who see it as a valuable social construct and those who do not. However, many writers who acknowledge that the private sphere – as opposed to privacy per se – promotes certain 'goods' consider that the protection of so-called privacy interests can be achieved by means other than an appeal to a difficult-to-define concept.

Judith Jarvis Thomson has claimed that there is nothing morally significant about the concept of privacy as such.[56] Instead, she argues that any right we may choose to claim as a privacy right can be more easily dealt with by reference to existing rights in other fields, such as property rights or rights over one's person – that problems can be resolved without having to refer to privacy at all. Thomson suggests, for example, that the reason that the actions of a Peeping-Tom are judged wrong is not because he invades our privacy, but because he breaches the personal right we all have not to be looked at. Similarly, if I read someone else's correspondence, I am not violating their right to privacy, but, rather, their property right in owning the papers, which in turn gives them the right to control access to those papers.[57]

Thomson's view is, however, clearly unacceptable in that it requires us to accept the existence of a plethora of ancillary rights which, in themselves, have little or no moral justification. What, for example, is the basis of a right not to be looked at? Even when one could appeal to another area of existing legally recognised rights, such as property rights, the important question remains as to whether the interests involved are adequately protected by the existing law. As we shall see in later chapters, established rights such as autonomy and confidentiality do not protect the interests surrounding genetic information adequately, and it is for that very reason that this work offers an alternative analysis focused on

---

[56] J. J. Thomson, 'The Right to Privacy' (1975) 4 *Philosophy and Public Affairs* 295. For a full critique of Thomson see T. Scanlon, 'Thomson on Privacy' (1975) 4 *Philosophy and Public Affairs* 315. See too, J. Inness, *Privacy, Intimacy and Isolation* (New York, Oxford University Press, 1992), ch. 3.

[57] This presupposes that I own the documents containing information about me. For personal correspondence that is likely to be true (although my correspondee will own other papers *from* me containing information *about* me), but in other contexts this model might be less helpful. In the health care setting, for example, it is now settled law in the United Kingdom that a doctor or a health board/authority and not patients own medical records – see *R. v. Mid Glamorgan Family Health Services Authority and Another, ex parte Martin* [1995] 1 WLR 110. Thus, on Thomson's analysis the doctor or health authority would have the right to control access. However, this right might be exercised in ways which offend me and my interests. In such cases Thomson's analysis offers no means of redress.

privacy. Thomson's approach would not necessarily lead us to disagree about the importance of protecting certain key individual interests; it is more a question of the means that are used to do so. While Thomson rejects privacy as a viable means of achieving that end, this work does not do so. One's view of privacy is, then, perhaps a question of faith.[58] Thomson's work should not be disregarded, but should be considered by way of being a comparative approach.

A similar sceptical treatment of privacy comes from William Prosser.[59] He has examined the US common law tort of invasion of privacy and has, as a result, outlined four distinct kinds of invasion of privacy and three different kinds of interests that are protected by the law. His approach is similar to that of Thomson, in that he identifies abstract interests in need of protection, for example, protection of reputation, avoidance of emotional stress and property interests. He concludes that all so-called privacy interests are adequately protected by the existing law. This view is clearly subject to the same criticism as has been made of Thomson's above. Even if an argument can be mounted that many privacy interests are already covered indirectly by other interests, it does not necessarily follow that unique and unprotected privacy interests cannot be found. Moreover, Prosser's approach has been questioned as being 'philosophically unsound'. As Wacks has observed,

> it is a singularly unrewarding and pointless exercise to comb through the case law in search of instances where courts have either employed the word 'privacy' or accorded protection to certain interests which are now (rightly or wrongly) conceived as privacy issues. Since this process requires distortions in the meaning of privacy and involves the application of past situations to present problems, it is both legally and philosophically unsound.[60]

This is true up to a point. To measure the breadth of understanding of privacy by the courts in a particular jurisdiction in order, then, to evaluate the sorts of interests currently protected may well be a valuable exercise.[61] But it is a non sequitur to draw the conclusion, as Prosser does, that all future privacy interests will necessarily find protection in

---

[58] P. Oliver, S. Douglas Scott and V. Tadros, *Faith in Law* (Oxford, Hart Publishing, 2000).
[59] W. Prosser, 'Privacy: A Legal Analysis' (1960) 48 *California Law Review* 338.
[60] R. Wacks, *The Protection of Privacy* (London, Sweet & Maxwell, 1980), p. 5.
[61] See, as an example, M. Hogg, 'The Very Private Life of the Right to Privacy' (1994) 2(3) *Hume Papers on Public Policy* 1.

existing areas of law. Moreover, it is an exercise of limited scope and value in the search for the ultimate nature and limits of privacy protection.

The approach of writers such as Thomson and Prosser has been called the reductionist model of privacy, that is, one which denies that there is anything worthwhile or distinctive about privacy that deserves specific protection. Some sceptics, however, go further and argue the negative nature of privacy.

Richard Wasserstrom has suggested that not revealing information about oneself may be equivalent in moral terms to deception and therefore normatively unacceptable.[62] He posits that individuals make themselves unnecessarily vulnerable in society by accepting the notion that there are thoughts and actions about which one ought to feel ashamed or embarrassed. He suggests that we would be less embarrassed and therefore less vulnerable if we were honest about our lives. By doing so we would realise that many other individuals share similar life stories. Such a view, however, fails to take account of considerable anthropological evidence which indicates that the desire to hide is culturally conditioned and is, therefore, unlikely to change without fundamental shifts in society itself.[63] Wasserstrom's position may well be correct for an ideal world, but it is not valid for the one in which we live.[64]

By contrast, Goffman has argued forcefully that a measure of privacy is necessary precisely because of the pressures and hypocrisy to which each individual is subjected by society.[65] Likewise, Murphy has put the case for the value of social distancing mechanisms, of which privacy is an important example. His view is that privacy is not only recognised and institutionalised in all societies – albeit in relation to different matters and to varying degrees – but that a measure of privacy is absolutely essential to the maintenance of both social relationships and one's own sense of self.[66] Macklin supports this in part when she

---

[62] R. A. Wasserstrom, 'Privacy: Some Arguments and Assumptions', in Schoeman, *Philosophical Dimensions of Privacy*, pp. 223–45.

[63] See, for example, B. Moore Jr, *Privacy* (New York, M. E. Sharpe Inc., 1984); R. F. Murphy, 'Social Distance and the Veil' (1964) 6 *American Anthropologist* 1257; A. Westin, 'The Origins of Modern Claims to Privacy', in Schoeman, *Philosophical Dimensions of Privacy*, pp. 56–74; and H. Arendt, *The Human Condition* (Chicago, University of Chicago Press, 1958).

[64] J. Rosen, *The Unwanted Gaze: The Destruction of Privacy in America* (New York, Random House, 2000).

[65] E. Goffman, *Stigma* (London, Penguin Books, 1963), also Goffman, *The Presentation of Self in Everyday Life*.

[66] Murphy, 'Social Distance and the Veil'.

writes: 'Although respect for privacy is much more a Western value, even in China and other Eastern cultures some respect for boundaries is an accepted norm.'[67] In her search for 'ethical universals', Macklin acknowledges that even when 'there is no word for privacy in Mandarin Chinese',[68] there is nevertheless a strong prohibition in all cultures on behaviour that displays disrespect for persons. Thus, while we may not share a common language or taxonomy to describe certain cultural phenomena, it does not follow that we do not experience those phenomena and describe them under another name, even if the ways in which they are experienced vary sharply between cultures and peoples. Westin has considered this sort of evidence at length and has concluded that 'privacy appears to be a cultural value in all known human communities, although the forms it takes vary enormously'.[69]

The tension between these various writers might best be explained as a tension between individualist and communitarian notions of privacy. Wasserstrom's negative view of privacy sees the concept as anti-social or anti-communitarian, and to a lesser extent anti-individual. This is because he sees the potential for harm rather than the potential for benefit that is identified by others. Yet the evident need of humans for a sphere of the private arguably forces us to go a long way towards recognising that need as a good thing.[70]

This having been said, there is no imperative that privacy should assume paramountcy in our value hierarchy, and it certainly does not mean that we need to accept protection of privacy if this is found to be harmful. It does suggest, however, that a core set of interests can be served by recognising the human need for a degree of privacy.

The polarisation of debate about the value or non-value of privacy is as unhelpful as it is inaccurate in its failure to reflect the realities of the diverse range of human communities in which privacy has a role to play. Too often a desire to protect privacy is portrayed as a 'Western' value that is symptomatic of the slow demise of a culture that has surrendered almost all of its values to the cult of the individual; in contrast,

---

[67] R. Macklin, *Against Relativism: Cultural Diversity and the Search for Ethical Universals in Medicine* (New York, Oxford University Press, 1999), p. 12.

[68] *Ibid.*, p. 13.

[69] A. Westin, *Privacy and Freedom* (London, The Bodley Head, 1970), p. 87. For criticism of Westin, see L. Lusky, 'Invasion of Privacy: A Classification of Concepts' (1972) 72 *Columbia Law Review* 693.

[70] Cf. H. Collins, 'The Decline of Privacy in Private Law' (1987) 14 *Journal of Law and Society* 91.

'Eastern' cultures are represented as essentially communitarian in nature, where there is neither a need nor a place for privacy. But, quite apart from their inherent inaccuracies, these representations of human society are not incontrovertibly antithetical,[71] nor do they respectively demand a wholehearted acceptance or rejection of privacy as a valuable asset.[72]

If this is accepted, then Wasserstrom and those who think like him can be seen as being not too far removed from Westin and his followers, for the question then becomes not one of whether privacy is good or bad, but rather one concerning the limits to the interests that should and will be protected, and the *degree* of privacy that can be expected.

Hixson has advanced an argument along this line, albeit one that ultimately comes down in favour of a narrow construction of privacy. Hixson considers privacy to be a privilege and thereby 'something well worth protecting', but 'not on the grand scale that claims for privacy are pressed today'.[73] He asserts that 'an open and democratic society cannot tolerate a high degree of privacy'.[74]

The value that Hixson attributes to privacy is based on the view of the relationship between society and the individual that favours society as representing the ultimate value. He considers that privacy threatens the American view of community, or what he calls 'collective individualism',[75] and that a commitment to 'public service' is more important than 'singularity'.[76] That such a view should emerge from what many would describe as the most individualistic of societies should not be as surprising as might first appear. A commitment to valuing individuals does not preclude the recognition of community interests. Indeed, this cannot be so, for it would signal the immediate downfall of the society in question. But privacy has been done no favours at all by our failure to recognise the symbiotic relationship between the individual and the

---

[71] Tam, for example, has argued that the polar opposite philosophies are individualism and authoritarianism, while his own version of communitarianism he offers as a 'third way' suitable for the social inclusion polices of twenty-first-century Britain: H. Tam, *Communitarianism: A New Agenda for Politics and Citizenship* (Basingstoke, Macmillan, 1998).

[72] T. M. Franck, 'Is Personal Freedom a Western Value?' (1997) 91 *American Journal of International Law* 593.

[73] R. F. Hixson, *Privacy in a Public Society* (New York, Oxford University Press, 1987), p. 4.

[74] *Ibid.*, p. 96.   [75] *Ibid.*, pp. 100–2.

[76] *Id.* Thus, rather than recognising and protecting a widely defined privacy right, Hixson proposes that the law should direct itself to the protection of specific instances of abuse concerning sensitive information.

community, or by the tendency to characterise certain kinds of society as revering one value system over another. De Bary, for example, has argued that even the most paradigmatic example of communitarian philosophy – Confucianism – is misconstrued if it is taken as requiring the subjugation of individuals to the collective will:

> the Confucian ideal was a balance of public and private, not an assertion of one over the other. In fact, from the Confucian point of view the state's responsibility for the public interest was to encourage private initiative. How to define what was legitimate remained an issue, and the state, historically, was not slow to assert its own authority in this respect . . . , but Confucians were just as ready to challenge any such claim on the part of the state bureaucracy (*guan*), asserting instead that the public interest (*gong*) consists in serving the legitimate desires and material needs of the people. A balance of public and private (*gongsi yiti*), not the person or individual subordinated to the collectivity or the state, remained the Confucian ideal.[77]

Etzioni, a professed communitarian, has also argued for balance. While being a stringent critic of what he sees as rampaging privacy protection (most particularly in the United States),[78] he, nonetheless, recognises the role of privacy in individuals' lives.[79] His point, however, is that the balance between social order and individual autonomy – of which privacy is an integral part – must be struck more evenly 'to prevent measures of liberalization from snowballing'.[80]

The approaches of Hixson, De Bary and Etzioni are informative because they demonstrate well how our view of privacy can change depending on our perspective, and their views are important because they avoid polarisation of the debate, even though the preference of each is ultimately for less privacy protection rather than for more. Their perspectives also show that protection is a matter of degree. It has already been put that privacy in essence concerns the boundaries of the society/individual relationship, and as Negley has pointed out, 'any consideration of whether privacy is a right of the individual will entirely depend

---

[77] W. T. De Bary, *Asian Values and Human Rights: A Confucian Communitarian Perspective* (Cambridge, MA, Harvard University Press, 1998), p. 29.

[78] Etzioni, *The Limits of Privacy*.

[79] A. Etzioni, *The New Golden Rule: Community and Morality in a Democratic Society* (London, Profile Books, 1996), pp. 53–7.

[80] *Ibid.*, p. 56.

on what definition of the individual we accept'.[81] That definition, in turn, depends on the definition of society we accept. But it is by the determination of those definitions, and so of the relative values that should be attributed to the individual and the community and vice versa, that each society will formulate its own unique character.

If our concern is for the individual in the Western liberal democracy, it is difficult to reject out of hand the idea that individuals have a core set of interests in the private sphere of their lives where they are entitled to be free from undue interference. That this is so is related to the commitment of the liberal society to notions of freedom, liberty and autonomy. Indeed, many of the so-called privacy interests that can be identified overlap with liberty and autonomy to such an extent that it becomes difficult to separate them. By the same token, we run the risk of compromising a correlative commitment to liberty and autonomy if we deny a degree of protection to privacy. The problem of overlap between these concepts will be discussed presently. For the moment, we can take it that the arguments of the privacy sceptics distil into arguments as to the degree of protection that should be afforded to privacy rather than into those that would deny privacy any value whatsoever. This leads logically to a consideration of which, if any, core interests are, in fact, privacy interests.

The fundamentalist approach

Many writers have searched for a fundamental, internally consistent and distinctive core to privacy concerns. This search has always been motivated by the notion that there is some particular aspect of human or moral character which can be called 'private' and which is overlooked by reductionist accounts.

Bloustein has postulated the idea of an inviolate personality that he associates with the 'right to be alone'.[82] Inviolate personality is taken to include such notions as individual dignity and integrity, personal uniqueness and personal autonomy. Bloustein's case is that respect for these values 'both grounds and unifies our concept of privacy'.

---

[81] G. Negley, 'Philosophical Views on the Value of Privacy' (1966) 31 *Law and Contemporary Problems* 319.

[82] See E. J. Bloustein, 'Privacy as an Aspect of Human Dignity: An Answer to Dean Prosser' (1964) 39 *New York University Law Review* 962. Also, *idem*, 'Privacy is Dear at Any Price: A Response to Professor Posner's Economic Theory' (1978) 12 *Georgia Law Review* 429; R. A. Posner, 'An Economic Theory of Privacy', in Schoeman, *Philosophical Dimensions of Privacy.*

Benn follows a similar line in asserting that the core element of privacy is a respect for persons as individual moral choosers.[83] His argument is essentially one of consistency – a commitment to values such as freedom and autonomy requires us to respect persons and to respect their choices, including those to be left alone or to be separate from others. Privacy interests should, therefore, also be respected and protected.

Other writers such as Gerety contend that privacy is concerned with control over the intimacies of personal identity,[84] and Jouard has posited that there are sound psychological reasons why individuals need privacy as an aspect of the control they have over others' perceptions and beliefs vis-à-vis themselves.[85] Others still, such as Fried,[86] Reiman[87] and Inness,[88] argue that the creation and maintenance of personal and social relationships are the key factors in unifying privacy interests.

Gavison asserts that privacy consists of three elements: *secrecy, anonymity* and *solitude*.[89] The functions served by this combination are considerable and include the development of individual autonomy, the growth and deepening of personality, the establishment of human relations, the promotion of liberty of action, and general support for the desirable ends of a free society.[90] Finally, Feldman has argued that privacy should best be seen as a civil liberty that consists of the following features: *secrecy* (which he considers is concerned with control of personal information), *autonomy* (which he classifies as being concerned with choosing the direction of one's life and social interactions) and *dignity* (which involves the giving and receiving of respect towards the choices and standards of oneself and others).[91]

It is clear that there is wide-ranging speculation on the fundamental nature of privacy concerns. Agreement is unlikely to be achieved.

---

[83] This argument is made in many areas of Benn's work, for example, S. I. Benn, *A Theory of Freedom* (New York, Cambridge University Press, 1988), and *idem*, 'Privacy, Freedom and Respect for Persons', in R. Pennock and J. W. Chapman (eds.), *NOMOS XIII: Privacy* (Atherton, NY, 1971), ch. 1. Also, *idem*, 'The Protection and Limitation of Privacy' in Schoeman, *Philosophical Dimensions of Privacy*.

[84] T. Gerety, 'Redefining Privacy' (1977) 12 *Harvard Civil Rights and Civil Liberties Law Review* 233.

[85] S. M. Jouard, 'Some Psychological Aspects of Privacy' (1966) 31 *Law and Contemporary Problems* 307.

[86] C. Fried, 'Privacy' (1968) 77 *Yale Law Journal* 475.

[87] J. H. Reiman, 'Privacy, Intimacy and Personhood' (1976) 6 *Philosophy and Public Affairs* 26.

[88] Inness, *Privacy, Intimacy and Isolation*.

[89] Gavison, 'Privacy and the Limits of Law'.   [90] *Ibid.*

[91] D. Feldman, 'Secrecy, Dignity, or Autonomy? Views of Privacy as a Civil Liberty' (1994) 47 *Current Legal Problems* 41.

Nevertheless, a strong commitment to the protection of privacy is conveyed by each of these writers. From the legal perspective this is a first, and very crucial, hurdle to overcome. The details of any particular legal protection measure become a matter for each jurisdiction, and this in turn depends on the aims of the particular legal system.

To acknowledge that privacy is an amorphous concept should not lead to the conclusion that it should go unprotected by law or that it cannot be so protected. Many ill-defined and indeterminate terms – such as good faith, recklessness, the public interest and the reasonable man – are used in the law.[92] The difficulty in achieving our aims should be no reason alone not to pursue our goals. And, if common aims in respect of privacy can be agreed, a sincere commitment to its protection will more easily follow. Such common aims can be identified in the above account of perspectives on the fundamental nature of privacy. Despite the broad range of views expressed about the specific nature of privacy, each is underpinned by common, clear and generalisable elements. These include an acceptance of the value of the public/private distinction, the recognition of the genuine human need of individuals to experience a degree of privateness, a commitment to coherent and consistent protection of individual interests, and the desire and need to strike a balance between individual rights and public interests. The legal issue then becomes a search for a particular definition.

The search for a definition of privacy

Benn and Schoeman have identified different categories of definition that have been advanced as possible means for explaining or protecting privacy.[93] These can be summarised:

- privacy as a right;
- privacy as a claim;
- privacy as an interest;
- privacy as an aspect of control;
- privacy as a state or condition.

---

[92] T. A. O. Endicott, *Vagueness in Law* (Oxford, Oxford University Press, 2000).

[93] Benn, *A Theory of Freedom*, pp. 266ff., and *idem*, 'The Protection and Limitation of Privacy' (1978) 52 *Australian Law Journal* 601, 686 (note that Benn also speaks of privacy as a *power* which is a form of control theory). See too Schoeman, *Philosophical Dimensions of Privacy*, ch. 1.

Benn notes that those who define privacy as a right automatically do not address the question as to whether anyone ought to have the power to deny access to any places or activities called private. His view is that a right only exists to provide someone with a normative capacity to choose whether or not to maintain or relax a state. A right is always something bestowed on a person by another (excepting natural rights) in order to provide protection and/or show acknowledgement of some capacity, state or entitlement, from which it follows that to classify privacy as a right immediately confers a value on the concept as something worth protecting. Whereas this is not an undesirable end point, many writers have warned against value bias in the search for a definition. For example, Lusky has pointed out that it is very simple to start with the idea that privacy is a good thing and then to claim that it must be protected. Such a beginning 'naturally demands affirmative justification throughout one's discussion and biases of this kind are the enemy of just balance'.[94] In other words, we must be careful about the use of value-laden language that presupposes value where it might not exist. We should not confuse the concept of a 'right to privacy' with privacy *simpliciter*. Even so, as Gavison has stated, 'Insisting that we start with a neutral concept of privacy does not mean that wishes, exercises of choice, or claims are not important elements in the determination of the aspects of privacy that are deemed to be of value'.[95]

To return to Benn: he notes that a 'claim' is often described as an argument that someone deserves something, and that a right is a justified claim. This too carries with it a value judgment.[96] Thus writers such as Westin, who describe privacy as a claim are presuming, as are those who use the term 'right', that privacy is of self-evident value and, equally self-evidently, is worth protecting.[97] Benn's objection to this is not that privacy is not or cannot be valuable but, rather, that such presumptions lack moral justification in the absence of legal definition.

Those who argue that privacy is an 'interest' are thought to be mistaken on two grounds. First, they perpetuate the error of evaluating

---

[94] Lusky, 'Invasions of Privacy: A Classification of Concepts', 697.
[95] Gavison, 'Privacy and the Limits of Law', 426.
[96] Wacks, *Personal Information, Privacy and the Law*, p. 14, also criticises this approach, quoting D. N. McCormick, 'Privacy: A Problem of Definition' (1974) 1 *British Journal of Law and Society* 75.
[97] Westin, *Privacy and Freedom*.

privacy before offering a neutral definition of it. Second, as Benn says, 'We cannot take for granted that giving people what they want is necessarily in their interests. Adults and children alike can be worse and not better off, for getting what they want.'[98] But, while Benn's view is undoubtedly factually correct – that is, it is certain that in some cases giving people what they want might make them worse off – it is less easy to reject the strong normative imperative in Western culture that leads us to believe that the best determination of an individual's interests are the wishes of the individual herself.

A control-based definition provides a different and popular option that has been advocated by Westin,[99] Lusky,[100] Fried,[101] Wasserstrom[102] and Feldman.[103] Along with others, the majority of these writers views privacy as a concern about personal information (and sometimes access to the person) and conclude that control of or access to such information is the key element in the recognition and protection of privacy. As Benn further points out, such theories appear more attractive because they avoid the moral question-begging provoked by definitions couched in terms of rights, claims or interests.[104] Despite these apparent benefits, however, control-based definitions have been heavily criticised.[105] In particular, Parent has argued that such theories fail because they are both conceptually and empirically too broad: 'To define privacy as the control over (all) information about oneself implies that every time I walk or eat in public my privacy is compromised.'[106]

Parent would still challenge this definition as unacceptable even if it were restricted to control over personal information: 'The comatose patient example should convince us that control over personal information is not a necessary condition of privacy.'[107] This point is of particular interest to this work. To classify privacy as being solely concerned either with personal information or its control excludes much of that which can legitimately be claimed under the privacy rubric, including

---

[98] Benn, *A Theory of Freedom*, p. 277.   [99] Westin, *Privacy and Freedom*.
[100] Lusky, 'Invasions of Privacy: A Classification of Concepts'.
[101] Fried, 'Privacy'.
[102] Wasserstrom, 'Privacy: Some Arguments and Assumptions'.
[103] Feldman, 'Secrecy, Dignity, or Autonomy? Views of Privacy as a Civil Liberty'.
[104] Benn, *A Theory of Freedom*, pp. 271–3.
[105] See in particular Gavison, 'Privacy and the Limits of Law'; Parent, 'Recent Work on the Concept of Privacy'; *idem*, 'A New Definition of Privacy for the Law', and Wacks, *Personal Information, Privacy and the Law*, p. 15.
[106] Parent, 'Recent Work on the Concept of Privacy', 344.   [107] *Ibid.*

spatial privacy interests.[108] However, Parent also discredits definitions which focus on control of access to the person. Inter alia, his argument relies once again on the example of the comatose patient.[109] If someone cannot exercise control, control-based theories offer us no option but to conclude that privacy has been compromised, yet this might not be the case. No third party may have personal information about the comatose patient nor access to her person. As Gavison has commented:

> 'control' suggests that the important aspect of privacy is the ability to choose it and see that the choice is respected. All possible choices are consistent with enjoyment of control, however, so that defining privacy in terms of control relates it to the *power* to make certain choices rather than the way in which we choose to exercise the power. To be non-preemptive (that is, non value-laden), privacy must *not* depend upon choice. Furthermore, the reasons why we value privacy may have nothing to do with whether the individual has, in fact, chosen it.[110]

Parent's overriding objection to control-based theories is that they all 'confuse the two distinct values of privacy and liberty or freedom'.[111] His definition of freedom/liberty is 'absence of coercion or restraint on choice'.[112] His point is that control issues are already dealt with by these other valuable concepts and that we must avoid conceptual confusion between them and privacy. Whether or not one should conclude that such concepts are, and need always be, mutually exclusive is a different matter, and is discussed further below.

Parent's solution is to conceive privacy as 'the condition of a person's not having undocumented personal information about himself known by others'.[113] This covers many things, among which the following are significant. First, he follows the lead of those who argue that privacy is concerned with personal information, and second, he opts for Benn's final category of candidates for best describing privacy, namely, privacy as a state or condition.[114]

---

[108] Wacks roundly criticises control-based arguments on this and other grounds in *The Protection of Privacy*, pp. 10–11.
[109] Parent, 'Recent Work on the Concept of Privacy', 345.
[110] Gavison, 'Privacy and the Limits of Law', 427–8.
[111] Parent, 'Recent Work on the Concept of Privacy', 345.
[112] *Ibid.*   [113] *Ibid.*, 346.
[114] Gavison also supports this; see generally 'Privacy and the Limits of Law'.

Parent defends his approach thus: by defining personal information as 'facts that most persons in a given society choose not to reveal about themselves (except to friends, family, advisors, etc.) or ... facts about which a particular person is extremely sensitive and which he therefore does not choose to reveal about himself',[115] he casts his net very wide and includes both objective and subjective assessments of the personal.[116] His view that personal information is crucial to privacy is motivated in large part by a desire not to confuse privacy with other social concepts such as liberty, autonomy, property, secrecy etc.[117] By choosing to see privacy in terms of personal information Parent provides it with a relatively clearly defined niche within the community or family of concepts. That he insists on conceptual clarity is not likely to be a point of contention. However, the fact that he focuses privacy concerns solely on personal information is more open to question. It has already been argued in chapter 1 that privacy interests relate both to informational and spatial interests. And, while it is not denied that these interests overlap to an extent with interests protected by other concepts such as confidentiality and autonomy, it is not immediately apparent why this raises a problem. Moreover, it is unclear that existing non-privacy concepts can protect all informational or spatial interests which exist. There is nothing fatal to the development of a clear concept of privacy in supposing that it can fill such gaps, or that, in doing so, we allow it to overlap in places with existing concepts. Indeed, it might lead to a better understanding of the relationships between this family of concepts that are thought to be so important in Western society.

Finally, Parent's choice of privacy as a condition is welcomed. Such an approach – which has also been advocated by Benn,[118] Gavison[119] and DeCew[120] – avoids the criticism associated with the use of value-laden language and allows us to see privacy for what it is, as distinct from what we think it ought to be. This is not to say, however, that value will not be attributed to privacy at some future time through one's conduct or

---

[115] Parent, 'Recent Work on the Concept of Privacy', 346–7.
[116] Parent refines his arguments about a subjective evaluation of 'personal information' in 'A New Definition of Privacy for the Law', 306.
[117] Parent, 'Recent Work on the Concept of Privacy', 347–8.
[118] Benn, *A Theory of Freedom.*   [119] Gavison, 'Privacy and the Limits of Law'.
[120] J. Wagner DeCew, 'The Scope of Privacy in Law and Ethics' (1986) 5 *Law and Philosophy* 145. Cf. *idem, In Pursuit of Privacy: Law, Ethics, and the Rise of Technology* (Ithaca, NY, Cornell University Press, 1997).

through laws, but to forecast this is a step beyond describing privacy and the function that it serves.

A core concern for privacy: personal information or beyond?

It is important at this juncture to address one of the most common features found in the literature concerned with the defence of privacy. This is the view that privacy is primarily concerned with personal information, and that this is the sole and proper subject of legal protection. We have already seen that Parent advocates such a position, but he is by no means alone.

The works of Raymond Wacks have made a significant contribution to the debate about the propriety and practicalities of privacy protection by legal means.[121] In particular, *Personal Information, Privacy and the Law* sets out 'to obviate the confusion that afflicts the question of "privacy" and obstructs the satisfactory legal protection of the interests with which it is concerned'.[122] Thus, while acknowledging that individuals might have a wide range of interests in privacy that can legitimately include, say, the use of contraceptives, termination of pregnancy, or homosexual conduct, he argues that in order to secure viable legal protection of privacy one must start with a workable and relatively narrow concept. Protection, he submits, cannot be achieved under the banner of a wide-ranging rubric. Rather, Wacks identifies concern with personal information as crucial to privacy interests: '"Personal information" consists of those facts, communications, or opinions which relate to the individual and which it would be reasonable to expect him to regard as intimate or sensitive and therefore to want to withhold or at least to restrict their collection, use or circulation.'[123]

This is an objective test. It determines the personal nature of information by reference to the reasonableness of the individual's expectations of privacy. Wacks argues that such an assessment is the only viable option, since a subjective assessment of personal information would not only

---

[121] See, for example, 'Privacy in Cyberspace: Personal Information, Free Speech, and the Internet' in P. Birks (ed.), *Privacy and Loyalty* (Oxford, Clarendon Press, 1997), ch. 4; *Privacy and Press Freedom* (Blackstone Press, London, 1995); *Personal Information, Privacy and the Law*; *The Protection of Privacy*; and 'The Poverty of Privacy' (1980) 96 *Law Quarterly Review* 73.

[122] Wacks, *Personal Information, Privacy and the Law*, p. 1.   [123] *Ibid.*, p. 26.

require the protection of 'spurious' privacy interests, but would also require the protection of illegitimate privacy claims, for example, the claim that the fact that X beats her children is personal information. In other words, Wacks' definition sees personal information as something that earns protection by a combination of its quality and the reasonableness of the expectation of the individual claiming protection.[124] The reliance on reasonableness is crucial here. In many ways this approach casts a wide net of protection. For example, as Wacks points out, a reasonableness-based assessment of what qualifies for protection allows an individual to claim that even if she has chosen to disclose personal information in one circumstance, it does not mean that she has forfeited protection for all circumstances. You might be happy to tell your doctor that you are infertile but would be very much aggrieved if your employer found out.[125]

Similarly, Wacks notes that his definition allows an individual to claim protection even if she has no idea that information about herself exists or has been used without authority. This is so because one can determine if the individual might reasonably be expected to view the information as sensitive or intimate 'if she were aware' of the unauthorised activities in question.[126] However, the obvious question that this approach needs to address is how the matter of reasonableness is to be determined. In turn, this question can be broken down into a number of related issues. For example, who is to answer the question of reasonableness? Are there any basic preliminaries that mean that the status of 'personal information' can be claimed for certain issues as a matter of course? And, is the determination of reasonableness open to influence from the interests of other individuals or from society at large?

Wacks' approach to the practical problem of how to protect personal information is to apply a model for assessing the normative degree of protection that can reasonably be expected by the subject. This model depends on the view taken of the sensitivity of the information in question, which he calls 'Information Sensitivity Grading'.[127] It works as follows. Different types of personal information are categorised into one of three indices: high, moderate, and low sensitivity. The purpose is to assist in determining the role of the law in regulating the collection and/or the use

---

[124] *Ibid.*, p. 24.   [125] *Ibid.*, p. 27.   [126] *Id.*   [127] *Ibid.*, pp. 226ff.

of such information. Information concerning how an individual voted at the last general election, how frequently she has sexual intercourse, her divergent sexual habits, her mental health, suicide attempts, misuse of drugs or alcohol and genetic predispositions to illness or congenital handicaps are classified as 'highly sensitive'. In comparison, information relating to an individual's previous address, the fact that she is adopted, her NHS number, her absences from work or her credit rating are examples of information of 'moderate sensitivity'. Finally, information of 'low sensitivity' includes sporting activities, membership of clubs, employer details, home address and the fact that an individual wears glasses. Wacks identifies six factors which assist in the categorisation of personal information.[128] These are:

- the reasonable expectations of the data subject;
- the recipient of the data;
- the scale of the disclosure;
- the age of the data;
- the context of the collection, use or disclosure;
- the purpose of collection, use or disclosure.

In this way he provides us with a means of measuring the reasonableness of a claim to protection of personal information through a range of objectively assessed criteria. Even so, the very general question of the reasonableness of the expectations of the data subject remains one of primary importance.

Wacks also accepts that his model is principally normative and not value-free because it classifies information by reference to existing norms and to attitudes towards certain kinds of information. Thus, as he notes, 'medical information accounts for the preponderance of "highly sensitive" data'.[129] He also concedes that such a model cannot be exhaustive and will never attract universal approval. This, however, he sees as an advantage rather than a disadvantage: the quality of information can shift as social and political norms themselves change.[130]

In essence, however, Wacks' classification system is based on a concern with harm. The over-arching question to be asked of information is this: to what extent will unauthorised use or disclosure of the information result in harm to the subject? Thus, the classification of personal

---

[128] *Ibid.*, pp. 227–9.   [129] *Ibid.*, p. 242.   [130] *Ibid.*, pp. 226–7.

information becomes a mechanism for risk management and damage limitation. While there is no obvious first-degree objection to this approach, it suggests that information cannot be classed as highly personal if – when objectively assessed – it is thought to cause little or no harm if misused. Such information is therefore unlikely to receive (strong) protection. But, in certain cases, the use or disclosure of particular information that falls outside Wacks' model or that has been classed as 'low sensitivity' might, nonetheless, be harmful for a particular individual, and Wacks' model is unlikely to protect against it. This is not to say that Wacks' adoption of an objective test is in itself wrong. It is simply to assert that a model that is concerned primarily with the avoidance of harm is weakened if it excludes cases where harm is actually likely to result, even if those cases do not fit neatly into the model that has been devised.[131] If Wacks' response would be that his list of six factors that determine the category into which any particular form of information should fall will operate in conjunction with the particular interests of the individual – for example, depending on how she views the purposes of disclosure, or how she sees the context of disclosure – then this involves the introduction of a subjective element to his assessment of personal information, and it should be recognised as such.

The consequence of Wacks' system is that the form of protection offered to personal information depends upon the category in which any particular piece of information is placed. He suggests that there is a strong case for holding that information of a highly sensitive nature should, perhaps, not be gathered at all. The implication is that if such information is not gathered, control cannot be lost and therefore harm cannot result from misuse or unauthorised disclosure. Wacks admits that it is difficult to argue that moderately sensitive information should not be collected at all; rather, he suggests that, once collected, it should receive a high degree of protection because 'the potential for harm is of a very high order'.[132] Finally, low sensitivity information concerns, in the main, biographical information about an individual, that is, information that is already available in the public domain (for example,

---

[131] Wacks himself admits that his model is concerned with the avoidance and/or reduction of harm: 'The threefold classification used in the above index of "personal information" is based on the extent to which the collection or use of the data holds a potential for *serious harm* to the subject', *ibid.*, p. 238.

[132] *Ibid.*, p. 229.

address, telephone number, employment details, etc). The collection of such information is of itself unlikely to cause harm, but the collocation of various pieces of information from different sources can create a category of personal information that is of a higher order of sensitivity. Low order information deserves a degree of protection in this respect.

Wacks' aim is admirable. He offers a model for dealing with personal information that is viable and which provides a relatively sound base for legal supervision. He is, however, fully cognisant of the objections that might be raised and does not purport to offer a definitive account of how personal information should be classified. But, as he himself says, 'the purpose is to demonstrate that personal information is susceptible of this sort of analysis, and that it might offer a more effective means of regulating the collection and use of such data'.[133]

This he does well, and it is not the intention here to criticise that attempt per se. However, there are two objections to the work that can be raised from the perspective of the present analysis. These are, first, the question of third party interests, and second, the restriction of his protection of privacy to personal information.

We have already asked to what extent the determination of reasonableness is open to influence from the interests of other individuals or from society at large. In the first instance, Wacks avoids saying that information in which others have an interest is no longer 'personal' or 'highly sensitive'. His model is designed to apply to all kinds of personal information irrespective of external factors such as third party interests.[134] However, he introduces these when discussing the question of whether highly sensitive information should be gathered or used at all. Indeed, he is led to conclude – using the example of persons afflicted by AIDS – that legitimate third parties' interests should be furthered if possible. He then argues that to say that highly sensitive personal information should not be collected at all is no answer to the question of its appropriate legal protection. His solution in the context of AIDS is anonymisation. In that way, he submits, the risk of harm to the individual is minimised but, at the same time, the public interest in statistical data on the spread of HIV and AIDS can be furthered. Unfortunately, such a solution cannot be applied across the whole health care spectrum. In particular, it is not open in the context of genetic information, where we are concerned with

---

[133] *Ibid.*, p. 230.   [134] *Ibid.*, pp. 226–7.

the interests of family members as well as those of the individuals who have been tested for genetic disease; we face the very difficult problem of determining to whom genetic information relates. This is explored further in chapter 5.

Wacks' analysis proceeds on the assumption that personal information concerns one person, who, as a consequence, should control the information in question. But as we will see in chapter 3, the position is considerably more complex in the case of genetic information when the essential nature of the information shifts from the personal to the familial. Wacks' model does not give us a means of assessing such circumstances. This can be seen, inter alia, from his views on the use of medical data. He posits that one approach to the problem of the legitimacy of using highly sensitive medical information is to argue that its use is in the patient's best interests.[135] He rejects this, however, as paternalistic and prefers instead the option of seeking the patient's consent. This is viable in the context of the single doctor/patient relationship, but individual patient consent provides us once again with a problem in the context of familial genetic information. Even if patient A refuses to allow access to genetic information, how are the interests of A's relatives, B and C, to be assessed when they might want or need to know the information? Wacks' model lacks the sophistication to address such problems.

The second objection to be raised to Wacks' thesis relates to his decision to restrict privacy protection to personal information. We have already considered his reasons for doing so: such a construct encompasses most concerns that are expressed in privacy terms, and Wacks suggests that such a concept is more amenable to effective legal protection. His aim is to strike 'the best deal' for a plurality of privacy interests. In the main, he puts forward a convincing and important argument, one that has a sound basis and which provides much of practical utility for those considering the problems of legal protection of privacy. However, it is a primary aim of this work to show that privacy concerns are not restricted simply to concerns about information and further that to fail to recognise this leaves many important non-informational interests unprotected. As an illustration of this consider two examples that cause problems for Wacks' model: the permanently insensate patient[136]

---

[135] *Ibid.*, pp. 242–3.
[136] The permanently insensate patient is, for example, one in irreversible coma or permanent vegetative state (PVS).

and the individual who does not want to know about her own genetic constitution.

In the case of the irretrievably insensate patient, how is such a person harmed by the taking of information about her? She is not conscious, she will never regain consciousness and the information that is obtained is completely beyond her control. Wacks' model would lead us to classify all information about such a person as of low or no sensitivity because the person cannot be injured by the misuse of the information. Yet intuitively we would still say that the patient's privacy had been invaded if, for example, newspaper reporters burst into her hospital room and took photographs and recorded details of her condition.[137] Surely, what is invaded here is not privacy in information, but rather privacy in the self – a sphere of physical privateness that others should not invade without authority and good reason. Moreover, such a sphere exists irrespective of whether the subject can control it or is conscious of its existence. This is so because that sphere is linked not just to information and fear of harm, but to individuality, dignity and respect for persons. This respect can be measured purely against the conduct of the aggressor, and can accordingly be found wanting, even when the aggressee is unaware of any intrusion into her private sphere. A harm-based analysis such as that of Wacks requires a degree of likelihood of harm before privacy interests are considered deserving of protection – no likely harm, no protection. Moreover, Wacks' step-like approach by way of the sensitivity of information does not help us here, because the person to whom the information relates is unaware, and unlikely ever to become aware, of any intrusion.[138] Thus, even on an objective analysis, there would be no likelihood of harm and therefore no reason to protect the information.

The individual who does not want information about her own genetic make-up is also unlikely to be protected by Wacks' analysis. His entire assessment of sensitivity is concerned with harm arising from unauthorised communication of personal information to third parties. However, the individual who does not want to know about familial genetic information is concerned that information *about* herself should not be communicated *to* herself. Moreover, and as will be argued further in chapter 3, it is not clear that the interest that an individual has in not knowing information is to be properly regarded as an informational

---

[137] Note the parallels here with *Kaye* v. *Robertson* [1991] FSR 62, discussed in ch. 1.
[138] Wacks, *Personal Information, Privacy and the Law*, p. 27.

privacy interest. Were it to be so, the nature of privacy would, once again, be reduced to a control-based concept. The individual's privacy argument would then be premised on a claim to control information about herself and, for the reasons articulated above, that is an unsatisfactory view of privacy. Furthermore, a claim to control personal information presupposes that the subject of the information knows the information to exist. The most likely scenario in this context is, however, one in which the subject has no idea about the information in question, for it will have been generated outside her immediate ambience, for example through the testing of relatives; and a person is powerless to exercise control over something about which she is ignorant. Rather, if privacy is seen as a state or condition – which it is submitted is the preferable view – then it becomes a sphere of separateness that deserves recognition as being inviolable, and not merely an issue of control of information. That state of inviolability, if respected, would protect an interest in remaining in ignorance of one's own genetic constitution. This view is akin to that of a spatial privacy interest, something which Wacks would not accept as part of his model.

The above comments should be taken not so much as criticisms of Wacks, but as defences of the approach adopted in this work, which is to argue a view of privacy that encompasses both informational and spatial privacy interests. The utility of this lies in the fact that it widens and, at the same time, crystallises the range of interests that are legitimately subsumed under the privacy rubric. Less ambitiously, it highlights the strong arguments that can be made against narrower constructs, even if in the short term it must be conceded that protection along the lines suggested by Wacks is a necessary and important first step. But, even if that is the case, we should not stop at that point. We should not rest on our laurels simply because we have found a way to protect *some* privacy interests. This work posits that the limits of the law can be pushed further forward in the pursuit of adequate protection for legitimate privacy interests. It paves the way for future and further steps along the privacy path. For these reasons, Wacks' narrow construction of privacy is rejected. And yet, the aim of this work and that of Wacks can be reconciled in the following paradoxical fashion. Wacks seeks to extract a narrow view of privacy from the literature in order to broaden the range of protection that can be afforded to privacy by law. This work examines a narrow area of privacy concern, namely genetic privacy, in order to broaden the privacy debate. The precise role for the law that emerges from this analysis will be examined more fully in later chapters.

Spatial and informational privacy: a medico-legal definition

Privacy was defined broadly in chapter 1 as a state of separateness from others. Such a state encompasses both physical or psychological separateness (spatial privacy), and separateness of personal information (informational privacy). The utility of this definition in the health care setting is examined here.

First, consider informational privacy. Undoubtedly patients have considerable interests in their own medical information, not only because it can be used against them by others with harmful outcomes such as upset, discrimination, or prejudice as envisaged by Wacks, but also by virtue of the simple fact that personal information is an intimate adjunct to individual personality. Respect for personal information is a means to demonstrate respect for the individual herself. Informational privacy implies the denial of access to personal (health) information to those to whom the information does not relate, and to attribute value to informational privacy, as we might do by legal means, is to recognise the interest of patients in maintaining information in a state of non-access and preventing unauthorised use or disclosure of that information to others. The question of what kinds of information qualify as 'personal information' need not lead us to an analysis such as that undertaken by Wacks. For present purposes, the information in question is health information, or, more particularly, genetic information that relates to the individual. Thus a concern about informational privacy is a concern about maintaining a state of non-access to personal health (genetic) information.

Second, let us examine spatial privacy. It has been suggested above that a concept of privacy that is defined solely in informational terms does not adequately reflect the privacy interests of patients and so cannot purport to protect such interests comprehensively. In particular, the notion of spatial privacy has been advocated as complementary to that of informational privacy. The concern of spatial privacy is not simply information. Rather, spatial privacy relates to the sphere of the self – a zone of privateness surrounding the individual that cannot and should not be invaded without due cause. Yet, such a sphere can be invaded either by unwarranted physical contact – which in the medical context can arise through unauthorised treatment or continued futile treatment – or by unwarranted observation, which can occur even when there is no trespass to the actual person. In the latter example it could, of course, be argued that it is the gathering of information that is offensive rather than the observation, but such a view requires us to conclude that there is no invasion of privacy if no information is gathered. This surely cannot be true. The better view is that the invasion of privacy arises from the unwarranted observation per se. However, this is defensible only if it is accepted that the interest that is compromised in such cases is a spatial privacy interest and not an informational privacy interest.[139] Moreover, in the context of genetic information, it has been argued that spatial privacy can be invaded by the revelation of genetic data about an individual to that self-same individual. This cannot appropriately be seen as an informational privacy issue because the latter concerns an interest in maintaining non-access vis-à-vis third parties. In the example under discussion, the concern is revelation of information about oneself to oneself.

Two concepts, not one?

The justifications for this two-fold conception of privacy are numerous. First, it accords to a high degree with what is understood in lay terms as being private. This is important because it goes a long way in the formulation of an effective law that can address actual social needs. For example, a number of reports have been commissioned in the United Kingdom to investigate the need for greater privacy protection, key among which is that of the Younger Committee which reported in 1972.[140] As part of its report the Committee published the results of a survey that had been conducted to determine the attitudes of members of the public towards various forms of invasion of privacy. The main reason given by respondents for feelings that privacy protection had declined was the increase in the number of requests to complete forms and this led to an impression that too much was known about individuals by a wide variety of organisations.[141] The second most common reason

---

[139] The basis for this interest is human dignity and respect; see above.

[140] Sir Kenneth Younger, *The Report of the Committee on Privacy*, Cmnd 5012 (London, HMSO, 1972).

[141] A shortened version of the survey report is contained in Appendix E of the Committee's report. The Committee discusses its conclusions about the survey in ch. 6, particularly paras. 98–102, 236, Table F; 239, Table J.

given for the perception that privacy had declined was that housing was considered to be crowded together, with consequent feelings of violation of personal space. While this survey was commissioned and carried out some three decades ago, there is nothing that has changed so radically in contemporary society that might lead us to expect that the results would be very different if the same survey were conducted today.[142] The two primary concerns disclosed mirror the twin concepts of informational and spatial privacy advocated here.[143]

Personal privacy in the United Kingdom has been under most threat in recent years from the vagaries of the news media, and in particular the press. During the late 1980s and the 1990s Sir David Calcutt was the central figure in a long-drawn-out saga concerning the need for tighter controls on the press in respect of the protection of individual privacy. In 1989 he was appointed Chair of the Committee on Privacy and Related Matters to investigate these concerns, and while, like the Younger Committee before it, the Calcutt Committee declined to recommend the introduction of a statutory right of privacy in the United Kingdom,[144] it felt none the less that there was a need for legislation to address the problem of intrusion into the lives of individuals by the use of surveillance technologies. It proposed criminal offences along the following lines.

- The following acts should be criminal offences in England and Wales:
  (a) entering private property, without the consent of the lawful occupant, with the intent to obtain personal information and with a view to its publication;
  (b) placing a surveillance device on private property, without the consent of the lawful occupant, with the intent to obtain personal information with a view to its publication;

---

[142] A recent study by Harris and Westin reveals that over 80 per cent of American adults consider that they have lost control of the collection and use of personal information by corporations; see A. C. Aman Jr, 'Information, Privacy, and Technology: Citizens, Clients, or Consumers' in J. Beatson and Y. Cripps (eds.), *Freedom of Expression and Freedom of Information* (Oxford University Press, Oxford, 2000), p. 339. This supports the thesis that the greatest current threat to privacy now comes from private enterprise and not the state.

[143] It should also be noted that of a category of seven civil and social rights (which included improving race relations, protecting the freedom of the press and giving equal rights for women) protecting people's privacy was ranked the most important. In this context it is submitted that a different outcome might well result today. This does not mean however that privacy concerns in se have diminished any, but simply that other concerns, such as accepting racial and sexual equality, have taken on increased importance since 1972.

[144] Sir David Calcutt, *Report of the Committee on Privacy and Related Matters*, Cm 1102 (London, HMSO, 1990), para. 12.5.

(c) taking a photograph, or recording the voice, of an individual who is on private property, without his consent, with a view to its publication and with the intent that the individual shall be identified.[145]

These criminal offences are premised on a binary view of privacy such as has been argued for above. It can be seen, for example, that although entry on to private property is necessary in the cases of (a) and (b), the same is not true of offence (c). Thus, actual physical intrusion is not always necessary for an invasion of privacy. Furthermore, in the cases of (a) and (b) no actual personal information need be obtained to constitute an invasion of privacy. It is sufficient that the private sphere has been penetrated and there is an intention to seek out such information for publication. That is, it is the invasion of the private space rather than the taking of private information that is thought to constitute the offensive behaviour. Similarly, as regards offence (c) it is not the obtaining of information in the guise of a photograph or a voice sample that is necessarily the invasion of privacy – for this could occur when the person was in public – but rather it is the obtaining of this information when the person is in the private sphere. It is important to note that there is no qualification that the information be personal or private. This suggests that the focus of the offence, as with (a) and (b), is the invasion of private space. Together these suggested offences reveal a perceived need for greater protection in the fields of both informational and spatial privacy.

While nothing came of these proposals, the recommendations made it clear that concerns with spatial interests are particularly important to members of the public and, perhaps more significantly, are thought to be the appropriate focus of legislative action. Also, the point is made indirectly by Calcutt that these interests cannot be subsumed in toto under the rubric of an informational analysis.

Privacy as a solid state of affairs

For the reasons outlined earlier, to define privacy as a state rather than a right or a claim helps to describe the concept while at the same time avoids imputing value to it, at least in the first instance.[146] While privacy

---

[145] *Ibid.*, para. 6.33.
[146] For a defence of a 'valued' approach to privacy, see Inness, *Privacy, Intimacy and Isolation*, ch. 4.

is defined as a state of separateness from others, this is not to say that other parties cannot enter that sphere, nor that individuals can act however they wish when in such a sphere, nor indeed that such a state necessarily protects undesirable activities. Rather, it is to say that, prima facie, a state of privacy places the individual apart from others. This notion can of course extend to the privacy of groups, but the common denominator is the state of separateness of a significant unitary entity. This having been said, merely to be apart from others will not always lead to the conclusion that a state of privacy has been attained. For example, to be marooned on a deserted island is certainly to be apart from others, but few would claim this to be privacy.[147] This is in part because privacy implies something more than mere separateness, which can sometimes be seen as undesirable. As Schoeman has said, 'the problem for such a person [on an island] is that he has too much privacy'.[148] However, it is equally arguable that a person in such circumstances has not achieved privacy at all, but is simply in a state of isolation. In order to be in a state of privacy there must be others from whom one can choose to be separate. This is not possible on a desert island, for one is alone. Isolation implies a state of enforced non-access to others. Privacy, on the other hand, is a state that can easily be relaxed or maintained because it occurs in a social context. Isolation concerns the removal of individuals from that context and therefore ought not to be described as privacy. Consider, then, the position of the prisoner condemned to solitary confinement. She has been removed from a social context – not simply society in general but also the community of the prison population – and has been placed in isolation. This person does not have privacy. However, a prisoner who retires to her cell to read does have privacy in that she is voluntarily separate from the rest of the prison community.

Similarly, simply to be in the presence of others does not necessarily mean that privacy interests cannot be claimed. For example, an interest in maintaining bodily integrity is an aspect of spatial privacy. It is not because I am in a crowd that unwarranted interferences with my bodily integrity are not offensive and cannot be classed as invasions of privacy. Mere jostling or accidental contact are examples of the *de minimis* principle, but intentional contact with my person can easily be seen

---

[147] Cf. Inness, *Privacy, Intimacy and Isolation*, p. 6.
[148] F. Schoeman, 'Philosophical Dimensions of the Literature', in *idem, Philosophical Dimensions of Privacy*, p. 3.

as an invasion of privacy. As a corollary, it would be difficult to maintain that the privacy interest in not being observed is invaded by being in a crowd. In such a case there is consent to a degree of observation, namely, that which flows directly and naturally from one's voluntary presence in the public sphere. However, a strong argument could be made that to record a person's movements clandestinely does indeed infringe her privacy interests.[149] There is a world of difference between the anonymity of the crowd and the specific identification of an individual within a crowd. In the former case any observation which occurs is merely incidental and can be readily anticipated by the individual in question. If, however, the individual is being observed clandestinely, not only can she not reasonably anticipate being the focus of someone else's attention, but she becomes a means to someone else's end, a factor which in itself is offensive and disrespectful of her.[150]

To describe privacy as a *state* and therefore to seek to offer a neutral description of the concept of privacy does not preclude us from attributing value *to* such a state. Nor does it prevent us from seeking to accord (legal) protection for such a state by reason of the good ends that it can further and for the interests that it can protect. It has already been argued that a state of separateness *can* protect good ends – both private and public. In essence, such a state is one in which the interests of the individual are paramount. To accord respect and protection to such a state evidences a degree of commitment to valuing individuals. However, the obvious question that arises from this is why should we seek to protect such a state of privacy when mechanisms for respecting individuals and protecting their interests already exist? The response is that such existing mechanisms cannot always provide adequate protection. Furthermore, the concept of privacy advanced here allows us to acknowledge a broad range of interests that might otherwise have gone unrecognised.

One criticism that might be levelled at the view of privacy presented here is that it confuses privacy with concepts such as autonomy, liberty or even confidentiality. For example, a state of separateness implies a state

---

[149] For recent recognition of this from the Supreme Court of Canada, see *Les Editions Vice-Versa Inc.* v. *Aubry* (1998) 5 BHRC 437.

[150] Strong counter-arguments can be made to justify such observation – for example, closed circuit television in shopping malls for security purposes or to further some other legitimate public interest. However, if such tapes are sold to broadcast media for entertainment purposes this would become an offensive use of the images obtained.

of non-interference, which is arguably simply one definition of liberty or freedom. Similarly, it might be contended that the state in question is one that depends largely on the notion of autonomy – the individual as self-ruler. This would be an important criticism, and the relationship between privacy and these related concepts must be examined.

Privacy and related concepts

Many writers associate the beginning of modern Western legal interest in privacy with the seminal article by Warren and Brandeis, *The Right to Privacy*, published in the 1890–91 volume of the *Harvard Law Review*.[151] This article was written at the instigation of Warren, a then notable Boston lawyer, who took umbrage at what he saw to be excessive press intrusion into his daughter's marriage. The US tort of invasion of privacy grew from such small beginnings.[152] Warren and Brandeis examined cases drawn from areas as diverse as defamation,[153] breach of confidence[154] and copyright,[155] and concluded that the common law recognised a general right to privacy.[156] This they classified as a 'right to be alone'.[157] This work, whose influence has been unimaginably far-reaching, has been much praised[158] and much criticised.[159] Here, it is not intended to do either but, rather, to offer it as an illustration of a common problem that arises in the field of privacy study. This is the problem of conflation of concepts and confusion of terminology.

[151] S. D. Warren and L. D. Brandeis, 'The Right to Privacy' (1890–91) 4 *Harvard Law Review* 193.

[152] For analysis see Prosser, 'Privacy: A Legal Analysis'.

[153] Warren and Brandeis, 'The Right to Privacy', 205.

[154] See, for example, *Abernathy* v. *Hutchinson* (1825) 3 L. J. Ch. 209, and *Prince Albert* v. *Strange* (1849) 1 McN. & G. 25.

[155] For example, *Tuck* v. *Priester* (1887) 19 QBD 639.

[156] It is often pointed out that ironically the authors relied heavily on English common law cases to support their argument, but no common law right to privacy was recognised in England until 2000: see ch. 5.

[157] The 'right to be alone' was first expounded by T. M. Cooley, *A Treatise on the Law of Torts*, 2nd edn (Chicago, Callaghan & Co., 1888), p. 29.

[158] For example, see R. Gavison, 'Too Early For A Requiem: Warren and Brandeis Were Right on Privacy vs. Free Speech' (1992) 43 *South Carolina Law Review* 437.

[159] For example, D. L. Zimmerman, 'Requiem for a Heavyweight: A Farewell to Warren and Brandeis' Privacy Tort' (1984) 68 *Cornell Law Review* 291; W. F. Pratt, 'The Warren and Brandeis Argument for a Right to Privacy' [1975] *Public Law* 161; E. J. Bloustein, 'Privacy, Tort Law and the Constitution: Is Warren and Brandeis' Tort Petty and Unconstitutional as Well?' (1968) 46 *Texas Law Review* 611; H. Kalven, 'Privacy in Tort Law: Were Warren and Brandeis Wrong?' (1966) 31 *Law and Contemporary Problems* 326.

The association of privacy with the 'right to be alone' has been made by many writers since Warren and Brandeis,[160] and all have been subject to the same challenge: by conceiving privacy as a right to be free from intrusion or interference they have equated privacy with liberty.[161] This is not only confusing generally, but it can also have adverse consequences for those who seek to argue positively about privacy. Fried has recognised that 'to present privacy only as an aspect of or an aid to general liberty is to miss some of its most significant differentiating features'.[162] Similarly, Posner has observed that 'we already have perfectly good words – Liberty, Autonomy, Freedom – to describe the interest in being allowed to do what one wants (or chooses) without interference. We should not define privacy to mean the same thing and thereby obscure its other meanings.'[163]

The United States' constitutional right of privacy

The conflation of privacy with liberty is a common problem in the United States. Indeed, this is the primary criticism levelled at the US constitutional right of privacy that was interpreted out of the Constitution by the Supreme Court in *Griswold* v. *Connecticut*.[164] This case concerned Estelle Griswold, who was the Executive Director of the Planned Parenthood League in that state. In defiance of a statute criminalising contraception and acts aiding and abetting the use of contraception,[165] Griswold provided information, instruction and medical advice to married couples as to the various means of preventing conception. She was successfully prosecuted under the law and fined $100. The constitutionality of the statute was immediately challenged and the case was ultimately heard by the Supreme Court. In a seminal decision, the Court 'interpreted out' of the US Constitution a right to privacy that is not expressly included therein. It did so by reference to what it called *penumbras*, 'emanations

---

[160] See, for example, L. Blom-Cooper, 'The Right to Be Let Alone' (1989) 10 *Journal of Media Law and Practice* 53.

[161] Parent warns against this very specifically in 'Privacy, Morality and the Law'.

[162] Fried, 'Privacy', 490.

[163] R. Posner, 'An Economic Theory of Privacy' in F. D. Schoeman (ed.), *Privacy: An Anthology*, pp. 274–5.

[164] *Griswold* v. *Connecticut* 381 US 479 (1965). For an account of the historical lead-up to *Griswold* see Rubenfeld, 'The Right of Privacy', 740–4.

[165] The provisions in question were paras. 53.32 and 54.196 of the General Statutes of Connecticut (1958 rev.).

from those guarantees [in the Bill of Rights] that help give them life and substance'. It was held that various guarantees create 'zones' of privacy. In other words, various rights expressly guaranteed in the Bill of Rights, such as the right of association,[166] the right against self-incrimination,[167] or the right not to have soldiers quartered in one's home during peacetime[168] – as applied to states through the due process clause of the Fourteenth Amendment[169] – create spheres of life which are protected and *private*. And, in order for that protection to be complete, the true extent of the zones of privacy that exist must be recognised, even if there is no express mention of their existence in the text of the Constitution. As the Court said in *Griswold*,

> The present case ... concerns a relationship lying within the zone of privacy created by several fundamental constitutional guarantees. And it concerns a law which, in forbidding the *use* of contraceptives rather than regulating their manufacture or sale, seeks to achieve its goals by means having a maximum destructive impact upon that relationship. Such a law cannot stand in light of the familiar principle [that] a 'governmental purpose to control or prevent activities constitutionally subject to state regulation may not be achieved by means which sweep unnecessarily broadly and thereby invade the area of protected freedoms'. ... Would we allow the police to search the sacred precincts of marital bedrooms for telltale signs of the use of contraceptives? The very idea is repulsive to the notions of privacy surrounding the marriage relationship.[170]

In this way the Court ruled the Connecticut statute unconstitutional and in doing so gave birth to the Constitutional Right to Privacy.[171] It is important to note that at this stage in its development the right was concerned with family life and its protection.[172] It was, however, soon extended to 'individual' rights and beyond, in cases such as *Eisenstadt* v. *Baird*[173] (in which prohibitions on contraceptive use by single persons

---

[166] Part of the First Amendment.   [167] Part of the Fifth Amendment.
[168] The Third Amendment.
[169] *Griswold*, 482–5. In all, the Court held that the penumbras emanated from the First, Third, Fourth, Fifth and Ninth Amendments.
[170] *Per* Justice Douglas, at 485.
[171] Heavy reliance was also placed on the Ninth Amendment (*per* Justice Goldberg, at 493) and the Fourteenth Amendment (*per* Justices White and Harlan, at 500–2, 502–8).
[172] In particular, Justice White made it clear that the policy behind the statute – namely, an attempt to ban 'illicit sexual relationships' (and by this was meant all forms of 'promiscuity' and sexual relations between non-married couples) – was perfectly permissible as a legislative goal.
[173] *Eisenstadt* v. *Baird* 405 US 438 (1972).

were held to be unconstitutional[174]), *Roe* v. *Wade*[175] (in which the right of privacy was held to be broad enough to encompass a woman's decision to terminate a pregnancy[176]), *Planned Parenthood* v. *Danforth*[177] (in which the Supreme Court held unconstitutional a statute requiring a woman to obtain her spouse's consent to abortion) and *Planned Parenthood of Southeastern Pennsylvania* v. *Casey*[178] (in which the Court reaffirmed the authority of *Roe* and *Danforth*[179]).[180]

These decisions extend considerably the rights of persons, and particularly women, in the area of reproduction. More generally, it can be seen how the right of privacy started as a 'family right' and became an

[174] *Per* Justice Brennan: 'If under *Griswold* the distribution of contraceptives to married persons cannot be prohibited, a ban on distribution to unmarried persons would be equally impermissible. It is true that in *Griswold* the right of privacy in question inhered in the marital relationship. Yet the marital couple is not an independent entity with a mind and heart of its own, but an association of two individuals each with a separate intellectual and emotional make-up. If the right of privacy means anything, it is the right of the *individual*, married or single, to be free from unwarranted governmental intrusion into matters so fundamentally affecting a person as the decision whether to bear or beget a child', *ibid.*, at 453.

[175] *Roe* v. *Wade* 410 US 113 (1973).

[176] *Roe* v. *Wade* is easily *the* most analysed US constitutional right of privacy case. As an example of the range of arguments which have been made surrounding it, consider J. H. Ely, 'The Wages of Crying Wolf: A Comment on *Roe* v. *Wade*' (1973) 82 *Yale Law Journal* 920.

[177] *Planned Parenthood* v. *Danforth* 428 US 52 (1976).

[178] *Planned Parenthood of Southeastern Pennsylvania* v. *Casey* 112 S.Ct. 2791 (1992); 505 US 833 (1992).

[179] Note, however, that the court also held certain restrictions on a woman's abortion decision to be constitutional in this case. The case concerned several provisions of the *Pennsylvania Abortion Control Act* which provided that (except in an emergency) a physician could not perform an abortion within twenty-four hours of a request, that such physicians had to furnish women seeking an abortion with information pertaining to the nature of abortion, the risks involved and available alternatives to abortion, the risks of continued pregnancy, and the age of the foetus. There were also provisions concerning parental consent, spousal notification and public recording of abortions performed. Although a majority of the Supreme Court held that 'the essential holding of *Roe* v. *Wade* should be retained and once again reaffirmed' (at 2804), it struck down only the provision of the Pennsylvania Act which concerned spousal notification. The remaining provisions were not 'unduly burdensome' on the woman and therefore acceptable in constitutional terms. This language is revealing. It represents a significant shift away from the language of *Roe* v. *Wade*, which required the state to show a 'compelling interest' to justify interference with the abortion decision. This shift in terminology is not mere sophistry. The need simply to avoid an 'unduly burdensome' provision means that states can legitimately give information to women about abortion and its risks and consequences in an attempt to persuade (but not coerce) them into opting out of abortion. Such an outcome, arguably, was not possible with the language of Justice Blackmun in *Roe* v. *Wade*.

[180] For critical comment on these and other right of privacy cases in the area of reproduction, see E. Keynes, *Liberty, Property and Privacy: Towards a Jurisprudence of Substantive Due Process* (University Park, PA, Pennsylvania State University Press, 1996), ch. 8.

'individual right' that guarantees many personal and sexual freedoms.[181] However, the right has not been without limits. This point was made quite categorically by the Supreme Court in *Bowers* v. *Hardwick*.[182]

Bowers v. Hardwick

In this case the constitutionality of a Georgia statute that criminalised sodomy was challenged by Michael Hardwick, who had been prosecuted under the law. He argued that his homosexual activity was 'a private and intimate association' beyond the legitimate reach of state intervention and protected by his Constitutional Right to Privacy. Justice White, who wrote the 5–4 majority opinion upholding the statute, framed Hardwick's case rather differently. He asserted that the essence of the case was whether 'the Federal Constitution confers a fundamental right upon homosexuals to engage in sodomy'.[183] Thus put, it is hardly surprising that Hardwick's case was unsuccessful.

Justice White noted that to date the constitutional privacy cases protected three categories of activity: marriage, procreation and family relationships.[184] Since the activities of homosexuals fall into none of these, he argued, their activities could not be protected by the privacy right. This is strange reasoning by anyone's standards. First, all that Justice White achieved in *Bowers* was a description of the nature of the Court's prior decisions on privacy. What he did not do, and yet what is surely fundamental to his argument, was to provide an explanation of the underlying doctrinal philosophy that ties these three areas together. In the absence of such an explanation, these three categories can only be taken as examples of the spheres of life protected by privacy; they cannot be seen as determinative in any way.

Second, Justice White failed to explain why he thought (as he and the majority obviously did) that the constitutional right of privacy should be restricted to areas of life that do not include homosexual conduct. This point should not be misinterpreted. It is not to suggest that no

---

[181] As Rubenfeld has noted, 'The great peculiarity of the privacy cases is their predominant, though not exclusive, focus on sexuality – not "sex" as such, of course, but sexuality in the broad sense of that term; the network of decisions and conduct relating to the conditions under which sex is permissible, the social institutions surrounding sexual relationships, and the procreative consequences of sex. Nothing in the privacy cases says that the doctrine must gravitate around sexuality. Nevertheless, it has', 'The Right of Privacy', 744.

[182] *Bowers* v. *Hardwick* 478 US 186 (1986).   [183] *Ibid.*, at 190.   [184] *Ibid.*, at 190–1.

justification for upholding the Georgia statute was advanced. Rather, it poses the question, why is privacy – which is clearly concerned with sexual conduct and sexuality – not concerned with the sexuality of all persons, including homosexuals? It is no longer possible to argue, for example, that the right of privacy is solely concerned with families and marital activity, for the Court's decision in *Eisenstadt* v. *Baird* permitted single people to have access to contraceptives, and this can only be seen to be about sex. *Bowers*, then, is inconsistent and unprincipled, for it fails to extend the authority from established cases that sexual freedom should be protected as a central element in the right to privacy, and offers no justifiable rationale for doing so.

Not surprisingly, the *Bowers* decision has been heavily criticised.[185] Those who analyse the aftermath primarily asked the question, what does privacy mean now? Many see privacy as being concerned with choices and decisions, but this is simply to avoid the question as to *which* choices and decisions are protected by privacy. And, as Rubenfeld has pointed out, 'On this point the Court has offered little guidance.'[186] He adds further:

> We are told that privacy encompasses only those 'personal rights that can be deemed "fundamental" or "implicit in the concept of ordered liberty"' [*Roe* v. *Wade* at 152], that it insulates decisions 'important' to a person's destiny [*Whalen* v. *Roe* 429 US 589, 1977, at 600], and that it applies to 'matters . . . fundamentally affecting a person' [*Eisenstadt* v. *Baird* at 438, 453]. Perhaps the best interpretation of these formulations is that privacy is like obscenity: The Justices might not be able to say what privacy is, but they know it when they see it.[187]

Rubenfeld himself argues, however, that this is an unsatisfactory state of affairs, leaving privacy open to allegations of conceptual confusion and ill-considered development. For him, the underlying principle that binds privacy cases together, and which provides a consistent and jus-tifiable rationale for them, is that of 'the fundamental freedom not to have one's life too totally determined by a progressively more normal-izing state'.[188] This is an aspect of liberty, but not the aspect commonly

---

[185] See, for example, Rubenfeld, 'The Right of Privacy', M. H. Kohler, 'History, Homosexuality, and Homophobia: The Judicial Intolerance of *Bowers* v. *Hardwick*' (1986) 19 *Connecticut Law Review* 129; and K. Thomas, 'Beyond the Privacy Principle' (1992) 92 *Columbia Law Review* 1431.
[186] Rubenfeld, 'The Right of Privacy', 751.   [187] *Ibid.*   [188] *Ibid.*, 784ff.

understood to prohibit laws which restrict specific conduct. Rather, Rubenfeld's thesis is that privacy concerns laws that 'take over' the lives of individuals because they are concerned with aspects of life that are profoundly and extensively affected by such laws. An individual's liberty or freedom is not merely restricted in certain aspects; her entire life is directed down a state–prescribed path. He puts it thus:

> laws against abortion, interracial marriage, non-nuclear family residences, and private education all involve a peculiar form of obedience that reaches far beyond mere abstention from the particular proscribed act. It is a form of obedience in which the life of the person forced to obey is thereafter substantially filled up and informed by the living, institutional consequences of obedience. The person finds himself in a new and sharply-defined, but also broadly encompassing institutional role because of their affirmative direction of individuals' lives, these roles – whether as mother, spouse, student or family member – have profoundly formative effects on identity and character.[189]

Moreover, this analysis explains and justifies the protection of rights in the *Bowers* v. *Hardwick* scenario. The obedience of anti-sodomy laws has the product of forcing homosexuals into relations with the opposite sex and requires that they adopt 'normalised' social roles as between themselves and the opposite sex. Undeniably, this has profound implications for the everyday lives of persons.[190]

The appeal in Rubenfeld's analysis is strong. Not only does he offer a unifying concept of privacy which provides consistent explanation of past cases and allows clear prediction for future cases, but he also establishes a valid theoretical basis on which to defend Hardwick's claim and to criticise the Supreme Court's rejection of it. The content of his right of privacy is a right 'not to have the course of one's life dictated by the state'.[191] As an aspect of a liberty argument, however, Rubenfeld's thesis is open to the criticism that is made so often of the Constitutional Right of Privacy and those who write about it, namely, that privacy is confused with, and conflated with, liberty.

But before examining this charge, there is a more obvious question that must be addressed. If, indeed, Rubenfeld and others are right, and it is liberty that is the issue and not privacy, why then would the Supreme Court create a privacy right?

---

[189] *Ibid.*, 792–3.   [190] *Ibid.*, 799–802.   [191] *Ibid.*, 807.

Judicial knot-tying

Gavison notes that the use of the language of privacy rather than liberty was deliberate on the part of the US Supreme Court.[192] This is primarily because a problem for the Court in *Griswold* was the need to distinguish 'the substantive due process rationale' established in *Lochner* v. *New York*.[193] This 1905 decision represents the extreme 'liberal' approach once adopted by the Court towards the legitimacy of state intervention in the lives of individuals. In that case the Court held unconstitutional a New York law that sought to restrict the hours that a bakery worker could work in any one day or any one week. The rationale behind the statute was that the state sought to develop consistent labour law policies and to protect the health and safety of workers. The Supreme Court, however, rejected these arguments and held by a majority that the principle of liberty of contract was unduly compromised by such an Act. Taking as its authority the due process clause of the Fourteenth Amendment, the Court opined that to uphold the constitutionality of such an Act would be effectively to deprive individuals of their liberty interests in contracting upon terms agreed privately between themselves and their employers.[194] The Court saw the case as an attempt to impose external constraints on economic relations rather than one truly concerned with worker welfare – an end not acceptable as a legislative goal in its eyes. The immediate consequence of this decision was that economic regulation was treated as an issue requiring strict scrutiny if contained in any statute, the implication being that freedom in economic matters was a fundamental freedom under the Constitution.

Post-*Lochner*, however, the Supreme Court was very heavily criticised. As an interpretation of 'liberty' in the Fourteenth Amendment, the decision is not only very broad, but it ignores the very real problem of inequality of bargaining power between employer and employee. The protection of individuals was seen to be abandoned to the vagaries of the marketplace.

Although the specific ruling in *Lochner* was overturned only twelve years later,[195] the effects of the decision continued to be felt long afterwards.[196] In particular, the protection of 'liberty' under the Constitution

---

[192] See Gavison, 'Feminism and the Public/Private Distinction', 31–2 and 34–5.
[193] *Lochner* v. *New York* 198 US 45 (1905).   [194] *Ibid.*, at 53.
[195] *Bunting* v. *Oregon* 243 US 426 (1917).
[196] The decision in *Nebbia* v. *New York* 291 US 502 (1934) signalled the beginning of the end-point of *Lochner*-type thinking towards the regulation of economic matters. Here the

as a matter of substantive due process came to be seen in a bad light
as a result of the *Lochner* economic rights analysis.[197] Thus, when the
Court came to decide *Griswold* in 1965, it was keen (i) to extend the
protected rights of individuals to include the use of contraceptives between married couples; but (ii) to avoid using the rationale of *Lochner*
(and therefore 'liberty' as it had been defined previously) for fear of
undermining the protection to be afforded.[198] As Gavison has observed,
'Privacy reasoning offered a way out of the *Lochner* dead end.'[199] Of
course, it should not be forgotten or allowed to be obscured that the
primary constitutional provision under which these cases are argued
remains the same, namely, the substantive due process clause of the
Fourteenth Amendment. This brings us to the crucial question: are
'liberty' and 'privacy' under *Lochner* and *Griswold et al.* the same thing
under different guises?

Various arguments have been advanced on both sides.[200] Some have
argued that the *Lochner* cases were concerned solely with economic interests and that the flaw regarding those cases is that the Court cannot,
and should not, act as a dictator of state economic policy. These cases
can be distinguished on the grounds that privacy cases do not involve
the Court in acting as a 'super legislature'. However, as Rubenfeld points
out, 'In its own eyes, the *Lochner* Court was not regulating economics;
it was protecting liberty – the liberty of contract.'[201] Furthermore, he
comments quite rightly that that which is 'private' can easily extend to
economic matters, even if the Supreme Court has thus far chosen to
restrict privacy cases principally to matters of sexuality.[202] Rather, his
defence of the two sets of cases focuses on the 'pre-political' nature of
the *Lochner* decisions. The concerns of those cases – that is, liberty of
contract cases – were property rights that pre-existed the Constitution

---

Court held that strict scrutiny was no longer necessary and that the law need only not be
'unreasonable, arbitrary or capricious' and the means selected to achieve the particular
legislative end should have a real and substantial relation to that end. Eventually, in *West
Coast Hotel Co.* v. *Parrish* 300 US 379 (1937) the Court upheld a statute requiring a minimum
wage for women even though it interfered with freedom of contract *because* the Court
recognised in real terms that there was a very great inequality of bargaining power between
the parties concerned.

[197] For account of the 'demise of substantive due process', see Keynes, *Liberty, Property and
Privacy*, ch. 6.

[198] To see how this is done see *Griswold* v. *Connecticut*, at 482.

[199] Gavison, 'Feminism and the Public/Private Distinction', 34.

[200] See, in particular Rubenfeld, 'The Right to Privacy', 802–5.

[201] *Ibid.*, 803.   [202] *Ibid.*

and so did not require its explicit protection. Privacy rights, however, have evolved because of 'creeping totalitarianism', and are thus political rights created in response to societal influences. Unfortunately, the utility of this analysis is limited for the purposes of the present discussion. Rubenfeld provides *a* means of distinguishing the privacy and liberty cases, but he does not address the criticism that his 'privacy' analysis is simply a 'liberty' analysis by another name. Similarly, Gavison provides us with an explanation of the Court's use of 'privacy' and not 'liberty', but this still does not address the question whether, ultimately, 'privacy' is not simply confused with 'liberty' as a general metaphysical concept.

While some state courts have extended privacy yet further, fashioning it into a fundamental interest in the medico-legal sphere that protects crucial life decisions affecting both individual liberty and autonomy,[203] the Supreme Court itself has experienced something of a volte face, and has rejected privacy as the key interest that protects these interests, preferring instead a return to a liberty analysis in recent years.[204] For some, such as Annas, this represents no serious problem: 'it should be noted ... that both rights [privacy and liberty] derive from the same source, and their content in this context is unlikely to be different'.[205] By the same token, Meisel notes,

> The Court's shift from a privacy analysis to a Fourteenth Amendment analysis is unlikely to have any impact in state courts on common-law or

[203] See most notably the approach of the Supreme Court of New Jersey in respect of withdrawal of life support provision: *In re Quinlan* 70 NJ 10 (1976), 355 A 2d 647; *In re Peter* 108 NJ 365, 529 A. 2d 419 (1987); *In re Farrell* 108 NJ 335, 529 A. 2d 404 (1987); *In re Jobes* 108 NJ 394, 529 A. 2d 434 (1987).

[204] In *Cruzan v. Director, Missouri Department of Health et al.* 497 US 261, 111 L Ed 2d 224 (1990) the Court held that: 'Although many state courts have held a right to refuse treatment is encompassed by a generalised constitutional right of privacy, we have never so held. We believe this issue is more properly analysed in terms of the Fourteenth Amendment liberty interest', at 242, n. 7. The court cited its own liberty jurisprudence in support: *Jacobson v. Massachusetts*, 197 US 11, 24–30, 49 L Ed 643, 25 S Ct 358 (1905) (in which the Court balanced the recognised liberty interest of the individual in refusing invasive vaccination with the state interest in protecting public health); *Washington v. Harper*, 494 US 210, 108 L Ed 2d 178, 110 S Ct 1028 (1990) (in which the Court held that the forcible injection of medication into a non-consenting person's body represents a substantial interference with the person's liberty); *Vitek v. Jones* 445 US 480, 63 L Ed 2d 552, 100 S Ct 1254 (1980) (in which the Court held that the transfer of a patient to a mental hospital coupled with mandatory behaviour modification treatment implicated liberty interests); and *Parham v. J. R.*, 442 US 584, 61L Ed 2d 101, 99 S Ct 2493 (1979) (here the Court held that a child, in common with adults, has a substantial liberty interest in not being confined unnecessarily for medical treatment).

[205] G. J. Annas, 'The Long Dying of Nancy Cruzan' (1991) 19 *Law, Medicine and Health Care* 52.

state constitutional grounds, as well as the federal constitutional right of privacy. This has been borne out in subsequent state court decisions, in which they have continued to rely on state constitutions, state statutes, and the common-law right to be free from unwanted interference with bodily integrity to provide the basis for the right to refuse medical treatment, the refusal of which will result in death.[206]

This suggests that the wide-ranging influence of the right to privacy is likely to remain in the medico-legal sphere, at least at the state level.[207] However, the continued confusion surrounding the legitimate boundaries and roles of concepts such as liberty, autonomy and privacy has done a great disservice to their ontological essence, and by far the most significant harm has been done to privacy, for it has long been seen as the poorest cousin in the family. Thus, while its continued existence is one thing, its legitimacy and scope are entirely different matters.

Conflation of concepts

Commentators criticise the US Constitution's privacy right on many different levels.[208] As has already been discussed, a major criticism that is frequently voiced is the alleged confusion of privacy with liberty. Parent, for example, shows deep concern:

> The defining idea of liberty is the absence of external restraints or coercion. A person who is behind bars or locked in a room or physically pinned to the ground is unfree to do many things. Similarly, a person who is prohibited by law from making certain choices should be described as having been denied the liberty or freedom to make them. The loss of liberty in these cases takes the form of a deprivation of autonomy. Hence we can meaningfully say that the right to liberty embraces in part the right of persons to make fundamentally important choices about their

---

[206] A. Meisel, 'A Retrospective on *Cruzan*' (1992) 20 *Law, Medicine and Health Care* 340.

[207] It is interesting to note, for example, that despite the Supreme Court's rejection of a privacy analysis in *Bowers* v. *Hardwick*, the Georgia State Supreme Court later struck down the sodomy law as 'violative of the privacy rights protected by the state's own constitution'; see T. M. Franck, *The Empowered Self: Law and Society in the Age of Individualism* (New York, Oxford University Press, 1999), pp. 192–3.

[208] L. Henkin, 'Privacy and Autonomy' (1974) 74 *Columbia Law Review* 1410, has argued that *Griswold* and its progeny have given rise to 'an additional zone of *autonomy* of presumptive immunity to governmental regulation'. This constitutional right of privacy, he considers, 'may not add much protection to "traditional value privacy"', 1424–5. A similar criticism has been advanced by H. Gross, 'Privacy and Autonomy', in J. Feinberg and H. Gross (eds.), *Philosophy of Law*, 2nd edn (Belmont, CA, Wadsworth, 1980), pp. 246–51.

lives and therewith to exercise significant control of different aspects of
their behaviour. It is clearly distinguishable from privacy, *which condemns
the unwarranted acquisition of undocumented personal knowledge.* (emphasis
added: Parent's definition of the concept of privacy)[209]

Parent is of the view that all of the US constitutional privacy cases
'conflate the right to privacy with the right to liberty'.[210] And, while
one may not agree with his particular definition of privacy, his point
on confusion of concepts is valid none the less.[211] DeCew offers the following explanation: 'Given early association of a legal right to privacy
as a right to be let alone and the well-known explanation of a concept
of negative liberty in terms of freedom from interference, it is hardly
surprising that privacy and liberty should often be equated.'[212]

There is, however, an additional problem which stems from the fact
that although one may accept wholeheartedly that privacy and liberty as
defined by Parent are completely separate, it does not necessarily follow
that the two concepts raise issues wholly unconnected with each other.
Furthermore, as DeCew points out in relation to the US cases, 'it is not
at all clear that Parent has shown that the constitutional privacy cases
involve no "genuine" privacy interests'.[213]

Clearly, however, the two concepts are by no means synonymous. As
DeCew herself comments, it is simple to show how a notion of privacy can be shown to be distinct from that of liberty. She offers the
example of an individual's privacy being constantly invaded by surreptitious surveillance of which she is unaware, thereby having no effect on
her liberty. To this could be added the example of genetic information
gathered about an individual through testing of her relatives when the
individual in question is unaware that knowledge about herself has been
generated. Both of these examples involve invasion of the private sphere
yet entail no impingement on liberty. Indeed DeCew states: 'While the
word "privacy" could be used to mean freedom to live one's life without
governmental interference, the [US] Supreme Court cannot so use it
since such a right is at stake in every case. Our lives are continuously
limited, often seriously, by governmental regulation.'[214]

---

[209] Parent, 'Privacy, Morality and the Law', 274–5.   [210] *Ibid.*, 284.
[211] Although this is by no means altogether novel; see, for example, H. Gross, 'Privacy and
Autonomy', *Nomos* XIII, 180–1, and Henkin, 'Privacy and Autonomy'.
[212] DeCew, 'The Scope of Privacy in Law and Ethics', 162.
[213] *Ibid.*, 161.   [214] *Ibid.*, 162.

In fact the Supreme Court has expressly rejected this idea.[215] However, we can once again accept that perhaps this particular conflation of privacy with liberty is wrong, yet this does not necessitate that we reject completely the possibility of a relationship between the two concepts. Just as DeCew gives examples of privacy issues that do not involve liberty, and vice versa, she equally gives examples of autonomy that exclude all mention of privacy.[216] She qualifies this immediately, however, by acknowledging

> [that] a subset of autonomy cases, certain personal decisions regarding one's basic lifestyle, can plausibly be said to involve privacy interests as well. They should be viewed as liberty cases in virtue of their concern over decision-making *power*, whereas privacy is at stake due to the *nature* of the decision. More needs to be said about which decisions and activities are private ones, but it is no criticism or conflation of concepts to say that an act can be both a theft and a trespass. Similarly, acknowledging that in some cases there is both an invasion of privacy and a violation of liberty need not confuse those concepts.[217]

She also comments that 'loss of privacy can diminish freedom. Nevertheless defending privacy cannot always protect liberty.'[218]

What a defence of privacy can do, however, is protect some forms of liberty; principally those relating to non-interference with the personal sphere of individuals' lives. This is true for autonomy and the same can be said of confidentiality in the case of personal information. This point cannot be stressed too strongly. Many commentators who concern themselves with the concepts of liberty or autonomy face problems of ideological confusion, difficulty of definition and ambiguities of scope. Beauchamp and Childress, for example, point out that autonomy is seriously conceptually confused – it is 'not a univocal concept in either ordinary English or contemporary philosophy and needs to be refined in light of particular objectives'.[219] Similarly, Dworkin considers a plethora of definitions of autonomy offered by writers in that field, almost none of

---

[215] *Paris Adult Theatre I et al. v. Slaton, District Attorney, et al.* 413 US 49 (1973). DeCew makes this point in 'The Scope of Privacy in Law and Ethics', 163–4.

[216] *Ibid.*, 164–5.   [217] *Ibid.*, 165.   [218] *Ibid.*

[219] T. L. Beauchamp and J. F. Childress, *Principles of Biomedical Ethics*, 5th edn (New York, Oxford University Press, 2001), p. 58.

which is in conformity with any other.[220] The same is true in the context
of liberty. For example, Berlin has noted that 'Almost every moralist in
human history has praised freedom. Like happiness and goodness, like
nature and reality, the meaning of this term is so porous that there is
little interpretation that it seems able to resist.'[221]

In the light of this, it is important to recognise the fact that the concepts of liberty, autonomy and privacy are *interrelated*. Indeed, we can
go as far as to say that they are interdependent, each relying on the other
to fulfil its true function in the most effective way possible.[222] Consider
the impossibility of making autonomous choices without a degree of
freedom from interference.[223] Consider the residual value of liberty if
life choices are never respected. And, consider whether it is feasible to
be truly free or fully autonomous without some element of privacy.

Neither liberty nor autonomy can properly fulfil their function or
potential in protecting individuals and their interests without a con-
comitant commitment to a respect for privacy. Each of these concepts
performs the same function, albeit in different ways: each represents
an expression of the fundamental respect that a liberal society has for
its citizens. However, each is also open to criticism as ill-defined, anti-
communitarian and conceptually obfuscated. This having been said, it
may be that we see liberty and autonomy as ends in themselves rather
than as means to an end,[224] while we may view privacy purely as a device
to reach a certain end. Even so, it is not necessary to show privacy to be

---

[220] Dworkin, *The Theory and Practice of Autonomy* (Cambridge, Cambridge University Press, 1988).

[221] I. Berlin, *Four Essays on Liberty* (Oxford, Oxford University Press, 1969), p. 121.

[222] This is supported inter alia by R. B. Hallborg, 'Principles of Liberty and the Right to Privacy' (1986) 5 *Law and Philosophy* 175, who argues for a view of privacy that is deduced from fundamental principles of liberty. This he does 'in order to obtain a right to privacy which is not easily defeasible, and a right which ought to be a permanent part of our legal system'. That is, he sees the essence and value of privacy as being derivative.

[223] Greenawalt has argued, for example, that 'Given a society in which many life-styles and points of view evoke *negative* reactions if publicly known, a substantial degree of freedom from observation is essential if there is to be any genuine autonomy; and real choice also depends on the ability of persons to enjoy states of privacy without intrusion'; see J. H. F. Shattuck, *Rights of Privacy* (New York and Skokie, IL, National Textbook Company in association with American Civil Liberties Union, 1977), p. 199. The original version of this material is to be found in K. Greenawalt, 'Privacy and its Legal Protections' (1974) 2 *Hastings Center Studies* 45.

[224] R. A. A. McCall-Smith, 'Beyond Autonomy' (1997) 14 *Journal of Contemporary Health Law and Policy* 23, 30ff.

a fundamental and ultimate value of itself in order to stake a valid claim to its protection. As Gavison points out,

> Privacy has as much coherence and attractiveness as other values to which we have made a clear commitment, such as liberty. Arguments for liberty, when examined carefully, are vulnerable to objections similar to the arguments ... [against] privacy, yet this vulnerability has never been considered a reason not to acknowledge the importance of liberty, or not to express this importance by an explicit commitment so that any loss will be more likely to be noticed and taken into consideration.[225]

But, for Gavison, the case for an explicit commitment to privacy is made by pointing out the distinctive functions of privacy in our lives. Thus, while privacy might well be complementary to autonomy and liberty, and while it might have as valid a response to criticisms as these related concepts, the strongest case for privacy protection appears when we can identify areas of our lives that are most appropriately described in terms of privacy. Are there, then, specific functions for privacy to perform over and above those constructs that are well established? It is submitted that this is indeed the case in the context of genetic information.

Conclusion

The purpose of this chapter has been to examine current thinking on privacy and to outline common themes and criticisms and certain key views that have been advanced to date. In the course of this, the elements that support the definition of privacy that has been offered in this work have been defended. This definition relates to a state of separateness from others that primarily protects two kinds of interest: informational privacy and spatial privacy. Privacy as so defined has its roots in a moral value system which places considerable emphasis on the protection of the rights and interests of individuals and presupposes such social norms as respect for individuals. In this it is allied to the related concepts of liberty and autonomy, and all three combine to perform essentially the same function – they prescribe the way in which individuals are to be treated in Western society, and they operate to establish and maintain boundaries between the individual and society. These constructs are all adjuncts to a view of human dignity that is prevalent in our society.

---

[225] Gavison, 'Privacy and the Limits of the Law', 468.

Moreover, they are concerned with more than mere protection from harm, for they also provide a means to accord respect to individuals, irrespective of the ability of such individuals to control, comprehend or command situations. To see privacy in such terms allows us to comprehend better why a state of separateness should be sought. It further supports the case for arguing that such a state should be protected, and that invasion of that sphere should only be permitted on grounds and for reasons that have been legitimated. Such a case can be made all the more forcefully when it is appreciated that this view of privacy can identify and protect certain human interests which liberty, autonomy and indeed confidentiality (as an additional cousin in the family) cannot. It is to a consideration of this case in the context of genetic information that we now turn.

3

Human genetics and genetic privacy

Good ethics and good law

Good ethics and good law begin with good facts.[1] This chapter therefore considers the current state of knowledge about human genetics and outlines the available options for its possible uses. The claims of persons and institutions with an interest in genetic information are examined and the potential conflicts explained. This is a crucial precursor to any discussion about the appropriate responses that ethics and law should have to any advances in genetic science and medicine.

The Human Genome Project

The idea of the Human Genome Project was endorsed by the US National Research Council in 1988,[2] and an internationally coordinated effort was under way by late 1990 with the aim of mapping and sequencing the entire chain of human DNA:[3] the human genome.[4] A double helical string of DNA is contained in the nucleus of every cell in every human being, except the gametes. DNA dictates the nature and function of all such cells,[5] and for this reason the human genome has been

---

[1] I am grateful to Professor Michael Grodin of the Department of Health Law, Boston University, for this useful aphorism.

[2] National Research Council, *Mapping and Sequencing the Human Genome* (Washington, DC, National Academy Press, 1988).

[3] Deoxyribonucleic acid.

[4] For general comment on the project and its aims compare J. D. Watson, 'The Human Genome Project: Past, Present and Future' (1990) 248 *Science* 44, and E. S. Lander, 'Scientific Commentary: The Scientific Foundations and Medical and Social Prospects of the Human Genome Project' (1998) 26 *Journal of Law, Medicine and Ethics* 184. For an accessible and comprehensive account of the work of the Human Genome Project and its consequences see W. Bodmer and R. McKie, *The Book of Man: The Quest to Discover Our Genetic Heritage* (New York, Little, Brown, 1994).

[5] It is estimated that a human being is composed of ten million million cells.

referred to as 'the master blueprint of us all'.[6] It is estimated that the work of the Human Genome Project will be completed by 2003.[7] International coordination of the project is undertaken by the Human Genome Organisation (HUGO).[8]

The project has proved to be a source of invaluable knowledge regarding the make-up, nature and function of the so-called 'double helix of life'.[9] The benefits that will accrue from this work are extensive. Several of these were outlined in the UK House of Commons Science and Technology Committee Report on Human Genetics which was published in July 1995.[10] They comprise:

- better understanding of human illness and the role of genetic influences in a great many conditions including psychiatric and neurological disorders;
- quicker and cheaper diagnoses of common diseases;
- better understanding of the 'biochemical or physiological mechanisms' involved in genetic disease: 'focusing on the mechanism involved may bring about cures';[11]
- improved techniques in the design of drugs to produce chemicals that can fit precisely with molecules implicated in disease (pharmacogenomics);
- gene therapy;[12]
- germ-line therapy.[13]

[6] See US Department of Energy and National Institutes of Health, *The Human Genome 1991–92 Program Report* (Washington, DC, Office of Energy Research and Office of Environmental Research, 1992), at iii.

[7] The completion of a full working draft of the human genome was announced in June 2000, see *Human Genome News*, 11, November 2000, p. 4. Its first publication took place in February 2001, see The Genome International Sequencing Consortium, 'Initial Sequencing and Analysis of the Human Genome' 409 *Nature* 860–921 (15 February 2001). For comment see G. Lindsey, 'Human Genome Project' in E. C. R. Reeve (ed.), *Encyclopedia of Genetics* (London, Fitzroy Dearborn Publishers, 2001), pp. 606–612.

[8] V. A. McKusick, 'The Human Genome Organisation: History, Purpose and Membership' (1989) 5 *Genomics* 385.

[9] The expressed aim of the Project is to acquire 'complete knowledge of the organization, structure and function of the human genome', see *Human Genome 1991–92 Program Report*, at iii.

[10] House of Commons Science and Technology Committee, *Human Genetics: The Science and its Consequences*, Third Report (London, HMSO, 6 July 1995), pp. 33–51, paras. 65–124.

[11] *Ibid.*, p. 36, para. 69.

[12] The Gene Therapy Advisory Committee (GTAC) was established in the United Kingdom in 1993 on the recommendation of the Clothier Committee (Clothier Committee, *Report of the Committee on the Ethics of Gene Therapy*, Cm 1788, 1992). Inter alia, the remit of the GTAC is: 'to consider and advise on the acceptability of proposals for gene therapy research on human subjects, on ethical grounds, taking account of the scientific merits of the proposals and the potential benefits and risks', http://www.doh.gov.uk/genetics/gtac.htm

[13] Germ-line therapy, which aims to modify the genetic make-up of human gametes and so carries the risk that it might affect future generations, is currently thought to be unacceptable

However, as the Committee pointed out, 'While genetics is likely eventually to transform medicine, it may take some while before treatments based on genetic knowledge become available ... [i]n the short term, the most widespread use of medical genetics will be, as now, in diagnosis and screening.'[14]

Thus test kits for genetic diseases and conditions are the first real and tangible benefits to emerge from this work.[15] These make the processes of identification and analysis of defective genes relatively inexpensive and increasingly commonplace occurrences.[16] Tests can detect an individual's genetic predisposition to a particular genetic disorder or her status as a carrier of a condition that might affect her progeny. Already 95 per cent of the most common genetic diseases can be tested for, together with several hundred rarer diseases, and, as one commentator has noted, 'This is likely to rise to a thousand or more ... as the human genome project bears fruit.'[17]

However, as the Science and Technology Committee has indicated, the development of therapies from the work of the Project is far less common, although some successes have already been achieved. The first attempt to treat a human being affected by an inherited genetic disorder using genetic engineering techniques was made in 1990.[18] The success

---

in ethical terms, primarily because the precautionary principle dictates that the unknown risks are too great to proceed at present. See Council of Europe, Convention for the Protection of Human Rights and Dignity of the Human Being with regard to the Application of Biology and Medicine: Convention on Human Rights and Biomedicine (Oviedo, April 1997), Article 13.

[14] *Ibid.*, pp. 36–7, paras. 71–2; as the Report makes clear, '*Diagnosis* is aimed at individuals; genetic *screening* is routine screening of populations, or identifiable subsets of populations (for example, men or women only, or ethnic groups at increased risk for particular diseases)' (*ibid.*).

[15] While there have been no direct clinical benefits from gene therapy to date, encouraging advances have been seen in the fields of severe combined immune deficiency (SCID–IX) and haemophilia. Over 400 clinical protocols involving more than 3,000 subjects worldwide had been approved by December 1999, although that year also heralded the first gene therapy treatment-related death in the United States. See the UK's Gene Therapy Advisory Committee, *Sixth Annual Report* (London, Health Departments of the United Kingdom, 2000), at i.

[16] It has been estimated that there are over 3,500 'established' and 2,500 'suspected' genetic disorders. Disorders are 'suspected' to exist principally because of a lack of familial data to substantiate the existence of more rare conditions; see V. A. McKusick, *Mendelian Inheritance in Man: Catalogs of Autosomal Dominant, Autosomal Recessive and X-linked Disorders*, 11th edn (Baltimore, Johns Hopkins University Press, 1993).

[17] See G. Vines, 'Gene Tests: The Parent's Dilemma' (1994) November *New Scientist* 40, 42.

[18] The technique was carried out by a team from the National Institutes of Health in Bethesda, Maryland USA, on a young girl suffering from SCID (Severe Combined Immune

of this procedure led to others using similar techniques,[19] and in 1994 specialists at the Jones Institute for Reproductive Medicine at the Eastern Virginia Medical School in the United States successfully completed the first genetic testing of an embryo for Tay-Sachs disease[20] prior to its implantation in its mother's womb.[21]

Most recently, the development of stem cell technology has made possible the creation of pluripotent cell lines from undifferentiated human cellular material taken from embryos and deceased foetuses. The potential therapeutic benefits of this form of cloning technique, such as the cultivation of replacement cells and tissues for diseased body parts, have proved very attractive to researchers and governments alike,[22] leading to the rapid moral and legal acceptance of the practice in many countries.[23] The UK House of Commons, for example, voted in

Deficiency). In this case, the condition was caused by an inherited inability to produce an enzyme (adenosine deaminase) essential to the proper functioning of the immune system. Most persons afflicted with the condition die in early childhood; normally by succumbing to a minor infection. The technique employed by the Bethesda team was as follows. A sample of the most affected cells (white blood cells or T cells) was extracted from the patient's body and subjected to genetic modification techniques which allowed the missing enzyme to be 'inserted' into the genetic make-up of each of the cells in the sample. Thereafter, the cells were allowed to divide and multiply until a sufficient quantity of the 'treated' sample was produced. This was then transfused back into the girl in the same way as an ordinary blood transfusion. Although apparently simple, this was the first time such genetically-modified material had been used in the treatment of a human being with a genetic disorder. For a fuller account of events see T. Wilkie, *Perilous Knowledge: The Human Genome Project and its Implications* (London, Faber & Faber, 1993), pp. 16–23.

[19] *Ibid.*

[20] Tay-Sachs disease is caused by the absence of an enzyme which breaks down fatty substances in neurons. It is a fatal disorder of the nervous system which invariably results in a slow, painful death within the first five years of life.

[21] This resulted in the birth of a healthy baby girl in January 1994. See J. Rennie, 'Grading the Gene Tests' (1994) 270 *Scientific American* 66.

[22] For an account of the science and ethics of this technique, see Nuffield Council on Bioethics, *Stem Cell Therapy: The Ethical Issues* (London, Nuffield Council, 2000).

[23] In the United States the National Bioethics Advisory Commission (NBAC) recommended limited approval of federally funded stem cell research on certain classes of human material, namely, cadaveric foetal tissue and embryos remaining after fertility treatment: NBAC, *Ethical Issues in Human Stem Cell Research* (Rockville, MD, NBAC, 1999). In 2000 the National Institutes of Health issued guidelines on this form of research and the legitimate use of federal funds in this regard. Thus, while NIH funds may be used to derive human pluripotent stem cells from foetal tissue, they may not be so used to derive human pluripotent stem cells from human embryos, unless the cells were derived from human embryos that were created not using federal funds and for the purposes of fertility treatment and when these embryos were in excess of the clinical need of the individuals seeking such treatment: National Institutes of Health, *Guidelines for Research Using Human Pluripotent Stem Cells* (Effective August 25, 2000, 65 Federal Register 51976; Corrected November 21, 2000, 65 Federal Register 69951).

December 2000 to legalise the creation of embryos purely for research to just such an end.[24]

Clearly, these advances have far-reaching implications for the future of medicine and the provision of health care. It is undeniable that they bring considerable benefits to humanity. It is also self-evident, however, that they will change incontrovertibly the way we consider the human species and the manner in which we consider ourselves as part of that species. In the preamble to the World Medical Association Declaration on the Human Genome Project, it was stated that 'This area of scientific progress will profoundly affect the lives of present and future members of society, bringing into question the very identity of the human individual and intruding upon the snail's pace of evolution in a decisive and probably irreversible manner'.[25]

The implications that these advances have for personal privacy are equally profound. While few would deny that genetic knowledge can be beneficial, it must also be recognised that genetic tests can give rise to considerable problems. Information concerning an individual's genetic make-up is of a highly personal and sensitive nature. To discover that one is likely to develop a debilitating condition in later life or that this might be passed to one's children must be an intense and possibly devastating experience.[26] Exposure to such knowledge can alter self-perception and challenge notions of identity,[27] and could adversely affect an individual in her social, professional and familial milieux. The mere availability of genetic information serves to heighten concerns about the uses to which the information might be put, uses which might in turn compromise the interests of the person who has been tested – the proband. For example, the disclosure of information to employers, insurers or other interested parties might lead to judgements being made which adversely affect or discriminate against the individual. Uniquely, genetic tests can also reveal information about blood relatives of the proband, with a corresponding threat to their interests and their privacy. Family

---

[24] 'MPs Give Go Ahead for Embryo Research', *The Times*, 19 December 2000. The House of Lords gave its approval on 22 January 2001.

[25] This declaration was adopted at the World Medical Association's 44th assembly in 1992; see (1993) 87 *Bulletin of Medical Ethics* 9.

[26] M. Levitt, 'The Ethics and Impact on Behaviour of Knowledge About One's Own Genome' (1999) 319 *British Medical Journal* 1283.

[27] This point is well made by the Danish Council of Ethics, *Ethics and Mapping the Human Genome* (Copenhagen, Notex, 1993), p. 52.

members might be loath to learn of a relative's predisposition to a particular genetic condition, given the likelihood that they carry a similar risk.

A number of public interests can also be furthered through judicious use of genetic information. The research value of genetic samples and information derived from them is axiomatic, but the achievement of this end requires a delicate balance between, on the one hand, gaining access to samples and information, and on the other, ensuring that research subjects are respected and protected from harm, including in particular endangerment of their privacy.[28]

Finally, the state itself can stake a claim to access genetic information in the name of the public interest given the ease with which many forms of this information may be used to identify individuals with high degrees of accuracy. There is, for example, a clear state interest in the establishment of forensic databases to assist in the investigation and prosecution of crime. The United Kingdom was the first country to establish a national DNA database for such purposes.[29] This was provided for in England and Wales by the Criminal Justice and Public Order Act 1994 which empowered the police to take samples and retain information derived from them even when the subjects were convicted on the basis of evidence derived other than from the samples. Similar provisions exist in Scotland[30] and in Northern Ireland,[31] and the national database has operated since April 1995. More recently, the UK government has sought to increase the potential of this database by reforming the law so as to permit the retention of samples even when no conviction has been secured against an individual.[32] Despite the considerable civil liberties issues that this measure raises, there is much popular support

---

[28] See generally Working Party of the Royal College of Pathologists and the Institute of Biomedical Science, *Consensus Statement of Recommended Policies for Uses of Human Tissue in Research, Education and Quality Control* (London, RCP, 1999), Medical Research Council, *Working Group on Human Tissue and Biological Samples for Use in Research: Report of the Medical Research Council Working Group to Develop Operational and Ethical Guidelines* (London, MRC, 1999), and Medical Research Council, *Public Perceptions of the Collection of Human Biological Samples*, (London, MRC, 2000).

[29] The national database is maintained by the Forensic Science Service in Birmingham. The legal foundation of the national database and guidance on its operational use are contained in a Home Office Circular HOC 16/1995: National DNA Database, as amended by HOC 25/2001.

[30] Criminal Procedure (Scotland) Act 1995.

[31] Police (Amendment) (Northern Ireland) Order 1995.

[32] Criminal Justice and Police Act 2001, s. 82.

for the move, presumably because most people expect that the DNA to be retained will be that of other people.[33] As a counterbalance, the House of Lords has recommended the establishment of an independent body to oversee the workings of the National DNA Database 'to put beyond doubt that individuals' data are being properly used and protected'.[34]

For all of these reasons, the existence and availability of genetic information about individuals gives rise to concerns about its use or possible misuse. Moreover, particular features of this information, or at least the perception that is often held of those features, might also lead other parties to stake a claim to the information. Thus a range of potentially interested parties emerges, but the claims of these parties are not homogeneous and, as a result, potential for conflict also arises. A first step towards the resolution of any possible conflict is an assessment of the legitimacy of the claims in question, and this in turn requires an understanding of the value that human genetic information is thought to have.

Human genetics and genetic disease

In seeking an appropriate response to advances in genetics it is trite to observe that we should proceed in a manner that is informed by ethical debate, which is morally sound and which reflects common societal values. But, first and foremost, proceeding in such a manner requires that we are apprised of the functional utility of genetic information. The starting point, then, in deciding whether the promised benefits of genetic advances are truly desirable is to understand what information of this kind can facilitate, and perhaps more importantly, what it cannot enable us to do.

The uniqueness of genetic information

Information is a unique entity, in that the same information can be used co-temporaneously by a large number of persons for a wide range of ends

[33] The People's Panel Quantitative Study conducted for the Human Genetics Commission and published in March 2001 showed that 46 per cent of participants supported retention of samples taken from acquitted individuals and 61 per cent condoned police access to non-police databases for cross-checking purposes: see Human Genetics Commission, *Public Attitudes to Human Genetic Information* (HGC, London, 2001), p. 39.

[34] Report from the House of Lords Select Committee on Science and Technology, *Human Genetic Databases: Challenges and Opportunities* (2001 HL 57) para. 7.66.

without any change in the nature of the information itself. Traditionally, however, when wc have asked where the control of information should be located and how it should be exercised, the answer has been that the person to whom the information belongs, or to whom it relates – that is, the source of the information – should exercise that control. But in relation to genetic information this answer is simplistic and often unsatisfactory.

The potential impact of the uses of genetic information on families, in addition to individuals, is often perceived as being unique to this area of inquiry. Indeed, this is frequently held out to be the case irrespective of the kind of genetic knowledge involved. The implications of this are far-reaching. The historical focus of both ethics and law in the United Kingdom and the United States – as paradigm examples of communities nurtured in the Western liberal tradition – has been the rights of the individual to determine for herself the course of her life, with minimal interference by others. This notion is challenged by increased availability of genetic information. At least, this is so if we take as our premise that genetic information relates not only to the person from whom it is derived, but also to the blood relatives of that person. This gives rise to special problems concerning how the information should be gathered, stored, accessed and used. For, while we might choose to locate control of a genetic sample with the person from whom it has been taken,[35] we cannot ignore the fact that genetic information derived from the sample might also reveal information about the relatives of the sample source. To locate the control of this information solely with the sample source might, therefore, seem to many to be an inadequate response to concerns about how it should be treated.

The intuitive response that we have to genetic familial relations is deep-rooted and has long formed part of our cultural heritage. We learn from an early age that genetic relationships are different from other kinds of union. It is no accident, for example, that Cinderella's wicked sisters are related only by marriage – we would view our heroine quite differently were it otherwise.[36] Each of us has an innate belief that we are marked by our genetic links, and, by extension, we feel set apart from those with whom we have no such connection. Thus, the

---

[35] See G. J. Annas, L. H. Glantz and P. A. Roche, 'Drafting the Genetic Privacy Act: Science, Policy, and Practical Considerations' (1995) 23 *Journal of Law, Medicine and Ethics* 360.

[36] 'Aschenputtel', in J. Grimm and W. Grimm, *Kinder- und Hausmärchen* (Lindau, Antiqua-Verlag, 1812, 1814), I, no. 2.1.

interconnectedness we feel because of genetic ties is very familiar. However, it has only been in recent years, as a result of increased knowledge
and understanding of the function of genes, that 'The Gene' has assumed
the status of cultural icon, and it is this process that has, in turn, led
to an increased examination of what the appropriate legal responses to
how genetic information and samples are used should be.

Concrete and abstract genetic knowledge

It is sometimes claimed that a family history is simply genetic information in a different guise, and therefore that a genetic test result is no
different to a known family history. Family history, however, is abstract
knowledge flawed by bad or failing memories, a lack of accurate data as
to why a family member has become ill or died, and an absence of understanding about the pattern of disease. In contrast, genetic test results can
offer a high degree of specificity, both in terms of predicting the likelihood of disease in other family members and of fleshing out a suspicion
hitherto unconfirmed. Concrete information of this kind brings with it
a number of realities that can include a degree of certainty about future
ill-health or even the mode and manner of one's own death. These realities can affect an individual's self-perception in ways that family history
cannot, for, with the latter, the individual has the relative comfort of living with an abstract threat that has always manifested to someone else.

Specific knowledge of one's own genetic constitution, especially when
it is accompanied by knowledge of future ill-health, requires individuals
to reassess themselves and their position within a family unit and to
look with fresh eyes upon their family history, which will have suddenly
assumed a different significance. Specificity of knowledge can deprive us
of the ostrich's 'head-in-the-sand' that can sometimes serve as a valuable
psychological coping mechanism.[37]

The perceived utility of genetic information

It is precisely because genetic knowledge is thought to offer a high degree of specificity in determining future ill-health that it is seen to have

---

[37] See, for example, M. Richards, 'Families, Kinship and Genetics', in M. Richards and
T. Marteau (eds.), *The Troubled Helix: Social and Psychological Implications of the New Human
Genetics* (Cambridge, Cambridge University Press, 1996), pp. 249–73.

a value not only for a proband and her relatives, but also for parties outside the family. Insurers, employers, researchers and the state can find
considerable use for genetic information when test results might affect
their own interests. It is important, however, to offer a word of caution
as to this perceived value of genetic information.

The genetic constitution of all human beings is contained in their
chromosomes. Normally, an individual has twenty-three pairs of chromosomes, half inherited from her mother and half from her father.[38]
Each chromosome carries a set number of specified genes. Genes are responsible for the functioning and operation of every cell in the human
body.[39] And yet, while it is the case that every individual carries several
'defective' genes within their genome, not every individual suffers from,
or will suffer from, a genetic disorder.[40] This is because genetic diseases
have a variety of causes.

On the one hand, monogenic diseases are the direct result of particular mutations in the genome. These diseases can be either recessive
or dominant. Recessive conditions such as cystic fibrosis or sickle cell
anaemia are caused when an individual inherits two copies of a defective
gene – one from each parent. Disease is not manifested if only one copy is
inherited, but the individual then becomes an asymptomatic carrier for
the condition. In contrast, dominant disorders are inherited when only
one copy of a disease-specific gene is passed on. Its influence overrides
the effects of its twin 'healthy' copy. Such dominant disorders differ from
recessive disorders in two important respects. First, many dominant disorders do not usually manifest themselves until later in life.[41] This means
that a family can be complete before there is any sign that an adverse
genetic trait has been inherited. Second, when disease does occur it is

---

[38] A genetic disease is generally of one of three kinds: (i) chromosomal disorders, which
involve the 'lack, excess or abnormal arrangement of one or more chromosomes, producing
excessive or deficient genetic material'; (ii) Mendelian or simply inherited disorders which
are determined by a single gene mutant; and (iii) multifactorial disorders which are 'caused
by an interaction of multiple genes and multiple exogenous or environmental factors', see
J. D. Wilson, E. Braunwald, K. J. Isselbacher, R. G. Petersdorf, J. B. Martin, A. S. Fauci
and R. K. Root, *Principles of Internal Medicine*, 12th edn (New York, McGraw-Hill, 1991),
p. 24.

[39] It is estimated that between 50,000 and 100,000 human genes exist, with an average length
of a few thousand base pairs.

[40] See S. M. Suter, 'Whose Genes Are These Anyway?: Familial Conflicts over Access to Genetic
Information' (1993) 91 *Michigan Law Review* 1854 at 1858: 'Everyone probably carries between three and nine deleterious or disease genes, most of which are recessive.'

[41] Around 50 per cent of dominant disorders are late-onset disorders.

often characterised by extreme variation in the symptoms experienced by family members.[42] This can further delay the recognition of a pattern of inheritance in a particular family.[43]

None the less, the predictability of disease in future generations is a relatively straightforward exercise in the case of both recessive and dominant disorders. For a recessive disorder where both parents are carriers, there is a 25 per cent risk in the case of each pregnancy that a child will be born affected, a 50 per cent risk that a child will be born as a carrier, and a 25 per cent chance that the child will be genetically normal. For dominant disorders, the chances of having an affected child are 50 per cent if one parent carries the relevant gene and 75 per cent if both do.

It is understandable that interested parties might attach considerable importance to test results in the light of such figures. However, it is of crucial importance to consider other forms of genetic disease, which, in fact, represent by far the greater category of genetic disorders that affect individuals and families.

Polygenic disorders are caused by the interaction of two or more defective genes.[44] Because of this, the chances of being affected are more difficult to predict, and only 5 per cent to 10 per cent of first-degree relatives are affected by such conditions.[45] Moreover, these disorders are part of the wider class of multifactorial conditions caused not only by genetic defects, but also by the interaction of those genes with external factors, all of which play their part in the disease process. Common non-genetic factors that influence the manifestation and/or progression of genetic disease include diet, exercise, stress, alcohol and drugs, and

[42] An additional complicating factor is that of non-penetrance. That is, although defective genes have been passed on to progeny, the individuals remain unaffected by the condition. The degree of penetrance of a particular gene depends, to a large extent, on the general genetic ambience.

[43] Additional differences between recessive and dominant disorders include the fact that parents of a sufferer from a recessive condition will in general be entirely free of the disease. At least one parent of a person afflicted with a dominant condition will also be affected (although it is possible in a small number of cases for an individual to suffer from the condition because of a mutation which has occurred). Further, recessive conditions do not in general pass through generations vertically. Only siblings are affected. With few exceptions, such disorders are rare because of the need for the conjunction of two individuals both of whom carry the defective gene and transmit it to their children.

[44] Examples are ischaemic heart disease and certain forms of diabetes.

[45] Wilson *et al., Principles of Internal Medicine*, p. 30. The precise number of genes responsible for polygenic traits is unknown: *ibid.*

exposure to toxic chemicals or radiation.[46] As with purely polygenic conditions, however, the predictability of the occurrence of multifactorial genetic conditions is very low compared with monogenic disorders.[47] For this reason the majority of research that has been carried out to date relates to the latter rather than the former. The already evident disproportion between multifactorial and monogenic disorders[48] leads one to suppose that, in the future, it will be possible to detect a genetic component in a great many disorders and conditions which today are seen as purely organic or as resulting from social, and not physiological, dysfunction. Examples of where this is already happening include some cancers, schizophrenia,[49] manic depression, and drug or alcohol abuse.[50]

Possibly because of such advances, genetic research is frequently portrayed as though it will reveal the essence of humanity and unlock the secrets of our destiny and who we are as human beings. This will not be so. Such a reductionist view sets too much store by the influence of genetics in the determination of the human condition.[51] It is fortunate, therefore, that the law has generally resisted such an approach. Arguments about genetic determinism in the commission of crimes have received short shrift in the US criminal courts, where the attempt to reduce an accused to little more than the sum total of his genes has been generally rejected.[52] In the celebrated case of *Mobley* v. *State*[53] the Supreme Court of Georgia rejected a plea by the accused to offer evidence based on 'very recently' published articles and scientific studies that suggested a possible genetic basis for violent and impulsive behaviour in certain individuals. The court upheld the finding that the theory behind the request would not have reached a scientific stage of verifiable certainty

[46] The study of such conditions has been named 'Ecogenetics': see G. E. Pence, *Classic Cases in Medical Ethics* 2nd edn (New York, McGraw-Hill, 1995), pp. 407–8.
[47] *Ibid.*
[48] Indeed, it is thought that 'only 3 percent of all human diseases are caused by defects in a single gene', see Rennie, 'Grading the Gene Tests', 96.
[49] M. Baron, 'Genetics of Schizophrenia and the New Millennium: Progress and Pitfalls' (2001) 68 *American Journal of Human Genetics* 299.
[50] The Nuffield Council on Bioethics announced an inquiry into the ethics of genetic research into human behavioural traits in January 2001: Nuffield Council on Bioethics, Genetics and Human Behaviour: The Ethical Context, http://www.nuffield.org/bioethics/index.html
[51] S. Sarkar, *Genetics and Reductionism* (Cambridge, Cambridge University Press, 1998).
[52] D. W. Denno, 'Legal Implications of Genetics and Crime Research', in Ciba Foundation, *Genetics of Criminal and Antisocial Behaviour* (Chichester, John Wiley & Sons, 1996), pp. 248–64.
[53] *Mobley* v. *State* 265 Ga. 292; 455 S.E.2d 61 (1995).

in the near future and that the accused could not show that such a stage would ever be reached.[54]

However, even within the scientific community there has been a tendency towards reductionist accounts of genetic knowledge. Researchers and clinicians often speak of the search for 'the gene for' a particular condition. In fact, it has become apparent as more work is done on the HGP that comparatively few 'genetic' diseases fall into the attractively straightforward category of monogenic disorders. Rather, most form part of the burgeoning category of multifactorial diseases, with numerous and complex causes. Thus the simple nature/nurture dichotomy, appealing though it might be, is an increasingly outmoded and inaccurate representation from which to make sense of the range of knowledge borne of the HGP. Nowhere is this more true than in the context of neurological disorders.[55]

Conditions such as Huntington's disease and phenylketonuria have to date been offered as paradigm examples of genetic neurological disorders, and the experiences of dealing with this kind of genetic knowledge (concerning dominant and recessive disorders respectively) and with the families affected by these diseases have served as a model for dealing with many other conditions in which the genetic constitution is an operative factor. However, more recent work on Alzheimer's disease and Parkinson's disease has shown that straightforward indices of risk – such as a 50 per cent risk of an individual with Huntington's having affected progeny, or a 25 per cent risk that a couple who are carriers for phenylketonuria will have an affected child – have little application to these conditions.[56] Although their aetiology might involve a genetic component, genes are neither necessary nor sufficient in themselves to cause the disease itself. Moreover, while so-called 'susceptibility' genes might have a role to play in the onset of diseases such as these, they are not necessarily any more significant or determinative in the causal mechanism than are other factors, such as the environment or the interaction of a number of genes. For example, the discovery that the ApoE 4 allele is present in 50 per cent of cases of late-onset Alzheimer's disease

[54] See generally, Symposium Issue, 'Genes and Justice: The Growing Impact of the New Genetics on the Courts' (1999) 83(3) *Judicature* November–December.

[55] See M. A. Grodin and G. T. Laurie, 'Susceptibility Genes and Neurological Disorders: Learning the Right Lessons from the Human Genome Project' (2000) 57 *Archives of Neurology* 1569.

[56] J. A. Todd, 'Interpretation of Results from Genetic Studies of Multifactorial Disease' (1999) 354 (supp. I) *Lancet* 15.

reveals no more than the fact that the variant is only responsible for around 15 per cent of susceptibility to the disease.[57] Moreover, it is estimated that few, if any, of the other susceptibility genes that are likely to be discovered will make more of a contribution to disease onset than the ApoE 4 allele has done.[58]

These observations allow us to draw certain conclusions as to the nature of genetics and genetic information. Certainly it is true that from some forms of information about an individual's genetic constitution can be inferred, with varying degrees of certainty, similar information about members of both their immediate and extended family. For relatives, the possibility that they already have a particular condition, or that there is an increased risk of developing such a condition or that they are carriers, can be revealed. However, the chances of any of these being the case can rarely be accurately predicted simply on the basis of test results of a single family member. Although some conditions carry a straightforward statistical probability of affliction, in most cases a number of variable factors influence one's genetic constitution. In certain circumstances the cooperation of family members is required to provide an accurate prediction of a genetic condition. Tests fall into one of two categories: linkage tests and genetic tests. The latter detect the 'defective' gene itself and can be carried out without familial cooperation. Linkage tests, however, merely detect markers that accompany genes, and for accurate results blood samples are required from both affected and unaffected members of the family. Test results are inconclusive without these, but the informed consent of all necessary relatives might be difficult to obtain.[59] The efficacy of the tests will clearly be affected if a number of relatives decline to cooperate.[60] More particularly,

---

[57] Working Group of the American College of Medical Genetics and the American Society of Human Genetics on ApoE and Alzheimer's disease, 'Statement on Use of Apolipoprotein E Testing for Alzheimer's Disease' (1995) 274 *Journal of the American Medical Association* 1627.

[58] Nuffield Council on Bioethics, *Mental Disorders and Genetics: The Ethical Context* (London, Nuffield Council, 1998), para. 4.7.

[59] It is the view of the Danish Council of Ethics that 'no unsolicited approach may be made by . . . health authorities in the case of examinations which may evince an hereditary disease in the family. This can create undue anxiety on the part of the relatives concerned and, at worst, encroach radically on their lives, through no wish of their own . . . the regard for family members' integrity weighs heavier than the understandable need of the counsellee to be diagnosed and to have future options for action set out', Danish Council of Ethics, *Ethics and Mapping of the Human Genome*, p. 23.

[60] See D. Ball, A. Tyler and P. Harper, 'Predictive Testing of Adults and Children', in A. Clarke (ed.), *Genetic Counselling: Practice and Principles* (London, Routledge, 1994), pp. 66–9. As the

this precludes the drawing of any concrete conclusions based simply on information from others.[61] As the Danish Council of Ethics has noted,

> [i]n many – possibly even most – cases, great uncertainty still attaches to ascertaining whether or not a disease is hereditarily conditioned. A long string of illnesses such as cancer and cardiovascular disease cannot be categorically classified as being hereditarily or environmentally conditioned, but must be assumed to be due to the – as yet only partly clarified – interaction of hereditary and environmental factors.[62]

The degree of uncertainty that accompanies such information might lead to considerable unease and concern among relatives about their own genetic status. The prospect of living with uncertainty is a daunting one for those who choose not to be tested, but, even for those who accept a test, benefits are neither immediate nor guaranteed. As Zimmern has observed,

> Although directly obtained DNA-based genetic information may in many circumstances be more predictive than indirectly obtained information for the inherited genetic disorders, the converse is likely to be true for common complex diseases. It is a matter of consensus, for example, that information about smoking, family history, blood pressure and cholesterol levels are together likely to be significantly more accurate in assessing cardiovascular risk than a knowledge of the genetic sequences and mutations in the relevant genes.[63]

authors state, 'Linked marker studies are normally the only means of genetic prediction for a disorder until the causative gene is identified and specific mutations isolated, whereupon direct mutational analysis becomes possible, allowing prediction to be made using a single sample from an applicant', p. 68.

[61]   Gostin points out that the sensitivity of testing is limited by the known mutations in a target population. As he states, 'Screening can detect only 75 per cent of CF chromosomes in the US population. Approximately one in every two couples from the general population identified by CF screening as "at-risk" will be falsely labeled. Predicting the nature, severity, and course of disease based on a genetic marker is an additional difficulty. For most genetic diseases, the onset date, severity of symptoms and efficacy of treatment and management vary greatly'; see L. O. Gostin, 'Genetic Privacy' (1995) 23 *Journal of Law, Medicine and Ethics* 320, 323, quoting N. Fost, 'The Cystic Fibrosis Gene: Medical and Social Implication for Heterozygote Detection' (1990) 263 *Journal of the American Medical Association* 2777.

[62]   Danish Council, *Ethics and Mapping of the Human Genome*, p. 10. See also A. Cavoukian, 'Confidentiality Issues in Genetics: The Need for Privacy', in Second Symposium of the Council of Europe on Bioethics, Strasbourg, 30 November–2 December 1993, CDBI-SY-SP (93) 5, 4.

[63]   R. Zimmern, 'What is Genetic Information?' (2001) 1(5) *Genetics Law Monitor* 9, 10.

Genetic information and testing

A wide range of genetic tests is now available.[64] In contrast, there are currently few cures for genetic disorders.[65] The usefulness of testing is therefore limited, and, since the knowledge from most tests can be used to avoid the onset of disease only in a very small number of cases, its value must be sought elsewhere.

Several arguments can be advanced in support of testing in the absence of cure. For instance, it has been argued that such knowledge can be used to inform individuals of possible risks to health that might be minimised by a change in lifestyle when the condition in question is multifactorial and heavily influenced by an environmental component.[66] Similarly, the discovery of one's status as a carrier for a particular condition means that any reproductive decision that is taken thereafter will be an informed one. It has also been argued that individuals can better prepare for hardship to come, both mentally and in other ways, if they are made aware of the risk of developing a disease later in life.[67] Such early prediction allows appropriate support mechanisms – such as counselling – to be set in place in advance of the onset of any disease.[68]

It must be borne in mind, however, that the efficacy of genetic tests is limited even in this context. Tests can predict neither the particular likelihood of the onset of a condition, nor the date when disease will

[64] Vines notes: 'All Britain's health regions have genetic testing and counselling centres, which can test for about 20 of the commonest inherited diseases, which together account for 95 per cent of all cases', 'Gene Tests: The Parent's Dilemma', 42.

[65] As one commentator has said, 'Forced analysis of the human genome will cause the gap between diagnostic ability and therapeutic failure to widen more than ever. We shall detect diseases with greater and greater precision, we shall learn to predict at the preclinical or prenatal stage without being able to do anything about the cause'; see J. Schmidtke, 'Who Owns the Human Genome? Ethical and Legal Aspects' (1992) 44 *Journal of Pharmacy and Pharmacology* 205, 209.

[66] See, for example, M. P. Ryan *et al.*, 'An Ethical Debate: Genetic Testing for Familial Hypertrophic Cardiomyopathy in Newborn Infants' (1995) 310 *British Medical Journal* 856, in which a view is put that early detection of this inherited weakness of the heart can mean that, 'The child can be raised with an emphasis on avoidance of energetic activities rather than be suddenly banned from an established sporting pursuit during adolescence, when the disease is diagnosed clinically', 857. See also P. Reilly, 'Rights, Privacy, and Genetic Screening' (1991) 64 *Yale Journal of Biology and Medicine* 43. However, the problem within the whole range of multifactorial conditions lies in knowing which aspects of one's lifestyle are causal to the onset of disease.

[67] See Ball *et al.*, 'Predictive Testing', pp. 63–94, especially p. 71; also, M. Z. Pelias, 'Duty to Disclose in Medical Genetics: A Legal Perspective' (1991) 39 *American Journal of Medical Genetics* 347.

[68] This of course presupposes that such support mechanisms exist.

develop, nor the severity of the condition that any one individual is likely to experience.[69] Further, mutations in disease-causing genes can themselves be responsible for disease. A test must be capable of detecting all such mutations if it is to be truly effective.[70] However, because longer genes are more likely to carry mutations, the difficulty of this task increases as the condition becomes more complex genetically. The BRCA1 gene[71] – thought to be responsible for 5 per cent of all breast cancers[72] – is unusually long.[73] Thus any diagnostic test that is developed is of limited efficacy: 'a negative result would be indeterminate and could be expressed only as a probability'.[74]

Genetic testing can be usefully performed in a wide range of circumstances and for purposes that include (i) pre-implantation diagnosis; (ii) prenatal diagnosis; (iii) newborn screening; (iv) carrier testing; (v) diagnostic analysis; (vi) confirmatory analysis; (vii) presymptomatic or predictive testing; and (viii) susceptibility testing. The US Department of Health and Human Services Secretary's Advisory Committee on Genetic Testing (SACGT) has highlighted the need to differentiate between these different kinds of genetic tests, and to educate the legal, medical and lay communities accordingly. Moreover, the Committee proposes that any regulatory oversight of genetic testing should be tailored to accommodate the range of factors that distinguish different categories of tests. Thus, as the Committee's report states,

> predictive tests require more scrutiny than do diagnostic tests. Similarly, tests for weakly penetrant mutations require more assessment than do those for highly penetrant genes. Tests for conditions for which no interventions are available would require more review than tests for conditions for which interventions exist. Thus, for example, a high scrutiny test would

---

[69] See K. Berg, 'Confidentiality Issues in Medical Genetics: The Need for Laws, Rules and Good Practices to Secure Optimal Disease Control', Second Symposium of the Council of Europe on Bioethics, Strasbourg, 30 November–2 December 1993, CDBI-SY-SP (93) 3, 4–5. See also Gostin, 'Genetic Privacy' 323.

[70] An example of this is the test for hypertrophic cardiomyopathy. Initial screening proved to be inaccurate until the discovery of a mutation of the cardial beta-myosin heavy chain gene MYH7, see Ryan *et al*, 'An Ethical Debate', 856.

[71] The discovery of the gene was announced on 15 September 1994 by a team at the University of Utah.

[72] For a statistical breakdown and comment see R. Eeles, 'Testing for the Breast Cancer Predisposition BRCA1' (1996) 313 *British Medical Journal* 572.

[73] The gene consists of 100,000 base pairs of nucleotides, which is ten times longer than the average gene.

[74] See Pence, *Classic Cases in Medical Ethics*, pp. 411–12.

be one that is predictive, detects a mutation that is weakly penetrant, and for which a proven intervention is not available. Similarly, a complex test, such as a linkage analysis for which interpretation is difficult, would require more oversight than a test measuring the presence or absence of a defined mutation. Conversely, lower scrutiny would be needed for tests performed solely to detect somatic mutations or to detect genotypic information used exclusively to direct clinical management of symptomatic patients.[75]

Reasoning such as this should bear directly on the nature, scope and limits of our ethical and legal responses to the generation of genetic knowledge. Primarily, it should lead us to reflect on how such information can be used, for this directly affects the ethical appropriateness of attempting to apply current models of dealing with genetic information to the vast amount of knowledge that is now being generated by the HGP. One thing is clear: no single model will be appropriate for all possible types and uses of genetic information. Furthermore, it is impossible to attach a uniform value to the practice of genetic testing for an entire range of conditions.[76]

These facts have not yet sufficiently penetrated the public's collective consciousness. In particular, the claims of third parties to gain access to genetic information are often based on a view of genetic testing that casts the practice as of homogeneous utility, when clearly this is not the case. The predictability value of testing will be affected by multiple considerations even when third parties restrict their interests to monogenic disorders in which the greatest utility might be found. Testing can only offer probabilities of the onset of disease. Importantly, it cannot give any indications of when disease will arise, nor of the degree to which any one individual will be affected (and this can vary considerably as between individuals), and tests cannot necessarily detect mutations for particular conditions. Accordingly, there can be a significant risk of false negatives.[77] All of these factors undermine the utility of genetic testing

---

[75] Health and Human Services Secretary's Advisory Committee on Genetic Testing, *Enhancing the Oversight of Genetic Tests: Recommendations of the SACGT* (Bethesda, MD, National Institutes of Health, 2000), pp. 20–21.

[76] See R. Hubbard and R. Lewontin, 'Pitfalls of Genetic Testing' (1996) 334 *New England Journal of Medicine* 1192.

[77] For example, current tests for cystic fibrosis can only detect up to 75 per cent of at-risk individuals in society. As Gostin states, 'Approximately one in every two couples from the general population identified by CF screening as "at risk" will be falsely labeled', see Gostin, 'Genetic Privacy', 323.

because they demonstrate that what is predictable is only so in a limited number of cases, which, in themselves, are subject to a further range of variables. Genetic knowledge is, therefore, a matter of probabilities rather than certainties.

What is genetic information?

There is a widespread perception that the nature of genetic information is unique and that it differs significantly from other forms of personal or medical data. The prima facie case for this position draws on elements already outlined above, and can be summarised as follows.

Genetic information relates to families and not just individuals;
genetic information can offer a degree of certainty in determining which of those persons is likely to be affected by genetic disease;
genetic information can provide a measure of predictability in the assessment of likelihood of ill health in particular individuals from an affected group;
genetic information can reveal secrets about future ill health, even in those who are currently well;
genetic information can help to determine future risks in future persons, i.e. one's progeny.

However, other examples of information which functions in one or more of these fashions can also be derived from non-genetic data, or at least from data that have not traditionally been considered to be genetic. For example, as the report *Genetics and Health* points out, 'High cholesterol levels [are] known predictors of cardiovascular disease, and high blood pressure of cerebrovascular disease risk . . . [and] . . . without recourse to genetic testing familial aggregation [is] discernible not only in the monogenetic disorders but also in a range of common disorders including heart disease, cancers and diabetes.'[78] Moreover, as we have seen, genetic information is not a homogeneous class of information, and at best only some limited sub-categories of that class are predictive of future ill health in any significant way. Many other forms of genetic information are no more predictive than is general health information. These factors militate against the argument that genetic data are in some way ontologically different from other forms of medical data. In fact,

[78] See the Nuffield Trust, *Genetics and Health: Policy Issues for Genetic Science and their Implications for Health and Health Services* (London, Nuffield Trust, 2000).

the one clear message to emerge from research on the human genome is that most diseases have a genetic component, thus potentially relegating most diseases to a sub-category of the ever broadening genus of 'genetic disease'.[79]

None the less, the debate about how law and ethics should respond to genetic advances has proceeded in large measure on the premise that genetic information is exceptional. But it is far from clear that the case for genetic exceptionalism has been made out satisfactorily.[80] While some have argued that our DNA acts as a 'future diary' revealing our genetic secrets in times to come,[81] others have pointed to the difficulties of defining 'genetic information' in law, and in separating what is genetic, and so deserving of special protection, from that which is not.[82] For example, Dutch insurers were recently accused of flouting a law prohibiting discrimination on the basis of genetic information, even when they had not specifically requested such data. A study had shown that families in which hypercholesterolaemia was prevalent had had difficulties in obtaining life insurance, despite the existence of legislation that prohibited direct questions about genetic information. The retort of the insurers was that no questions had been asked about hereditary conditions. They had simply asked if candidates had high cholesterol levels – classically a non-genetic question. Nevertheless, by asking this question, they indirectly came to know of the potential existence of an inherited genetic disorder.[83]

Thus, it should also be borne in mind that the means by which information is gathered can lead to an inference that the information is genetic in nature, or at least that it should be treated as such. For example, in the United Kingdom, the Medical Research Council in conjunction with the Wellcome Trust and the Department of Health have

---

[79] As the chair of the US Task Force on Genetic Information and Insurance has said, 'Genetic information is special because we are inclined to treat it as mysterious, as having exceptional potency or significance [and] not because it is different in some fundamental way from all sorts of information about us.'

[80] L. O. Gostin and J. G. Hodge Jr, 'Genetic Privacy and the Law: An End to Genetic Exceptionalism' (1999) 40 *Jurimetrics* 21.

[81] See generally G. J. Annas and S. Elias, *Gene Mapping: Using Law and Ethics as Guides* (New York, Oxford University Press, 1992).

[82] Contrast G. J. Annas, 'Genetic Privacy: There Ought to Be a Law' (1999) 4 *Texas Review of Law & Policy* 9, and M. A. Rothstein, 'Why Treating Genetic Information Separately is a Bad Idea' (1999) 4 *Texas Review of Law & Policy* 33.

[83] T. Sheldon, 'Dutch Insurers Flouting Law on Genetic Disease, Researchers Say' (2000) 320 *British Medical Journal* 826.

proposed the establishment of a Population Biomedical Collection that will involve gathering samples from 500,000 volunteers in order to determine the genetic influences that might have a bearing on their future health. Thereafter, all health information gathered from these subjects will be seen in the light of the original genetic findings, even when the information itself might not be 'genetic' in origin.[84] None the less, these data will help to fill in the overall genetic picture, and as such might well be classified as 'genetic knowledge'.

A definition of genetic information that is too narrow might prove to be useless in protecting any interests at all, while an overly broad definition might, for example, encompass data of relevance to important research, with the resultant risk that such work might be unduly hampered if access to the information is to be restricted. Indeed, such a definition might include taking a simple family history, if, as has been suggested above, a family history is seen as revealing familial genetic information.

In recognition of these problems the US Task Force on Genetic Testing, a joint working group of the Department of Energy and the National Institutes of Health, has offered a working definition of genetic test information that seeks to strike a balance between protecting legitimate interests in test results while, at the same time, avoiding the conclusion that any kind of medical test is, in fact, a genetic test.[85] The definition restricts genetic testing to 'processes which are carried out for the direct analysis of human DNA and other compounds such as RNA, chromosomes, proteins and certain metabolites, with a view to achieving a number of clearly identified end points, namely, the prediction of inherited disease, the detection of carrier status or the diagnosis of actual inherited disease'.[86] This, then, encompasses not only the testing of individuals but also the screening of at-risk populations, and includes pre-conception and antenatal screening and the testing of families with recognised histories of genetic disease.

This also means that the contents of an individual's medical file do not necessarily include genetic information and that testing for certain

---

[84] Medical Research Council website: http://www.mrc.ac.uk/
[85] US Task Force on Genetic Testing: A Joint Working Group of the Department of Energy and the National Institutes of Health. See N. Holtzman and M. Watson, *Final Report of the Task Force on Genetic Testing:: Promoting Safe and Effective Genetic Testing in the United States* (Baltimore, MD, Johns Hopkins University Press, 1998).
[86] *Ibid.*, p. 6.

conditions in which a genetic factor is operative, such as diabetes or ischaemic heart disease, will not be classified as genetic testing unless there
is a high probability that a mainly genetic form of the disease is involved.
While it is the case that all human cellular material contains a complete
copy of the genome (with the exception of the gametes), tests that do
not involve the direct analysis of the DNA, but rather concern other
components of the cells, will not be deemed to be genetic tests. The Task
Force definition specifically excludes, inter alia, tests conducted purely
for research, tests for somatic mutations (compare heritable mutations),
and tests for forensic purposes. On this basis, the genetic information
that the Task Force would seek to protect would not include abstract
data about family history.

Many different forms of genetic information exist, and these can be
generated from any number of human samples. The paradigm example
of a genetic sample and genetic information is direct analysis of DNA
taken from a person's blood; it is often on this basis that 'genetic' diseases
are categorised. But, in the light of the above discussion and given the
fact that genetic information can be derived from any tissue sample that
is provided, a starting premise must be that the term 'genetic' is, to a
large extent, a false construct.

A definition such as that proposed by the US Task Force would certainly be a possible starting point in developing specific genetics-related
legislation. However, this does not detract from the fact that the difficulty
of drawing a clear distinction between different kinds of information seriously undermines the feasibility of law designed solely to protect *genetic*
information. All personal data are worthy of respect and protection by
virtue simply of the fact that they relate to an inherently private sphere
of our lives. In the same way that each of us deserves respect as human
beings possessed of human dignity, so too must that respect extend to
intimate adjuncts of our personalities, such as personal information,
whether it be genetic or not.

This is not to deny that certain elements of certain forms of genetic information derived from samples throw up particular problems.
Monogenic disorders provide a clear example of the impact that information about them can have on families affected by them. But, as
the Nuffield Trust has identified, there is a view that 'If special levels
of protection [are] required then it should be in respect of monogenic
disorders of high penetrance and not genetic information in general,

whether that information came from the results of testing or from other sources.'[87]

The common unifying factor between this approach and that which suggests that genetic data generally are unique is the appeal to the harm principle. That is, the underlying motivation in defining some forms of information as a class apart is to minimise the potential for harm that may be associated with the use of that information. There is, however, nothing unique in itself about the information for which protection is sought, save that its use is perceived to be exposed to a greater risk of exploitation than is the use of other forms of information.

However, if the concern is with harm then it must be appreciated that potential for this arises as much from factors external to the nature of the information as it does from any essential quality. For example, the potential for discrimination – which is the differential treatment of different individuals or groups for irrelevant or irrational reasons – is a constant threat in modern society that needs no foundation in fact to become a reality. The risk of discrimination between groups on the basis of perceived genetic differences is as much a threat whether or not there is any scientific or logical basis for the belief that differences are meaningfully discernible. The potential for harm arises out of the perception that there is a difference, not out of the essential nature of the information that is seen to justify the differential treatment. Indeed, to perpetuate the belief that genetic information is highly predictive serves only to increase the risk of discrimination on 'genetic' grounds. But to what extent should we legislate for perceptions? And should not our concern be directed towards the eradication of discrimination in all of its many guises, rather than to the identification of particular classes of information as deserving of *extra* protection?

The creation of computerised databanks greatly facilitates the rapid processing and manipulation of data and as such represents another potentially significant source of harm through use or misuse of information – in particular, the establishment of genetic databanks has given rise to particular concerns and calls for specific protection.[88] However, it is the structuring, operation and, indeed, the very rationale behind databanks which generates risk of harm, and not the core nature of the

[87] The Nuffield Trust, *Genetics and Health*, p. 27.
[88] C. Kapp, 'WMA Drafts Guidelines on Genetic Databases' (2000) 355 *The Lancet* 1704.

data that they contain. In most cases, data are meaningless in the absence of a context. This is particularly true of those derived from DNA analysis, which in their raw state are intelligible only to highly trained individuals.

Thus, abstract DNA data only pose a threat if linked to other data that can identify the individual to whom the DNA relates. It is the confluence of these data sources that creates the potential for harm, and it is undeniable that this is considerably assisted by the existence and operation of databanks. Harm arises when two or more sources are brought together. Each thereby has a potential to make the other more significant, but the protection of either, or both, can equally avoid the harm in question. If our primary concern is the avoidance of harm, then, it is not at all obvious that data classified as genetic deserve greater protection than those which are not.

When our concern is with harm, the significance of any information about us becomes largely secondary to the significance of the moral position we enjoy as human beings deserving of respect. Respect for persons may be demonstrated by showing respect for information about them, but the moral significance of information is largely stripped away when it is no longer identifiably connected to any individual or set of individuals. The potential for harm remains – as must the imperative of respect – so long as the connection is maintained. However, information that is decontextualised loses much of its moral worth, and so too its potential for harm. This process invites too, in varying degrees, claims to use the information for its residual value, particularly in the sphere of research.

This having been said, the question arises whether the moral connection between individuals and their personal (genetic) information can ever be severed completely. Arguably, so long as information remains personal in any sense, it preserves a moral resonance that requires, inter alia, that it be treated with adequate respect. Information is personal if, in and of itself, it points the way to a particular individual. Thus, if it is accepted that an individual's complete genome as identified by direct DNA analysis is unique to her – even if, in percentage terms, this is only so to a few tenths of a percentage point as compared to the rest of humanity – then such data will always be personal information and should always be subject to stringent control as to their generation, storage and use. The same might not be true for other forms of information, including other forms of genetic data. I am not the only person to live in my street or at my address, nor am I the only person to work at the University of Edinburgh, or to wear size 46 shoes, or to have green eyes (a form of genetic data). These facts do not, in and of themselves, point a way to me. Their collocation might, however, do so, and so long as this is so then they too should be respected as personal information.

In order to appreciate the significance of this distinction it is important to understand the difference between harm and disrespect. While it is certainly true that it is respectful of persons not to harm them, and indeed to seek to avoid harm to them, the avoidance of harm is not the only way in which to accord respect. When our only concern is to avoid harm, then our moral task in relation to personal information is reduced to ensuring adequate security of the information. The moral significance of the information diminishes as the potential for harm diminishes. If we can eliminate the harm, we eliminate the significance of the information in moral terms. This may be achieved, in large part, by depersonalising or decontextualising the information, for example, through anonymisation.[89] If, however, we recognise an inherent connection between information and the person to whom it relates, an obligation of respect in relation to the information remains. This goes beyond the mere avoidance of harm, and encompasses other obligations of respect, such as ensuring that the information is obtained in an appropriate manner with valid and informed consent from the subject, and warranting that the uses to which the information is to be put are legitimate. Moreover, it can include recognition of possible future obligations arising out of uses of the information. For example, research might reveal a possible future health benefit to the subject from whom the information was initially derived. If this is so, a strong argument can be made that the benefit should go to the subject in question. This is more than a simple negative obligation to avoid harm. It is a positive obligation to do something good.

This latter point demonstrates too that the significance of information may change over time. Its value and utility may increase as more knowledge is gained and applied through its use, say, in a clinical or research setting. But, since that value and utility might accrue to parties

[89] Just such an approach underpins the decision of the English Court of Appeal in *R. v. Department of Health, ex parte Source Informatics Ltd.* [2000] 1 All ER 786, discussed in ch. 4.

other than the subject of the information, the need to protect the information and the interests of the subject is an ongoing process that must be the focus of thorough and regular review.

Until now, policies concerning the treatment of genetic information have tended to focus on the harm principle. A plethora of reports,[90] guidelines,[91] statements[92] and declarations[93] have been produced highlighting the harms that may derive from misuse of genetic information, yet there is little coherence or consistency between them as to what is meant by genetic information. The distinction between genetic and other forms of personal or health information is often treated as a given. Moreover, there is usually little attempt to differentiate between the different types of genetic information which have already been discussed. Finally, it is frequently assumed that the problem lies with genetic information itself, and that this should properly be the focus of our attention. While this is arguably so, it is not self-evident, and considerably more thought is needed as to the best policy strategy to adopt.[94] If we are to make genetic information the focus of our efforts, then we must be clear

[90] For example, in the UK alone, the Nuffield Council on Bioethics has devoted more than half of the investigations and reports in its first decade of existence to issues surrounding genetics: *Genetics Screening: Ethical Issues* (1993); *Mental Disorders and Genetics: The Ethical Context* (1998); *Genetically Modified Crops: The Ethical and Social Issues* (1999); *Genetics and Human Behaviour: The Ethical Context* (Consultation Document, 2001). During their existence of some three years (1996–9), the Human Genetics Advisory Commission and the Advisory Committee on Genetic Testing produced five reports between them on matters ranging across genetic issues in insurance and employment, cloning, and genetic testing for prenatal and late onset disorders.

[91] Some example include, in the UK, Advisory Committee on Genetic Testing, *Code of Practice and Guidance on Human Genetic Testing Services Supplied Direct to the Public* (September 1997), and Advisory Committee on Genetic Testing, *Advice to Research Ethics Committees: Points to Consider in Ethical Review of Research Involving Genetic Testing* (October 1998); in the wider European context, French National Bioethics Committee, *Avis et Recommandations sur 'Génétique et Médecine: de la Prediction à la Prévention'* (FNBC, October 1995), European Society of Human Genetics, *Guidelines for the Provision of Genetic Services in Europe* (ESHG, September 2000); and internationally, World Health Organisation, *Proposed International Guidelines on Ethical Issues in Medical Genetics and Genetic Services*, 1997, WHO/HGN/GL/ ETH/98.1, and UNESCO, *Guidelines for the Implementation of the Universal Declaration on the Human Genome and Human Rights* (1999).

[92] See, for example, American Society of Human Genetics, 'Statement on Informed Consent for Genetic Research' (1996) 59 *American Journal of Human Genetics* 471, and World Health Organisation, *Statement of the WHO Expert Consultation on New Developments in Human Genetics* (WHO, Geneva, 2000).

[93] On the international plane, see UNESCO, *Universal Declaration on the Human Genome and Human Rights* (Paris, November 1997).

[94] T. McGleenan, 'Genetic Information and the Challenge to Privacy' (1998) 12 *International Review of Law, Computers and Technology* 535.

on what this term means – and this, as we have already seen, is no easy task. Zimmern offers a useful starting point: 'A conceptualisation which distinguishes on one dimension DNA based from other sources of genetic information, and on another dimension inherited genetic disorders from common complex diseases, provides one approach to how policy might be determined and how a regulatory framework might be more closely applied to situations of differing ethical and social implications.'[95]

Ultimately, the debate as to whether it is a good thing to attempt to differentiate between genetic information and other types of health information must be widened. Within the remit of this work, however, it is legitimate to concentrate on actual and perceived notions of genetic information, if for no other reason than because of the adverse consequences for the proband and her relatives that may accompany the assumptions made. There is also the added fact that, while genetic information is not unique, the ways and means of dealing with it may pose ethical and practical problems in a particularly acute form; as a result, genetic information provides an ideal context in which to consider the range of options that are available to address such problems. For example, Lemmens and Austin have argued that three factors in particular should lead us to reassess our current regulatory approaches. These are (i) the volume of information that can be extracted from one sample which can be kept indefinitely; (ii) the speed of testing; and (iii) the link between genetics and computer technology.[96]

Lessons we cannot (currently) learn from genetic information

A further important rider to this discussion concerns the knowledge that genetic advances cannot currently provide, except in a few, rare instances. Primarily, this is knowledge about how to treat or cure a genetic disorder for which a test has been developed. How, then, should we respond to this limitation? If the pursuit of better health is our goal, then how can our current knowledge base still assist in achieving that end? The answer that is most often given is preparedness. Undoubtedly, some individuals will better prepare for decisions about reproduction when

---

[95] Zimmern, 'What is Genetic Information?', 11.
[96] T. Lemmens and L. Austin, *Of Volume, Depth and Speed: The Challenges of Genetic Information*, Report prepared for the Canadian Biotechnology Advisory Committee (Ottawa, CBAC, 2001).

armed with proper information about the genetic risks of procreating or the lifestyle changes that might minimise the health implications of carrying a defective gene. It is, however, by no means certain that genetic knowledge will achieve satisfactory psychological preparedness – indeed, psychological health may be damaged, rather than improved, by such disclosures. This is explored further below. The immediate lesson, however, is that we should not expect too much of this type of knowledge in our quest to improve our lives. To do so may mean that we achieve nothing more than the frustration of our own efforts.

A final crucial lesson to be learned is that we cannot know all of the ends to which genetic information might be put. Illegitimate uses of this information, which result in harm, discrimination and stigmatisation, must clearly be guarded against. However, the question of where the boundary lies between legitimate and illegitimate use, or indeed between legitimate and illegitimate claims with respect to genetic information, is not answered by the new knowledge that genetic science gives us. We must determine for ourselves where these limits are to be drawn – but how are we to decide where the boundaries of legitimacy begin and end? Intuitively, access to information for the purposes of socially useful research stands in contra-distinction to, say, access for insurance purposes, but is the former a legitimate end and the latter not?

How these and similar ends are to be accommodated, if at all, is a question to be answered in a context-specific manner. The fundamental issue of whether we should ensure baselines of protection for the initial source of the information applies throughout. We can progress from there only by, first, accepting that we must be careful about what we mean when we seek to discuss genetic information and, second, considering the nature and content of claims to genetic information within the context in which those claims are made and in respect of the kind of information that is sought.

The interested parties

This section will consider the claims of various parties who might have an interest in the genetic information of an individual. These parties are: (i) the individual herself; (ii) relatives of the individual; (iii) those employing or insuring the individual or seeking to do so; (iv) researchers; and (v) the state. The nature of these interests will be examined within the rubric of a common language, so as to facilitate a comparison of the various, and at times competing, claims.

An *interest* is defined here as a claim that a benefit can come to the party in question by recognising that she or he has a significant, or a potentially significant, relationship with the subject of our attention, which in this case is genetic information. The basis of that relationship might be

- *personal*: the information is about the person and/or might affect her in her personal capacity;
- *economic*: the information can influence economic interests, either adversely or positively;
- *societal*: social or collective utility might arise from gaining access to, or using, the information in question;
- *paternalistic*: the party with the information is in a position to use it to protect the individual source or others from harm.

The question of whether a party has an interest in genetic information is an evaluative matter. Inherent in the notion of interest is the idea that it is *in* the party's interest to recognise the relationship, and that to do so will normally lead to the conclusion that it is *in* the party's interest to know, and to have access to, the information in question. However, as is explained further below, whether or not this is the case depends on the perspective adopted.

The individual

It is axiomatic that a person who has been tested for one or more genetic conditions has a significant interest in knowing, and determining what happens to, the resulting information. As we have seen, such information can help an individual to make informed decisions about her health and lifestyle and this in turn can prevent future disease. Knowledge of one's genetic status facilitates informed decisions about future reproductive choices.[97] And, while it has already been established that personal health information is inherently connected to, and part of, the private sphere of an individual's life, some forms of health information are special to the individual in other ways. For example, as Suter has noted,

---

[97] See M. Petrou *et al.*, 'Long-term Effect of Prospective Detection of High Genetic Risk on Couples' Reproductive Life: Data for Thalassaemia' (2000) 20 *Prenatal Diagnosis* 469.

[w]hile contracting chicken pox has virtually no effect on identity, the knowledge that one carries a disease gene may influence one's self-perception and definition of 'one's own concept of existence' in a way most infectious diseases do not.[98]

Furthermore, and again unlike conventional health information, DNA-based genetic information cannot be completely anonymised. It is a unique marker pointing the way to a single individual. As Gostin puts it,

> Genomic data are qualitatively different from other health data because they are inherently linked to one person. While non-genetic descriptions of any given patient's disease and treatment could apply to many other individuals, genomic data are unique. But, although the ability to identify a named individual in a large population simply from genetic material is unlikely, the capacity of computers to search multiple data bases provides a potential for linking genomic information to that person. It follows that non-linked genomic data do not assure anonymity and that privacy and security safeguards must attach to any form of genetic material.[99]

Finally, many forms of genetic information not only provide us with information about an individual's medical past, which is the case with most medical records, but can also furnish us with knowledge about her medical *future*. This knowledge might be vague, in that we know only that the person *may* develop disease, or it can be certain; we know that given time, disease *will* develop. Either way, the person who holds that knowledge can make judgements about the individual's future. Thus the individual herself can make future life decisions based on this information. By the same token, insurers or employers might change their attitudes towards the individual in the light of predictive data, and such shifts might not always be to the individual's advantage.

For these reasons and those that have already been advanced in chapter 1, an individual has a very strong claim to determine what happens to such information. In essence, individuals have an interest in the information because it relates to them and can affect their lives. And, because of their status as moral agents, respect is due to them, their wishes, and their interests concerning such inherently personal material.

---

[98] See Suter, 'Whose Genes Are These Anyway?', 1893.
[99] Gostin, 'Genetic Privacy', 322.

Family members

In an entirely unique way, the same reasons can be advanced by the blood relatives of an individual to claim an interest in the latter's genetic test results, since these might also reveal information about themselves.[100] Indeed, as Andrews and Elster say of the prospect of human reproductive cloning, 'Even in cases where the donor waives privacy rights and releases private genetic information, the privacy rights of the clone are necessarily implicated due to the fact that the clone possesses the same nucleic genetic code.'[101] And, while meaningful data for other family members are likely to emerge only from tests for highly penetrant inherited disorders, this does not preclude the possibility of demands being made none the less in respect of other test results, perhaps through misperception or an ill-placed faith in the significance of genetic information as a broad class of knowledge. The task is to evaluate the relative strengths of the respective claims.

One significant difference, however, between an individual who has been tested for a genetic condition and a blood relative is that the proband has made a conscious decision to acquire the information. The same will probably not be true of relatives – at least initially. However, questions of security, access and control arise once such information exists. The protection of the interests of relatives also falls to be considered when these might be compromised through particular uses of the information, and this is true whether or not the relatives are aware of the existence of the information. Different problems emerge when relatives are cognisant of the information. These include balancing the competing interests if the individuals to whom the information relates do not agree collectively on how it should be treated.[102] A final complicating factor is

[100] The existence of this interest has been recognised by a variety of bodies, including the Nuffield Council on Bioethics, *Genetic Screening*, ch. 5; the Royal College of Physicians of London, *Ethical Issues in Clinical Genetics: A Report of the Working Group of the Royal College of Physicians' Committees on Ethical Issues in Medicine and Clinical Genetics*, 1991, para. 4.19, and the Danish Council of Ethics, *Ethics and Mapping of the Human Genome*, p. 62.

[101] L. B. Andrews and N. Elster, 'Regulating Reproductive Technologies' (2000) 21 *Journal of Legal Medicine* 35, 61.

[102] Because of technological advances in the last fifty years in the field of computers the means now exist to store and access all forms of information for indefinite periods of time. In this way, genetic information could also prove relevant for future generations of the same genetic line. See B. Barber, 'Securing Privacy in Medical Genetics', Second Symposium of the Council of Europe on Bioethics, Strasbourg, 30 November–2 December 1993, CDBI-SY-SP (93) 2 at 6; and K. Berg, 'Confidentiality Issues in Medical Genetics: The Need for

the potential claims of non-blood relatives, such as spouses, who might assert an interest in a partner's genetic information, inter alia, for reasons related to an informed reproductive choice. The complexities are well illustrated through the following example.

The French glaucoma studies

In the late eighties and early nineties the French Institut National D'Etudes Démographiques (INED – National Institute for Population Studies) conducted research into instances of hereditary glaucoma near Boulogne-sur-Mer, in the northern Pas-de-Calais *département*, where the number of reported cases of this condition was unusually high as compared with the rest of the country. The Institute was able to trace the antecedents of three families whose members were known to be sufferers from glaucoma back fifteen generations to a blind couple who lived in a small village in the region in the sixteenth century. Having done so, it was then relatively easy to retrace the descendants of the couple forward to the present day in order to identify those individuals who were currently at increased risk of developing glaucoma. The nature of the condition is such that, if caught in its pre-symptomatic or early stages, its progress can be halted simply with a prescription of eye-drops. However, it can eventually lead to blindness if it is not diagnosed at this stage, and the only treatment available for late-stage disease is surgery. The INED decided to consult the National Data Protection Agency to determine the correct procedure to be followed in order to inform the individuals at high risk. The Agency responded that the Institute should not, in any circumstances, take steps to inform these people of what they had discovered. To do so, it was said, would be a breach of their privacy. This caused outcry throughout France.[103] Of particular interest in this work is the nature of the questions to which the scenario gives rise.

For example, why should relatives not be informed of test results, especially if the results reveal a predisposition to a serious condition? Should the wishes of the tested person be taken into account? Should the wishes of relatives be taken into account? Should a relative be able to demand disclosure of such information? Does the absence or presence of

Laws, Rules and Good Practices to Secure Optimal Disease Control', Second Symposium of the Council of Europe on Bioethics, *ibid.*, 3.
[103] See *L'Express*, 20 March 1992.

a cure or a therapy make a difference? Could a relative refuse to receive such information – that is, could such a person have a claim *not* to know of a genetic predisposition? Might an interested third party such as the state have a claim in *requiring* that they know such information? Does the health care professional who has performed the test owe a duty of disclosure to relatives of a tested person, even if they are not her patients? If so, what is a professional to do if those to whom the duty is owed disagree about how the information should be treated? All of these questions have implications for the privacy of the persons concerned.

Familial issues and interests in genetic information

In November 1997 the General Conference of the United Nations Educational, Scientific and Cultural Organisation (UNESCO) adopted the Universal Declaration on the Human Genome and Human Rights, of which Article 7 provides: 'Genetic data associated with an identifiable person and stored or processed for the purposes of research or any other purpose must be held confidential in the conditions set by law.' Article 9 states: 'In order to protect human rights and fundamental freedoms, limitations to the principles of consent and confidentiality may only be prescribed by law, for compelling reasons within the bounds of public international law and the international law of human rights.'[104]

This atomistic approach generates a potential for considerable intra-familial tension. It is, therefore, important to distinguish the various interests involved. These can be distilled into the following categories.

The individual – an interest in the genetic information resulting from a test

For the reasons already outlined above, the individual who has consented to a genetic test has a significant interest in the results. This is so even if the test reveals information that was not expected; for example, a test for an inherited disease A also reveals a predisposition to disease B. This assertion is based on the individual's right to be respected as a moral

---

[104] UNESCO Resolution 29/C17, *Implementation of the Universal Declaration on the Human Genome and Human Rights*, November 1997. On 9 December 1998 the United Nations General Assembly endorsed the Declaration in Resolution A/RES/53/152, *The Human Genome and Human Rights*.

agent. However, it is entirely contingent on her agreeing to receive the information.

The individual – an interest in keeping information in a state of non-access

Because of potentially harmful consequences for an individual if personal information is not kept secure, the individual has an interest in keeping the information secret or private, that is, limiting access to those whom she nominates.

Wolf has warned that our society runs a serious risk of applying a reductionist approach to genetic information.[105] This, she posits, will adversely affect individuals and will lead to what she terms *geneticism*. Using the context of health insurance, she points out that too often individuals are seen 'as their genes'.[106] This in turn 'subdivid[es] communities by their genetic characteristics, and promot[es] the idea that genetic differences are real, biological, and neutral grounds for different treatment'.[107]

Wolf further warns that, although genetic knowledge in itself may be neutral, the uses to which it is put are not necessarily also so. Our recent past teaches us that genetic information can be seen as building scientific, and thereby supposedly credible, foundations for long-held prejudices and deeply ingrained bigotry. As more becomes known about the human genome it cannot be guaranteed that such information will always be used for entirely neutral ends. Consider, for example, recent discussion about the desirability and utility of a search for a so-called gay gene.[108] On the one hand, scientific proof that homosexuality has a genetic basis brings credence to the argument that homosexuals *are* made that way, and that homosexuality is not simply a lifestyle choice. By the same token, scientific proof of a genetic influence on sexuality would undoubtedly also strengthen the resolve in some quarters

[105] S. M. Wolf, 'Beyond "Genetic Discrimination": Towards the Broader Harm of Geneticism' (1995) 23 *Journal of Law, Medicine and Ethics* 345.
[106] *Ibid.*, 346.   [107] *Ibid.*
[108] As an example of the discussion which surrounds this subject see G. Vines, 'Gene Tests: The Parents' Dilemma' (1994) November *New Scientist* 40; S. LeVay and D. H. Hamer, 'Evidence for a Biological Influence in Male Homosexuality' (1994) May *Scientific American* 20; W. Byne, 'The Biological Evidence Challenged' (1994) May *Scientific American* 26; and U. Schuklenk, E. Stein, J. Kerin and W. Byne, 'The Ethics of Genetic Research on Sexual Orientation' (1997) 27 *Hastings Center Report* 6.

that homosexuals had been quite rightly treated as deviants, for such a gene could easily be seen as a mutation from the 'normal'. Such divergent viewpoints not only call into question the appropriateness of such research but also indicate that individuals have a strong interest in maintaining control and security over the knowledge that they possess such a gene. The same holds true for research into a genetic element in intelligence.[109]

However, the possibility of resulting harm is not the only reason for claiming an interest in informational security. In chapter 1 it was contended that individuals deserve respect and that this extends both to their person and their personal information. Deference to the wishes of individuals is one of the utmost forms of respect, and an expressed wish that security be maintained should be sufficient justification for its observance. The individual's interest lies in having her wishes respected, and it is therefore related only tangentially to the information itself.

Family members – knowledge and security of genetic information

For the same reasons as are argued above, and in the context of highly predictive genetic data, blood relatives can have an interest both in knowing the test results from a proband *and* in ensuring that that information is not noised abroad without authority. The question of whether or not their interest is as strong as that of the proband is more difficult to answer. Certainly, the risk of being affected by a particular condition is reduced with the distance of relationship because of the increasingly varied genetic and environmental factors which operate.[110]

A spouse or partner can gain no knowledge at all about his or her own genetic constitution by knowing the test result of their significant other, but could nevertheless claim several interests in having the information. Such knowledge gives an indication as to possible future risks to their progeny, and could also weigh heavily in any decision of the partner to remain in the relationship.

[109] A. Newson and R. Williamson, 'Should We Undertake Genetic Research on Intelligence?' (1999) 13 *Bioethics* 327; and M. J. Reiss, 'The Ethics of Genetic Research on Intelligence' (2000) 14 *Bioethics* 1.

[110] See Wilson, *Principles of Internal Medicine*, p. 30: 'as the degree of relation becomes more distant, the likelihood of a relative inheriting the same combination of genes becomes less. Moreover, the chances of any relative inheriting the right combination of genes decrease as the number of genes required for the expression of a given trait increases.'

First-degree relatives of the person who has been tested, who have the highest likelihood of genetic similarity with the proband, have the strongest interests. Such relatives include the children of a proband who might want to know of any risk of disease which might affect themselves or their progeny. Siblings, too, have a strong interest in a brother or sister's test results given their common parentage.[111]

This having been said, it is important to stress once again that the concern with genetic information involves more than a simple desire to avoid harm. Even if test results show no risk of disease, it should not be presumed that individuals will automatically be happy to surrender control of that information. Relatives will still have an interest in each other's genetic make-up even if it contains nothing sinister. Such information is intimately connected with their private sphere and possibly their sense of self, and therefore requires respect in the same manner as for the proband.

It is clear that conflict will arise, for example, when the proband wishes to keep the data *private* and the family wishes to invade that private sphere or, perhaps, become part of that sphere. Even more complex patterns of conflict can develop when the converse is true, that is, when the proband or another seek to impart genetic knowledge which relatives do not choose to know.

The individual and the family – an interest in not knowing?

Most discussion on how to handle familial genetic test results proceeds on the assumption that both the individual who has been tested and her family desire to know the information that has been generated. However, the question arises of whether any of these individuals have an interest in *not* knowing test results. For example, the proband might agree to be tested but then change her mind. Equally, relatives might be approached by a proband willing to reveal test results but they might refuse to accept the information. Let us consider, then, the possible interests that individuals might have in *not* knowing.

---

[111] This is particularly true for identical twins. It should be noted, however, that the knowledge of a sibling's test result will *not* give any further information about *one's own* risk of ill health. The odds of being affected are the same for each sibling, e.g. a 50 per cent chance of being affected by a dominant disorder or a 25 per cent chance of being affected by a recessive disorder (50 per cent chance of being a carrier). Matters are altogether more complicated with multifactorial conditions.

Genetic knowledge can undoubtedly bring many benefits to individuals. It can signal current or future ill health and if a cure is available it can be sought pre-emptively. Even if a cure is not available, knowledge can serve several ends. Because multifactorial conditions are influenced by many factors including the non-genetic, knowledge of a predisposition to such a condition can provide individuals with the opportunity to change aspects of their lifestyle, and this might, in turn, influence the onset of disease.[112] Similarly, the discovery of hereditary disease, or a predisposition to such, means that any subsequent reproductive decision will be an informed decision. Moreover, it has even been argued that with knowledge comes preparedness for the risk of developing disease at a later stage in life.[113] All of this has been covered above. Unfortunately, all such arguments suffer from one fundamental weakness. They proceed on the assumption that only benefit can result from knowledge, but this is by no means a clear given.[114]

The availability of a cure carries with it the certainty that disclosure can incontrovertibly avert harm.[115] In the vast majority of cases this can only be seen as a good thing for a third party to whom disclosure is made.[116] This might also be true of some therapies, but here the case is less clear-cut: 'If ... the treatment is ineffective, painful or difficult to come by, the grounds are less firm.'[117] Moreover, few cures or minimally invasive and effective therapies are currently available for genetic conditions. And if disclosure is made to avoid an ancillary harm such as psychological upset there is less of a guarantee that the harm in question will, de facto, be avoided. Evidence exists from empirical studies

[112] See Ryan, 'An Ethical Debate', and Reilly, 'Rights, Privacy, and Genetic Screening'.
[113] See Ball, Tyler and Harper, 'Predictive Testing of Adults and Children'; and Pelias, 'Duty to Disclose in Medical Genetics: A Legal Perspective'.
[114] L. B. Andrews, *Future Perfect: Confronting Decisions About Genetics* (New York, Columbia University Press, 2001), ch. 3.
[115] That said, in circumstances where a cure *is* available but an individual would not choose to take it – perhaps for religious reasons – it is hard to see how disclosure could ever be justified, because the perceived harm could not be avoided. Of course, one could argue that faced with the reality of the situation the individual might nevertheless accept treatment, but this is to adopt a strong paternalistic perspective, the ethical propriety of which is extremely doubtful.
[116] It is recognised that this might be a different matter for the individual who has had their genetic information revealed to others. However, both legally and ethically disclosure is justified, because it can further the public interest in avoiding harm.
[117] T. Takala and H. A. Gylling, 'Who Should Know About Our Genetic Makeup and Why?' (2000) 26 *Journal of Medical Ethics* 171.

that both supports[118] and refutes[119] the benefits in disclosure in facilitating preparedness. Most recently, for example, Almqvist *et al.* found
in an international study that the suicide rate among persons given a
positive genetic test result for Huntington's disease was ten times higher
than the United States average.[120] While this rate is no greater than that
for the population showing the symptoms of Huntington's disease (nor
indeed, is it vastly greater than the rate for persons with other debilitating and progressive diseases), it is significant that the survey primarily
focused on the two years after test results were given. This would tend
to indicate that the deaths were more directly related to the disclosure
of the genetic information, rather than to some other factors, such as
the onset of disease itself.[121]

Thus it is entirely possible that individuals might be loath to learn of a
relative's genetic status because of the implications that this knowledge
can have for their own wellbeing. Indeed, the Danish Council of Ethics

---

[118] J. Buxton and M. Pembrey, 'The New Genetics: What the Public Wants to Know' (1996)
4 *European Journal of Human Genetics (Suppl.)* 153; M. Hietala *et al.*, 'Attitudes Towards
Genetic Testing Among the General Population and Relatives of Patients with a Severe
Genetic Disease: A Survey from Finland' (1995) 56 *American Journal of Human Genetics*
1493; Ball, 'Predictive Testing of Adults and Children', quoting several others including
M. R. Hayden, 'Predictive Testing for Huntington's Disease: Are We Ready for Widespread
Community Implementation?' (1991) 40 *American Journal of Medical Genetics* 515; and
J. Brandt *et al.*, 'Presymptomatic Diagnosis of Delayed-Onset with Linked DNA Mark-
ers: the Experience of Huntington's Disease' (1989) 261 *Journal of the American Medical
Association* 3108.

[119] See D. Kevles, *In the Name of Eugenics: Genetics and the Uses of Human Heredity* (London,
Penguin Books, 1985), p. 298; E. Almqvist *et al.*, 'Risk Reversal in Predictive Testing for
Huntington Disease' (1997) 61 *American Journal of Human Genetics* 945; J. Fanos and
J. Johnson, 'Perception of Carrier Status by Cystic Fibrosis Siblings' (1995) 57 *American
Journal of Human Genetics* 431; L. Andrews, 'Legal Aspects of Genetic Information' (1990)
64 *The Yale Journal of Biology and Medicine* 29, 38; D. Craufurd, A. Dodge, L. Kerzin-Storrar
et al., 'Uptake of Presymptomatic Predictive Testing for Huntington's Disease' (1989) 2
The Lancet 603; C. Lerman *et al.*, 'Psychological Side Effects of Breast Cancer Screening'
(1991) 10 *Health Psychology* 259; and C. Hayes, 'Genetic Testing for Huntington's Disease –
A Family Issue' (1992) 327 *New England Journal of Medicine* 1449.

[120] See E. Almqvist *et al.*, 'A Worldwide Assessment of the Frequency of Suicide, Suicide
Attempts, or Psychiatric Hospitalization after Predictive Testing for Huntington Disease'
(1999) 64 *American Journal of Human Genetics* 1293. The authors surveyed 100 centres in
21 countries and gathered data on 4,527 individuals who had undergone predictive genetic
testing for Huntington's disease. Of those reviewed, 1,817 people had received a positive
result, of whom five had taken their own lives. This extrapolates to 138/100,000 suicides per
year, compared with the United States average of 12–13/100,000 per year. See T. Bird, 'Outrageous Fortune: The Risk of Suicide in Genetic Testing for Huntington Disease' (1999) 64
American Journal of Human Genetics 1289.

[121] Bird, 'Outrageous Fortune'.

has warned of the risk of *morbidification*: 'the notion of falling victim to some inescapable fate through knowledge about risk of disease'.[122]

The possible adverse effects of knowledge of genetic predisposition have been well documented by Hoffman and Wulfsberg.[123] They cite three examples of child screening programmes in Sweden, the United States and Wales involving, respectively, alpha$_1$-antitrypsin deficiency,[124] cystic fibrosis,[125] and Duchenne muscular dystrophy.[126]

The Swedish government initiated a nationwide screening pro-gramme of newly born babies in 1972. As part of the programme parents were (i) told whether or not the child had alpha$_1$-antitrypsin deficiency; (ii) counselled to protect the child from environmental factors such as smoking or high dense-particle atmospheres which could exacerbate the child's health problems; and (iii) followed to determine the psychologi-cal impact of the information. Follow-up studies showed that more than half of the families with affected children suffered adverse psycholog-ical consequences, some of which continued for five to seven years.[127] Indeed, in some cases the knowledge exacerbated the problems because worried parents began to smoke more and so contaminated further the child's environment. These factors led directly to the abandonment of the programme in 1974.[128]

---

[122] Danish Council, *Ethics and Mapping of the Human Genome*, p. 60. Whereas this is arguably true of all disease, the problem can be particularly acute with genetic disease, because individuals can have *future* ill health predicted. Thus a person can be affected even when they are perfectly healthy. With non-genetic disease usually one is actually affected by the disease before suffering psychological sequelae. An obvious example where this is not true is in the case of asymptomatic HIV infection leading to AIDS.

[123] D. E. Hoffman and E. A. Wulfsberg, 'Testing Children for Genetic Predispositions: Is it in Their Best Interest?' (1995) 23 *Journal of Law, Medicine and Ethics* 331.

[124] This is a genetic enzyme deficiency which is common in persons of Scandinavian descent. Those with the gene have a high risk of developing adult-onset emphysema.

[125] Cystic fibrosis is the most common recessively inherited disorder in the United Kingdom. It results in thick secretions in the lungs and pancreas which lead to chronic pulmonary and digestive disease.

[126] This condition is typified by chronic muscle wasting. The disease usually manifests itself in children of between two and four years old. Death normally results by the middle teenage years.

[127] Hoffman and Wulfsberg cite the following articles as authority: T. Thelin *et al.*, 'Psycho-logical Consequences of Neo-natal Screening for Alpha$_1$-Antitrypsin Deficiency (ATD)' (1985) 74 *Acta Paediatrica Scandinavica* 787; and T. F. McNeil *et al.*, 'Psychological Effects of Screening for Somatic Risk: The Swedish Alpha$_1$-Antitrypsin Experience' (1988) 43 *Thorax* 505. Most recently, see T. Sveger *et al.*, 'Neonatal 1-Antitrypsin Screening: Parents' Views and Reactions 20 Years After the Identification of the Deficiency State' (1999) 88 *Acta Paediatrica* 315.

[128] As an example, and for an account of the problems of prenatal testing from a French perspective, see N. Lenoir, 'Aspects Juridiques et Ethiques du Diagnostic Prénatal: Le Droit

In like manner, Hoffman and Wulfsberg note that in the United States cystic fibrosis screening programmes, which commenced as early as 1968, have been abandoned because 'many people think (even in cases where there is a familial risk of the disease) that early detection has no value and may, in fact, cause the family significant psychological distress prior to the time when the individual might become symptomatic'.[129] The authors assert that for these reasons the United States has not instituted a programme of screening newly born babies for Duchenne muscular dystrophy (DMD), unlike Wales, where such a programme has run for both DMD and cystic fibrosis on an evaluative basis for over a decade.[130]

Similar evidence is available for adults. Citing several studies, Kevles has noted that 'The revelation of genetic hazard has been observed to result not only in repression but in anxiety, depression, and a sense of stigmatization.'[131] Also, Andrews has written that 'deaths due to suicide are four times as prevalent among Huntington's disease patients than among the corresponding US Caucasian population', mirroring the finds of Almqvist above.[132] It has even been observed that confirmation of one's status as a *non-affected* person can have adverse psychological effects. Huggins *et al.*[133] and Wexler[134] have carried out studies in families affected by genetic disease whose results show that 'Many may suffer "survivor guilt", particularly characteristic of wartime soldiers who live while their buddies are killed.'[135]

The possibility that any or all of these forms of harm can result means that individuals can cite a strong interest in not knowing genetic information about themselves.[136] However, not only private interests are at stake. In the context of research, for example, the Medical Research Council has found that no clear view emerged on the propriety of feeding

et Les Pratiques en Vigueur en France et dans Divers Autres Pays', in O. Guillod and P. Widmer (eds.), *Human Genetic Analysis and the Protection of Personality and Privacy* (Zurich, Schulthess Polygraphischer Verlag, 1994).
[129] Hoffman and Wulfsberg, 'Testing Children', 333.
[130] For further information, see the University of Wales Medical Genetics Services website: http://medico.uwcm.ac.uk:10080/study/medicine/medical_genetics/service/laboratory.html
[131] Kevles, *In the Name of Eugenics*, p. 298.
[132] See Andrews, 'Legal Aspects of Genetic Information', 38.
[133] Huggins, 'Predictive Testing for Huntington Disease in Canada'.
[134] N. Wexler, 'Genetic Jeopardy and the New Clairvoyance' (1985) 6 *Progress in Medical Genetics* 277.
[135] *Ibid.*
[136] Cf. R. Rhodes, 'Genetic Links, Family Ties, and Social Bonds: Rights and Responsibilities in the Face of Genetic Knowledge' (1998) 23 *Journal of Medicine and Philosophy* 10.

research results back to subjects when those results revealed bad news. Indeed, a number of survey participants expressed the view that they would prefer not to be told bad news that resulted from the donation of samples for research purposes.[137] The deterrent effect of this prospect, were it significant, could be damaging to the research community's chances of recruiting suitable subjects, and so, in turn, damaging to the public interest in research.

Furthermore, and as with the arguments put above, we should not imagine that potential harm is the only reason for claiming an interest in not knowing genetic information. The question of respect also arises.[138] To disclose genetic information to someone who has not indicated a desire to know it is disrespectful in at least two ways. First, if the individual has expressly stated that she does not wish to know, to furnish the information nevertheless disregards their wishes and is an affront to them as moral 'chooser'.

Second, and by extension, the absence of a prior expressed wish should not necessarily lead to the conclusion that the individual has an interest in knowing. That an individual has not expressed a view about her desire to know genetic information is very likely, given that so many different conditions can manifest themselves with such irregular patterns through families. She might not know that there is anything to know. But, even if no tangible harm results from the disclosure, the fact that the individual's private sphere is invaded by such information – information which can alter considerably perceptions of herself, her children and her role in society – is potentially disrespectful in itself. It requires the individual to take on board information which then cannot be unknown. The knowledge becomes a factor that will necessarily form part of many of her future life decisions. She is coerced into self-reflection and forced to evaluate and re-evaluate her *self*. Moreover, the information is given for reasons that are not her own. It might be argued, of course, that it is in her best interests to know, but this is to make an evaluative judgement that does not consider the actual wishes of the individual or the full gamut of her interests, including that in not knowing.[139] At the very least, such

[137] Medical Research Council, 'Public Perceptions', para. 6.9.
[138] J. Raikka, 'Freedom and a Right (Not) to Know' (1998) 12 *Bioethics* 49, and T. Takala, 'The Right to Genetic Ignorance Confirmed' (1999) 13 *Bioethics* 288.
[139] Of course, we might take into account what we believe the wishes of the individual to be, but this is not the same as taking into account the individual's *actual* wishes.

disclosure requires strong justification, and it is in this regard that our current models for dealing with genetic knowledge are deficient.[140] The overriding imperative in modern medicine is to disclose information. The paradigm example of this is the doctrine of informed consent, now embraced wholeheartedly by the health care professions. But, while this is entirely proper in many circumstances, it is not so in all circumstances. And, in the present context, it is certainly not unquestionably the most respectful course of action.

Thus, it can be seen that both the proband and her relatives could have an interest in not knowing genetic information. This is not a fanciful argument. The interest has been recognised by the Council of Europe in its *Convention for the Protection of Human Rights and Dignity of the Human Being with Regard to the Application of Biology and Medicine*, chapter III of which states (Article 10):

1. Everyone has the right to respect for private life in relation to information about his or her health.
2. Everyone is entitled to know any information collected about his or her health. *However, the wishes of individuals not to be so informed shall be observed.*
3. In exceptional cases, restrictions may be placed by law on the exercise of the rights contained in paragraph 2 in the interests of the patient.[141] (emphasis added)

Similarly, the Universal Declaration on the Human Genome and Human Rights provides that, 'The right of each individual to decide whether *or not* to be informed of the result of genetic examination and the resulting consequences should be respected' (emphasis added).[142]

The recognition of this interest complicates matters considerably. The most obvious conflict arises when one party wants to impart genetic information and another does not wish to receive it. Given that this can have implications for family members further down the genetic line, the respective claims require very close scrutiny. While no attempt has

---

[140] American Society for Healthcare Risk Management, *Perspective on Disclosure of Unanticipated Outcome Information* (Chicago, ASHRM, 2001).

[141] Council of Europe, *Convention for the Protection of Human Rights and Dignity of the Human Being with Regard to the Application of Biology and Medicine: Convention on Human Rights and Biomedicine*. The Convention was adopted by the Committee of Ministers on 19 November 1996 (reference DIR/JUR (96) 14), and opened for signature in Oviedo, April 1997. Eight member states of the Council of Europe had ratified the Convention as of June 2001 (Denmark, Georgia, Greece, Romania, San Marino, Slovakia, Slovenia, and Spain).

[142] UNESCO, *Universal Declaration on the Human Genome and Human Rights*, Article 5c.

been made so far to evaluate the respective merits of these interests, or to determine the weight that each should receive relative to another, it should be noted that the identified interests correspond to privacy interests of the nature defined in chapter 1. First, an interest in keeping information secure and in a state of non-access is an example of an interest in *informational privacy*. Second, an interest in not knowing genetic information is an example of an interest in *spatial privacy*. This second example cannot also be an instance of an informational privacy interest because that interest is premised on knowledge of the existence of the information. As we have seen, an interest in not knowing does not require such knowledge. Rather, the interest in question is protection of the private sphere around one's *self*.[143] As the eminent philosopher and jurist James Fitzjames Stephen wrote in 1873, 'Privacy may be violated not only by the intrusion of a stranger, but by compelling or persuading a person to direct too much attention to his own feelings and to attach too much importance to their analysis.'[144]

Invasions of privacy occur, in the case of informational privacy, when disclosures of information are made to unauthorised parties. Spatial privacy interests are invaded by unsolicited disclosure of genetic information to the proband or relative him- or herself.[145]

What can we meaningfully conclude from the abundance of evidence that genetic information might benefit *or* might harm those to whom it is disclosed, save that matters are largely inconclusive? Well, at the very least this should lead us to question any underlying assumption that it is always in an individual's interests to know information about herself. Any coherent and ethically sound information disclosure policy must accommodate this consideration. Moreover, to the extent that this does

---

[143] That is, one's *self* in the sense of one's personality, body, mind etc.

[144] J. F. Stephen, *Liberty, Equality and Fraternity* (London, Henry Hold & Co, 1873), p. 160.

[145] As further recognition of the potential problem, and as an indication of a possible solution, consider the US President's Commission for the Study of Ethical Problems in Medicine and Biomedical and Behavioral Research, which recommended that disclosure to relatives should be made only if (i) reasonable attempts to persuade the proband to disclose have proved to be unsuccessful; (ii) there is a high probability of serious (that is, irreversible or fatal) harm to an identified third party; (iii) there is reason to believe that disclosure will prevent harm; (iv) the disclosure is limited to the information necessary for diagnosis and treatment. This tries as far as possible to cater for the interests of the proband but fails to consider the possible spatial privacy interests of relatives which exist *even if* a cure is available. See President's Commission for the Study of Ethical Problems in Medicine and Biomedicine and Behavioral Research, *Screening and Counseling for Genetic Conditions* (Washington, DC, United States Government Printing Office, 1983).

not appear to be the case in current practice, this should lead us further to examine how we might construct a model for dealing with such a nuanced approach. In turn, this calls for an examination of the tools that might be used in the construction of that model, and in the medico-legal workshop there is no shortage of candidates. Primary among these is autonomy, which has come to be equiparated with individual choice in contemporary bioethics. Indeed, the facilitation of choice as a reflection of respect for individual autonomy is rapidly assuming the mantle of the ethical panacea to all of the dilemmas we face in modern medicine. Thus, for example, when UNESCO and the Council of Europe show respect for the interest in not knowing (above), they do so by reference to the individual's *choice* not to know. But this is self-evidently inadequate as a complete answer to the problem, for how can there be an exercise of a choice not to know when one might be unaware that there is anything to know? And how can an appeal to choice protect an interest in not knowing when a meaningful choice can only be made in the light of information about the content of all possible choices? The straightforward answer is that it cannot do so. We are left therefore to wonder what further assistance is available in the construction of our model. One answer is privacy, as the rest of this book will seek to demonstrate. Its wider utility in the context of other competing interests is explored further below.

Insurers and employers

The range of parties with an interest in genetic information is not restricted to those directly affected. Genetic information has been perceived – rightly or wrongly – as a useful predictive tool, and much interest in the results of genetic tests has been expressed by bodies such as employers and insurers.[146] That such bodies could have an interest in

---

[146] See L. Andrews and A. S. Jaeger, 'Confidentiality of Genetic Information in the Workplace' (1991) 17 *American Journal of Law and Medicine* 75; L. O. Gostin, 'Genetic Discrimination: The Use of Genetically Based Diagnostic and Prognostic Tests by Employers and Insurers' (1991) 17 *American Journal of Law and Medicine* 109; T. H. Greely, 'Health Insurance, Employment Discrimination and the Genetic Revolution', in D. J. Kevles and L. Hood (eds.), *The Code of Codes* (Cambridge, Cambridge University Press, 1992), ch. 12; P. S. Harper, 'Insurance and Genetic Testing' (1993) 341 *The Lancet* 224; M. A. Rothstein, 'Genetic Discrimination in Employment: Ethics, Policy and Comparative Law'; and H. D. C. Roscam Abbing, 'Predictive Genetic Knowledge, Insurances and the Legal Position of the Individual', in Guillod and Widmer, *Human Genetic Analysis and the Protection of Personality and Privacy*. See also H. Nys *et al.*, *Predictive Genetic Information and Life Insurance: Legal*

gaining access to genetic information is not surprising – the possible risk of future ill health is not to their financial advantage. This section will examine the nature of this financial interest together with other possible interests that employers and insurers can claim in personal genetic information.

Insurance

Genetic testing and insurance have one important feature in common: both are concerned with the evaluation of risk. We have already considered the nature of genetic testing. The nature of the insurance industry – at least in the context of mutuality-based insurance – has been concisely summed up by Roscam Abbing:

> Insurance firms work with homogeneous risk groups. These are groups whose members have risks that are approximately similar (risk-classification). Private insurers generally base their decisions on actuarial calculations of the likelihood of loss or damage. Premiums ought to be consistent with the risk being insured. Underwriting is fundamental to insurance. It involves the careful assessment of the risk so that the rate of premium commensurate with that risk can be charged. Therefore, insurance companies need information of proposals, including medical information, in order to assess the risk and to take decisions on the issuing of policies, the charges and the conditions accordingly. In case a person represents a high risk, the insurance company will either demand a higher premium, or lay down special conditions (exclusions) or even will turn down the application.[147]

There are many different kinds of insurance, but those of most current relevance to genetic testing are life insurance and health insurance.[148] In the United States, where there is a very limited scheme of public health

Aspects – Towards European Community Policy? (Maastricht, Rijkuniversiteit Limburg, 1993). For comment on the latter, see P. Gannon and G. T. Laurie, 'Review: Predictive Genetic Information and Life Insurance: Legal Aspects – Towards European Community Policy?' (1995) 2 *European Journal of Health Law* 282.

[147] Roscam Abbing, 'Predictive Genetic Knowledge', p. 146.

[148] O'Neill has pointed out, however, that 'The initial concentration of the UK debate on genetics and life insurance . . . has in fact focused on the easy case. Life insurance is unlike other forms of personal insurance in that it is mainly bought in the prime of life by healthy people; other sorts of personal insurance are most needed by the less healthy. The most difficult debates may lie ahead', O. O'Neill, 'Insurance and Genetics: The Current State of Play' (1998) 61 *Modern Law Review* 716, 723. An obvious and difficult example is that of long-term care insurance.

provision, private health insurance is essential.[149] In the United Kingdom private health insurance is currently less important because of the existence of the National Health Service, which, as a form of solidarity-based insurance, takes no account of the particular risks brought to the pool by individuals, and distributes resources according to need. In contrast, life insurance is required for certain types of loans, including mortgages for the purchase of property. Moreover, life insurance provides individuals with the best means to fulfil their responsibilities and to protect their loved ones in the event of their own death. Finally, an increasingly important option is long-term care insurance which addresses the problems of inadequate pensions and longer life spans. In these ways, insurance touches the lives of most of us. Denial of insurance can, therefore, have far-reaching consequences for both individuals and families.

Genetic information may clearly be important to insurers in the assessment of risk and the establishment of premiums. It is entirely fair to say and to recognise that insurers have an economic or financial interest in relevant information. In particular, there are two ways in which genetic information becomes of relevance. This occurs, first, when the prospective insured already has knowledge about her genetic make-up. This might be in the form of a family history of genetic disease or a specific genetic test result. Either way, because the nature of the insurance contract requires *uberrima fides* – utmost good faith – the prospective insured must disclose such knowledge as relevant and material information. If she fails to do so the insurer can render the contract void at any time.

Second, if no such information is available the insurer might nevertheless require the insurance candidate to undergo genetic testing. Although at the present time insurance companies do not as a matter of course require prospective insured to undergo such testing – indeed, the Association of British Insurers (ABI) has repeatedly stated that it does not intend in the foreseeable future to require that life insurance candidates undergo genetic testing, and it has issued a Code of Practice to its members that makes this explicit[150] – there is a fear that the increased

---

[149] For an overview see Academy Task Force on Genetic Testing in Health Insurance, *Genetic Information and Medical Expense Insurance* (Washington, DC, American Academy of Actuaries, 2000).

[150] Association of British Insurers, *Genetic Testing: ABI Code of Practice* (London, ABI, 1999). In the United States a study carried out by the Office of Technology Assessment has suggested

availability of tests for a whole range of genetic conditions will lead to the 'development and proliferation of predictive genetic testing'.[151] This will, allegedly, 'be employed as a loss avoiding device by insurers'.[152] Thus, we have a paradigm example of a potential conflict of interests. But what is the precise nature of the interests at stake?

The interests of the insurance industry

The concept of insurance is based on two principles: *mutuality* (or equity) and *solidarity*. The principle of mutuality provides that the contribution of individuals should approximately reflect their level of risk. The more likely I am to claim insurance the higher my premium should be. The principle of solidarity, however, requires that the burden of bearing risks is spread throughout the general body of the insured.

From this we can identify two general interests of insurance companies in genetic information: (i) the interest in making money; and (ii) the interest in spreading the cost of insurance as widely as possible. That is, genetic information can assist the industry in calculating individual premiums but at the same time should not, where possible, discourage individuals from being tested. To do so would not be in the long-term interest of the industry. This having been said, an interesting paradox faces the insurance industry with genetic information. For just as the increased certainty that some forms of genetic information can bring permits the industry to identify high risk individuals, too much certainty could signal the downfall of the industry itself. As one expert on the economics of insurance has put it, 'The insurance industry cannot cope with certainty.'[153] This is explained by Alper and Natowicz:

> Traditionally, an insurance policy affords protection against very large costs resulting from the occurrence of an undesirable event whose probability is small. If the probability of loss is the same for each person then each will pay the same premium. But if the insurance company has information

that most insurers would not force individuals to undergo testing: Office of Technology Assessment of the US Congress, *Genetic Tests and Health Insurance: the Results of a Survey* (Washington, DC, US Government Printing Office, 1992).

[151] R. Chadwick and C. Ngwena, 'The Human Genome Project, Predictive Testing and Insurance Contracts: Ethical and Legal Responses' (1995) 1 *Res Publica* 115, 115.

[152] *Ibid.*, 116.

[153] See the evidence of Dr Nicholas Barr of the London School of Economics to the House of Commons Science and Technology Committee, 'Human Genetics', at para. 237.

about the relative risk to each person it might charge premiums proportionate to the risk. In the extreme case, where there is sufficient knowledge to predict definitively to whom events will occur, the traditional concept of insurance breaks down.[154]

A related interest of insurance companies concerns their public image. In particular, two perceptions among the public could have adverse consequences for the industry. First, if individuals feel that they will not receive fair treatment from insurance companies this might act as a disincentive to being tested. And, if individuals do not choose to be tested then no information will be available on which to calculate better the risk against which the individual seeks to insure. It might be argued that family history will still be a guide, which after all has always been part of the material information to be disclosed. Perhaps so, but the unpredictability of many genetic conditions means that family history can often give no indication of an individual's particular risk. For example, in one study concerning Tay-Sachs disease, '82 per cent of the incidents of the disease were initial occurrences within the kindred'.[155]

The risk of individuals being deterred from seeking testing has been considered to be significant. The House of Commons Science and Technology Committee commented: 'We accept that the insurance industry has collectively tried to deal with genetics in a responsible way; nonetheless we are concerned there is a real danger that people could decide to decline testing, even when such testing would be advantageous to them, because of the possible insurance implications'.[156] Indeed, a number of other bodies have noted a concern among the public about the potential uses which the insurance industry might make of genetic data. For example, while the Human Genetics Advisory Commission went out of its way in its 1997 report on genetics and insurance to praise the ABI for

---

[154] J. S. Alper and M. R. Natowicz, 'Genetic Testing and Insurance' (1993) 307 *British Medical Journal* 1506, 1507.

[155] Andrews, 'Legal Aspects of Genetic Information', 35, quoting M. M. Kaback and J. L. Zeigler, 'The John F. Kennedy Institute Tay-Sachs Program: Practical and Ethical Issues in an Adult Genetic Screening Program', in B. Hilton et al., *Ethical Issues in Human Genetics: Genetic Counseling and the Use of Genetic Knowledge* (New York, Plenum Press, 1973).

[156] House of Commons Science and Technology Committee, 'Human Genetics', at para. 242. The Committee continued: 'Not only will this act to the detriment of those directly concerned, but such reluctance could also hinder research which will be needed if genetic knowledge is fully to benefit society.'

introducing its Code of Practice,[157] the Commission also noted a strong sense of unease among the public about the potential uses to which the industry might put genetic information. Similarly, the Human Genetics Commission (HGC) has been asked by the government to examine the position in respect of genetics and insurance, without any clear steer on its own policy in this area, largely because of the apparent air of concern among the public. This has been borne out by the HGC's MORI poll on public attitudes to human genetic information published in March 2001, which showed that the use of genetic information to set insurance premiums was thought to be the least appropriate possible use of that information. Four out of five respondents said that it should not be used for that purpose.[158] As a corollary, a number of surveys, both in the United Kingdom and abroad, have found very little evidence of discriminatory practices in insurance.[159]

Second, if individuals are apprehensive about the security of the information given to insurance companies – for example, if they fear that it will be passed on to employers or other parties without authority – this once again might deter them from being tested for genetic conditions. Clearly, this has implications not just for the insurance industry but also for the individuals and the families of individuals involved.

One solution that has found favour in certain quarters is a moratorium on the use of genetic information.[160] For example, Cook-Degan has stated that insurance companies 'may choose not to use such underwriting information because using it would cause too much of a public outcry, or would call the entire industry into question'.[161] Certainly, many

[157] Human Genetics Advisory Commission, *The Implications of Genetic Testing for Insurance* (1997).

[158] Human Genetics Commission, 'Public Attitudes', 33. As the report indicates, 'This is in keeping with data from the 1999 British Social Attitudes study, where 75 per cent said insurance companies should not be allowed to use genetic tests when determining premium rates, and suggests that opinion is relatively constant on this issue', *ibid.*

[159] See, for example, P. Billings *et al.*, 'Discrimination as a Consequence of Genetic Testing' (1992) 50 *American Journal of Human Genetics* 476; J. Alper *et al.*, 'Genetic Discrimination and Screening for Hemochromatosis' (1994) 15 *Journal of Public Health Policy* 345; L. Geller *et al.*, 'Individual, Family and Social Dimensions of Genetic Discrimination: A Case Study Analysis' (1996) 2 *Science and Engineering Ethics* 71; L. Low *et al.*, 'Genetic Discrimination in Life Insurance: Empirical Evidence from a Cross-sectional Survey of Genetic Support Groups in the UK' (1998) 317 *British Medical Journal* 1632.

[160] T. McGleenan, 'Legal and Policy Issues in Genetics and Insurance' (2000) 3 *Community Genetics* 45.

[161] R. M. Cook-Degan, 'Public Policy Implications of the Human Genome Project' in Z. Bankowski and A. Capron (eds.), *Genetics, Ethics and Human Values: Human Genome*

countries have seen insurance companies self-impose a moratorium on requesting genetic testing.[162] Nys *et al.* reported in 1993 that of all the countries which had legislated on the matter none considered that genetic testing solely for the purposes of insurance was acceptable.[163] Furthermore both the European Parliament[164] and the Council of Europe[165] have taken a firm stand in decreeing as unacceptable either the use of genetic information *or* genetic testing. However, 'the insurance industry's objections to a moratorium on the use of genetic information are based on the fear of adverse selection'.[166]

Adverse selection refers to the phenomenon of individuals taking out insurance for excessively high sums on learning of an increased risk that the event to be insured against will occur. Given the strict full disclosure nature of insurance contracts, adverse selection is unproblematic at the present time. A failure on the part of the individual to reveal her knowledge of increased risk automatically entitles the insurance company to avoid the contract. If, however, a full moratorium were imposed on both requests for genetic tests *and* access to medical history, the insurance industry has a genuine fear that adverse selection will result. Unfortunately, no clear evidence exists that self-selection of this kind is likely to occur. As Harper has pointed out, 'the concerns of the insurance industry do not mirror the concerns of individuals and families. For the former, the fear is of high sum claims being made by high risk individuals. For the latter, the concern is with obtaining insurance at ordinary levels for basic life and health cover.'[167] This would tend to suggest that the fears of the industry are overstated.

Mapping, Genetic Screening and Therapy, Proceedings of the 24th CIOMS Conference (Tokyo, 22–7 July 1990), p. 64.

[162] Nys, 'Predictive Genetic Information and Life Insurance'.

[163] *Ibid.,* pp. 6–15. Note, however, that in 1992 California introduced a bill which would allow insurers to test persons seeking an individual life insurance policy. Also, Canada would consider genetic testing in relation to excessively high policies. The British Genetics and Insurance Forum tracks international developments: http://www.geneticsinsuranceforum.org.uk/InternDev/menu.asp

[164] European Parliament, *Resolution on the Ethical and Legal Problems Concerning Genetic Engineering,* 16 March 1989, *Official Journal of the European Communities,* 17.4.1989, Nr C 96, p. 168.

[165] Council of Europe, *Recommendation on Genetic Testing and Screening for Health Care Purposes,* No.R (92)3, 1992.

[166] House of Commons Science and Technology Committee, 'Human Genetics', para. 244.

[167] Harper, 'Insurance and Genetic Testing', 226. See also Chadwick and Ngwena, 'The Human Genome Project, Predictive Testing and Insurance Contracts', 119–21.

A hybrid approach has been adopted in the United Kingdom, where the government has established the Genetics and Insurance Committee (GAIC) – a body charged with the task of approving access to certain genetic test results that are thought to have a clear actuarial significance. So far, only the test for Huntington's disease has been approved in the context of life insurance, and the industry has agreed a moratorium in respect of other results until approval is given by the Committee.[168] However, in order to assuage the continuing concerns of the public, the House of Commons Select Committee on Science and Technology made a series of stringent recommendations in its Fifth Report in April 2001,[169] included in which was a recommendation to reconsider the membership of the GAIC – and in particular to exclude ABI-nominated experts from the Committee – and for the reformed GAIC to re-examine its approval of the use of Huntington's disease test results. The Committee also called for greater transparency on the part of the insurance industry as a whole with respect to its policies on genetic test results and its practices in performing actuarial calculations. It urged that there be more evidence from the industry that its Code of Practice is being complied with and that it is capable of maintaining self-regulation. Finally, the Committee recommended that 'The best way forward for the Government and industry would be a voluntary moratorium on the use of all positive genetic test results by insurers for at least the next two years.' This would allow more research on the scientific and actuarial relevance of genetic test results to the assessment of premiums, and the societal consequences of allowing or denying insurers access to any, or all, such results. The Human Genetics Commission responded in May 2001 with a recommendation of an immediate moratorium on the use by insurance companies of adverse results of genetic tests for all classes of insurance.[170] The HGC proposed that the moratorium last for a period of not less than three years 'to allow time for a full review of regulatory options and afford the opportunity to collect data which is

---

[168] Department of Health, 'Committee Announces Decision on Use of Genetic Test Results for Huntington's Disease by Insurers' (13 October 2000); see http://www.doh. gov.uk/genetics/gaic.htm. For an account of the work of the Committee and its remit, see Genetics and Insurance Committee, *First Annual Report: April 1999–June 2000* (London, Department of Health, 2000).

[169] House of Commons Science and Technology Committee Fifth Report, *Genetics and Insurance* (2001 HC 174).

[170] Human Genetics Commission, *The Use of Genetic Information in Insurance: Interim Recommendations of the Human Genetics Commission* (London, HGC, 2001).

not currently available. The moratorium should continue if the issues have not been resolved satisfactorily within this period.'[171] On the same day, the Association of British Insurers agreed to extend its self-imposed moratorium for two years and it will now not ask for any genetic test results from applicants for any insurance policies up to £300,000. Above that level, only tests approved by the Genetics and Insurance Committee will be taken into account.[172]

Individual and familial privacy interests

Insurance is a cultural phenomenon. Like law, its existence and its nature are dictated by the norms of the society in which it operates. Different forms of insurance develop in different social and cultural contexts. The nature of Western social structure dictates that individuals must rely heavily on insurance in order to receive many basic services. This is seen most acutely in the United States where health care provision is not a social given, and consequently health care insurance becomes a social necessity. The same is less true in most European countries, where a highly developed sense of social justice is generally prevalent with respect to health care, and where, accordingly, solidarity-based national health provision diminishes the importance of personal, mutuality-based health insurance. None the less, for many other forms of insurance, such as life insurance, pensions, long-term care insurance and travel insurance, the element of individual choice is largely removed from the equation, for if individuals wish to enjoy anything approximating an acceptable or bearable standard of living, some or all of these forms of insurance may be required at one time or another. As a result, the prospective insured finds herself in a considerably weaker bargaining position compared with the prospective insurer. Standard term contracts are the norm and there is precious little scope for negotiation. This has several implications for the personal interests of individuals seeking insurance and their relatives.

First, the principle of *uberrima fides* requires full disclosure of all material facts known to the prospective insured and likely to influence the

---

[171] *Ibid.* An exception is recommended for policies greater than £500,000 to address the concern about adverse selection, but even then only test results approved by GAIC should be considered.
[172] Correspondence from Mary Francis, Director General of the ABI, to Baroness Helena Kennedy, Chair of the Human Genetics Commission, 1 May 2001.

grant of insurance. This obviously includes medical history and therefore requires that highly personal and private details be disclosed. To assert that this occurs *voluntarily* is to stretch considerably the meaning of the word. This is not to say that such information should not necessarily be disclosed – for one might prefer the freedom of contract of the insurer to the curtailment of the freedom of the individual – rather, it is simply to state that the interests of the individual in the information are strong. These extend to seeking and receiving from those who now hold it guarantees about the security of the information. When this information includes genetic information the interests of relatives of the prospective insured are potentially also involved. Thus, the informational privacy interests of both an individual proband and her relatives are pertinent here.

Second, for insurance companies to require individuals to undergo genetic testing places the individuals in a position of having to receive information they might not otherwise wish to know. This potentially offends against the interest that individuals have in not knowing information about their own genetic constitution, that is, the interest in spatial privacy. Moreover, because this information might also reveal genetic data about relatives of the proband, the spatial privacy interest of such relatives in not knowing is also invoked.

Discrimination

Discrimination is defined here as treating different individuals or groups differently for irrational or irrelevant reasons. A US study that addressed the issues surrounding genetic discrimination concluded that genetic conditions are

> regarded by many social institutions as extremely serious, disabling or even lethal conditions without regard to the fact that many individuals with 'abnormal' genotypes will either be perfectly healthy, have medical conditions which can be controlled by treatment, or experience mild forms of the disease. As a result of this misconception, decisions by such institutions as insurance companies and employers are made solely on the basis of an associated diagnostic label rather than on the actual health status of the individual or family.[173]

---

[173] P. R. Billings, 'Discrimination as a Consequence of Genetic Testing' (1992) 50 *American Journal of Human Genetics* 476, 481.

This would suggest that the fear of discrimination by insurers in possession of genetic information has some basis. The United Kingdom's House of Commons Science and Technology Committee certainly found evidence that insurers had given genetic test results a predictive significance that could not be scientifically justified. Indeed, the ABI itself had expressly recommended in 1998 that insurers use test results in respect of four conditions which it now acknowledges are neither relevant nor reliable.[174]

Axiomatically, individuals have an interest in seeking to minimise instances of discrimination wherever possible, principally by retaining control of their own genetic information. Relatedly, individuals and their relatives have an interest in not being deterred from seeking genetic information should they wish to do so. As has been highlighted, deterrence can be an unlooked-for consequence of certain insurance practices. If individuals are deterred from seeking genetic information this can affect them in many ways. If a cure or treatment is available, non-diagnosis deprives the individual (and potentially her family) of such a benefit. The absence of knowledge can adversely affect future progeny if uninformed decisions to reproduce are taken, and deterrence deprives the individual of the chance of discovering a low risk, or non-risk, of genetic disease. This could not only positively affect her insurance premium but could also offer a degree of psychological stability and more certainty about her future.[175] Nor, of course, should we overlook the important public interest that might be damaged if in a high number of cases insurers set premiums inaccurately and must later pay out prematurely.

Further public interests

A discussion of insurance takes the debate about genetic information outside the health care setting. In turn, this has implications beyond the relationship between the insurer and the insured, for repercussions of

---

[174] House of Commons Science and Technology Committee, 'Genetics and Insurance', para. 33: 'The tests for familial adenomatous polyposis and hereditary motor and sensory neuropathy are irrelevant to insurers owing to their, typically, early onset; that for myotonic dystrophy is apparently not sufficiently predictive, and multiple endocrine neoplasia has too wide an age of onset.'

[175] This is premised on the fact that the individual *wants* to be tested but is deterred by fear of insurance consequences. The same arguments would not necessarily apply if the individual had no desire to know his or her own genetic constitution.

the policies and practices that govern that relationship are unavoidably felt in the wider community. This is particularly true for health care professionals from whom information about patient genetic health will be requested and for whom that information can also represent a certain value. Two particular interests in genetic information are discussed here.

If insurance practices deter individuals from seeking genetic testing, this can have considerable adverse consequences for genetic research. Statistical and epidemiological data are of fundamental importance in the fight against any disease, and this is equally true of genetic disorders.[176] It is therefore imperative that clinicians continue to receive source data from individuals and families affected by genetic disease. The importance of this public interest has been taken on board by insurers in the United Kingdom, and the ABI has confirmed that it will advise its members not to seek research results when assessing policies.[177]

Health care professionals have certain obligations to their patients that can be compromised by insurance practices. For example, requests for medical history might be viewed by clinicians as requests to breach patient confidentiality.[178] Similarly, if patients do not seek genetic tests

[176] See Nanula, who makes such an argument in the context of HIV/AIDS: P. J. Nanula, 'Protecting Confidentiality in the Effort to Control AIDS' (1986) 24 *Harvard Journal on Legislation* 315.

[177] House of Commons Science and Technology Committee, 'Genetics and Insurance', para. 48.

[178] There is some empirical evidence to substantiate this. In the 1980s Wertz and Fletcher carried out a survey of 295 geneticists in the United States. They found that the vast majority (88 per cent) would not disclose genetic information to insurers without patient permission, see D. C. Wertz and J. C. Fletcher (eds.), *Ethics and Human Genetics* (New York, Springer Verlag, 1989). More recently, Geller *et al.* have conducted a comprehensive survey to determine the frequency with which various groups of health care professionals (HCPs) would disclose confidential genetic information to family members and unrelated third parties. 65 per cent of a random sample of 1,759 obstetricians, paediatricians, internists, family practitioners and psychiatrists, and 79 per cent of medical geneticists and genetic counsellors in ten geographically representative US states responded to the survey. The results make interesting reading. Inter alia, the HCPs were asked if they would disclose a patient's known risk of Huntington's disease to a health insurance company without the patient's permission. None of the genetic counsellors and the medical geneticists would disclose the information. Only 2.9 per cent of the physician group would do so. More interestingly, when asked if they would disclose the fact that both members of a couple had tested positive for cystic fibrosis *when they had the couple's permission to disclose*, only 32.8 per cent of physicians said that they would automatically disclose the couple's carrier status. The remaining 67.2 per cent responded that they would discuss completion of the insurance form with the couple first. It is important to note that no legal obligation is imposed on professionals to do anything other than disclose information if patient consent has been given. The response to the survey would tend to suggest that the majority of physicians felt a

for fear of insurance consequences, doctors might feel that they are denied the opportunity to care for their patients as best they can. Also, if individuals are required to undergo examination and testing in locales chosen by insurance companies, doctors might feel concern about the adequacy of counselling that their patients will receive. Genetic counselling is an extremely important part of the testing procedure. Failure to offer or to perform it properly can have severe consequences for tested individuals on receipt of their results. All of these concerns relate to a health care professional's interest in the sanctity of the therapeutic relationship with patients. Requests by insurance companies for individual genetic information can place the parties in opposition to one another. The patient might consider disclosure by the doctor to be a breach of confidence, and/or this can disempower the professional and thereby weaken the relationship she has with her patient. Given the benefits that can flow from a strong doctor/patient relationship, there is arguably a strong interest for both parties to the relationship in avoiding any unwarranted intrusions or any externally imposed restraints. Matters are complicated further when the health care professional is acting for the insurance company, where there might be a direct conflict of interest as between her duties to the insurer and her professional duties to the prospective insured. At the very least, the precise nature of the relationships in play should be made clear to the prospective insured from the outset.

Assessing insurance interests in genetic information

Insurance companies have a financial interest in some forms of genetic information because these might minimise the damage of a bad risk. An abundance of accurate information, however, is not in the industry's interests, because this removes all element of risk from the enterprise. Fortunately for the industry, genetic testing cannot furnish such accurate information. The nature of genetic disorders is such that only a few are caused solely by a single gene dysfunction. The majority of disorders are polygenic and multifactorial. This means that test results for

moral or professional obligation not to disclose the information without first ensuring that all care had been taken to minimise any possible harm which could arise from disclosure: see G. Geller *et al.*, 'Physicians' Attitudes Toward Disclosure of Genetic Information to Third Parties' (1993) 21 *Journal of Law, Medicine and Ethics* 238.

most genetic disorders reveal little that is concrete about future risk. In particular, they reveal nothing about the likelihood of onset, or the date of onset, or the severity of affliction.[179] Even for disorders such as Huntington's disease or Duchenne muscular dystrophy, which are single gene dominant disorders and therefore carry a 50 per cent risk of affliction for first degree relatives in each case, a positive test result cannot give any indication about onset or degree of affliction. Thus genetic tests do not and cannot provide a means of infallible predictability for the insurance industry. And, given that most conditions are not monogenic, the fact that several members in one family have died of heart disease is likely to say more about the lifestyle of those individuals than it does about a pattern of genetic disease. This limited value of testing and analysis of family history must be set against the privacy interests of individuals in keeping secure and/or not knowing their genetic constitution.[180]

The two forms of privacy interest in genetic information – informational privacy and spatial privacy – correspond to the two ways in which the insurance industry may have access to genetic information; namely, through family history or other pre-existing knowledge and through requests to undergo genetic testing. To request a family history or to ask for the results of genetic tests is to ask about personal information known to the individual. Questions arise about the desire of the individual to surrender such information and the subsequent security that it will enjoy. These are clearly issues of informational privacy. To ask an individual to undergo genetic testing to determine genetic risk raises questions of spatial privacy, because the individual is placed in a situation where she will receive information that she might not wish to know. In both of these circumstances an element of coercion is present, in that information is revealed or discovered solely for the purposes of obtaining insurance. The powerful position of the insurer means that

---

[179] J. P. Evans, C. Skrzynia and W. Burke, 'The Complexities of Predictive Genetic Testing' (2001) 322 *British Medical Journal* 1052.

[180] One thing should be made clear. The better understanding that genetic testing can give us of individual genetic risk does *nothing* to affect the incidence of genetic disease in the community as a whole. Genetic testing can simply give a more accurate indication of risk, and even that is restricted. As Roscam Abbing has argued: 'Not using genetic information in principle (except in cases of adverse selection) is not a threat to the solvency of the insurance company: genetic risks have thus far (implicitly) been included in the coverage', in 'Predictive Genetic Knowledge, Insurances and the Legal Position of the Individual', 153.

often individuals have no real choice about complying with these demands. However, does the ethical propriety of insurers' requests come down entirely to a matter of consent? That is, is it sufficient to validate an insurer's request that a prospective insured person has consented to revealing personal details or to undergoing testing? To the extent that that consent is fettered, the answer must be returned in the negative. Thus, even if consent is given it does not follow that it has been ethically obtained. The problem of the consent model, however, is that consent does not call us to question the legitimacy of the initial request itself. Consent provides a possible ex post facto legitimation, but it cannot erect a barrier to inappropriate requests. But due respect for an individual's privacy can do so, because before an individual's private sphere is invaded with a request, a justifiable prima facie case for intrusion must be made out.

In contrast, and in a single respect, the interests of all parties concerned come together. No one wishes individuals to be deterred from seeking genetic testing. This could have adverse individual, familial and social consequences and deprive the industry of the perceived benefit of additional information. But in order to avoid this, concerns about discrimination and security of information must be addressed. This can be achieved in the context of discrimination and access to information by ensuring that individual and familial informational privacy is adequately protected.[181] More problematic, however, is the industry itself. As the Nuffield Council has commented, 'The Association of British Insurers emphasises that over 95 per cent of life insurance policies are obtained at standard premium rate, while less than 1 per cent of proposals are declined due to the mortality risk being too high. [However] the concern is that widespread use of genetic testing might sharply alter this balance.'[182]

The proposal of the Council is that those individuals with a known family history who decide to be tested and who test positive should not be treated any differently by an insurance company compared with other family members. That is, they will still be assessed as being at the same risk as those family members who have not been tested.[183]

---

[181] For an account of the US position see K. H. Rothenberg, 'Genetic Information and Health Insurance: State Legislative Approaches' (1995) 23 *Journal of Law, Medicine and Ethics* 312.

[182] Nuffield Council on Bioethics, 'Genetic Screening', para. 7.18.

[183] *Ibid.*, 7.28.

The rationale behind this is that since testing is most likely to occur in families with a known risk,[184] and because the industry tends to interpret family history cautiously, 'there is unlikely to be a major difference in insurability between an individual with a family history of a genetic disorder and an individual who has had a positive genetic test result'.[185] By extension, the Council envisages that an individual who tests negative should benefit from this result and be treated in the same way as someone with no family history.[186] In this way the Council hopes that individuals will not be deterred from having genetic tests and also that insurers will not be adversely affected, since they can continue their present practice based on family history.[187] This latter view has most recently been endorsed by the House of Commons Science and Technology Committee, and indeed, there is some evidence that this policy is already in place among a small number of British insurers.[188]

From one point of view this solution serves many interests, not only those of individuals who seek testing and the insurance industry, but also those of health care professionals and researchers who can gain access to test results if correct procedures are followed. However, it is important to note that the recommendations of the Council are somewhat different concerning population screening programmes. In such cases the majority of those taking part would not be aware of any family history of disease. The Council considers that,

> If insurers were to demand access to the results of population screening for polygenic or multifactorial disease (for example, for genetic predisposition to breast cancer), and premiums were increased for those who tested positive, many people would clearly be discouraged from participating in such programmes. This could have adverse consequences both for the health of individuals and for the public health.[189]

---

[184] For example, the Council notes that, 'Tables used by the insurance industry show that insurers treat a 5 per cent risk of developing Huntington's disease in the same way as a 50 per cent risk: such individuals may be declined insurance or offered insurance at an increased premium, depending on their age at the time of application. Insurance prospects for individuals with a family history of Huntington's disease only improve when the risk is below 5 per cent', *ibid.*, 7.23.

[185] *Ibid.*, 7.27.   [186] *Ibid.*, 7.29.   [187] *Ibid.*

[188] House of Commons Science and Technology Committee, 'Genetics and Insurance', para. 40.

[189] Nuffield Council on Bioethics, 'Genetic Screening', 7.31.

The conclusion of the Council is that it is not acceptable for insurers to have access to genetic test results that arise from a population screening programme.[190] Furthermore, because of the principle of free and informed consent, genetic testing should not be made a prerequisite for obtaining insurance.[191]

Thus, it can be seen that on one point the Council is emphatic. Genetic testing solely for the purposes of assessing insurance risk is not acceptable. This is true both for those who have a family history and for those who have no knowledge of their genetic constitution.[192] Indirectly, this shows due deference to the interest that individuals have in not knowing information. The language used by the Council is that of free and informed consent which relates to the principle of autonomy, but the interest in not knowing, and thereby the interest in spatial privacy, is protected nevertheless.

In contrast, the Council's recommendations about revealing existing knowledge diverge according to whether the information results from (i) knowledge of family history; or (ii) population screening. If there is no family history knowledge but screening reveals a genetic condition or predisposition, then there is no need to disclose this information. If, however, a family history is known but no effort has been made to confirm one's genetic status, the Council considers that nevertheless the history should be revealed. Thus, in one case genetic information about a specific individual can be withheld from the insurer while in another non-specific information must be disclosed.

The justification for this disparity seems to be the fear of dissuading individuals from seeking testing. For those with a family history of disease this is thought to be avoided by the scheme outlined above; namely,

---

[190] *Ibid.*, 7.32. That said, it was recommended that an upper limit be put on the moratorium. No sum was offered, but approval was expressed of the Dutch system which imposes a ceiling of 200,000 guilders, *ibid.*, 7.33.

[191] *Ibid.*, 7.35.

[192] This view is endorsed at the international level, inter alia, by the Council of Europe *Recommendation* on the Protection of Medical Data (1997, No. R (97)5), paras. 4.7 and 4.9 of which provide that genetic data collected and processed for preventive treatment, diagnosis or treatment of the data subject or for scientific research should only be used for these purposes or to allow the data subject to take free and informed decisions on these matters. Outside these purposes, the collection and processing of genetic data should, in principle, only be permitted for health reasons and in particular to avoid any serious prejudice to the health of the data subject or third parties. However, the collection and processing of genetic data in order to predict illness may be allowed for in cases of overriding interest and subject to appropriate safeguards defined by law.

those who are not tested are judged on the basis of the family history, and this is also true for those who are tested and test positive, but those who test negative should be treated as though there is no family history. It is submitted that this is to place too much emphasis on family history. Furthermore, it is to do so at the expense of the privacy interests of individuals within a family. What this solution does not do is give due weight to an individual's interest not to know their own genetic constitution. By offering the incentive of possible lower premiums to those who seek testing and test negative, the Council makes a clear division between those who do, and those who do not, want to know. Those who do not want to know are judged on the basis of family history, and this works in favour of the industry. These individuals can do nothing to improve their chances of benefiting from insurance or lower premiums. It might be argued that such a balance is fair because the insurance industry does not have any more accurate information on which to proceed and therefore it is entitled to judge based on existing knowledge of family history. However, given the risk of overreaction to genetic information and the possibility of individuals receiving an unfair deal at the hands of insurance companies that fail to interpret family history properly,[193] it might equally be argued that it is not acceptable to leave individuals' fate to the whim of the industry.

If it is accepted that people can have a strong interest in not knowing their own genetic constitution, we should surely not consider as acceptable a policy that prejudices that interest. Moreover, it should not be forgotten that a family history belongs to a collective of individuals, each one of whom has an informational privacy interest in the security of the information and a spatial privacy interest in not knowing information. By the same token, it should not be thought that a common history means that knowledge of that history is necessarily held in common. Many members of a family might be ignorant of the existence of a pattern of disease threading itself through the generations. But for such knowledge to be placed in the hands of insurers means that these individuals might be faced with the knowledge at some future

[193] Note, in addition, that evidence to the House of Commons Science and Technology Committee suggests that 'witnesses were concerned that ... insurers were not able to interpret the relatively simple genetic information available to them. While there were no comprehensive studies of the extent to which genetic information was misinterpreted to a person's disadvantage, several cases in which this clearly had occurred were drawn to our attention', 'Human Genetics', 239, referring to Memorandum (Volume III) at 1, 5, and 6–7.

date. Databases allow insurance firms to establish connections between individuals with common histories, and this is a self-evident threat to a family member's interest in not knowing genetic information. Given this, perhaps a solution different from that proposed by the Nuffield Council is called for.

One suggestion that was put to the House of Commons Science and Technology Committee was that (i) insurance companies should not ask for any information on genetic tests at the time the contract was made; (ii) if the insured dies of a genetic disease on a list maintained by an appropriate authority as predictable by a genetic test, then the sum paid by the insurance company need not exceed a ceiling specified at the time of the contract; and (iii) insurance companies would re-insure in an industry pool against the risks of deaths from genetically identifiable causes on the list.[194] As was stated, 'the effect of this would be to spread the cost of payments from the genetically determined diseases on the list over the whole population of the insured'.[195]

The advantages of such a scheme are that informational privacy of genetic test results, however obtained, can be upheld, and that individuals would not be dissuaded from taking otherwise desirable tests for fear of the cost of later insurance. What is not clear is whether this scheme would extend to individuals who have a family history of disease but who have not taken a test. If it did not, then the objections raised above would apply. Given that the scheme specifically mentions information on genetic tests it is unlikely that it would extend to such persons.

A final possible approach would be to ban altogether the use of genetic information by insurers, whether it be specifically related to an individual – that is, a genetic test result, or whether it be of a more vague familial nature, such as family history. Support for such an approach has been advocated by various commentators.[196] For example, Roscam Abbing has argued that restrictive measures on insurance companies should include (i) a ban on genetic predictive testing for serious diseases without the prospects of treatment; (ii) a restriction on the possibility of

[194] House of Commons Science and Technology Committee, 'Human Genetics', 246.
[195] *Ibid.*
[196] See Roscam Abbing, 'Predictive Genetic Knowledge, Insurances and the Legal Position of the Individual', and L. R. Churchill, *Self-Interest and Universal Health Care: Why Well-Insured Americans Should Support Coverage for Everyone* (Cambridge, MA, Harvard University Press, 1994) who argues that a system of universal coverage is a viable way forward to address the problems of US health insurance cover.

obtaining existing genetic predictive information on serious diseases without prospect of treatment, provided the insurance will not exceed an equitable ceiling (in order to prevent adverse selection); and (iii) a restriction on asking for family history in the framework of medical underwriting if the insurance would not exceed a certain ceiling.[197]

These recommendations are linked to two relevant factors: the availability of a cure and the setting of a ceiling limit. The latter ensures that insurance companies do not suffer excessively should adverse selection prove to be a problem. The former recognises that the interests of individuals in knowing information change depending on whether anything can be done for their condition. The view taken is that to test people when there is no prospect of a cure for the condition solely to assess insurance risk is too great a burden for the individual to bear. However, if a cure is available, testing can not only assist with insurance assessment but can also alert the individual to the possibility of disease. This approach is appealing because it considers the privacy interests of individuals in both specific genetic information and family history. Such information need only be revealed in rare circumstances which reflect the concerns of the insurance industry. The relevance of a cure or treatment to the recommendations is interesting and the sense of the arguments is self-evident. This writer would add, however, that one should not overlook the possibility that individuals might *not* wish to know information about their genetic make-up even if a cure or treatment were available. The basis of an objection to receiving genetic information in such circumstances would be that it offends against one's spatial privacy interests. Thus, it might not be enough simply to require that a cure be available or that a ceiling limit be set, because such restrictions on the use of genetic information do not protect against invasions of spatial privacy.

Some countries have gone further still and imposed outright bans on the use of genetic information by insurers. In Europe, these countries are Austria, Belgium, Denmark, France, and Norway.[198]

Examples of the position advocated by Roscam Abbing are to be found in the current approaches of Sweden and the Netherlands. The Swedish

---

[197] Roscam Abbing, 'Predictive Genetic Knowledge, Insurances and the Legal Position of the Individual', 164.

[198] For discussion see European Society of Human Genetics, *Genetic Information and Testing in Insurance and Employment: Technical, Social and Ethical Issues*, Background Document (November 2000).

government and the Swedish Insurance Federation signed an agreement in 1999 restricting insurers' access to, or use of, genetic test results and 'family particulars' in decisions to grant insurance or calculate
premiums.[199] There is also an express prohibition on asking prospective insured to undergo testing as a precondition of insurance. Access
to genetic data is allowed, however, if the sum insured exceeds a certain
amount, and this is calculated by reference to the 'price base amount' – a
device used in Swedish social security provision that is tied to economic
fluctuations and is adjusted annually. In this way, an ad hoc balance of
interests is thought to have been achieved. The current agreement will
remain in force until 31 December 2002 (absent any breach on the part
of insurers) – whereupon it is open for renewal on a further two-year
cycle.

In the Netherlands, the Medical Examination Act of 1 January 1998
follows very precisely the model proposed by Roscam Abbing, linking
the legitimacy of a request to a ceiling limit for the sum insured. This
is variable depending on the type of insurance policy; for example for
life policies the limit is NLG 300,000, and for disability policies the
limit is NLG 60,000. An insurer cannot require an individual to undergo
testing if this might reveal that she is suffering from an incurable genetic
condition, nor can any questions be asked about a known condition if
this has not already manifested itself in the individual to be insured. In no
circumstances can questions be asked about the health status of relatives
with respect to hereditary conditions, even if the relatives already suffer
from the condition, nor can there be any request to disclose pre-existing
genetic test results from either the individual or her family.

A single problem with each of these approaches, however, lies in finding workable definitions of the focus of the laws or agreements in question; namely, what do we mean by *genetic information* and *genetic testing*?
For example, the Swedish Agreement offers a tautologous definition of
'genetic testing', which is said to mean 'genetic tests carried out prior to
the appearance of symptoms; genetic tests carried out for predictive purposes; and genetic tests carried out in order to demonstrate or exclude
the possibility of people being genetically predisposed to a hereditary
disorder or disease that manifests itself only in subsequent generations'.

[199] Agreement Between the Swedish State and the Swedish Insurance Federation Concerning
Genetic Testing (May 1999).

A flaw in the Dutch law has already been highlighted in this chapter. Recent reports show that Dutch insurers have been accused of breaching the 1998 law by asking prospective insured about cholesterol levels – a non-genetic question – but indirectly an affirmative answer furnishes the insurers with knowledge about familial hypercholesterolaemia.[200] If this is an infringement of the law, then is it meaningful to continue to view that law as dealing solely with *genetic* information?

Such problems do not fundamentally undermine the validity of these solutions, but they should nevertheless lead us to question the appropriateness of the current focus of our attention. That is, are *genetic information* and *genetic testing* really the problem? An alternative view is to consider the genetic context merely as a conduit to a better understanding of more fundamental concerns, such as those surrounding the personal interests that are at stake. If our true concern lies with vital privacy and autonomy interests, then solutions should be addressed towards their protection in a more generalised or universalised sense. For example, is it not more coherent to address our laws to *any* form of discrimination against prospective insured persons? Is it not more consistent to protect individuals from *any* imposition of unwanted and potentially harmful personal information?

Employment

In ways similar to those concerning the insurance industry, current and future employers can have a use for genetic information that has either been derived from a person's family history or obtained directly by subjecting the individual to testing. The interests of individuals in their own genetic information have already been outlined in detail above, and these remain constant in the employment context. The task is to consider whether and how a balance can be struck between these interests and the interests of employers as outlined below.

Financial interest

The ill health or potential ill health of employees can have numerous adverse financial consequences for employers. For example, ill health can lead to early retirement or redundancy, requiring large payments to

---

[200] Sheldon, 'Dutch Insurers Flouting Law on Genetic Disease'.

employees. This in turn means frequent turn-over of personnel with clear implications for continuity and efficiency. Ill health during employment means days lost, with consequent disruption to the work environment. Furthermore, in the United States much health insurance cover is provided by employers, and this means that ill employees can represent a considerable added financial burden. Given that employers clearly have an interest in reducing as far as is practicable undue personnel costs, the supposedly predictive nature of genetic information is a very attractive tool in workforce management. As one body has put it, 'Healthy workers cost less – they are less often absent through illness, there are lower costs for hiring temporary replacements, and there are fewer precautions which would need to be taken to deal with health and safety risks.'[201] Some jurisdictions, such as Denmark,[202] have identified the need to protect *all* forms of health data from misuse in the workplace, but in most countries the issues are only now being addressed, in response to developments in genetics, because these have sharply focused attention on the matters at hand.

Employers can seek and use genetic information at one or both of two different times to advance their financial interests. This can happen when an employer is deciding whether to employ a particular individual, or this can occur at some later point when the individual is in employment. Moreover, as has been said, the source of the information can either be existing knowledge possessed by the individual qua her suitability as an employee or future employee, or testing or screening to reveal previously unknown genetic conditions.

Let us first consider pre-employment requests for information. This is the most effective means of reducing costs for the employer for several reasons. First, there is little expenditure incurred in obtaining the information; either the prospective employee is asked simply to reveal existing knowledge or she is asked to take a relatively inexpensive test. Second, the individual has not been provided with training or fringe benefits and so there is no previously incurred expenditure that would be lost if the genetic knowledge proved to be disadvantageous. Third, no future expenditure need be incurred in providing for the job applicant because there is no obligation to do so absent an actual employment contract.

[201] The Nuffield Council on Bioethics, 'Genetic Screening', para. 6.4.
[202] Act on the Use of Health Data etc. on the Labour Market, Act No. 286 of 24 April 1996.

With the exception of the first of these factors, an employer who seeks genetic information from a current employee is in a very different position. This is because she may well have spent time and money training someone who cannot now do the job, and also because an employment contract cannot simply be terminated without good reason; either the individual must be found another position or financial provision must be made, for example through early retirement.

All of this means that if an employer intends to use genetic information as a basis for managing her workforce, it is very much in the employer's financial interests to seek genetic information from potential future employees, rather than from actual employees. Of course, whether or not it is legitimate to seek genetic information at all, either before or during employment, is another matter.

Protecting third party interests

Certain onerous burdens are placed on the shoulders of employers in Western jurisdictions. They must provide acceptable standards of care and conditions for their workers, they must ensure health and safety at work, they must bear the cost of work-related accidents and they must take responsibility for the careless conduct of employees who cause harm or injury in the course of their employment. Moreover, it is frequently the case that employers are liable to third parties for any harm or damage occurring on the former's premises or as a result of their operations. And, because so much of this harm can occur at the hands of employees, once again genetic information is perceived as a useful tool in determining any potential future mishap or liability.[203] For example, if a worker who operates heavy machinery is found to be suffering from a genetic condition that makes her prone to a sudden heart attack beyond the age of forty-five, then her employer can take steps to ensure that the worker is given another less dangerous task to perform. Similarly, if an employee is found to have a predisposition to a particular condition that is exacerbated by environmental factors, the employee can be placed in working conditions from which such factors are absent. For example, an environment that is dense with heavy particles is very bad for individuals

---

[203] This interest is acknowledged both by the Nuffield Council on Bioethics, 'Genetic Screening', paras. 6.8–6.10, and the House of Commons Science and Technology Committee in its third report, 'Human Genetics', para. 232.

suffering from or prone to alpha$_1$-antitrypsin. In this way employers can act more responsibly and minimise risk both to individuals who are likely to have their own health affected by working conditions, and to other parties such as co-workers or customers who might be harmed if ill health strikes at an inopportune time. And, perhaps better still from the perspective of the employer, it might be argued that future employees can, and should, be excluded from employment if information about their genetic constitution becomes available and this reveals either the presence of a genetic disease or a predisposition to developing such a condition which means that they are likely to pose a risk to others if employed.

Protecting the employee and the prospective employee

It can also be argued that employer access to genetic information will further not only the interests of employers themselves but also the interests of individuals, either as employee or as job applicant. As an example, consider screening programmes for employees and potential employees. Not only might test results give the employer a better idea of who might be a suitable worker in a particular environment, but also such knowledge might allow the individual herself to make informed decisions about the desirability of such employment. As the Nuffield Council on Bioethics has stated, 'Employees would, in principle, be empowered to avoid occupations which would increase the risk of ill health and which in the long run might be life threatening. In this way they could protect the economic security of themselves and their families'.[204]

Of course, one would like to think that genetic information that could predict ill health would do so accurately enough to ensure the best interests of all concerned. However, as we know, the accuracy of genetic predictive information is far from assured, and the very factors that concern employers, such as date of onset and degree of affliction, are not currently known to us, and may never be. Also, the sensitivity of this information and the apparent public misunderstanding that surrounds genetic information mean that there is a very legitimate fear that the information could be used to exclude individuals from employment or to terminate employment contracts even when the employees in question

---

[204] Nuffield Council on Bioethics, 'Genetic Screening', para. 6.6.

are not affected by disease and are unlikely to be so for some time. The question therefore arises as to whether access to genetic information is an acceptable way of ensuring the interests of employers and those of employees or job applicants.

It should be evident from what has been said previously that each of the three interests postulated above raises serious problems of privacy for employees or prospective employees. Both the informational and spatial privacy interests of individuals are affected. Informational privacy interests are compromised because personal information may be requested, disclosed and utilised in circumstances where the individual is not in a position to object by virtue of her weaker bargaining position, nor is she in a position to control the uses to which the information might be put at some future date. Spatial privacy interests are interfered with because individuals might be given previously unknown information, again in circumstances where they might otherwise not have chosen to know, but their freedom of choice is restricted by the desire to begin or remain in employment.

The privacy implications of employer requests for genetic information have been recognised in the United Kingdom by a number of bodies, including the Nuffield Council on Bioethics,[205] the House of Commons Science and Technology Committee[206] and the Human Genetics Advisory Commission.[207] Relying heavily on the recommendations of the Nuffield Council, the Science and Technology Committee recommended that legislation be introduced to protect the privacy of genetic information. It suggested that the legislation be drafted so as to forbid employers testing for genetic conditions other than those which might put the public at direct and substantial risk. Furthermore, any genetic testing for employment purposes should be strictly limited to specific conditions relevant to the particular employment and samples provided for testing should not be examined for evidence of other conditions: 'as a general principle, the individual's right to privacy should prevail'.[208]

In coming to such recommendations, the Committee agreed with the Clinical Molecular Genetics Society that 'decisions on employment

[205] Ibid., paras. 6.20–6.23.
[206] House of Commons Science and Technology Committee, 'Human Genetics', paras. 231–3.
[207] Human Genetics Advisory Commission, The Implications of Genetic Testing for Employment (London, Department of Health, 1999).
[208] House of Commons, 'Human Genetics', paras. 231–2.

should be based on current ability to do the job'.[209] The clear message is that access to genetic information must be justified on the grounds that the knowledge can have a direct bearing on the job of work to be done. If not, there is no legitimacy to a claim to have access to an individual's genetic information. In other words, for an employer to seek access to information – either pre-existing or previously unknown information – simply to further financial interests is not acceptable. This is all the more true when that access is sought to identify some future risk, because such a future possibility does not affect the individual's current ability to perform her job of work.

It is also interesting to note that there is evidence that employment-based screening can actually be counterproductive, in that it can increase rather than reduce employers' costs. For example, studies have shown that screening for hypertension has led to an increased sickness absence, increased anxiety and reduced self-perceived health status among persons found to be hypertensive. This is so even when their condition proved to be so mild as not to warrant treatment.[210] This further weakens any economic arguments that employers could put in support of claims for access to genetic information.

What, however, of the argument that genetic information should be revealed to protect the interests of employees and job applicants themselves? Once again, the Science and Technology Committee agreed broadly in this regard with the recommendations of the Nuffield Council,[211] and concluded that

Genetic screening for employment purposes should be contemplated only where:
(i) there is strong evidence of a clear connection between the working environment and the development of the condition for which the screening is conducted;
(ii) the condition in question is one which seriously endangers the health of the employee;

---

[209] Ibid., quoting Memorandum (volume II) p. 52.
[210] See S. Stewart-Brown and A. Farmer, 'Screening Could Seriously Damage Your Health' (1997) 314 British Medical Journal 533, quoting (i) M. F. Johnstone et al., 'Effects of Labelling on Income Work and Social Function Among Hypertensive Employees' (1984) 37 Journal of Chronic Diseases 417, and (ii) R. B. Haynes et al., 'Increased Absenteeism from Work After Detection and Labelling of Hypertensive Patients' (1978) 299 New England Journal of Medicine 741.
[211] Nuffield Council, 'Genetic Screening', para. 10.13.

(iii) the condition is one for which the dangers cannot be eliminated or significantly reduced by reasonable measures taken by the employer to modify or respond to the environmental risks.[212]

Importantly, the Committee stressed that 'employees should have the right to decide whether or not to participate in such screening'.[213] What neither the Committee nor the Council recommend, however, is that anti-discrimination provisions be introduced to protect those persons who choose not to know. We shall return to this below. It is also unclear whether the recommendations are intended to extend both to current employees and job applicants. No convincing argument could be put that this should not be the case, but it is significant that the Committee only mentions *employees*. However, the interest of employees *and* job applicants in not knowing has been articulated by the Nuffield Council: '[Genetic screening] could operate to restrict job opportunities to those who, with few employment prospects, or for personal reasons, were prepared to assume the risk of ill health. It could provide a convenient excuse for employers to refuse either to take the reasonable steps necessary to accommodate those at higher risk or to employ certain categories of people able to work normally for an indefinite period.'[214]

The recommendations fail to distinguish between testing for conditions in individuals who are likely to be affected when there is clear evidence, for example family history, to this effect and the comprehensive screening of groups such as current employees or job applicants. This is a very important distinction for several reasons. To screen widely and randomly is tantamount to a fishing expedition. In such circumstances it is hard to reject the conclusion that screening is done primarily out of financial motive. For, given the interest in not knowing, it is more difficult to argue in such cases that screening is done in the individual's (best) interests. Whether or not screening is done in the interests of third

---

[212] House of Commons, 'Human Genetics', para. 233. The Committee added, however, that there should be defences for employers against action taken by employees who had exercised their right to refuse genetic screening and developed a work related illness to which they were particularly susceptible. It should also be noted that the Council's recommendation is premised on the requirement that employers consult with employee representatives and possibly also seek the approval of the Health and Safety Commission.

[213] *Ibid.* The Nuffield Council is less clear about this matter. It simply states that any programme should be 'accompanied by safeguards for the employee', Nuffield Council, 'Genetic Screening', para. 10.13.

[214] Nuffield Council, 'Genetic Screening', para. 6.7.

parties is a question of fact, but as Rothstein has correctly pointed out, 'To justify genetic testing or subsequent exclusion, the danger should pose a *direct and immediate threat* of harm to the individual or third parties. Otherwise, genetic testing and exclusions will be justified by future risks – possibly years away.'[215]

Rothstein criticises the recommendations of the Nuffield Council – which, as has been indicated, were largely adopted by the Science and Technology Committee – for being 'not nearly strong enough'.[216] These recommendations require simply that the genetic condition 'seriously endangers' the health of the worker or third parties. This is clearly not the same as a 'direct and immediate threat of harm'. The number of conditions likely to pose such a 'direct and immediate threat' are few. If Rothstein's stricter language is accepted, the circumstances in which employment testing is justifiable are severely limited.[217] This latter approach is to be preferred primarily because of the privacy implications that surround employer requests for genetic information.[218]

More recently, however, the British Human Genetics Advisory Commission recommended in its report, *Implications of Genetic Testing for Employment*, that 'there are situations where it might be appropriate for genetic test results to be used in employment . . . it would not be in anyone's best interests to ban the use of genetic test results from employment purposes completely'.[219] It devised a series of policy guidelines which, it recommended, should be adhered to if ever employment testing were to be instituted. These include (i) the right not to know (and so not to be required to take a test); (ii) no compulsion to disclose prior results unless there is clear evidence that the information is needed to assess current ability to perform a job safely or to determine a susceptibility to harm from doing a particular kind of job; (iii) the active offer of testing by employers where it is known that the working environment which

---

[215] Rothstein, 'Genetic Discrimination in Employment', 138–9.

[216] *Ibid.*, 138.

[217] For a similar argument see L. Andrews and A. S. Jaeger, 'The Human Genome Initiative and the Impact of Genetic Testing and Screening Technologies: Confidentiality of Genetic Information in the Workplace' (1991) 17 *American Journal of Law and Medicine* 75.

[218] Geller *et al.*, 'Individual, Family and Social Dimensions of Genetic Discrimination', note that when health care professionals were asked if they would disclose genetic information about patients to employers without permission, 0.5 per cent of physicians, 0.7 per cent of medical geneticists and 0 per cent of genetic counsellors said that they would do so.

[219] Human Genetics Advisory Commission, 'Implications of Genetic Testing for Employment', paras. 3.14–3.15.

they provide could pose a serious risk to certain persons. Moreover, in jobs where an element of public safety is in question, an employer should be able to refuse to employ a person who refuses to take a genetic test. While these measures are designed to strike a balance between the various interests, they follow the lead of the Nuffield Council in tipping that balance in favour of the employer and away from Rothstein's more stringent, and arguably more justifiable, approach.[220]

Discrimination

There is currently no specific legal regulation of genetic testing and screening in the United Kingdom, nor any direct protection against discrimination in this regard. In contrast, the majority of states in the United States have introduced anti-discrimination legislation directly tailored to problems arising from uses of genetic information, and usually these measures are concerned with the harm caused by discrimination in both the employment and insurance contexts. Two key features have driven these developments. First, the cultural importance of insurance in the United States weighs particularly heavily, given the relative absence of social support mechanisms such as a national health service. In relation to this, a tradition of linking health insurance cover to employment benefits means that employers must often bear the brunt of insurance costs for employees, thereby compounding the potential financial burden to employers and heightening their interest in the possible, or perceived, utility of genetic information as a means to reduce that burden. The concurrent potential for misuse is high,[221] and the push for anti-discrimination measures becomes inevitable. Most action has occurred, however, at the state level.

Of the few federal measures that currently exist, the Health Insurance Portability and Accountability Act 1996 is of special significance in its application to employer-based and commercially provided group health insurance. The Act prohibits the use of either genetic test results or family history to exclude individuals from group health cover, but

---

[220] Further policy guidance is offered by the Recruitment Society, *Proposal for a Code of Practice for Genetic Testing for Employers* (London, Recruitment Society, 2000).

[221] D. Martindale, 'Pink Slip in Your Genes: Evidence Builds that Employers Hire and Fire Based on Genetic Tests' (2001) January *Scientific American* 19. This article highlights a study of 1,500 genetic counsellors and physicians that found that 785 patients had reported having lost their jobs or insurance because of adverse reactions to genetic knowledge about them.

does not protect individuals in the wider insurance market. In February 2000 President Clinton signed an Executive Order which prohibits federal government agencies from obtaining genetic information from employees or job applicants and from using genetic information in hiring and promotion decisions.[222] Three bills were introduced in the 107th Congress in an attempt to extend this sort of protection to the private sector.[223]

As of February 2001, the National Human Genome Research Institute reported that most states had enacted legislation to conform with the Health Insurance Portability and Accountability Act. Moreover, thirty-seven states had enacted state legislation on genetic discrimination in health insurance, and twenty-four states had enacted provisions against genetic discrimination in the workplace. In the legislative session for 2000, over 100 anti-discrimination bills were introduced into state legislatures.[224]

Beyond all of this, it is also argued that the Americans with Disabilities Act 1990 (ADA) is sufficiently robust in its protection of citizens to guard against genetic discrimination,[225] although the terms of the Act do not specifically deal with this eventuality. The Act was accordingly the subject of a congressional hearing in July 2000, during which Commissioner Paul Steven Miller of the US Equal Employment Opportunity Commission urged Congress to enact further specific measures to protect against genetic discrimination, and pointed out a number of lacunae in the 1990 Act, including the fact that

> The ADA does not protect workers from requirements or requests to provide genetic information to their employers. Under the ADA, an employer

---

[222] *The Executive Order To Prohibit Discrimination in Federal Employment Based on Genetic Information* (8 February 2000): 'In general, protected genetic information means: (1) (a) information about an individual's genetic tests; (b) information about the genetic tests of an individual's family members; (c) or information about the occurrence of a disease, or medical condition or disorder in family members of the individual. (2) Information about an individual's current health status (including information about sex, age, physical exams, and chemical, blood, or urine analyses) is not protected genetic information unless it is described in subparagraph (1).'

[223] HR602 Genetic Nondiscrimination in Health Insurance and Employment Act, S318 Genetic Nondiscrimination in Health Insurance and Employment Act, and S382 Genetic Information Nondiscrimination in Health Insurance Act of 2001.

[224] National Human Genome Research Institute, *Health Insurance and Employment Discrimination* (Bethesda, MD, National Institutes of Health, 2001).

[225] See M. A. Rothstein, 'Genetic Discrimination in Employment and the American with Disabilities Act' (1992) 29 *Houston Law Review* 23.

generally may not make medical inquiries about a job applicant prior to extending a conditional offer of employment. However, once a conditional offer of employment has been extended, but before the individual begins work, the employer may obtain extensive medical information about the applicant, including genetic information. During this period, the ADA may not prohibit an employer from, for example, obtaining genetic information of job applicants, requiring genetic screening as a condition of employment or purchasing genetic information about applicants from a genetic information data bank.[226]

In April 2001 the US Equal Employment Opportunity Commission (EEOC) settled its first court action in which it had challenged the conduct of an employer in using genetic information and requiring genetic testing of employees to handle claims for work-related injuries.[227] The Burlington Northern Santa Fe railway (BNSF) had implemented a programme of genetic testing of previously donated samples, without the knowledge or consent of employees, to investigate worker claims for injuries based on carpal tunnel syndrome. Furthermore, at least one worker had been threatened with termination for refusing to submit to testing. The settlement ensures that the employer shall not directly or indirectly require its employees to submit blood for genetic tests, nor shall it analyse any blood previously obtained. The settlement is enforceable by the relevant district court, although the court in question was at pains to point out that it offered no ruling on the respective arguments of the parties under the ADA.

In stark contrast to the US position, discrimination in the United Kingdom is outlawed only in three discrete areas, and under three pieces of legislation: the Sex Discrimination Act 1975, the Race Relations Act 1976, and the Disability Discrimination Act 1995. Under the 1975 and 1976 acts, the protection afforded against discrimination is restricted to the precise remits of the acts, that is, sexual or racial discrimination.[228] In the light of the fact that many genetic conditions are sex-linked or affect particular ethnic and racial groups, instances of different treatment of

[226] Statement Of Commissioner Paul Steven Miller US Equal Employment Opportunity Commission Before The Committee On Health, Education Labor And Pensions US Senate July 20, 2000.
[227] United States Equal Employment Opportunity Commission, Press Release, 18 April 2001: http://www.eeoc.gov/press/4-18-01.html
[228] Other recourse might, of course, be available to the individual, for example, unfair or constructive dismissal procedures.

afflicted individuals could amount to discrimination within the terms of these acts, probably as examples of indirect discrimination. It is not clear, however, how successful such arguments would be, there being no cases on the point. More chances lie with the 1995 Act.

The Disability Discrimination Act 1995 is the first piece of UK legislation to deal directly with discrimination against disabled people. The Act outlaws discrimination in a wide range of fields such as employment, the provision of goods, facilities and services, the sale and let of property, education and public transport. The Act defines 'disability' and 'disabled persons' as follows.

1(1) Subject to the provisions of Schedule 1, a person has a disability for the purposes of this Act if he has a physical or mental impairment which has a substantial and long-term adverse effect on his ability to carry out normal day-to-day activities.

1(2) In this Act 'disabled person' means a person who has a disability.

In the context of employment, the provisions of the Act ensure that it is unlawful for an employer to treat an individual less favourably than she would treat others for a reason that relates to the individual's disability and when she cannot show that the treatment in question is justified.[229] Discrimination can occur, inter alia, in respect of (i) the arrangements which an employer makes for the purpose of determining to whom she should offer employment;[230] (ii) the terms in which she offers employment;[231] (iii) the refusal to offer, or deliberately not offering, employment;[232] (iv) the refusal to afford an employee opportunities for promotion, a transfer, training or receiving any other benefit, or treating the employee differently in such opportunities;[233] (v) the dismissal of an employee, or subjecting her to any other detriment.[234]

These provisions could clearly go a long way to preventing discrimination against individuals based on information about their genetic constitution.[235] Note particularly how pre-employment discrimination is also outlawed.[236] However, the question arises of whether the

---

[229] s.5(1)(a) and (b).   [230] s.4(1)(a).   [231] s.4(1)(b).
[232] s.4(1)(c).   [233] s.4(2)(b) and (c).   [234] s.4(2)(d).
[235] One limiting factor is the exemption for small business under s.7. The provisions of the Act do not apply to an employer who has fewer than twenty employees.
[236] The remedies provided by the Act in the context of employment are contained in s.8. The Act provides that cases can be heard before an industrial tribunal, which has the power to order compensation to be paid, and/or to order the respondent to take action to obviate or reduce the adverse effect on the complainer.

provisions of the Act extend to persons whose genome contains defective genes which might, but do not yet have, a bearing on their ability to do their job. Clearly, persons who are already affected by a genetic condition come within the definition of *disabled person*. But what of a person who merely has a predisposition to ill health? A literal interpretation of s.1(1) clearly excludes such a person, for it speaks of one who '*has* a physical or mental impairment which *has* a substantial and long-term adverse effect on his ability to carry out normal day-to-day activities'.[237] This section must, however, be read in conjunction with Schedules 1 and 2, which allow for regulations to be made that will clarify the definitions in Section 1. In particular, paragraph 8 of Schedule 1 concerns progressive conditions. The examples given of such conditions are cancer, multiple sclerosis, muscular dystrophy or infection with the human immunodeficiency virus. The paragraph provides that (i) the Secretary of State can issue further regulations which can include or exclude other conditions as progressive; and (ii) someone who suffers from such a progressive condition will be treated as disabled provided that their condition results in an impairment which at least has (or had) an effect on their ability to carry out normal day-to-day activities, even if that effect is not a substantial adverse effect.[238] Note, however, that the individual must still in some way be symptomatic, thus still excluding those who will always be asymptomatic, such as carriers, or who have at the relevant time merely a predisposition to disease. This means that discrimination against persons in the latter two categories is, by inference, not illegal under the Act. In the parliamentary debates this disparity and the question of genetic testing were raised, but the minister in charge stated:

> except in a few well-publicised cases, genetic tests are not as yet a useful indicator of future actual disability. Their inclusion would open up the [Act] to large numbers of people who are clearly not, and may never become disabled . . . we cannot wander into a situation whereby, for some reason or another, potentially the entire population could claim protection under the [Act].[239]

This is clearly a nonsense. It is certainly true that genetic tests are by no means accurate at the present time, but that does not mean that such

---

[237] See above.   [238] Schedule 1, para. 8(1)(a)(b) and (c).
[239] *Hansard*, H.C., Volume 257, col. 887.

tests cannot be misused by employers and others nor that they will not be used to exclude people from jobs and other services for irrelevant and irrational reasons. The provisions of this Act as they currently stand are inadequate and clearly prejudicial to persons likely to develop conditions stemming from genetic disorders later in life. It is to be hoped that the Secretary of State will use the powers given under the Act to expand the definition of disability to include such persons as soon as possible. The ludicrousness and dangerousness of the current provisions were accurately summed up by Baroness Jay in the House of Lords:

> The paradox which is possible in the present situation is that where genetic counselling, genetic testing and identifying genetic markers is [sic] potentially one of the most exciting and liberating developments in medical science at the end of the twentieth century, if it becomes the case that people feel that identifying those markers in their own personal situation will lead to discrimination, they will be less likely to take advantage of those extraordinary scientific advances which may help their own condition and in which medical science may be able to help future generations of children.[240]

By way of comparison, the Australian Disability Discrimination Act 1992 defines 'disability' to include 'a disability that: (h) presently exists; or (i) previously existed but no longer exists; or (j) may exist in the future; or (k) is imputed to a person'.[241] This inclusive approach has been criticised in the context of genetics, because it is pointed out that each of us has 'defective' genes in our genome, and so each of us technically has a disability. This, it is argued, renders such forms of legislation ineffective.[242] But this is to miss the point. Discrimination, by definition, is about treating people adversely for bad reasons or irrational reasons, or indeed for no reasons at all. It is the absence of justification that renders differential treatment unacceptable, and so discriminatory. In the genetics context the greatest problem stems from misconceptions about the significance of genetic differences and the importance of genetic information. There need be no foundation in fact for those perceptions. Indeed if there were, differential treatment might be justifiable. In other circumstances, differential treatment is never justifiable largely because

---

[240] *Hansard*, H.L., Volume 564, col. 1713.   [241] Disability Discrimination Act 1992, s.4(1).
[242] B. Lennox, 'Genetic Discrimination in Insurance and Employment: Spoiled Fruits of the Human Genome Project' (1997) 23 *University of Dayton Law Review* 189, 205.

it is morally and socially unacceptable. If I were to treat X differently because I perceived him to be less intelligent than Y, this would remain discriminatory whether or not there was any basis for my view. The fact that we are all possessed of intelligence, but to varying degrees, does not render meaningless any legal prohibition on my using intelligence as a factor in my dealings with people, when, and if, we decide that this is not a good reason to do so. Disability is just such an example. And, an effective disability discrimination Act should outlaw *all* forms of discrimination that are based on grounds of disability, whether that disability is actual *or* perceived, current *or* future.[243]

Evaluating employment interests in genetic information

The general consensus of commentators and official bodies is that access to genetic information by employers is acceptable only in very rare circumstances: 'decisions on employment should be based on current ability to do the job'.[244] Where the ability of individuals becomes affected by genetic or genetic-related disease it is very likely that they themselves will have knowledge of the fact. This militates against arguments supporting employer-based genetic testing. Arguments about the predictive value of such testing and its possible benefits for employers, employees and job applicants must be seen in the context of potential conflict with individual privacy interests. Testing puts at stake the spatial privacy interests of employees and potential employees. Access to existing genetic information by employers puts at stake the informational privacy interests of these persons. It should therefore only be permissible when no other means of assessing risk are available. However, even if access is granted, the privacy interests of employees or potential

---

[243] J. Beckwith and J. S. Alper, 'Reconsidering Genetic Antidiscrimination Legislation' (1998) 26 *Journal of Law, Medicine and Ethics* 205.

[244] House of Commons Science and Technology Committee, 'Human Genetics', para. 232, quoting favourably the evidence of the Clinical Molecular Genetics Society. Most recently the UK's Data Protection Commissioner has issued a draft Code of Practice on *The Use of Personal Data in Employer/Employee Relationships* (October 2000), which endorses the position of the HGAC in its 1999 report and admits a role for genetic information in limited circumstances. Testing is only permissible when an employee is likely to represent a 'serious safety risk to others', or a voluntary screening programme can be established if the working environment or practice will pose specific risks to employees with genetic variations, *ibid.*, p. 41.

employees remain and must be respected by the employers now in possession of the information. Measures such as the EC Directive on Data Protection will undoubtedly assist in this regard.[245] This is now implemented throughout the European Union and requires high standards of security of personal information by those who process it, including employers. But, overarchingly, the question of discrimination in the United Kingdom requires to be addressed more forcefully than at present.

Researchers

To the extent that medical research is scientifically sound and ethically conducted, it is trite to confirm that there is a significant public interest in its continuation. Crucial to that process is the active participation of volunteers, drawn from the various classes of the healthy and the ill, the male and the female, the young and the old, and the capable and the incapable. However, public confidence in the aims of research and the motivations of researchers has been undermined in recent years, and a number of factors have conspired to bring this about. Notable among these is the serious attitudinal shift towards the medical profession in the light of a number of so-called scandals involving less than respectful treatment of patients. An additional factor is the rise in the role and control of the private sector in medical research, which has been met with a great deal of scepticism on the part of the public. Matters have been compounded further by the entry into the arena of intellectual property claims, and the patenting of biotechnological inventions has proved to be extremely controversial, especially in Europe. Most interesting, however, are the findings of the Medical Research Council's public survey into perceptions of the collection of human biological samples, published in October 2000.[246] While the Council found confirmatory evidence of public cynicism towards the medical profession,[247] most people

---

[245] European Directive 95/46/EC on the Protection of Individuals with Regard to the Processing of Personal Data and on the Free Movement of Such Data; see further ch. 5.

[246] Medical Research Council, 'Public Perceptions'.

[247] Particular examples cited were the abuses of the Human Tissue Act 1961 at Alder Hey Trust where organs of deceased children were removed and retained without the informed consent of parents, and the saga of Dr Harold Shipman, convicted of murdering fifteen of his elderly patients, *ibid.*, para. 1.2.

continued to find medical research to be worthy and worthwhile.[248] There was, however, disparate knowledge and understanding of the meaning and the goals of genetic research, and where understanding was lacking, there was considerable evidence of negative associations with the research.[249] As the report states:

> Underlying these negative associations was a feeling that genetics research can make people feel vulnerable about themselves. It was believed to be about seeking to perfect the human body, for good or bad ends, and that it could induce concern about individuals' own imperfections . . . Alongside this was a feeling expressed by a few that genetics research, if put to these sorts of uses, conflicts with the (beneficial) diversity of the human race. Though it would be a good thing to attempt to eliminate genetically linked diseases and conditions, this is likely to go hand-in-hand with other development that will make it possible to produce 'perfect' people.[250]

The Human Genetics Commission's People's Panel Quantitative Study of March 2001 produced very similar results. Over one third of those surveyed considered genetics research to be 'tampering with nature' and so unethical.[251]

We have, then, a serious problem of perception. Indeed, this confirms much of the discussion so far, in that many of our problems stem from misconceptions about genetics. It is not clear to what extent, however, the law can address such a problem. While further or more stringent regulation of public and private research might force transparency and accountability – the buzz words of our twenty-first-century 'name, blame and shame' culture – there is no guarantee that this process alone will resolve the public's crisis of confidence in genetics and genetic research. Indeed, it might simply compound it, for there is little evidence from other quarters that greater openness and scrutiny serves to engender greater public trust.[252] It is easier to criticise than to construct, however. Certainly, there is no straightforward answer to the problem of involving the public in furthering the public interest in genetic research. Although regulation might be part of the answer – and judgement should be reserved on this point – in no way does it provides a complete answer. The final picture in this puzzle remains obscured for now, but two essential

[248] *Ibid.*, para. 2.1.   [249] *Ibid.*, para. 2.2.   [250] *Ibid.*
[251] Human Genetics Commission, 'Public Attitudes', pp. 20–2.
[252] See O. O'Neill, 'Autonomy and Trust in Bioethics', The Gifford Lectures, University of Edinburgh (2001).

pieces must take their rightful place. The first is education. There must be wider, deeper, better, more accessible and more informed debate about all of the issues that concern this book. The second crucial piece of the puzzle is, unsurprisingly, privacy. At this stage the privacy concerns of those who become directly involved in research almost do not require mention. Informational privacy protection must necessarily be part of any solution to the current crisis. However, privacy protection has an additional role to play in furthering this particular public interest. This is a role that serves the dual purpose of promoting both research and the interests of research subjects. Unlike the other examples that we have considered, this solution does not set interest against interest but seeks to bring about a confluence of public and private interests. In this sense it is a unique construct. This is examined in more detail in chapter 5.

The state

The preceding sections have identified many varied interests that individuals, groups and institutions might have in genetic information. Two key concerns emerge from this analysis. These are, first, a desire to minimise or eliminate harm and, second, an inclination to reduce costs wherever possible. These concerns are also central to the interests that governments might claim in the genetic information about their citizens. In addition and related to this point, the state has a role in protecting and advancing the public good, that is, the collective interests of society as a whole. This section outlines the nature of these interests that the state might have in genetic information. To the extent that privacy arguments are relevant to this discussion these will merely be highlighted in passing; the foundations of the arguments have already been laid.

Health care and social interests

Protection of public health

One of the most obvious state interests in the health care setting is the interest in securing public health. In chapter 1 it was shown how forceful arguments legitimise measures designed to contain contagious disease which at the same time curtail the rights and interests of infected individuals. In like manner, some have argued that freer access to genetic information could be justified on the grounds of halting the spread of genetic disease. It has also been posited that mandatory testing might achieve the same end where specific genetic information is not readily available.[253] The point is made that even if little or nothing can be done for those already afflicted by genetic disorders, disclosure might prevent the transmission of defective genes to future persons. Against this, however, are the problem of generating meaningful genetic data, as has been pointed out above, and the potential infringement of privacy interests which such practices would represent. In particular, it is highly questionable that the mere giving of information will necessarily lead to more informed or responsible reproductive choices. And, to the extent that a state is unwilling to enforce such choices – and ideally it should be true of all states – then the efficacy of a testing or disclosure policy is seriously in doubt.[254] The attendant potential infringement of an interest in not knowing such matters is an additional reason to call such a policy into question.

Enhanced patient choice

Even if the state is not so draconian as to require its citizens to know their genetic constitution, it can be argued none the less that the state has an interest in facilitating individual choice. The state can adopt a more pastoral role towards individuals by providing them with information that can assist in the making of important life decisions, such as the question of whether or not to have a child when both partners are cystic fibrosis carriers. Not only does this arguably make individuals more independent as moral choosers, but it might also have the desired social end of preventing further spread of genetic disease. Ball *et al.* have noted that this view is held by the Royal College of Physicians: '[the] Royal College of Physicians report suggests that as long as individuals have the right to decide for themselves whether to bear children it could be

---

[253] See Suter, 'Whose Genes Are These Anyway?', 1897, citing H. P. Green and A. M. Capron, 'Issues of Law and Public Policy in Genetic Screening', in D. Bergsma (ed.), *Ethical, Social and Legal Dimensions of Screening for Human Genetic Disease* (New York, Stratton Intercontinental Medical Book Corporation, 1974). See also M. Shaw, 'Conditional Prospective Rights of the Fetus' (1984) 5 *Journal of Legal Medicine* 63, in which it is argued that prospective parents should face mandatory screening for certain conditions.

[254] For a sensible approach to policy see European Society of Human Genetics, *Population Genetic Screening Programmes: Recommendations of the European Society of Human Genetics* (Birmingham, ESHG, 2000).

argued that such individuals should have access to the fullest possible information, including genetic, pertinent to that decision and therefore this should not be withheld'.[255]

This would imply that the state could seek to further its interest in facilitating choice by providing comprehensive screening programmes and wider availability of genetic tests accompanied by suitable counselling services. Presumably, this would have to be accompanied by other support mechanisms such as easy access to abortion. Cost implications aside, this would certainly further both individual and state interests by making free choice a market commodity. If such programmes were also free of coercive measures the risk of conflict of interests is almost entirely eliminated.[256]

There can be, however, a fine line between coercion and choice. The residual concern about such a policy has been highlighted by the Nuffield Council: 'the availability of prenatal screening and diagnosis, together with the termination of seriously affected pregnancies, both reflect and reinforce the negative attitudes of our society towards those with disabilities. Indeed medical genetics may add a new dimension if genetic disorder came to be seen as a matter of choice rather than fate'.[257]

As this quote indicates, increased focus on choice in health care might not always be to the advantage of patients. Choices may easily be labelled as good *or* bad. As more prenatal testing becomes available, and particularly if it is presented as routine, then an increasing number of women will be faced with the choice of what to do with an adverse genetic test result. Not only does this place an undue burden on the shoulders of pregnant women, who are unlikely to have been fully informed of the possible consequences of being tested, but it also leads to questions of what constitutes responsible reproductive health.[258] For example, the UK Abortion Act 1967 provides that a termination of pregnancy is

[255] See Ball *et al.*, 'Predictive Testing', p. 77, referring to the Royal College of Physicians of London, *Ethical Issues in Clinical Genetics: A Report of the Working Group of the Royal College of Physicians' Committees on Ethical Issues in Medicine and Clinical Genetics* (London, RCPL, 1991).

[256] The British National Health Service announced plans in April 2001 to offer screening services for cystic fibrosis in all neonates, see http://www.doh.gov.uk. For commentary, see W. W. Grody and R. J. Desnick, 'Cystic Fibrosis Population Carrier Screening: Here At Last – Are We Ready?' (2001) 3 *Genetics in Medicine* 87.

[257] Nuffield Council, 'Genetic Screening', para. 8.11.

[258] T. M. Marteau and R. T. Croyle, 'Psychological Responses to Genetic Testing' (1998) 316 *British Medical Journal* 696.

permissible within twenty-four weeks if, 'continuance of the pregnancy would involve risk, greater than if the pregnancy were terminated, of injury to the physical or mental health of the pregnant woman or any existing children of her family'.[259] Indeed, termination is justifiable until full term if, 'there is a substantial risk that, if the child were born, it would suffer from such physical or mental abnormalities as to be severely handicapped'.[260] Many, if not all, genetic diseases would fall within this latter provision,[261] and it is difficult to see how another (disabled) child would not pose a risk for a family in one way or another. Women who decided not to terminate in such circumstances might therefore come to be seen as irresponsible. And this would be particularly true in the case of women less financially able to care for the child. The perceived burden of a disabled child both on the family and on the health service would make it difficult for counsellors not to modify the advice given to poorer clients compared with the advice given to clients who are more financially secure and so better able to shoulder the burden of rearing a disabled child.[262] Stigmatisation might result against those women who choose not to abort, and who then come to be seen as a drain on the finite resources of a perennially debilitated health service. One must contemplate too the treatment that disabled children born to such women might receive. A supreme effort must be made to ensure that these hypotheticals do not become a reality. As an example of the kind of initiative that is required, consider the recent statement by the US Society of Human Genetics in which it, 'deplores laws, governmental regulations, and any other coercive effort intended to restrict reproductive freedom or to constrain freedom of choice on the basis of known or the anticipated genetic characteristics, health, or capacities of potential offspring'.[263] The Society calls for an international and interdisciplinary effort to protect reproductive freedom through education and the struggle against discrimination and stigmatisation.[264]

---

[259] Abortion Act 1967, s.1(1)(c).   [260] *Ibid.*, s.1(1)(d).

[261] For argument on this point, see I. Kennedy and A. Grubb, *Medical Law*, 3rd edn (London, Butterworths, 2000), pp. 1427–8.

[262] A. Clarke, 'Is Non-Directive Genetic Counselling Possible?' (1991) 338 *Lancet* 998.

[263] Board of Directors of the American Society of Human Genetics, 'Statement: Eugenics and the Misuse of Genetic Information to Restrict Reproductive Freedom' (1999) 64 *American Journal of Human Genetics* 335.

[264] Consider too the eminently sensible recommendations of the European Society of Human Genetics, *Population Genetic Screening Programmes* (ESHG, 2000).

Post has argued in the context of Huntington's disease that to test for this condition prenatally is ethically abhorrent.[265] It is argued, inter alia, that to deny a person years of asymptomatic life by preferring death to life is an abuse of the limits of the abortion decision. Along similar lines, Lippman has suggested that to offer a range of genetic antenatal tests and to label a foetus as malformed is to fail to appreciate that it might be society which is malformed in being unable to, 'accommodate the disabled in its midst'.[266] This latter point is a very important one. Although it might be possible to legalise the abortion of countless foetuses by liberal interpretation of abortion legislation and by offering a wide range of antenatal genetic tests, it should not go unquestioned what the motivation for such testing actually is, nor should we imagine that a woman's choice of abortion is necessarily an unfettered one. The offer of antenatal testing for multifactorial and/or late-onset disorders of itself encourages abortion. As the Science and Technology Committee noted, 'providing a prenatal screening test for a genetic defect, in the absence of any treatment for that defect, gives a signal that many people, at least, may consider the condition so serious it justifies termination of a pregnancy. If that is not the case, offering prenatal screening is a waste of resources'.[267] The conclusion of the Committee was that 'The objection to termination for late onset disorders may be so great that it outweighs the desire of parents to spare their child eventual suffering.'[268]

Uses of genetic information in the criminal justice system

DNA fingerprinting

DNA fingerprinting has revolutionised the process of crime detection. The technique was invented and developed in 1984 by Professor Alec Jeffreys, a biologist at the University of Leicester. DNA fingerprinting allows the identification of one individual among millions by simple analysis of a spot of blood, a few strands of hair, a sample of sperm or a drop of saliva. The method involves analysis of fragments of DNA that

---

[265] S. G. Post, 'Huntington's Disease: Prenatal Screening for Late Onset Disease' (1992) 18 *Journal of Medical Ethics* 75.

[266] A. Lippman, 'Prenatal Genetic Testing and Screening: Constructing Needs and Reinforcing Inequalities', in Clarke, *Genetic Counselling*, p. 160. See also V. Schubert-Lehnhardt, 'Selective Abortion after Prenatal Diagnosis' (1996) 15 *Medicine and Law* 75.

[267] House of Commons Science and Technology Committee, *Human Genetics*, para. 90.

[268] *Ibid.*

repeat certain sequences in abstract and complex patterns and serve as a unique marker for the individual in question.[269] In decrypting the order of these sequences biologists can produce images on radiographic film akin to bar codes. Each individual produces a separate and unique pattern of lines: a genetic identity card of the individual. Minute samples of evidence from the human body left at the scene of a crime can help to identify a particular individual within very small margins of error. Scientific establishments that carry out such tests normally work with and for the police and justice departments. In order to be accepted in court, genetic evidence must be accompanied by statistical data relating to the probability of another individual having the same genetic fingerprint as the accused. To calculate such probabilities experts must have at their disposal considerable amounts of genetic data in a readily accessible form, such as on a computer, for comparison purposes. This is why most laboratories keep detailed data banks of genetic information that are updated regularly with new genetic profiles. These are used for comparison with criminal profiles, yet often profiles are kept together without distinction between the private clients and those obliged by law to take the test. Concerns have therefore arisen about the security of genetic information kept in such files together with the possible uses to which it is put. None the less, most legislation providing for the establishment and operation of forensic databases allows for the retention of information derived from samples once these have been taken, even if no conviction has been secured against an individual.[270] In this way the data derived from them bolster the statistical efficacy of the database as a research tool, and this is justified as being in the public interest.[271] Indeed, it has already been pointed out that the British government has extended the power of its national database by allowing the retention of all samples once obtained and irrespective of the outcome of any criminal proceedings against the individual providing the sample.[272]

---

[269] Save identical twins.

[270] See *Attorney General's Reference No.3 of 1999* [2001] 2 WLR 56, HL.

[271] See, for example, in the United Kingdom, the Police and Criminal Evidence Act 1984, s.64(3B), as amended by the Criminal Justice and Police Act 2001, and in Australia the Crimes Amendment (Forensic Procedures) Act 1998, Division 8, s.23 (although the data must be anonymised). In Canada, the DNA Identification Act 1998, s.17 will permit the collecting of samples from certain specified offenders after conviction, unless the threat to their privacy would be 'grossly disproportionate' to the public interest to be achieved.

[272] Criminal Justice and Police Act 2001, s.82. By March 1999 over 500,000 DNA profiles from suspects were held on the British databases, and over 50,000 profiles were held which had

The 1985 Schengen Agreement proposed the abolition of border controls and the development of closer relations between the police forces of signatory states with a correlative sharing of criminal information.[273] The Schengen Information System that was born out of the Agreement has been described as 'the most spectacular novelty' of the instrument.[274] It is a computerised system based in Strasbourg that links national authorities and facilitates access to information and reports for the purposes of border checks and police enquiries. Police forces and immigration services Europe-wide potentially will have access to information on the 330 million individuals who live within the borders of the European Union.[275] Baldwin-Edwards and Hebenton have noted the clear implications of this for personal privacy.

> The real danger lies not so much in the arcane details of data protection provisions but in what Schengen presents as the key practice of policing in the future: essentially this focuses on 'unwanted and undesirable' individuals and groups as the end-point in European police-work. In our view, effective policing requires public confidence: this can only be achieved with appropriate standards of transparency, accountability and judicial review. The standards of Schengen will amount in practice to little more than a complex, almost impenetrable, legitimation of state and inter-state invasion of personal privacy. The underlying trend is without doubt towards 'Big Brother'.[276]

The perceived success of the British National DNA Database led to the establishment of the European DNA Profiling Group (EDNAP), which had as its original aim the harmonisation of procedures and approach

---

been obtained from samples taken from crime scenes. By this date over 40,000 matches of suspects to a crime had been made, as well as over 7,000 cross-crime scene matches, see P. J. Lincoln, 'From ABO to DNA . . .' (2000) 40 *Medicine, Science and the Law* 3.

[273] Named after the Agreement signed at Schengen, Luxembourg in 1985 relating to the free movement of persons within the European Community.

[274] See J. E. Schutte, 'Schengen: Its Meaning for the Free Movement of Persons in Europe' (1991) 28 *Common Market Law Review* 549, 559.

[275] The system will contain, inter alia, data about persons wanted for arrest for extradition purposes, data relating to aliens, data relating to persons whose whereabouts are to be reported (e.g. missing persons), data concerning witnesses or suspects summoned to appear before a criminal court, personal information in police reports including name, sex, date and place of birth, nationality, identifying physical features, and propensity for violence.

[276] See M. Baldwin-Edwards and B. Hebenton, 'Will SIS Be Europe's Big Brother?' in M. Anderson and M. Den Boer (eds.), *Policing Across National Boundaries* (London, Pinter Publishers, 1994), ch. 8. See also, in the same volume, C. D. Raab, 'Police Co-operation: The Prospects for Privacy', ch. 7.

between forensic laboratories, so that results could meaningfully be compared; and most recently there has been the creation of the European Network of Forensic Science Institutes (ENFSI), which is also designed to further the operational processes of DNA technology in the forensic setting.[277] Such initiatives will undoubtedly assist the coordinated efforts of police forces around Europe and the world in pursuing their activities. The consequent threats to civil liberties remain very real, and for the moment, significantly under-addressed.[278]

Legal obligations of disclosure to prevent or detect crime

Because the public interest in crime detection and prevention is considerable, disclosure of private information can be required in some circumstances. The following UK examples are typical: (i) the Road Traffic Act 1991, Section 21, requires that 'any person' in possession of information which might lead to the identification of a driver thought to be involved in an offence under the Act must disclose this to the relevant authorities; (ii) the Data Protection Act 1998, Section 29, exempts the processing of personal data from certain key protections of the Act if this is done for the purposes of the prevention or detection of crime; (iii) the Terrorism Act 2000, Section 19, makes it an offence not to disclose knowledge or a suspicion of terrorist activities to a constable as soon as is reasonably practicable; and (iv) more generally, the lawful order of a competent court can compel disclosure of personal information.[279]

While none of these examples is specific to genetic information, all extend to cover such information if its disclosure could further the ends of the particular legal provision or order.

Genetic determinism and crime

A recent Ciba Foundation Symposium considered the extent to which an individual's propensity towards criminality may be genetically determined.[280] A major conclusion of the symposium was that far more work must be done to establish the role of genetics in crime and criminal

---

[277] Lincoln, 'From ABO to DNA...', 6.
[278] P. Reilly, 'Legal and Public Policy Issues in DNA Forensics' (2001) 2(4) *Nature Reviews* 313.
[279] This extends even to health care professionals, see *Hunter* v. *Mann* [1974] 2 All ER 414.
[280] Ciba Foundation Symposium 194, *Genetics of Criminal and Antisocial Behaviour* (Chichester, John Wiley & Sons, 1996).

behaviour, but nonetheless a nexus could not be ruled out. Evidence of a genetic element in criminal behaviour presents the Western state with a series of interesting dilemmas.[281] For example, if an individual commits crime because she has a predisposition to do so – in much the same way as one might have a predisposition to developing ischaemic heart disease – then to what extent, if at all, should that individual be held to blame for her crimes? If a system of criminal justice professes to be equitable and fair because it only punishes those who choose to exercise their free will in the commission of crimes, and if it excuses those whose will is somehow overcome or affected by uncontrollable factors, should not the genetically driven also avail themselves of an excuse? In principle, the answer must be returned in the affirmative. By extension, how can the state ensure that those who are more likely to lose control because of their genetic constitution will not simply become those most likely to be absolved of crime and therefore those most likely to be released back into the community potentially to do more harm? There are no easy answers to these questions, but it is certainly arguable that if a genetic component proves to have a significant role in criminal behaviour then the state has a strong claim to an interest in knowing which individuals are likely to be affected. At the moment we have a long way to go. The US criminal courts have not, in the main, been open to arguments about genetic determinism,[282] demanding more evidence of the role of genetics than is available. However, from the current state of understanding and the trend that seems to be emerging about the nature of genetic knowledge and its near all-pervasive but subtle influence in many spheres of human existence, it looks unlikely from our present

---

[281] C. Wells, ' "I Blame the Parents": Fitting New Genes in Old Criminal Laws' (1998) 61 *Modern Law Review* 724.

[282] *Mobley* v. *State* 265 Ga. 292; 455 S.E.2d 61 (1995). Stephen Mobley shot and killed a pizza store manager after robbing the till in February 1991. He confessed to the crime one month later. At his trial, Mobley's lawyers sought to lead evidence that his behaviour was heavily influenced by his genetic make-up. This, they argued, did not affect his guilt but should be taken into account to mitigate his possible sentence from the death penalty to life imprisonment. Evidence was led that Mobley's family history displayed four generations of pattern violence. Mobley was characterised as a man who 'had an inability to control his impulses or to internalize any kind of value system'. However, the Court's view of such evidence was that 'The theory of genetic connection ... is not at a level of scientific acceptance that would justify its admission'. On 20 February 1994 the jury found Mobley guilty and he was sentenced to death. An appeal was, however, immediately lodged; see D. W. Denno, 'Legal Implications of Genetics and Crime Research' in Ciba Foundation Symposium, 'Genetics of Criminal and Antisocial Behaviour', pp. 248 *et seq.*

standpoint that genetic influences will be shown to be so great as to meet the stringent requirements for criminal excuse.[283]

Financial interests

Any state or government has an interest in economic efficiency. Genetic information can assist in this goal in several ways.

Testing to establish paternity

DNA fingerprinting is not reserved for use by the police or for medical statistics. One obvious advantage of genetic fingerprinting over old methods of blood testing is that it can identify a particular individual, whereas traditional tests could only establish who was not present or who was not involved. This has obvious implications for paternity suits, because it is now possible to determine precisely who is the father of a child rather than determining simply who is not. Immigration officers in the United Kingdom have since 1985 used the technique to reunite families, establishing with relative certainty the genetic link between immigration candidates and their supposed relative already resident in the country. The test is even carried out in the country of origin. For example, the British embassies in Pakistan and Bangladesh have the necessary tools to carry out the test on suspect visa applicants even before they leave their respective countries. This relieves the United Kingdom of the problem of detaining, processing and possibly returning the individuals in question.[284]

In 1991 the Swedish social services department set up a programme to combat one of the biggest drains on its resources in recent years: the holiday romance syndrome. In the previous decade statistics had shown that some 14,000 Swedish women had returned from holiday pregnant, principally from Mediterranean countries such as Spain, Italy and France. The Swedish government therefore decided to initiate a programme to identify these 'Latin lovers' in an attempt to recover some of the monies it had paid out in child maintenance and support. The unmarried mothers were asked to name the fathers of their children. In all, 942 Spaniards, 550 Italians and some 60 Frenchmen were identified in this way. They

---

[283] J. D. McInerney, 'Genes and Behavior: A Complex Relationship' (1999) 83(3) *Judicature* 112.
[284] *L'Express*, 20 March 1992, 48.

were then offered the choice of either signing a document acknowledging paternity – and thereby accepting to pay maintenance – or of
giving a sample of blood for genetic analysis. Almost two thirds of the
Spanish accepted to pay, with the remaining 383 being summoned to the
Swedish embassy in Madrid to undergo the test, where they were joined
by 172 of the Italians. The French, it would seem, accepted their fate
without question.[285] This is indicative of an ever increasing demand to
use such fingerprinting techniques in paternity cases outside the judicial
system.

In cases of uncertain paternity in Germany heavy reliance is placed
on evidence to determine the identity of the biological father. Around
22,000 cases arise each year requiring either traditional blood tests or
genetic fingerprinting.[286] This, however, is relatively minor compared
with the situation in the United States, where 160,000 tests are carried
out annually. However, unlike the United States and most other countries, Germany considers the truth about a person's hereditary descent
to be so important that its laws provide for compulsory examinations to
furnish the requisite evidence from reluctant parties.[287] Such measures
date from the time of the National Socialists, but they are thought to
represent such an ingrained attitude of the German people towards heritage that they have remained part of the law ever since.[288] Indeed, the
German Federal Constitutional Court (Bundesverfassungsgericht) has
held that there is a human right to know one's parentage under Articles
1 and 2 of the German Constitution (Grundgesetz).[289]

No such view prevails in England and Wales, but the Child Support
Act 1991 none the less provides for the possibility of legally obliging a
single mother to reveal the identity of the father of her child; failure to
do so may mean her sacrificing certain social security allowances and
benefits.[290] Moreover, the Child Support, Pensions and Social Security

---

[285] *Ibid.*, 49.

[286] For an account of the German position and that in many other countries see European
Commission, *Studies on the Socio-Economic Impact of Biotechnology – Genetic Fingerprints:
Scientific Truth and Filiation Law* (Luxembourg, Office for Official Publications of the
European Communities, 1996).

[287] §372a of the German Civil Procedure Code (ZPO).

[288] For a comparative analysis, see R. Frank, 'Compulsory Physical Examinations for Establishing Parentage' (1996) 10 *International Journal of Law, Policy and the Family* 205.

[289] Bundesverfassungsgericht, 31 January 1989, BVerfGE 79, 256.

[290] There is also the question of the 'right' of the child to know: see K. O'Donovan, 'A Right
to Know One's Parentage?' (1988) 2 *Journal of Law and the Family* 27.

Act 2000 now makes it lawful for the Secretary of State to assume a person to be the parent of a child for the purpose of making a maintenance calculation under that Act if the alleged parent refuses to take a scientific test – including a DNA test – that would be relevant to determining the child's parentage.[291]

Clearly, each of these states has a significant financial interest in requiring individuals to take responsibility for their acts.[292]

Finally, for children who are unwanted by their natural parents the role of genetic testing in limiting or determining their future has been a source of concern in some quarters, and in particular for the American Society of Human Genetics and the American College of Medical Genetics. These bodies have issued a Joint Statement on genetic testing in adoption which stresses in the strongest terms the unacceptability of indiscriminate testing of children as part of the adoption process. The statement recommends that genetic testing of newly born babies and children should be limited to testing for conditions that manifest themselves during childhood or for which preventive measures or therapies may be undertaken during childhood. In particular, the statement makes it clear that it is not appropriate to test newly born babies or children for the purposes of detecting genetic variations of, or predispositions to, physical, mental, or behavioural traits within the normal range. The statement is a response to reports from geneticists in the United States that prospective adoptive parents and adoption agencies have been requesting an increasing range of genetic tests before, during and immediately after the adoption process.[293]

Testing to prevent social benefit fraud

A further financial interest of the state lies in the reduction of fraud at the hands of unscrupulous citizens. Genetic testing or access to genetic information could verify the existence of actual or potential disease and

[291] Child Support, Pensions and Social Security Act 2000, s.15(1).

[292] See B. M. Knoppers *et al.*, 'Les Tests Génétiques à des Fins D'Identification' in Guillod and Widmer, *Human Genetic Analysis and the Protection of Personality and Privacy*, pp. 57–105, for a discussion of the validity of genetic test results in the context of both penal policy and paternity suits.

[293] M. A. Rothstein and M. Z. Pelias, 'Genetic Testing in Adoption: Joint Statement of the American Society of Human Genetics and the American College of Medical Genetics' (2000) 66 *American Journal of Human Genetics* 761.

thereby legitimise individual claims for state assistance. By extension, such testing and access could defeat fraudulent claims and thereby save the state considerable sums of money. The United Kingdom has recently expanded the powers of investigators to investigate instances of alleged fraud.[294] While these provisions guard against self-incrimination on the part of the alleged defrauder or her spouse, they represent a further incremental encroachment of enforcement bodies on the lives of citizens in the name of the public interest. They erect no obvious barrier for the protection of more personal information, such as that relating to one's genetic constitution.

The state as employer

It has already been shown that in the United Kingdom the only employer currently making regular use of genetic testing is the armed forces.[295] The rationale is to ensure that at risk individuals are not placed in dangerous situations, but in turn this measure saves the government money in not training those who are unlikely to perform their duties with the requisite degree of efficiency. In the United States, the administration instituted in 1991 a programme of compulsory genetic screening of military personnel, which information is held on computerised databases.[296] Never again will there be an unknown soldier.[297] Such databases facilitate quick, efficient and low-cost access to information about personnel with potential multifactorial uses. The mandatory DNA collection policy was, however, challenged in 1995 by two servicemen on the basis of the Fourth Amendment,[298] but unfortunately the men left service before proper argument could be made, and the case was dismissed as moot.[299] A possible avenue of challenge to the policy accordingly remains open.

---

[294] Child Support, Pensions and Social Security Act 2000, s.67 and Schedule 6.

[295] The Health and Safety Executive has determined that one third of employers require pre-employment health checks, see Health and Safety Executive, *Health Surveillance in Great Britain*, HSE Contract Research Report No.121 (London, 1996).

[296] The database was established by the US Defense Department and it is estimated that a profile of all personnel in current service will be held by the end of 2001: Deputy Secretary of Defense Memorandum, No. 47803, 16 December 1991.

[297] For comment and criticism of the system, see E. Reiter, 'The Department of Defense DNA Repository: Practical Analysis of the Government's Interest and the Potential for Genetic Discrimination' (1999) 47 *Buffalo Law Review* 975.

[298] *Mayfield* v. *Dalton* 901 F. Supp. 300 (D. Haw. 1995).

[299] *Mayfield* v. *Dalton* 109 F. 3d. 1423 (9th Cir. 1997).

Summarising state interests

One can see from the above account that a broad range of roles is adopted by the state in its relationship with its citizens. We see the state as protector from harm, facilitator of choice, social regulator and employer. To many, these roles will seem entirely beneficent, but as was pointed out in chapter 1, such roles also typify the interventionist Western state. This has clear implications for the division between public and private life, and by extension for the privacy of individuals. The legitimacy of these beneficent roles of the state must be subject to close scrutiny not only to determine whether they do in fact impinge on individual interests to an unacceptable degree, but also to establish where the boundary can and should be drawn between public and private, and therefore between legitimate and illegitimate involvement of the state in the lives of individuals.

Future persons

Lastly, one further interest might deserve recognition. Given the obvious implications for reproductive choices linked to genetic information, and given the possible consequences of a decision to reproduce even when test results reveal bad news – namely, the birth of a child with genetic defects – it is possible to argue that an interest might exist with regard to the progeny of affected individuals. Such an interest might arise in one of two ways. First, an argument could be made that the interests of future progeny should be weighed in the balance of overall interests,[300] even if we do not consider that such interests can, or should, trump those of existing persons.[301] Second, the state might claim a valid interest in the outcome of individuals' reproductive choices if this will result, with a relatively high degree of certainty, in the birth of a child that will be

---

[300] J. C. Heller, *Human Genome Research and the Challenge of Contingent Future Persons: Towards an Impersonal Theocentric Approach to Value* (Omaha, NE, Creighton University Press, 1996).

[301] Ngwena and Chadwick have argued that it might be possible to take account of the interests of the unborn in such circumstances; see C. Ngwena and R. Chadwick, 'Genetic Diagnostic Information and the Duty of Confidentiality: Ethics and Law' (1993) 1 *Medical Law International* 73, 85. Glannon has argued further that the testing and selective reduction of genetically damaged embryos is the only medically and morally defensible way to prevent the existence of people with severe disability; see W. Glannon, 'Genes, Embryos, and Future People' (1998) 12 *Bioethics* 187.

a drain on valuable resources.[302] This latter point has been explored to some extent above. We shall revisit both arguments in due course.

Interests in genetic information: a conclusion

Clearly there are a considerable number of potential interests that exist in relation to genetic information. To recap, the interested parties include

- the individual and her interest in her own genetic information;
- the relatives of this person (and their relatives);
- the insurance industry;
- employers and potential employers;
- researchers;
- the state;
- future persons (and their representatives).

As we have seen, there is much potential for conflict, but also much scope for compromise. The next step is to consider how best to weight these respective interests, reach acceptable balances where possible, and choose between interests where this is not possible. In order to do this it is necessary to consider the relevant principles and values that bind together much of the fabric of Western society. These must be examined, together with those relevant factors about genetic information and disease that we can extrapolate from earlier discussion and which can also serve to tip the balance. The ultimate objective of this exercise is to consider what should be the optimal legal and social responses to developments in genetics. But this can only be determined by reference to the key features of the value system in question, and in the Western liberal tradition this means a reconsideration of the position of 'the individual' within that system. Accordingly, this will provide a focus for the subsequent chapters of this book.

---

[302] The Bush administration announced plans in July 2001 to allow states to redefine foetuses as 'targeted low-income children' who would then qualify for prenatal care under the Children's Health Insurance Programme (Chip); see J. Borger, 'Alarm as Bush Plans Health Cover for Unborn', *Guardian*, 7 July 2001, p. 5.

4

Autonomy, confidentiality and privacy

Challenging medico-legal paradigms

Much ink has been spilled discussing the ramifications of genetic advances for individuals, communities and society at large. As we have seen, a central concern has been the problem of regulating access to, and control of, the genetic information that has been produced as a result of rapid progress in the fields of genetic research and genetic testing. To date, discussion has rightly focused on the uses to which genetic test results should be put, and, indeed, on the logically prior question of whether genetic information should be sought at all in certain circumstances. Debate has, however, tended to polarise the issues under scrutiny, setting the individual against the state or other interested parties such as insurers or employers. Moreover, from the perspective of the individual, the interests that have been identified as being at stake have centred on the autonomy of persons and the 'right' that they have to control personal genetic information. While these are important starting points, it should be realised that the discourse has barely begun on the appropriateness of social, ethical and legal responses to the challenges that are thrown up by such scientific advances.

We have examined the nature of the interests at issue to determine precisely which factors, values, perceived benefits and adverse consequences should be assessed when deciding how genetic information should be handled. At first sight, the most obvious interest focuses on knowing genetic information, and, on this basis, arguments for a 'right to know' are frequently founded, particularly in the context of individuals and their relatives with respect to their own genetic information. The argument in favour of a 'right *not* to know' genetic information, which may equally protect personal and familial interests, also merits analysis. Only then can a proper assessment be made of the appropriateness of any use of the information in question. While it is possible to make a strong argument in favour of knowing based on existing ethical and legal models, it is sub-mitted that proper recognition of the interest in not knowing is urgently needed. Furthermore, in order properly to protect such an interest by legal procedures or other means, a paradigm shift in medico-legal norms is required. This is revealed by an assessment of the role of more tra-ditional concepts, such as autonomy and confidentiality, in providing a suitable basis on which to found the claim not to know. As will be argued, these are wanting in the present context, and a viable alternative must be sought. That alternative is privacy.

Autonomy

There is one book in the medico-legal sphere that desperately requires to be written. That is a history of the adolescent lives of the disci-plines of medical law and bioethics.[1] While these fields of scholarship remain in a nascent state, they have already each enjoyed a satisfying existence, marked by many controversies and battles. Key among these has been the struggle over the recognition, nature and content of pa-tients' rights.[2] And central to that struggle, in turn, has been the concept of patient autonomy, as manifested primarily through the doctrine of informed consent. Indeed, such has been the success of the autonomy and consent-based argument that it has come to be seen as something of an ethical panacea for the dilemmas that we face in contemporary medicine. A recent and striking example of this in the United Kingdom is the response of official bodies established to investigate allegations over the removal and retention of organs from deceased children in the absence of adequate parental consent.[3] Without exception, each body

---

[1] These disciplines began to emerge as discrete areas of enquiry in the late 1960s and early 1970s.

[2] For a seminal work from the United States, see G. J. Annas, *The Rights of Patients* (Carbondale, IL, Southern Illinois University Press, 1989), first published in 1975 as *The Rights of Hospital Patients*. In the United Kingdom, for equivalent influential works one would look to the writings of S. McLean (S. McLean, *Legal Issues in Medicine* (Aldershot, Gower, 1981), and S. McLean and G. Maher, *Medicine, Morals and the Law* (Aldershot, Gower, 1983)) and J. K. Mason and R. A. A. McCall-Smith, *Law and Medical Ethics*, 5th edn (Edinburgh, Butter-worths, 1999 [1983]).

[3] See The Bristol Royal Infirmary Inquiry, *Interim Report: Removal and Retention of Human Ma-terial* (London, The Stationery Office, May 2000); M. Redfern *et al.*, *The Report of the Royal Liverpool Children's Inquiry* (London, The Stationery Office, January 2001); Advice from the Chief Medical Officer, *The Removal, Retention and Use of Human Organs and Tissue from*

that made recommendations did so by almost exclusive reference to the principle of informed consent, urging that the optimal ethical solution to the public crisis of confidence was to elicit more and better consent to post-mortem examination from relatives of deceased persons. This approach has been criticised, however, as departing to an unacceptable degree from the true meaning of consent – which should be a reflection of an individual's wishes about her own condition – and for setting too much store by the ability of consent and autonomy to legitimise all dealings with patients and their families in the health care setting.[4]

Baroness Onora O'Neill has recently argued that 'The supposed triumph of autonomy in bioethics is an unsustainable illusion.'[5] O'Neill posits that the modern view of autonomy and its equiparation with informed consent does a disservice to Kantian notions of principled autonomy, which is concerned with the universalisability of principles of conduct by which we can live a morally good life.[6] The contemporary conception of autonomy is flawed in this and a number of other respects, most notably because it is highly individualistic to the point of exclusion of our relational obligations to others, and second, because the conflation of autonomy with consent robs the former of much of its meaning and strips it of much of its ethical credibility. One can add to this a caution against seeing autonomy or consent as universally appropriate ethical and legal solutions. While this is not to deny the general validity and importance of autonomy and consent in medical law and ethics, it is none the less a call to consider wider ethical and legal options in the search for a resolution to contemporary medico-legal dilemmas. More particularly, the limits of an autonomy-based approach can be

---

Post-mortem Examination (London, Department of Health, 2001); Chief Medical Officer, *Report of a Census of Organs and Tissues Retained by Pathology Services in England* (London, Department of Health, 2001); Health Services Directorate, *Report of Content Analysis of NHS Trust Policies and Protocols on Consent to Organ and Tissue Retention at Post-mortem Examination and Disposal of Human Materials in the Chief Medical Officer's Census of NHS Pathology Services* (London, Department of Health, 2000). In Scotland, see S. McLean *et al.*, *Report of the Independent Review Group on the Retention of Organs at Post-mortem* (Edinburgh, The Scottish Executive, January 2001).

[4] See J. K. Mason and G. T. Laurie, 'Consent or Property? Dealing with the Body and its Parts in the Shadow of Bristol and Alder Hey' (2001) 64 *Modern Law Review* 710.

[5] O. O'Neill, 'Autonomy and Trust in Bioethics', The Gifford Lectures, University of Edinburgh (2001).

[6] See further J. B. Schneewind, *The Invention of Autonomy: A History of Modern Moral Philosophy* (Cambridge, Cambridge University Press, 1998).

well demonstrated in the context of genetics through an analysis of its suitability to protect certain core interests, such as the interest in not knowing.

The principle of autonomy in contemporary medical law and ethics

What is autonomy? What does it mean to be autonomous? The term *autonomy* is derived from the Greek words *autos* (self) and *nomos* (law or rule). As several writers remind us, it was first used to refer to self-rule in Greek city states whose citizens legislated for themselves and were not subject to some conquering power.[7] Applied to an individual, autonomy has been taken to mean a number of things. For example, to call an individual autonomous can refer to the fact that she is independent and makes her own choices, or that she has the capacity to make choices. Clearly, this precludes a number of classes of individual. A person in a coma has no capacity to choose. Equally, infants, children, and persons suffering from serious mental dysfunction might not have the capacity to make choices, and so might not be considered autonomous. According to this conception a person must possess certain characteristics or traits before she can be called autonomous. These usually include reason and ability or competence.[8] Sometimes, however, it is argued that an individual is only autonomous if certain strict criteria – such as consistency in decision-making, resistance to external influence, and self-sufficient independence in the establishment of personal values and beliefs – are met.[9] Other conceptions of autonomy perceive it as an ideal,[10] or as the sovereign authority to govern oneself, akin to political independence enjoyed by states.[11]

Unfortunately, these different conceptions do not provide us with a unifying definition of the principle of autonomy.[12] Nevertheless, certain

---

[7] See G. Dworkin, *The Theory and Practice of Autonomy* (Cambridge, Cambridge University Press, 1988), pp. 12–13; T. L. Beauchamp and J. F. Childress, *Principles of Biomedical Ethics*, 5th edn (New York, Oxford University Press, 2001), pp. 57–8; and J. Feinberg, *Harm to Self* (Oxford, Oxford University Press, 1986), at 28, n. 1.

[8] See, for example, R. S. Downie and E. Telfer, 'Autonomy' (1971) 15 *Philosophy* 301.

[9] See, for example, S. I. Benn, 'Freedom, Autonomy and the Concept of a Person' (1976) 76 *Proceedings of the Aristotelian Society* 123. See also J. Raz, *The Morality of Freedom* (Oxford, Clarendon Press, 1986), pp. 379–82.

[10] For example, see R. S. Downie *et al.*, *Health Promotion: Models and Values* (Oxford, Oxford University Press, 1991), p. 139.

[11] See Feinberg, *Harm to Self*, pp. 27 *et seq.*

[12] This point is cogently made by Dworkin, *Theory and Practice*, pp. 5–6.

common elements can be identified, and these have become core features of the working model that is used in the contemporary Western health care setting.

First, central to the principle of autonomy seems to be the idea of *choice*.[13] To be respected as an autonomous individual is to have one's choices respected. Second, crucial to this respect is *non-interference*. In order to make one's own choices – that is, for those choices to be autonomous – one must be free from unwarranted interference by others.[14] Bound up with all of this is possession of the *capacity* to make those choices.[15] Finally, to be meaningful these choices must be *informed*, that

---

[13] See, for example, Feinberg, *Harm to Self*, p. 54: 'The kernel of the idea of autonomy is the right to make choices and decisions ... put compendiously, the most basic autonomy right is the right to decide how to live one's life'. In a discussion of positive liberty, Berlin puts forward the view that this sense of liberty derives from the wish on the part of the individual to be his own master. As he says, 'I wish my life and decisions to depend on myself, not on external forces of any kind', I. Berlin, *Four Essays on Liberty* (Oxford, Oxford University Press, 1969), p. 131. Similarly, Dworkin, *The Theory and Practice of Autonomy*, p. 20, defines autonomy as 'a second-order capacity of persons to reflect critically upon their first-order preferences, desires, wishes and so forth and the capacity to accept or attempt to change these in light of higher-order preferences and values'. For Raz, to be autonomous is to be 'the author of one's own life'. The autonomous life is opposed to coerced choices; and further, to be autonomous a person must not only be given a choice but he must be given an adequate range of choices, see Raz, *The Morality of Freedom*, pp. 370–3. Downie and Calman opine that: 'To be an autonomous person is to have the ability to be able to choose for oneself or more extensively to be able to formulate and carry out one's own plans or policies', see R. S. Downie and K. C. Calman, *Healthy Respect: Ethics in Health Care*, 2nd edn (Oxford, Oxford University Press, 1994), p. 52.

[14] See Beauchamp and Childress, *Principles*, pp. 58–60; Berlin, *Four Essays*, p. 131; and Dworkin, *The Theory and Practice of Autonomy*, pp. 18–19. Raz, *The Morality of Freedom*, pp. 408–11, argues that although autonomy is a valuable thing, and a constituent element of 'the good life', he does not include in his conception of autonomy as valuable the right to make bad choices. He argues that restrictions can be placed on autonomy and the making of autonomous choices if to fail to do so would result in harm to others, or even harm to the individual in question in the future.

[15] Dworkin, *The Theory and Practice of Autonomy*, p. 20, considers capacity as a constituent element of his definition of autonomy. For Raz, *The Morality of Freedom*, p. 408, the autonomous person has the capacity to control and create his good life. He argues elsewhere that 'a person is [not] autonomous if he is paralysed and therefore cannot take advantage of the options offered to him', see J. Raz, 'Autonomy, Toleration, and the Harm Principle', in R. Gavison (ed.), *Issues in Contemporary Legal Philosophy* (Oxford, Clarendon Press, 1987), p. 314. Downie and Calman, *Healthy Respect*, p. 52, consider that autonomy includes not only choice but the ability to choose. Beauchamp and Childress, *Principles*, pp. 69–77, discuss the role of competence to take decisions and note that 'Competence judgments serve a gatekeeping role in health care by distinguishing persons whose decisions should be solicited or accepted from persons whose decisions need not or should not be solicited or accepted', p. 69. They point out, however, that 'A person should rarely be judged incompetent with respect to every sphere of life', *ibid.*, p. 70.

is, based on information that is understood. Otherwise there is no reason to imagine that a bare choice is a reflection of the individual's will.[16]

It is not necessary for a working model of autonomy to conceive of the principle as a condition achievable only on the attainment of certain elusive characteristics or qualities.[17] Although autonomy has come to be concerned almost exclusively with choice and the exercise of that choice in relation to life decisions, realistically it must be accepted that no person can control, at all times, all aspects of her life.[18] That this is so does not mean that no person can be autonomous. In like manner, simply because some influence is exerted on an individual in making a choice,[19] or because the individual has diminished capacity in some aspects of her life,[20] does not mean that such a person is not autonomous or that she cannot take autonomous decisions. For a working model of autonomy it is only necessary that a certain degree of autonomy is reached and that capacity to make a choice is evidenced in relation to the choice that is to be taken. In practical terms the standard that is required is always a question to be answered by reference to the facts and circumstances of each case. What is important is that autonomy be respected where it is achievable, and, ancillary to this but in no way less necessary, that autonomous choices be equally respected.

In the context of medical ethics, Downie and others have argued that the concept of autonomy is a basic and guiding principle which is presupposed by other principles.[21] That is, autonomy is a fundamental ethical principle from which other ethical principles derive their authority.[22] For Downie and Calman, for example, to respect the autonomy of an individual is to employ the four core ethical principles

[16] See, generally, S. A. M. McLean, *The Patient's Right to Know: Information Disclosure, the Doctor and the Law* (Aldershot, Gower, 1989).

[17] See, for example, Beauchamp and Childress, *Principles*, pp. 58–9.

[18] See Raz, 'Autonomy, Toleration, and the Harm Principle', p. 314.

[19] Indeed, arguably no one has an entirely influence-free life since we live in communities and families, are subject to cultural, religious and moral influence and are conditioned by our education and surroundings.

[20] I may not have the capacity to run because I am disabled, I may not have the capacity to vote because I am too young, I may not have the ability to understand quantum physics because my IQ is too low, but none of these limitations means that I cannot exercise my autonomy in other aspects of my life; see P. D. G. Skegg, *Law, Ethics and Medicine* (Oxford, Clarendon Press, 1984), pp. 56–7.

[21] See, for example, Downie and Calman, *Healthy Respect*, ch. 4 and Downie *et al.*, *Health Promotion*, chs. 9 and 10.

[22] Downie and Calman, ch. 4.

for dealing with others, namely, those of beneficence, non-maleficence, justice and utility.[23]

Downie and Calman maintain that in the first instance the best way to accord respect to others is to leave them alone and do them no harm: the principle of non-maleficence. However, as they note, 'sometimes plans and projects go wrong and then benevolence [beneficence] might become appropriate'.[24] By this is meant a compassionate attitude and behaviour towards a person which involve empathy or sympathy, positive help and imaginative understanding.[25] In turn, these authors comment that the principle of justice can have at least two meanings in this context. First, it can require that all autonomous individuals are treated equally, in that they are accorded the same level of respect. Thus, even if we ultimately treated persons differently, we respect them because they have been considered on an equal basis and a defensible justification is offered for any different treatment that might occur. Second, on a purely individual level, justice can mean treating individuals appropriately in the light of their own wants, needs and merits.[26] As the authors say, 'Justice or fairness in this sense is sometimes expressed by the concept of deserts. For example, we might say "He deserves better care than he got".'[27] Thus, to respect the individual is to treat her fairly. Finally, the principle of utility is considered to be less amenable to respecting individuals, for 'The principle of utility tells us that we ought to seek the best possible consequences, or the greatest happiness, for the greatest number of people. In other words, utility is not concerned with individuals but with majorities, with aggregates.'[28] None the less, the authors still consider that the principle draws its authority from the principle of autonomy: 'there can be no sense in promoting the interests or happiness of aggregates of people unless one is already presupposing the supreme value of the persons who make up these aggregates'.[29]

Not all ethicists agree with this analysis of ethical principles or on the pivotal role of autonomy. For example, Beauchamp and Childress consider that 'construing respect for autonomy as a principle with priority over all other moral principles, rather than one principle in a framework of prima facie principles, gives it too much weight'.[30] However, beyond such disputes about the relative role of autonomy lies the deeper significance of its central position in the theoretical and practical framework

---

[23] *Ibid.*, pp. 54 *et seq.*   [24] *Id.*   [25] *Ibid.*, p. 56.   [26] *Id.*   [27] *Id.*
[28] *Ibid.*, pp. 57–8.   [29] *Id.*   [30] Beauchamp and Childress, *Principles*, p. 104.

of modern bioethics. The principles of non-maleficence, beneficence, justice, utility and autonomy underpin the entire ethos of current ethical thinking. Even if one ultimately rejects this particular approach to ethical discourse,[31] the strong influence of principlism on the discipline is undeniable.[32] Further key factors that have moulded bioethics include an increase in concern for human rights in the post-Second World War era, rapid advances in technology that have considerably expanded the limits of medical science, and a rejection of the attitude that health care professionals have authority to act as sole arbiters in questions involving health care provision. All of these changes have impacted considerably on the lives of individuals throughout Western society, and as a result bioethics and notions of personal autonomy are more relevant and more pertinent to our lives than ever before. In the health care setting respect for individual autonomy is required by the common ethical principles that constitute medical ethics and which dictate the appropriateness of the conduct of health care professionals towards their patients.

And yet, it is easy to imagine situations when an individual might wish to exercise her autonomy in a manner that will interfere with the autonomy of others or cause them harm or treat them unfairly. And, as Beauchamp and Childress point out,

> Respect for autonomy . . . has only prima facie standing and can be over-ridden by competing moral considerations. Examples include the following: If our choices endanger the public health, potentially harm innocent others, or require a scarce resource for which no funds are available, others can justifiably restrict our exercises of autonomy. The principle of respect for autonomy does not by itself determine what, on balance, a person ought to be free to know or do or what counts as a valid justification for constraining autonomy.[33]

Thus, autonomy is not an absolute value, and nor should it be.[34] None the less, its emergence as the guiding principle in ethical discourse in the health care setting is unprecedented, and its normative and emotional

---

[31] See, for example, B. Gert, C. M. Culver and K. D. Clouser, *Bioethics: A Return to Fundamentals* (New York, Oxford University Press, 1997).

[32] For a defence of the methodology of principlism, see R. Macklin, *Against Relativism: Cultural Diversity and the Search for Ethical Universals in Medicine* (New York, Oxford University Press, 1999).

[33] Beauchamp and Childress, *Principles*, p. 65.

[34] R. A. A. McCall-Smith, 'Beyond Autonomy' (1997) 14 *Journal of Contemporary Health Law and Policy* 23.

appeal now goes largely unquestioned. The significance of this view of autonomy has equally been reflected in the law.

Autonomy in law

The classic legal formulation of patient self-determination was offered by Justice Benjamin Cardozo in *Schloendorff* v. *Society of New York Hospitals*.[35] This case dealt with an operation that was carried out despite the patient's express wishes to the contrary, and which resulted in the patient suffering physical injury. Although the action was unsuccessful on its facts,[36] Justice Cardozo affirmed categorically in his judgement the legal importance of autonomy in medical treatment: 'Every human being of adult years and sound mind has the right to determine what shall be done with his own body; and a surgeon who performs an operation without his patient's consent commits an assault, for which he is liable in damages.'[37]

This reflects current thinking in society generally, for the idea of the human body as an inviolate entity is now common in the laws of Western states. In cases where the body has been violated, the law provides that a civil action in assault or battery can be brought by the victim, and, usually, that criminal prosecution is also possible at the discretion of the state. In this way, respect for autonomy is a legally prescribed phenomenon. In like manner, failure to inform a patient sufficiently about the nature of a procedure to be endured, its risks, and any alternatives may vitiate any apparent consent that is subsequently given. This leaves the health care professional open to an action for damages in negligence that will reflect the measure of affront to the personal integrity of the patient, and will seek to compensate for any physical harm that might otherwise have been avoided if the patient had been fully informed and had consequently chosen not to proceed with the medical intervention.[38]

---

[35] *Schloendorff* v. *Society of New York Hospitals*, 211 N.Y. 125 (1914). For an excellent discussion of this case in the context of informed consent see R. R. Faden and T. L. Beauchamp, *A History and Theory of Informed Consent* (New York, Oxford University Press, 1986), ch. 4.

[36] For a discussion see Faden and Beauchamp, *A History and Theory of Informed Consent*, p. 123.

[37] *Schloendorff*, 128.

[38] The classic rulings in this regard from various jurisdictions include, from the United Kingdom, *Chatterton* v. *Gerson* [1981] QB 432, [1981] 1 All ER 257; *Hills* v. *Potter* [1983] 3 All ER 716, [1984] 1 WLR 641; and *Sidaway* v. *Board of Governors of the Bethlem Royal Hospital* [1985] AC 871, [1985] 1 All ER 643, HL. From Canada, see *Reibl* v. *Hughes* (1980) 114 DLR

The importance of the role of the law in protecting patient autonomy has often been reiterated since Cardozo's statement in 1914. An
assessment of the current position across a range of jurisdictions finds
individual autonomy and patient consent and refusal as trump cards
in the medico-legal sphere. Numerous rulings affirm a legal conception of patient autonomy that holds out individual unfettered choice
as a supreme value, irrespective of the consequences for the individual chooser. As the English Court of Appeal has confirmed, 'A man or
woman of full age and sound understanding may choose to reject medical advice and medical or surgical treatment either partially or in its
entirety. A decision to refuse medical treatment by a patient capable of
making the decision does not have to be sensible or well-considered.'[39]

In the United Kingdom, those not of full age or sound understanding
and who cannot exercise autonomy have traditionally been treated in
their own best interests. To many this is an inimical approach in the
modern era, requiring a paternalistic stance and avoiding such questions
as who should decide best interests and on what basis. Indeed, Scots law
has recently rejected this approach in the context of incapacitated adults,
admitting a system whereby proxy decision-makers can be appointed
with the power to consent on behalf of an incapax person.[40] In England
and Wales, however, no one – not even a court – can consent or refuse
of behalf of an incapacitated adult.[41] By way of contrast, many US states
permit the use of substituted judgements to deal with the problem of
incapacitated persons. That is, decisions are taken in the name of the
incapax by a court or those close to the person, usually relatives, in a
manner that reflects what the individual would have chosen had she been
able to do so.[42] The obvious limitation is that the test is highly artificial
and indeed inappropriate for minors or the life-long incompetent when

(3d) 1, and from the United States see *Canterbury* v. *Spence* 464 F 2d 772 (DC, 1972) and
Cobbs v. *Grant* 8 Cal. 3d 229 (1972). For evidence of a shift towards a more patient-oriented
approach see the Australian case of *Rogers* v. *Whitaker* (1993) 109 ALR 625.

[39] *Re T (Adult: Refusal of Medical Treatment)* [1992] 4 All ER 649, 664.

[40] See Adults with Incapacity (Scotland) Act 2000. Note, however, that there is no corresponding right to refuse treatment, nor does the Act give any indication of the basis upon which
decisions should be taken. For critical appraisal see G. T. Laurie and J. K. Mason, 'Negative
Treatment of Vulnerable Patients: Euthanasia By Any Other Name?' (2000) *Juridical Review*
159.

[41] *Re F (Mental Patient: Sterilisation)* [1990] 2 AC 1.

[42] See, for example, the ruling of the Supreme Judicial Court of Massachusetts in *Re Moe* 432
NE 2d 712 (1982).

there is no evidence whatsoever of what these persons would want.[43] None the less, the general thrust of this approach attempts to reflect as closely as possible the value of giving effect to individual autonomy.[44]

In the hardest of cases – when capacity is neither wholly present nor absent but in serious doubt – courts have to decide between, on the one hand, respecting the degree of autonomy that is present but reduced, and on the other, treating the person in a paternalistic fashion. This is seen most sharply in the treatment by British courts of minors who seek to refuse medical treatment. In *Re S (A Minor)(Consent to Medical Treatment)*,[45] the Family Division of the English High Court of Justice was concerned with a 15½-year-old girl who was suffering from a form of thalassaemia that alters the formation of haemoglobin in the body so that red blood cells are destroyed. Affected persons must receive monthly blood transfusions and daily abdominal injections in order to survive. *S* had been receiving such treatment since birth. In 1989 she and her mother began to attend meetings of Jehovah's Witnesses, and in May 1994 *S* refused a blood transfusion. An order was sought by the local authority requesting the court to authorise treatment under its inherent jurisdiction. In authorising the treatment the court held that although it had the power so to do, it must start from the premise that the patient's wishes should be respected unless the circumstances strongly indicated intervention. To be weighed against the wishes of the patient (her refusal) are her own best interests. In determining such best interests the court held that it must examine the extent to which the decision to refuse treatment had been reached independently, and this must be based on a proper understanding of the illness and the consequences of refusal. In the particular circumstances of *S*, the court held that because the child entertained a hope of a miracle cure she did not fully understand the nature or implications of her choice. She was not, therefore, competent to make the decision and the treatment could go ahead contrary to her wishes.[46]

---

[43] For a rejection of the test in the context of an incapax child by the Illinois Supreme Court, see *Curran* v. *Bosze* 566 NE 2d 1319 (1990).

[44] For a discussion of the origins of the approach and its attendant difficulties, see J. Robertson, 'Organ Donations by Incompetents and the Substituted Judgment Doctrine' (1976) 76 *Columbia Law Review* 48.

[45] *Re S (A Minor)(Consent to Medical Treatment)* [1994] 2 FLR 1065.

[46] Consent and refusal cases concerning minors in England and Wales are governed by the House of Lords decision in *Gillick* v. *West Norfolk and Wisbech Area Health Authority* [1986] AC 112; [1985] 3 All ER 402, HL.

This case seems to uphold the principle of autonomy, for prima facie the patient's wishes must be respected. However, an analysis of the
judgement reveals that in practice it will be very difficult for minors
to choose for themselves when that decision goes against the views of
attending health care professionals. The court overturned the refusal of
the minor on the authority of previous case law which clearly established a best interests analysis for the treatment of minors.[47] What is of
importance, however, is the nature of the test that the court laid down to
establish best interests. It is hard to reject the view that what is in someone's best interests should ideally be determined by the person herself,
provided, of course, that she has capacity to do so. In the present case
the court held that because the child entertained an irrational belief in
a cure, and because she failed to appreciate 'the manner of the death
and pain and the distress' which her decision would entail, she was not
competent to refuse. This is to set a very high standard. Indeed, some
would argue that it is an impossibly high standard.[48] Johnson J held
that it was not enough simply that the child had 'an understanding that
she will die'. What is required is not only a fairly detailed understanding of the processes of one's demise, but also evidence of having come
to terms with one's own end. This standard is unlikely ever to be met
by any child. Indeed, as one commentator has pointed out, it is also
unlikely to be met by most adults.[49] Thus, this case tends to indicate
that minors will rarely, if ever, have the capacity to refuse, and will accordingly be treated in their own best interests as determined by others.
Further jurisprudence substantiates this view,[50] to the extent that the
position in England and Wales now seems to be that provided a court
can find *a* consent to authorise medical treatment, then treatment of
a minor will be lawful. Such consent can come either from the child,
or if she refuses, it can come from the parents, who retain a residual
right to consent. Indeed, by virtue of its wardship jurisdiction, the High
Court itself can consent for the child, always of course in the child's best
interests.

---

[47] See *Re R (A Minor)(Wardship: Medical Treatment)* [1991] 4 All ER 177, CA, and *Re W
(A Minor)(Medical Treatment)* [1992] 4 All ER 627, CA. For comment see M. Brazier
and C. Bridge, 'Coercion or Caring: Analysing Adolescent Autonomy' (1996) 16 *Legal
Studies* 84.

[48] See M. Gunn, 'The Meaning of Incapacity' (1994) 2 *Medical Law Review* 8.

[49] A. Grubb, 'Commentary' (1996) 4 *Medical Law Review* 84 at 86.

[50] See, for example, *Re E (A Minor)* (1990) 9 BMLR 1.

Such a paternalistic approach might be more defensible were it not for the fact that the courts have held in another line of authority that the 'mature minor' is a meaningful concept in English law. That is, children not of full age might nevertheless have the capacity to take their own medical decisions which deserve to be respected.[51] But the reality is that this is only so in respect of *consent* to medical assistance that is offered. No correlative right to refuse such assistance is admitted, as the above cases demonstrate. This does an extreme disservice to the notion of individual autonomy. If it is recognised that I have capacity to make my own decisions and to act autonomously in respect of my own health, why should this only be true when I agree with medical advice, and not true when I reject that advice? If a right to consent is to be meaningful exercise of autonomy, it must include an attendant right not to consent, that is, a right to refuse.[52] If this is not so, then my autonomy is neither properly recognised nor fully protected.

Paternalism

One cannot talk of the principle of autonomy in either ethics or law without reference to the concept of paternalism. A strong conception of autonomy considers respect for individual choice to be even more important than individual wellbeing, so that it is irrelevant if in the exercise of the former the latter is jeopardised. The case for such a view is based on pragmatism and the logical extension of the beliefs that underpin the modern view of autonomous individuals. If autonomy relates to an individual's right to take decisions affecting her life uninhibited by interference because, after all, it is her life, then the nature of the decisions taken should be of no consequence. What has become important is the fact that in at least three senses of that word persons *can* take these decisions: they have (i) the ability, (ii) the capacity and (iii) the unfettered opportunity to exercise that capacity, to do so.[53] Generally, however, such a view is not followed in Western democracies. Rather, a compromise solution is reached that allows unchallenged exercises of

---

[51] This is a line of authority that began with the case of *Gillick* v. *West Norfolk and Wisbech Area Health Authority* [1986] AC 112, leading to the concept of the *Gillick competent* child.

[52] For a defence of the alternative approach see J. K. Mason and R. A. A. McCall-Smith, *Law and Medical Ethics*, 5th edn (Edinburgh, Butterworths, 1999), pp. 260–1.

[53] This view is discussed by Feinberg, *Harm to Self*, p. 59. See also J. Feinberg, 'Autonomy, Sovereignty, and Privacy: Moral Ideals in the Constitution' (1983) 58 *The Notre Dame Law Review* 445 at 457–61.

autonomy only in certain circumstances.[54] If, for example, an exercise of
one's autonomy will directly harm others or if there is the possibility of
harm to oneself, and some dubiety about the autonomy of the individual
can be inferred, then such exercises of autonomy will not be tolerated.[55]
Certainly, when capacity is in doubt intervention is justified in the individual's perceived best interests.[56] And it sometimes also happens that
an assessment of best interests is used to decide for others even when
those persons have the capacity to decide for themselves. It is the act
of deciding for and acting ostensibly in another's best interests that is
commonly known as paternalism.[57]

Our forbearance towards paternalism has diminished dramatically in
recent years, in a manner inversely proportional to the rise and supposed
success of autonomy in regulating relations between patients and medical professionals. Paternalism has come to be seen as the very antithesis
of autonomy and self-determination because implicit in its operation is
a disregard for the wishes of the subject towards whom the paternalism
is directed. Paternalism can take a variety of forms, and in most but
not all cases the patient is deemed to be incapax and therefore unable
to exercise her autonomy. This is not to say, however, that the patient's
wishes are not known or cannot be ascertained. Some examples serve to
illustrate the gamut of potential paternalistic practices.

First, let us consider the situation where a patient is unconscious and
treatment is required to avert a threat to her life. To carry out such
treatment without first attempting to ascertain the wishes of the patient
is paternalistic, not only because it is done in what are considered to be
the best interests of the patient, but because it is done irrespective of her
wishes. However, in such cases the law presumes that the urgency of the
situation provides the health care professional with a defence of necessity
and no action brought subsequently by the patient will succeed.[58] An
example of this is the case of *Marshall* v. *Curry* in which a Canadian court

[54] A classic example is *St George's Healthcare NHS Trust* v. *S (No.) 2; R* v. *Collins, ex parte S (No.2)*
[1998] 3 WLR 936.
[55] For a discussion of this latter point see A. Grubb, 'Treatment Decisions: Keeping it in the
Family', in A. Grubb (ed.), *Choices and Decisions in Health Care* (Chichester, John Wiley
& Sons, 1993), pp. 37–96.
[56] This approach is very similar to a model discussed by Feinberg in 'Autonomy, Sovereignty,
and Privacy', 460–1. This model is not, however, supported by him, *ibid*.
[57] For commentary on paternalism see Dworkin, *The Theory and Practice of Autonomy*, ch. 8,
J. Kleinig, *Paternalism* (Manchester, Manchester University Press, 1983), and A. Buchanan,
'Medical Paternalism' (1978) 7 *Philosophy and Public Affairs* 370.
[58] See Mason and McCall-Smith, *Law and Medical Ethics*, pp. 220–1.

denied a claim in battery brought because a doctor removed a patient's diseased testicle during the course of a hernia operation.[59] The court was of the opinion that it would have been unreasonable to delay the operation in order to seek the patient's specific consent.[60]

Second, paternalistic approaches to patient treatment have been legally sanctioned even in circumstances where the patient has expressed wishes against treatment prior to lapsing into an incapacitated state. In the US case of *Werth* v. *Taylor* a civil action in battery failed against a health care professional who had authorised a blood transfusion to one of the plaintiffs despite her having signed a Refusal to Permit Blood Transfusion form.[61] The fact that the patient had been unconscious at the time when the transfusion became necessary was decisive for the court. The refusal of the patient was not informed because it was not made at a time contemporaneous with the threat to her life. This meant that her refusal could be overridden. The difference between this and the first scenario is the evidence of a patient's wishes. However, the similarity between the two scenarios lies in the paternalistic practice of disregarding those wishes. In the first it is not sought, which is a form of disrespect in itself. In the second it is ignored. Thus, absent from each scenario is the patient's consent, which we take to be the ultimate expression of autonomy and self-determination in the health care setting.

A third example concerns disclosure of information to a patient. If a health care professional considers that for a patient to hear that she has a terminal disease will merely advance her condition and seriously affect her mental state, then to omit to convey this information will undoubtedly be an act of paternalism, but it might nevertheless be legally justifiable.[62] In the United Kingdom this practice has long been condoned by the courts, which have considered that no legal action should lie for non-disclosure of medical information provided that the judgement of the health care professional in withholding information was in accordance with 'a responsible body of medical opinion'.[63] That is,

---

[59] *Marshall* v. *Curry* [1933] 3 DLR 260.   [60] Cf. *Murray* v. *McMurchy* [1949] 2 DLR 442.

[61] *Werth* v. *Taylor* 475 NW 2d 426 (1991).

[62] On this matter see S. Bok, *Lying: Moral Choice in Public and Private Life* (New York, Vintage Books, 1989), pp. 220–41.

[63] See *Bolam* v. *Friern Hospital Management Committee* [1957] 2 All ER 118, *Chatterton* v. *Gerson* and *Sidaway*. It is thought that the position in Scotland is the same, see *Hunter* v. *Hanley* 1955 SLT 213; *Moyes* v. *Lothian Health Board* [1990] 1 Med. L.R. 463; *Goorkani* v. *Tayside Health Board* [1991] 3 Med. L.R. 33; and *Gordon* v. *Wilson* 1992 SLT 849.

the standard against which the paternalistic conduct is tested has been one set by the medical profession itself. Most recently, however, there is evidence that this position is shifting as the courts become more willing to assume the role of ultimate arbiters of adequate levels of disclosure. The standard that seems to be emerging requires that patients be given enough information to permit a reasonable patient to reach a balanced judgment.[64] However, even in jurisdictions where standards of information disclosure are governed by what a prudent patient would wish to know, health care professionals retain a therapeutic privilege to withhold from patients information that is perceived to be potentially damaging.[65]

Fourth, the courts might deem that a patient is not sufficiently autonomous to merit respect of their wishes even if these can be expressed, and in such cases medical care will be approved, once again, in the best interests of the patient. This point has already been made above concerning children and mentally incapable adults. Also, those who are subjected to undue influence, or who are ignorant of the consequences of their acts, can be deemed incapax for the purposes of legitimising medical intervention. For example, it is common for mental health legislation to sanction compulsory detention and treatment of individuals suffering from prescribed disorders, although normally the treatment is restricted to that which is directed to the mental condition in question. But, in such cases, and indeed in all cases when a patient's competence is in question, it should be borne in mind that it is not the case that, because an individual suffers from incapacity in some respects, she is automatically incapax regarding all aspects of her life, and therefore incapable of making autonomous choices concerning those aspects.[66]

These examples demonstrate a number of matters. For example, it is clear that autonomy is not, and cannot be, the complete answer to the question of how health care professionals should treat their patients. For, sometimes, the necessary conditions are simply not present. Furthermore, there are many circumstances in which paternalistic treatment of patients has been sanctioned by the courts because autonomy has been in doubt, and in each case it is tempered by the requirement that

---

[64] See, for example, *Pearce* v. *United Bristol Healthcare NHS Trust* (1998) 48 BMLR 118.
[65] *Canterbury* v. *Spence* 464 F 2d 772 (DC, 1972).
[66] *Re C (Adult: Refusal of Treatment)* [1994] 1 WLR 290.

patients be treated in their own best interests. This is ethical, notionally at least, because it pays lip-service to the principles of beneficence and non-maleficence. However, the problem surrounding paternalism arises not so much from these relatively straightforward examples, but rather from the fact that paternalism has come to be seen as a signally and fundamentally unacceptable attitude that is inherently contrary to the ethical underpinnings of the principle of respect of autonomy. Taking this view, paternalism is considered to be prima facie unethical. However, this attitude is premised on the mistaken assumption that paternalism and a desire to respect patient autonomy are necessarily mutually exclusive. Paradoxically, the runaway success of autonomy and the desire to place patient choice at the centre of the dealings that health care professionals have with their patients have led to the belief that information disclosure is an imperative in the doctor/patient relationship.[67] The assumption has arisen that it is an entirely good thing to disclose information to patients in order to help them to make health care choices. While this is not necessarily challengeable in and of itself, it is no less paternalistic either. It betrays a belief that it is better to know, that it is in a patient's best interests to know, and therefore that knowledge should be imparted. But, when the concern is with *facilitating* choices, the justifications lie just as much in paternalistic practices as do other decisions to treat patients in their own best interests.[68]

Facilitating choices

An example from chapter 3 illustrates this point well. It has been noted that the state might have a strong interest in the genetic health of its citizens, and that this is an end that might be furthered by making genetic testing more available. The attractiveness of genetic testing as a means to facilitate choice is seen most clearly in the context of prenatal testing. Reproductive freedom is often hailed as the value that underpins the claims of prospective parents to have access to a battery of tests to assure themselves of their baby's health. The social implications of allowing unfettered access to testing cannot, however, be ignored. In the absence

---

[67] Cf. M. S. Pang, 'Protective Truthfulness: The Chinese Way of Safeguarding Patients in Informed Treatment Decisions' (1999) 25 *Journal of Medical Ethics* 247; and A. Akabayashi *et al.*, 'Family Consent, Communication, and Advance Directive for Cancer Disclosure: A Japanese Case and Discussion' (1999) 25 *Journal of Medical Ethics* 296.

[68] Gert *et al.*, *Bioethics: A Return to Fundamentals*, ch. 9, especially pp. 211–12.

of an effective therapeutic intervention, a positive test for a genetic condition or an indication of increased susceptibility to disease facilitates
only one choice: that to continue or to terminate the pregnancy. And,
although we need not go as far as to restrict a woman's right to choose
to continue or terminate her pregnancy, we should not remain blind
to the possibility of coercive uses of genetic testing.[69] While large-scale
eugenic practices are likely to have been consigned to the annals of history, less obvious but no less invidious policies designed to eliminate
the unhealthy or undesirable from society may emerge in a piecemeal
fashion under the guise of choice and reproductive freedom. Facilitating
reproductive decision-making by offering choice, when the only choice
available is between carrying a foetus that has been labelled less than
normal and the termination of the pregnancy, is for many a choice that
cannot be exercised free of undue influence. Indeed, the prospect of the
wholesale introduction of state screening programmes for incurable or
immutable conditions betrays an attempt to bring societal influence to
bear on a woman's right to choose.[70] The availability of prenatal susceptibility testing would equally send out a message that it is acceptable
to abort even when the risk of disease is minimal and to ignore other
causal factors that often have more to do with disease than genetics. Such
testing practices give an illusion of enlightened control, when in fact the
only control, at present, is termination. Furthermore, in circumstances
where such control is not exercised, there is a real risk that women will be
stigmatised for their 'irresponsible' decisions to carry a 'defective' child
to term. This compounds a cultural phenomenon whereby the language
that we use predisposes us towards certain value judgements against
persons and their actions. It is no more legitimate when presented in
the guise of choice.[71]

Confirmation of these concerns is found in the context of institutional responses to Huntington's disease. This is a late-onset dominant
condition that carries a 50 per cent chance of affecting each child of an
affected individual.[72] No cure is available. The severity of the disease is

---

[69] A. Lippman, 'Choice as a Risk to Women's Health' (1999) 1 *Health, Risk and Society* 281.

[70] L. Shepherd, 'Protecting Parents' Freedom to Have Children with Genetic Differences'
(1995) 4 *University of Illinois Law Review* 761.

[71] Cf. M. T. White, 'Making Responsible Decisions: An Interpretive Ethic for Genetic Deci-
sionmaking' (1999) 29 *Hastings Center Report* 14.

[72] If both parents are affected by Huntington's disease, a child's chances of developing the
condition are increased to 75 per cent in each case.

such that it is not unusual for prenatal testing to be offered solely on the condition that a positive test result will be followed by abortion. However, to do so places considerable moral and social pressure on parents and is tantamount to a subtle form of coercion to abort.[73] As the House of Commons Science and Technology Committee reported, 'We heard in Edinburgh that if after counselling a prospective parent with Huntington's Disease insists on pre-natal testing for the condition this will only be offered on the understanding that the pregnancy will be terminated if the test proves positive; to do otherwise would burden the child with knowledge of its early death.'[74]

Equally, the acceptability of postnatal testing for Huntington's disease is highly questionable. Because minors are incapax in law, parents can only legitimately request that their child be tested if it is in the child's best interests to do so. But it is far from clear that it is in a child's best interests to determine a predisposition to develop an extremely debilitating and ultimately fatal disease in adulthood when nothing can be done to avert this outcome, and when the child will remain asymptomatic throughout childhood. Even if the child is not informed of the result, it can be upsetting for the parents and can lead to the child being treated differently as a result. As Wertz et al. have poignantly noted:

'Planning for the future', perhaps the most frequently given reason for testing, may become 'restricting the future' (and also the present) by shifting family resources away from a child with a positive diagnosis... In families with a chronically ill child, there is less socialization to future roles for the children, including those who are 'healthy'. Parents are less likely to say 'When you grow up ...' or 'When you have children of your own ...' to any of their children, because they cannot say these words to the ill child... 'Alleviation of anxiety', another reason commonly given by parents for predictive genetic testing, does not necessarily benefit the children. A positive diagnosis may create serious risks of stigmatization, loss of self-esteem, and discrimination [by] family or by institutional third parties such as employers or insurers. Testing may disrupt parent–child

---

[73] For comment see Clarke, 'Is Non-Directive Genetic Counselling Possible?'; R. F. Chadwick, 'What Counts for Success in Genetic Counselling?' (1993) 19 *Journal of Medical Ethics* 43; and A. Clarke, 'Response to: What Counts as Success in Genetic Counselling?' (1993) 19 *Journal of Medical Ethics* 47.

[74] House of Commons Science and Technology Committee, 'Human Genetics', para. 90.

or sibling bonds, may lead to scapegoating a child with a positive result
or to continued anxiety over a child despite a negative result ... [75]

In other words, such practices can have serious implications for the
child's privacy interests – both spatial and informational. However, the
principle of autonomy cannot help children in such circumstances. As
minors, the respect due to them and their wishes is furnished through
their guardians, who must act in their best interests. But the best interests
of a child are not served by a parent who requests a test for a condition
such as Huntington's disease. There is no reason not to delay testing until
the child can understand the implications of testing and can decide for
herself whether or not to know. This view is supported by bodies such
as the House of Commons Science and Technology Committee,[76] the
International Huntington's Disease Association and the World Federation of Neurology.[77]

The British Medical Association has also considered the merits of the
introduction of screening for Duchenne muscular dystrophy (DMD). In
evidence to the House of Commons Science and Technology Committee
the argument was put thus: 'One of the advantages of early screening
is that it warns parents of the risk of recurrence in subsequent children ... potential carriers in the family can be informed of the risk. The
knowledge would also avoid a delay in diagnosis ... and would enable
parents to prepare themselves for the future, such as modifying their
home to accommodate a wheelchair.'[78]

Each of these justifications is open to question. First, a positive or
negative diagnosis in one child tells us nothing about future risk in future
children. If present, the condition might be the result of spontaneous
pathology; if a negative result is returned, this might simply be because
the test is unable to detect a particular mutation. Second, early diagnosis
and preparedness are not always beneficial, as we have seen with the
example of Huntington's disease. Third, the test is done not in the best

---

[75] See D. C. Wertz et al., 'Genetic Testing for Children and Adolescents: Who Decides?' (1994)
   272 Journal of the American Medical Association 875, 878.
[76] House of Commons, Human Genetics, at 80.
[77] See D. Ball, A. Tyler and P. Harper, 'Predictive Testing of Adults and Children' in A. Clarke
   (ed.), Genetic Counselling: Practice and Principles (London, Routledge, 1994), pp. 69–74.
[78] House of Commons, Human Genetics, Memorandum, Volume II, at 116. The Association
   did also note disadvantages: 'Parents are told that their son will develop a fatal condition
   for which there is no cure, years before the first symptoms appear', ibid.

interests of the child, and certainly not to protect the privacy interests of the child, but rather to favour the reproductive autonomy of the parents. The acceptability of this is questionable, and leads us to wonder how the interests of children are best protected. These challenges would render a screening programme for DMD unacceptable and probably unethical.[79] And, as has already been argued, because the principle of autonomy is less strongly invoked for minors, the claim on behalf of the minor to prevent such an interference with her interests is less well grounded if it is grounded solely in the principle of autonomy.

But, even in the case of adults, the perceived utility of autonomy-based arguments extends beyond circumstances in which a meaningful choice is within the grasp of an individual. For, even in cases where no choice has been made or where no meaningful choice is possible for want of information, autonomy is frequently advanced as a reason to put individuals in a position whereby they can choose. As has been suggested, the facilitation of choices is generally a given good in contemporary health care.[80] However, it is important to distinguish between cases in which the doctor–patient alliance has been established at the behest of the patient, and those in which an individual is approached by a doctor, or some other party, with information that is perceived to be of benefit to the individual's future health. In the former case, an alliance has been established whose goals have been agreed by the parties, and where the promotion of the patient's health and autonomy is among those goals. In the latter case, there is no mutually agreed alliance, and unilateral efforts to 'optimize [someone else's] future health'[81] are ontologically and ethically different. Indeed, Malm has gone so far as to argue in the context of speculative screening that while a recommended treatment for a patient should be justified on the 'preponderance of the evidence' as embodying a benefit, in the case of preventive medicine 'the evidence must show it to be beyond reasonable doubt that the recommended

---

[79] The Science and Technology Committee recommended that 'There should be no mass screening for public health reasons in childhood unless a treatment for the disorder exists', *ibid.*, para. 92.

[80] See J. Katz, *The Silent World of Doctor and Patient* (New York, The Free Press, 1984), p. 141, who argues that 'The inevitable conflict that such insistence [on disclosure and conversation] creates between the values of autonomy and privacy should be resolved in favour of autonomy. Such invasions of privacy must be tolerated in order to enhance patients' psychological autonomy through insight and not allow it to be further undermined by too hopeful promises, blind misconceptions and false certainties.'

[81] B. Charlton, 'Screening Ethics and the Law' (1992) 305 *British Medical Journal* 521.

procedure will benefit the patient on balance'.[82] The Council of Europe has recommended that unexpected findings from genetic analysis should not be communicated to potentially affected parties unless the person himself/herself has asked for the information, and the information is not likely to cause serious harm to his/her health (including that of family members) or the information is of direct importance for his/her medical treatment.[83]

Autonomy and genetic information

The broader relevance to genetic information of what has been said about autonomy should be obvious. It has been argued that such aspects of the self as the body and personal information require respect under the principle of autonomy. The principle also dictates that individuals deserve respect concerning the choices that they make about what happens to their bodies and their personal information. Thus the principle prescribes that choices concerning genetic information are equally deserving of respect. Several problems, however, become immediately apparent. First, given that some forms of genetic information have direct impact on a number of individuals in a family, how can the principle of autonomy help to resolve conflicts that might arise about the control and use of the information? For example, if patient A is tested and found to be a carrier of cystic fibrosis, does his pregnant sister have a right to the information so that she can make an appropriate and autonomous choice about her pregnancy? In other words, what is to be done when two autonomies conflict?

Second, it has been noted that there exist in both ethics and law certain basic criteria that must be met for someone to qualify as an autonomous individual. Central to the modern conception of autonomy is *choice*, and in particular, choices must be taken free from interference and by those who have the capacity to do so. But, in turn, fundamental to such choices is knowledge. One cannot choose in a meaningful sense if one is not informed of the parameters within which one must choose. This is why informed consent is crucial to ethically and legally

---

[82] H. Malm, 'Medical Screening and the Value of Early Detection: When Unwarranted Faith Leads to Unethical Recommendations' (1999) 21 *Hastings Center Report* 26, 36.

[83] Council of Europe, Recommendation on the Protection of Medical Data (1997, No. R (97)5), para.170.

acceptable health care. However, in the context of genetics this causes a problem. If in order to choose one must have knowledge, then the giving and receiving of knowledge become crucial to the proper operation of the principle of respect for autonomy. But in many circumstances the problems surrounding genetic information are precisely concerned with the absence of knowledge. This is the basis of the claim to respect the interest in not knowing genetic information. In such cases, the choice is one about knowing itself. The choice, then, is whether to receive or not to receive information about oneself. This is problematic for the concept of autonomy because it is difficult to see how one can exercise meaningfully a choice not to know unless one has a certain degree of knowledge about the subject matter of one's choice. An obvious practical solution would be to approach the individual and ask, 'do you want to know this information?', but as Wertz and Fletcher have pointed out, 'There is no way . . . to exercise the choice of not knowing, because in the very process of asking, "Do you want to know whether you are at risk . . . ?" the geneticist has already made the essence of the information known.'[84]

This is not to say that one cannot simply state: 'I wish to know no information about my genetic make-up whatsoever', nor is it to suggest that such a wish should not be respected. However, the requirement that autonomous choices be informed choices tends to imply that the credibility of an uninformed choice is more easily questioned. It leaves the way open for it to be argued that actual knowledge about circumstances might nevertheless affect the chooser who might then choose differently if furnished with relevant information. The situation might be seen as analogous to the problem of the incapax. The individual who is incapax cannot choose for herself and so choices must be made for her. In the same way, the individual who is ignorant of genetic information might be seen as a pseudo-incapax, and therefore it might be assumed that it is legitimate to make choices about the genetic information on her behalf. At present and as we have seen, choices for the incapax are to be made in her best interests. It is far from clear, however, how one would determine an individual's best interests concerning genetic information. The ethical principles of non-maleficence and beneficence are largely unhelpful. These principles require that harm should be avoided and

---

[84] See D. C. Wertz and J. C. Fletcher, 'Privacy and Disclosure in Medical Genetics Examined in an Ethics of Care' (1991) 5 *Bioethics* 212, 221.

benefit conferred wherever possible. It is not clear, however, that best interests are clearly discernible on the facts of any given case once the interest in not knowing is acknowledged as a factor, for an appeal to beneficence and non-maleficence could both countenance and weaken a case for disclosure. One might, of course, seek to maximise the felicific calculus, but that in itself is a value-laden exercise, and if autonomy is given the importance that it has received to date, then disclosure is likely, because the bias is to allow persons to decide for themselves by knowing the options that are available. Not only is this a paternalistic assumption, but it also ignores the fact that an additional interest at stake is that concerning whether to receive knowledge at all. This seriously undermines the ability of an appeal to autonomy to protect individual privacy interests.

More particularly, law is generally blind to these privacy interests. Certainly, the law in the United Kingdom that protects individual autonomy provides no guidance for a disclosure dilemma. And, if disclosure occurs and harm results, there is no existing legal remedy that would entitle any person so harmed to claim a breach of an interest not to know.

The myth of consent as an ethical panacea

On the whole, the modern expression of autonomy is found in the imperative to obtain consent which is the first line of defence in any dealings between a health care professional and a patient. This is also true in the research context. The principle of respect for patient autonomy requires that consent be given both for the release of personal information – which has informational privacy implications – and for the collection of information – for example by testing – which has spatial privacy implications. Unfortunately, in many contexts and especially in those of employment and insurance, the individual from whom consent is to be obtained is in a substantially weaker position than the party seeking consent. This is also true in the doctor–patient relationship, albeit the motives of the health care professional are different from those of, say, employers or insurers. None the less, the imbalance of power in these relationships distorts their dynamics, leaving one party holding most, if not all, of the cards. Consent is treated as the ethically legitimating factor for the establishment and regulation of these relationships, but the reality is that the sole defence that consent provides to the individual is the power to refuse. However, the exercise of that power in the vast majority of cases is neither meaningful nor in the individual's interests, for to refuse will simply mean the end of the relationship, and so the end to any potential benefit that it might bring, such as health care provision, employment or insurance. Consent, then, is neither an effective nor adequate protection of individual interests on its own. Indeed, consent can be seen to legitimise requests and practices that are unacceptable in themselves. But where is the protection to ensure that such requests or practices are objected to long before consent enters the arena? Wherever that protection may be found, it will not stem from the principle of respect for autonomy alone.

The focus of modern autonomy discourse on individual choice also tends to ignore the fact that individual choices cannot be taken in isolation. The impact on a wider community should also be examined.[85] Consider, for example, the negative impact of consensually based screening programmes for sickle-cell disease that took place in the United States in the 1970s.

Sickle-cell disease is a recessive condition that affects particular ethnic groups,[86] and although incurable, it is treatable with blood transfusions if necessary. None the less, population screening programmes for this condition in the United States had to be abandoned because of the serious adverse consequences that resulted for the racial groups who were the focus of the programmes. Members of the relevant groups experienced racial and general discriminatory treatment, were denied insurance and employment, and suffered a high degree of stigmatisation. Furthermore, through public ignorance, even those who proved not to be affected by the condition were treated in this way, as were those who did not choose to participate in screening.[87]

---

[85] R. R. Sharp and M. W. Foster, 'Involving Study Populations in the Review of Genetic Research' (2000) 28 *Journal of Law, Medicine and Ethics* 41, and E. T. Juengst, 'Commentary: What "Community Review" Can and Cannot Do' (2000) 28 *Journal of Law, Medicine and Ethics* 52.

[86] The condition primarily affects Afro-Caribbeans. When the trait is homozygous the condition is known as sickle-cell disease.

[87] This experience is recounted by the Nuffield Council on Bioethics in its report on *Genetic Screening: Ethical Issues* (NCB, London, 1993), ch. 2, paras. 8.13–8.14. Skene also notes that similar discrimination and stigmatisation has arisen in Greece as a result of sickle-cell anaemia screening programmes: see L. Skene, 'Mapping the Human Genome: Some Thoughts for Those Who Say "There Should Be a Law On It"' (1991) 5 *Bioethics* 233, 238.

From the perspective of autonomy, the argument that individuals must be allowed to choose whether or not to know information about themselves carries all the more weight in such a context, given the potential for serious adverse consequences that can arise from the fact of having been tested. But, more worryingly, it is important also to note that such group-centred programmes can lead to discrimination against persons even if they have not been tested, because the mere existence of the programme gives cause to treat such persons differently solely because of their membership of a perceived high risk group. This has implications for individual autonomy, albeit in an indirect way. Screening programmes can adversely affect all of the persons who constitute such a group, because wider societal reactions to the programmes can lead to a shutting down of options and a closing off of avenues, all of which restrict choice and the ability of group members to act as autonomously as they would like. It is not enough to protect against such eventualities simply to say that screening programmes are consensual. The ethical propriety of screening programmes does not turn only on obtaining consent from those who choose to participate, because the mere existence of such programmes might also have consequences for those who choose not to participate. These experiences teach us valuable lessons about offering screening for conditions such as sickle-cell anaemia. To avoid such outcomes screening should not be implemented without corresponding public education programmes and other measures such as anti-discrimination laws to ensure that the US experience is never repeated. But perhaps this is an attempt to treat the symptom rather than the cause. A priori, the establishment of screening programmes must rest on surer ground than the facilitation of individual choice and individual autonomy, and the onus must be on those who advocate the establishment of such programmes to provide such justification. The wider impact of facilitating individual choice cannot be ignored.

Matters can best be summed up by this passage from Ngwena and Chadwick in the context of familial interests:

> what has to be taken into account is the fact that respecting the autonomy
> of one person may have implications for the autonomy of others. As
> the Royal College of Physicians argue, 'Blood relatives have an interest
> in knowing the truth which has nothing to do with influencing their

behaviour towards affected individuals in their families, but as a necessary means to finding out the truth about themselves' . . . How is the choice between the autonomy of different people made? . . . What is clear is that the decision cannot be taken *on autonomy grounds*.[88] (emphasis added)

This suggests that the inherent conflict that can arise in such a situation is irresolvable if one appeals simply to the principle of autonomy. Autonomy and consent are not universal panaceas to the ethico-legal dilemmas that we face in contemporary society.

Autonomy and the right not to know

The particular limitations of autonomy in the context of genetics are best seen when attempting to make sense of, and to protect, an interest in not knowing.[89] The challenge to this application of autonomy has been set out above. Presently it will be contrasted with the suitability of the concept of confidentiality to serve this role, and ultimately both confidentiality and autonomy will be set against the concept of privacy advocated in this book in a defence of this last's adeptness at promoting and protecting the interest not to know. First, however, it is apposite to explore further the limited role of autonomy in this regard.

Jorgen Husted has argued that a right not to know can be based on the principle of autonomy provided that one adopts a 'thick conception' of autonomy.[90] By this he means a view of the autonomous individual as one who takes direct responsibility for her life, and for the decisions that form and shape that life.[91] Central to this conception is the idea of *self-definition*: 'what makes a life *ours* is that it is fashioned by our choices, is selected from alternatives by a human being taking his or her life seriously and wanting to be, and be recognised as by others as [sic],

---

[88] See C. Ngwena and R. Chadwick, 'Genetic Diagnostic Information and the Duty of Confidentiality: Ethics and Law' (1993) 1 *Medical Law International* 73, 77. This point is also made by Chadwick in 'The Philosophy of the Right to Know and the Right Not to Know' in R. Chadwick, M. Levitt and D. Shickle (eds), *The Right to Know and the Right Not to Know* (Aldershot, Avebury, 1997), p. 15.

[89] See also J. Raikka, 'On the Morality of Avoiding Information', in V. Launis *et al.* (eds.), *Genes and Morality* (Amsterdam, Rodopi B. V., 1999), ch. 6.

[90] See J. Husted, 'Autonomy and a Right Not to Know', in Chadwick *et al.*, *The Right to Know and the Right Not to Know*, pp. 55–69.

[91] He contrasts this with the 'thin conception' of autonomy which, 'aims to explain the autonomous person and the autonomous life by way of explaining the kind of choice characteristically made by the former and defining the latter, *viz*. the autonomous individual choice', *ibid.*, p. 59.

the kind of person who makes decisions and accepts the responsibility for them'.[92]

Husted argues that the imposition of unwarranted information is an autonomy issue, because choices and decisions must now be taken in the knowledge of information never previously requested, and thereby the individual loses the ability to direct her life as she might otherwise have wished.[93] This argument is not entirely convincing, however, because it requires us to adopt a view of autonomy that is unrealistic. It is a view that requires us to say that informed choice is not autonomous choice. Consider this passage:

> in many cases [of unsolicited information] what were initially very valuable options for the person to choose (for one set of reasons) or not to choose (for a different set of reasons) were being closed down by disclosure. Of course, the option still remained open for the person, but the reason why he or she did not choose it was not that another one was considered more valuable. The reason was that she or he could not take the responsibility for choosing it, i.e. choosing it being aware of the genetic warning, because it would be a morally wrong thing to do, e.g. start building a family knowing in advance what kind of suffering this project of one's is bound to create for other people. Where the person concerned was formerly pondering the various options for trying to make something worthwhile out of life, accepting the normal hazards of life, she or he may now be struggling for survival. And as a result of this the history of that person's life may very well not be the history of an autonomous life, a life whose contents, for a significant part, are freely chosen among different and morally valuable alternatives. The history of that person's life might rather come to resemble the life of a person who had to become an electrician in order not to have to murder someone else[94] – a life of morally forced choices.[95]

This is a perplexing view of autonomy for several reasons. First, it is not the case that decisions taken in the light of knowledge (solicited or otherwise) are not autonomous decisions. All of the decisions that we take are taken in the light of the information and options available to

---

[92] *Ibid.*, pp. 61–2.   [93] *Ibid.*, p. 66.

[94] This example of the person who must choose between becoming an electrician or a murderer is a reference to a discussion that occurs earlier in the chapter concerning Joseph Raz's view of autonomy. Raz opines that autonomous choices must be choices between moral 'goods' and that a choice between good and evil is not an autonomous choice, *ibid.*, p. 62.

[95] *Ibid.*, pp. 66–7.

us, and while it is correct to say that we may choose differently once exposed to certain knowledge, it is not accurate to imply that choices in the light of unasked-for knowledge are somehow, by that fact alone, not *our* decisions.

Second, it is difficult to see how one can resolve the problem posed by Husted from within an autonomy model. He advocates a view of autonomy that is predicated on 'free' choices, but this seems to suggest that it is entirely possible to make free choices about the direction of one's life. This is simply not accurate, or at least one must accept that 'freedom' in this context is a relative term. No choices are completely unfettered, and few choices are taken in a moral vacuum. And, while one's choices can certainly be adversely influenced by pressure from others, it is not clear that there is a significant enough degree of pressure from merely offering people information to warrant the conclusion that this somehow interferes unacceptably with their autonomy. It does not, to the extent that these persons can still make choices for themselves according to their own values and moral code. The situation would be different if the information was accompanied by a prescribed course of conduct, for example, the offering of an antenatal test for Huntington's disease on the condition that the pregnancy be terminated if the result is positive, as discussed above.

Finally, Husted does not draw any distinction between choices not to know and no choices at all. For it is accepted that to offer unsolicited information to a person who has expressed a wish not to know it is to disrespect the autonomy of that person. In the circumstances spoken of by Husted, however, when there is no previously expressed wish in respect of the information – that is, an exercise of autonomy – then it is unconvincing to argue that to offer the information is an unwarranted interference with autonomy.

The general sentiment expressed by Husted is a central theme of this book; namely, that it is unacceptable in many circumstances to give individuals unsolicited genetic information. However, it is argued here that the interference is with the spatial privacy interests of the individuals in question, rather than with their autonomy *per se*. This reveals both an overlap and a division between the concepts of privacy and autonomy. So far, we have considered the extent to which autonomy can help to protect privacy interests. The conclusion must be that autonomy can achieve this to an extent. But to attempt to subsume privacy interests under a modified view of autonomy is unacceptable for at least two reasons. First, it further distorts autonomy and perpetuates the erroneous view that autonomy is the trump ethical principle in modern medical law and ethics. Second, it denies a further and better possibility, namely that protection for privacy in itself is a preferable option. This is not to say in any way that the two concepts are or should be mutually exclusive, but it does recognise that the two might be complementary, and that autonomy should not necessarily be our first or last port of call in the search for resolution to contemporary bioethical dilemmas.

The ultimate example of misplaced faith in the powers of autonomy to protect the interest in not knowing can be seen by examining the international response. While both the UNESCO Universal Declaration on the Human Genome and Human Rights and the Council of Europe Convention on Human Rights and Biomedicine seek to protect the interest in not knowing, both do so through the mechanism of autonomy. For example, Article 10(2) of the Council of Europe Convention states: 'Everyone is entitled to know any information collected about his or her health. However, the wishes of individuals not to be so informed shall be observed.' Similarly, the UNESCO Declaration provides in Article 5c: 'The right of every individual to decide whether or not to be informed of the results of genetic examination and the resulting consequences should be respected.' This is admirable as far as it goes, but here the interest in not knowing is only protected when the individual can exercise the choice not to know. If, however, she truly does not know that there is anything to know, how can such a choice be meaningfully exercised? The answer is that it cannot, and a mechanism that focuses on choices must accordingly be condemned as inadequate in fully protecting an interest not to know.

Confidentiality

In the search for a robust theory of genetic privacy it is essential to examine the role of the medico-legal concept of confidentiality. And, as a starting point, it is important to stress that confidentiality should not be taken as a synonym for privacy. While the two overlap in many ways, they are by no means identical. Confidentiality, for example, is concerned as much with the protection of a relationship as with personal information, while the invocation of privacy requires no relationship and is concerned with interests that encompass, but also extend beyond, security of personal information. In particular, while confidentiality cannot protect the interest in not knowing, as this section will demonstrate a properly designed right to privacy may do so.

Conceptual underpinnings of confidentiality

Confidentiality is concerned with security of information. To be precise, it is concerned with the security of confidential information. To be confidential, information must be in a state of limited access from individuals, groups, bodies and institutions generally. Confidentiality is characterised by a relationship involving two or more individuals, one or more of whom has undertaken – explicitly or implicitly – not to reveal to third parties information concerning the other party to the relationship. It is widely accepted that health care professionals owe a duty of confidence to their patients and that only rarely should disclosure without patient consent be made. Although exceptions to the duty exist in most countries, no breach is made lightly or without good cause. In sum, confidentiality is the duty of the health care professional and the right of the patient.

While medical confidentiality is the classic exemplar of the duty of confidence, the legal basis for that duty has been extrapolated at a much broader level of abstraction, so that the fundamental principles that underpin obligations of confidence cut across many areas of life.[96] Thus, certain threshold principles are common to the creation of all such obligations. For example, information that is in the public domain cannot be confidential and therefore cannot be protected by confidentiality. Similarly, once information moves from the private sphere to the public sphere, it loses the necessary quality of confidence, and so any continuing duty of confidence falls. Indeed, it would appear that almost any form of information can come within an obligation of confidence provided that it has 'the necessary quality of confidence'.[97] Thus trade secrets,[98]

---

[96] For an historical account of the action of breach of confidence, see R. G. Toulson and C. M. Phipps, *Confidentiality* (London, Sweet & Maxwell, 1996), ch. 1, and F. Gurry, *Breach of Confidence* (Oxford, Clarendon Press, 1984).

[97] See Megarry J in *Coco* v. *A N Clark (Engineers)* [1969] RPC 41. This does not, however, cover 'trivial tittle tattle', *ibid.*, at 48.

[98] See *Printers and Finishers Ltd.* v. *Holloway* [1965] 1 WLR 1.

business practices,[99] and government data,[100] as well as personal information, can be confidential.

Professional and ethical sources of the duty of confidence are also frequently invoked. The British General Medical Council[101] and the American Medical Association[102] issue explicit guidelines to their members on the importance of patient confidentiality and the sanctions that are attendant on breach. In turn, these professional guidelines are founded on the ethical parameters that support the prima facie imperative to respect confidences.

Although confidentiality does not form one of the core principles of ethics that have been outlined earlier, for many the concept has nevertheless been 'elevated to the status of a principle of Medical Ethics'.[103] Ethical justifications for the duty of confidentiality are found in principles considered to be fundamental to our social value system. These appeal both to public and private interests in security of personal information. For example, Ngwena and Chadwick argue cogently that justifications for protecting confidences are found both in the principle of utility and the principle of autonomy.[104] They contend that considerable utility can flow from respecting confidentiality since this can protect individuals from harm. Discrimination and stigmatisation can result from disclosure of sensitive personal information of any kind, and this is certainly true of genetic information. Moreover, to keep confidences fosters trust in the health care relationship, which can only be seen as a 'good

---

[99] See *Faccenda Chicken* v. *Fowler* [1986] 1 All ER 617.

[100] See *Attorney General* v. *Guardian Newspapers No.2* [1990] 1 AC 109, and *Lord Advocate* v. *Scotsman Publications Ltd.* 1989 SLT 705, HL.

[101] The GMC outlines several principles which form the basis of its guidance on confidentiality, in *Confidentiality: Protecting and Providing Information* (London, GMC, 2000). As it states in Section 1.1, 'Patients have a right to expect that information about them will be held in confidence by their doctors. Confidentiality is central to trust between doctors and patients. Without assurances about confidentiality, patients may be reluctant to give doctors the information they need in order to provide good care.'

[102] Principle IV of the American Medical Association Code of Medical Ethics states: 'A physician shall respect the rights of patients, of colleagues, and of other health professionals, and shall safeguard patient confidences within the constraints of the law.' See also Council on Ethical and Judicial Affairs, 'Fundamental Elements of the Patient-Physician Relationship' (1990) 264 *Journal of the American Medical Association* 3133: 'The patient has the right to confidentiality. The physician should not reveal confidential communications or information without the consent of the patient, unless provided for by the law or by the need to protect the welfare of the individual or the public interest.'

[103] See Ngwena and Chadwick, 'Genetic Diagnostic Information and the Duty of Confidentiality', 74.

[104] *Ibid.*, 74–9.

thing'.[105] By the same token, and as has already been argued, adherence to an autonomy model of health care requires respect not only of individual patients themselves but also of their interests, including interests in personal information. To protect confidentiality is, therefore, to respect the individual.

Raanan Gillon endorses this view. As he has stated,

> [The principle of autonomy] requires us to consult people and obtain their agreement before we do things to them. As an individual we do not have any general obligation to keep other people's secrets, but health care workers, explicitly or implicitly, promise their patients and clients that they will keep confidential, the information confided to them. In other words, medical confidentiality is another implication of respecting people's autonomy. Without such promises of confidentiality, patients are far less likely to divulge the often highly private and sensitive information that is needed for their optimal care; thus maintaining confidentiality not only respects patients' autonomy but also increases the likelihood of our being able to help them.[106]

An appeal to principles such as autonomy and utility is important, because it provides strong justification for protecting personal health information through the concept of confidentiality. It imbues confidentiality with a value of its own for the interests that it serves and protects. This sets the concept up as being of prima facie value and worthy of respect, in much the same way as the principle of autonomy. However, this view does not hold confidentiality out as a supreme value. If to maintain confidentiality risks harm to others the principle of non-maleficence might be invoked to justify a departure from this practice. Similarly, if to disclose personal details without the consent of the patient is thought to be in the patient's medical interests, justification for this can be found in the principle of beneficence. Each case will depend on its own circumstances, but the process is in the nature of a balance of interests, and this in turn is reflected in law.[107]

In most countries the legal duty of confidentiality is not absolute, and certain exceptions are admitted, including actions to prevent harm

---

[105] *Ibid.*, 75.

[106] R. Gillon, 'Medical Ethics: Four Principles Plus Attention to Scope' (1994) 309 *British Medical Journal* 184 at 185.

[107] P. Moodie and M. Wright, 'Confidentiality, Codes and Courts: An Examination of the Significance of Professional Guidelines on Medical Ethics in Determining the Legal Limits of Confidentiality' (2000) 29 *Anglo-American Law Review* 39.

to third parties.[108] While the sources of this duty in law are many and
varied,[109] in each case the duty arises with respect to the specific relationship that the professional has with patients qua patients.[110] In
the United States, however, it is not thought to be the case that legal duties arise merely by virtue of the fact that an individual comes
into possession of personal information about another.[111] Thus, absent some specific customary or professional, contractual or impliedly
contractual relationship,[112] a duty to maintain confidences is unlikely
to exist.[113] By way of contrast, the law in the United Kingdom is such
that a duty of confidence can arise provided that a reasonable person
would realise, or should have realised, that she was receiving information in circumstances that imported a duty of confidence.[114] This tends
to suggest that British health care professionals come under a duty of
confidence whenever they receive personal information about patients
in a professional capacity, even if they have no direct relationship with
those patients. More questionable, however, is the legal basis for this
duty.

Libling has argued that if time, money and effort are expended in
obtaining or creating information, this is a 'valuable entity' which can

[108] For example, in *Hague* v. *Williams*, 181 A. 2d. 345, 349 (1963), it was stated: 'Although
ordinarily a physician receives information relating to a patient's health in a confidential capacity..., where the public interest or the private interest of the patient so demands,...disclosure may, under...compelling circumstances, be made to a person with
a legitimate interest in the patient's health.'

[109] For an account of the situation in the United States, see W. Roach, Jr, *Medical Records and
the Law*, 3rd edn, (Gaithersburg, MD, Aspen Publishers Inc., 1998), pp. 91 *et seq.*

[110] In the UK, Caldicott Guardians are appointed in each NHS health organisation to ensure
due respect for the handling of patient-identifiable information; see Caldicott Committee,
Report on the Review of Patient-Identifiable Information (London, NHS Executive, 1997).

[111] See Note, Alan B. Vickery, 'Breach of Confidence: An Emerging Tort' (1982) 82 *Columbia
Law Review* 1426.

[112] In *Quarles* v. *Sutherland* 389 S.W. 2d 249 (Tenn. 1965) the provision of free medical treatment meant that no contractual duty arose between physician and patient, and so no duty
of confidentiality. In *Macdonald* v. *Clinger* 446 N.Y.S. 2d. 801 (N.Y. App. 1982) the court
stated: 'We believe that the relationship contemplates an additional duty springing from
but extraneous to the contract that the breach of such duty is actionable as a tort.' This is a
fiduciary relationship arising from the contractual nature of the relationship: *Hammonds*
v. *Aetna Cas. and Sur. Co.*, 243 F. Supp. 793 (N.D. Ohio 1965).

[113] In *Darnell* v. *Indiana* 674 N.E. 2d 19 (Ind., 1996) a physician–patient privilege statute was
construed narrowly to exclude nurses from the duty of confidentiality; similarly, in *Evans* v.
Rite Aid Corp., 478 S.E. 2d 846 (S.C. 1996) and *Suarez* v. *Pierard* 663 N.E. 2d. 1039 (Ill. App.
1996) pharmacists were held to have no duty in the absence of a contractual obligation.

[114] See *Attorney General* v. *Guardian Newspapers, (No.2)* [1990] AC 109 (henceforth *Spycatcher*);
Lord Advocate v. *Scotsman Pub. Ltd.*, 1989 SLT 705; *Stephens* v. *Avery* [1988] Ch 449.

be the subject of a property right.[115] By extension it could be argued that the basis of the action of breach of confidence is a desire to protect the property interest in the information. However, a property analysis of information suffers from serious problems. For example, what if the information arises from a relationship between two or more persons or bodies? Who *owns* the information? Is it an example of common or joint ownership? If so, who should control the information? Moreover, how are disputes between parties to be resolved given that the parties to the relationship can simultaneously and yet independently possess and control the valuable entity in its entirety? For these reasons and others, Jones has argued that property cannot be the basis of the action of breach of confidence.[116] Rather, he posits that the basis of the action is the 'broad equitable principle of good faith', namely, that 'he who has received the information in confidence shall not take unfair advantage of it'.[117] This relates, in part, to the general notion that we should not be allowed to take unfair advantage of others. This avoids the problems of trying to fit a concept such as information into an existing and rigid set of rules such as the law of property.[118] Because good faith is based on abstract principles this facilitates the development of the legal protection of confidential information along its own lines into something of a sui generis form of protection.[119] This is certainly the view taken by the English and Welsh Law Commission in its 1981 report: 'the courts do not confine

[115] D. F. Libling, 'The Concept of Property: Property in Intangibles' (1978) 94 *Law Quarterly Review* 103.

[116] G. Jones, 'Restitution of Benefits Obtained in Breach of Another's Confidence' (1970) 86 *Law Quarterly Review* 463, at 464–5. He notes that 'A cursory study of the cases, where the plaintiff's confidence has been breached, reveals great conceptual confusion. Property, contract, bailment, trust, fiduciary relationship, good faith, unjust enrichment, have all been claimed, at one time or another, as the basis of the judicial intervention. Indeed some judges have indiscriminately intermingled all these concepts. The result is that the answer to many fundamental questions remains speculative.'

[117] *Ibid.*, at 466 quoting *Seager* v. *Copydex Ltd* [1967] 2 All ER 415, at 417 and *Fraser* v. *Evans* [1969] 1 All ER 8, at 11.

[118] Another view is that the law seeks to protect the relationship rather than the information *per se*, S. Wright, 'Confidentiality and the Public/Private Dichotomy' (1993) 7 *European Intellectual Property Review* 237. However, this argument is seriously undermined by the reality outlined by the House of Lords in *Spycatcher* and its Scottish equivalent *Lord Advocate* v. *Scotsman Publications*. In neither case was there any form of relationship between the confider (the government) and the third party coming under an obligation of confidence (the newspapers).

[119] See also G. Wei, 'Surreptitious Takings of Confidential Information' (1992) 12 *Legal Studies* 302, who states that 'the majority view is that the action is founded on equitable notions of good faith'.

themselves to purely equitable principles in solving the problems which arise in breach of confidence cases and it would seem more realistic to regard the modern action as simply being *sui generis*.[120]

However, the ruling of the House of Lords in the *Spycatcher* case – which clarified considerably the modern law of confidence in the United Kingdom and which gave authority to the position that an objective assessment of circumstances can give rise to a duty of confidence – also gives considerable weight to the argument that the basis of the action lies in the law of Equity.[121] Most recently, Toulson and Phipps have suggested that the foundation of the action of breach of confidence in England and Wales is indeed an equitable obligation, binding in conscience, and arising from the circumstances in which one receives the information.[122] They agree with Jones that the law of confidence is sui generis in that it has developed a unique niche for itself in law, but they argue none the less that the foundational basis of the action is clear and lies in Equity.[123]

An irony for Scots law arises from this. The House of Lords confirmed in *Lord Advocate* v. *Scotsman Publications Ltd* that the law in respect of confidentiality was the same in Scotland as in England and Wales, but to locate the foundation of confidentiality in good faith or equity poses a problem for the Scottish courts. First, to found the action in a general obligation not to treat others unfairly lacks substance in both Scots and English law. There is, for example, no law of unfair competition as this is understood in other jurisdictions. Second, to imply that the basis of the action is founded in the English law of Equity tells us nothing about the Scottish source, for Scots law has no conception of the law of Equity and such a law is of no standing in the Scottish legal system. Nevertheless, as Lord Keith stated in *Lord Advocate* v. *Scotsman Publications Ltd*, 'While the juridical basis may differ to some extent in the two jurisdictions, the substance of the law in both of them is the same.'[124]

[120] Law Commission, Breach of Confidence, Law Com. no.110, Cmnd 8388 (1981), p. 11.
[121] See, for example, Lord Keith at 255E, Lord Griffiths at 268A and Lord Goff at 281D–E. For comment, see D. Capper, 'Damages for Breach of the Equitable Duty of Confidence' (1994) 14 *Legal Studies* 313.
[122] Toulson and Phipps, *Confidentiality*, ch. 2 generally, and specifically at paras. 2.12–2.24.
[123] *Ibid.*
[124] *Lord Advocate* v. *Scotsman Pub. Ltd.*, 1989 SLT 705 at 708. A similar position subsists in Australia, see *Smith Kline & French Laboratories (Australia) Ltd.* v. *Secretary to the Department of Community Services and Health; Alphafarm Pty Ltd.* v. *Secretary to the Department of Community Services and Health* (1991) 99 ALR 679, and there is also some supporting authority in the United States, see *E I Dupont de Nemours Powder Co.* v. *Masland* 244 US 100 (1917).

Despite the above, one common and unifying source for the duty of confidentiality can be identified from the case law. That source is the public interest. In both *Spycatcher* and *Lord Advocate* v. *Scotsman Publications Ltd* the House of Lords made it clear that the protection of confidences finds considerable justification in the public interest. For example, Lord Keith in *Spycatcher* stated that 'as a general rule, it is in the public interest that confidences should be respected . . . '.[125] Similarly, Lord Goff commented in the same case that

> I start with the broad general principle . . . that a duty of confidence arises when confidential information comes to the knowledge of a person (the confidant) in circumstances where he has notice, or is held to have agreed, that the information is confidential . . . The existence of this broad general principle reflects the fact that there is such a public interest in the maintenance of confidences, that the law will provide remedies for their protection.[126]

Confidentiality in health care

Legal decisions on medical confidentiality stress the important public interest(s) served by respecting patient confidences. For example, the case of *X* v. *Y* concerned the disclosure to a reporter from a national newspaper of personal health information of two general practitioners with AIDS by an employee of a health authority.[127] The health authority sought and obtained an order restraining the publication or use of the confidential information. Nevertheless, an article was published and a further item was intended. The plaintiffs therefore sought, inter alia, an injunction restraining the defendants from identifying the two doctors and an order from the court requiring the newspaper to disclose its sources. In reply, the defendants argued that publication was justified in the public interest and that the public had a right to know that doctors were continuing to treat patients while infected by AIDS.

Rose J refused to authorise disclosure in the public interest. He held that the plaintiffs were entitled to a permanent injunction against the defendants to prevent them from publishing the confidential information in any form. Whereas he did not deny that there was a public interest

---

[125] *Attorney General* v. *Guardian Newspapers (No.2)* [1990] AC 109 at 256A.
[126] *Ibid.*, at 281B–C.   [127] *X* v. *Y* [1988] 2 All ER 648.

in public health, he did not accept the argument that this interest would
be furthered by disclosure of the sensitive, personal and confidential information. Indeed, his view was that the public interest that formed the
basis of the protection of confidence in the first place would be compromised to an unacceptable degree if the confidences were not respected.
He noted that public health was not under threat from doctors who
continued to practise general medicine, although the situation might
be different if they were engaged in invasive procedures. While there
was a clear public interest in freedom of the press this was not sufficiently strong in the circumstances of the present case to merit breach
of confidence.[128] Finally, Rose J drew a very important distinction concerning the meaning of the public interest: 'There is a wide difference
between what is interesting to the public and what it is in the public
interest to make known.'[129]

Several observations can be made of this decision. First, and axiomatically, there is a strong public interest in protecting patient confidences.
Second, there is no absolute duty to do so, but when conflict arises the
balance must be between competing public interests, and most notably
between the public interest in maintaining confidences – which will be
taken as a given – and the challenging public interest. In particular, it is
important to note that the balance is not between the patient's private
interest in keeping her information secret and the public interest that
would justify disclosure. Such a balance would always weigh in favour
of the latter interest.[130] Third, to be acceptable the breach of confidence must assist in furthering the competing public interest. This was
clearly not possible in *X* v. *Y*. Moreover, if some other means of furthering the public interest can be found which does not involve a breach
of confidence then that option should be preferred. Also, confidential
information should only be released to the extent that is required to
further the public interest in question, and disclosure should only be

---

[128] *Ibid.*, at 658d–661g.
[129] This is the frequently cited quote from Lord Wilberforce in *British Steel Corporation* v.
Granada Television Ltd [1981] AC 1096 at 1168.
[130] *X* v. *Y*, at 660–1, and *W* v. *Egdell* [1990] 1 All ER 835, in which Sir Stephen Brown commented: 'in so far as the [first instance] judge referred to the "private interest" of W, I do
not consider that the passage in his judgement accurately stated the position . . . Of course
W has a private interest, but the duty of confidence owed to him is based on the broader
ground of public interest described by Rose J in *X* v. *Y*', at 846g–h; also *per* Bingham LJ at
849d–e.

made to those parties that are in a position to further that interest.[131] Finally, in determining legitimate public interests, some tangible benefit to the public must be demonstrated and not mere titillation or entertainment.

The value of this case is found in its defence of the private and public interests that support strong legal protection of confidentiality. Its weakness lies in the failure to express more clearly the precise nature of the concept of public interest. Such lack of clarity in the law has been compounded by subsequent decisions that have served to reinforce the point that the duty of confidence is a relative notion which depends on a just balance between competing interests. At the same time these rulings have resolutely failed to specify when and how a legitimate public interest defence might be raised. Thus, in *W* v. *Egdell* the Court of Appeal unhelpfully pointed out that 'a doctor has a duty not only to his patient but also to the public',[132] and went on to hold that it was a defence to a breach of confidence action for a psychiatrist to reveal his assessment of a prisoner to the relevant authorities to block the prisoner's move to a less secure unit. This was so despite the fact that Dr Egdell was the only psychiatrist to take a negative view of the prisoner's mental state, and the fact that the patient would remain within a criminal and medical control environment.

The matter of public interest even arises at the stage of disposal, as was demonstrated in *R. v. Crozier*.[133] In criminal proceedings the accused, Peter Michael Anthony Crozier, pleaded guilty to the attempted murder of his sister. When sentence was pronounced one week later no psychiatric report was available to the defence even although the accused had undergone evaluation. The judge therefore proceeded in the absence of medical evidence and sentenced Crozier to nine years' imprisonment. As this was happening the doctor who had most recently assessed the accused entered the court and was alarmed to hear that a custodial sentence was to be imposed. He approached counsel for the Crown and disclosed the contents of his report which concluded that the accused was suffering from a mental illness of a psychopathic nature and that he should be detained under the provisions of the Mental Health Act 1983. As a result the Crown sought a variation of the sentence under

---

[131] See also *Lion Laboratories* v. *Evans* [1985] QB 526 at 536.
[132] *W* v. *Egdell*, at 852h–853a.   [133] *R. v. Crozier* (1990) 8 BMLR 128.

Section 47(2) of the Supreme Court Act 1981 to replace the custodial sentence with a hospital order. At the third hearing counsel for the appellant argued that the judge should disregard the evidence contained in the psychiatric report because it should never have been placed in the hands of the Crown as a confidential document between the appellant and the examining physician. Rather, it should have been a matter for the appellant and his counsel to decide whether or not to disclose the report. Had correct procedure been followed neither the Crown nor the judge would have been aware of the report's contents. The judge ruled, however, that justice demanded that he consider any medical evidence put before him. An appeal was lodged to the Court of Appeal challenging the trial judge's disposal and arguing that it was invalid because it took into account a report which was released in breach of patient confidentiality.

The Court of Appeal asked two fundamental questions: did the psychiatrist (Dr McDonald) breach confidentiality, and, if he did, was he justified in doing so?[134] Quoting heavily from the dicta of Bingham LJ in *W* v. *Egdell*, the court regarded Dr McDonald as very much in the same position as Dr Egdell. That is, the clinician was in possession of information that he felt was of vital importance concerning the treatment of one who had previously committed violent crime. As in Egdell's case, it was held that there was a strong public interest that favoured disclosure. Dr McDonald was, therefore, acquitted of any 'impropriety' and the disposal confirmed.[135]

Typically for a medical confidentiality case, *R.* v. *Crozier* does not contain any deep analysis of the content of the public interest. The Court of Appeal relied exclusively on the decision in *W* v. *Egdell*, but the facts of the two cases are not on all fours. In *Egdell* the decision that was to be taken concerned the first move in the process of release of the patient. In *Crozier* there was no question of the release of the accused; rather it was a matter of the appropriateness of disposal. There could not have been any immediate or even foreseeable danger to the public arising from the instant decision of the trial court. Certainly, a difference in the two proposed disposals is the question of time limits: the initial imprisonment was for a period of nine years, whereas the hospital order could be imposed without limit of time. But it is surely better and more credible

[134] *Ibid.*, at 134.   [135] *Ibid.*, at 136.

to argue that a hospital order was in the *patient's* (better) interests rather than in the *public* interest. Unfortunately, the law of confidence does not seem to provide for this. Another distinction between the cases concerns the relative threat that the respective patients posed to the public interest. Unlike patient *W* who had attacked and killed several individuals randomly, Crozier's crime was person-specific and arose from particular circumstances within his family.[136] From this it is arguably less clear that Crozier posed as great a threat, or indeed any threat, to the general public. What the court says about the public interest defence is in effect very little, except perhaps that it can be used to justify breaches of confidence when there is no immediate threat to the public interest and where it is far from clear how dangerous the individual in question actually is.

This judgement also calls us to question several other aspects of the duty of confidentiality. For instance, what is the difference between a breach of confidence for which there is a defence – for example, the defence of public interest – and the disclosure of confidential information in circumstances that do not amount to a breach of confidentiality even when the confider objects to disclosure? Does the latter imply that no duty exists in those circumstances? In other jurisprudence the Court of Appeal has suggested, for example, that it is possible for information to be disclosed without a confider's consent and that this would not amount to a breach of confidence. This is not an issue of mere sophistry. It matters very much whether or not a prima facie duty is owed but breach is justified or whether no duty is owed at all. For one thing, it means that patients are not entitled to expect that as a matter of course their confidences will be respected. Furthermore, it has consequences for evidential burdens. If no prima facie duty is owed then the task of proving breach of confidence becomes correspondingly more difficult for the plaintiff. Clearer explication of the parameters of the duty and indeed of when such a duty comes into being, or ceases to be, is required. Perhaps the closest indication of the true position comes in the Court of Appeal's ruling in *Re C (A minor)*.[137] This case concerned a general practitioner who disclosed the contents of a woman's file without her consent in support of an argument that she was not fit to object to the adoption of her newborn child. Of this, Stuart-Smith LJ said:

[136] He attacked his sister with an axe when, as co-trustee for a trust set up for Crozier's daughter, she disputed his management of the monies.
[137] *Re C (A Minor)(Evidence: Confidential Information)* (1991) 7 BMLR 138.

It seems to me that the doctor was plainly under a duty to treat the information given by the patient in confidence *in general terms*. For example, she would plainly be in breach of that duty to disclose any matters to the press or people who were not concerned. The court is concerned with the breach of the duty. I am by no means satisfied that, in the circumstances of this case, there was any breach of that duty in disclosing these matters to those who were concerned with the welfare of the child, namely the court and the solicitors for the adopters.[138] (emphasis added)

It is reasonable to interpret this passage as meaning that the duty owed by doctors to patients is one of a general nature that does not necessarily extend to specific circumstances, an example of which arose in the instant case. If this is true it removes the prima facie assumption that health care professionals owe their patients a duty of confidentiality over all information received as soon as the therapeutic alliance is formed.[139]

Further limits to the duty of confidence are revealed by one of the Court of Appeal's latest offerings.[140] In *R. v. Department of Health, ex*

---

[138] *Ibid.*, at 144.

[139] Although it is not argued in the case, support for such a view can be found (albeit tentatively) in the dicta of Lord Goff in *Attorney General* v. *Guardian Newspapers Ltd (No.2)*, where at 281 he says: 'I start from the broad general principle (which I do not in any way intend to be definitive) that a duty of confidence arises when confidential information comes to the knowledge of a person (the confidant) in circumstances where he has notice, or is held to have agreed, that the information is confidential, *with the effect that it would be just in all the circumstances that he should be precluded from disclosing the information to others*' (emphasis added). By extension this would mean that in certain circumstances justice would dictate that a duty need not arise. On the facts of this case, the interests at stake as articulated by counsel for the appellant were those in maintaining confidentiality and those of justice. Rather than balancing the two (as counsel argued) one might choose, on the authority of Lord Goff, to submit that justice requires that no duty be seen to arise in the first place. This is borne out if one accepts the arguments that, in England and Wales at least, the duty of confidence is based in equity. What this means is that a court can recognise a right but refuse to protect it in particular circumstances because the rights are discretionary. See, for example, R. Wacks, *Privacy and Press Freedom* (London, Blackstone Press Ltd, 1995), p. 96. This would certainly provide an explanation for the decision of the Court of Appeal in *Re C*, even if the judges in that case do not choose to articulate their judgements in such terms. This explains nothing from the Scottish perspective. Finally, it is interesting to note that Toulson and Phipps, *Confidentiality*, are of the opinion that 'no obligation of confidence exists in contract or equity, in so far as the subject matter concerns a serious risk of public harm (including but not limited to cases of "iniquity") and the alleged obligation would prevent disclosure appropriate to prevent such harm', *op. cit.*, at 6.11. At 6.19–6.20 they discuss *W* v. *Egdell* and conclude that 'The danger to the public was such that, although there was a confidential relationship between the parties, the duty of confidence impliedly undertaken by the defendant *did not extend* to withholding information about the plaintiff's state of health from the responsible medical authorities' (emphasis added).

[140] For an expansionist view of the duty see *Venables and Another* v. *News Group Newspapers Ltd. and Others* [2001] 1 All ER 908.

parte Source Informatics Ltd the court was asked to rule on the legality of disclosing anonymised prescribing data to a firm that wished to sell them to pharmaceutical companies to facilitate the marketing of their products.[141] Pharmacists had been requested to provide details of general practitioners' prescribing habits, and all data were stripped of patient identifiers before being passed on. None the less, the Department of Health issued a policy statement to the effect that this practice was a breach of patient confidentiality, there being no provision in the process to obtain patient consent, nor could this be implied from the circumstances in which the information was originally generated. The Court of Appeal held, however, that there could be no breach of confidentiality because 'The concern of the law here is to protect the confider's personal privacy. That and that alone is the right at issue in this case.'[142] In the court's view patient privacy was not under threat because there was no realistic possibility that patient identity could be revealed. Moreover, because the obligation of confidence binds in conscience as an equitable doctrine, and because a reasonable pharmacist's conscience 'would not be troubled by the proposed use made of patients' prescriptions',[143] such treatment of patient information was entirely legal as a fair use.

This decision challenges the law of confidence at its very core. On extremely uncertain legal authority, the ruling shifts the basis of the duty of confidence from the public interest to the question of fairness of use. Furthermore, the court saw fit to re-assess the basis upon which a duty will arise and also how far it will extend, and thereby conflated the establishment of a duty with its scope. Yet, while the former is clearly founded in Equity in English law – where a proper role for the question of fairness might arise – the latter has traditionally been treated as a logically subsequent issue, and not one that is bound up with notions of equity.[144] But, in the light of the decision in *Source Informatics* the position now seems

---

[141]   *R* v. *Department of Health, ex parte Source Informatics Ltd.* [2000] 1 All ER 786.
[142]   *Ibid.*, at 797a.   [143]   *Ibid.*, at 796f.
[144]   For a legally enforceable right of confidentiality to arise several factors must be satisfied. First, the information must have the necessary quality of confidence about it; second, the information must be imparted in circumstances which import a duty of confidence; and finally, the information must be disclosed or used by the confidant without authority from the confider or without lawful excuse, as per the classic dicta of Megarry J in *Coco* v. *A N Clark (Engineers)* (1969) 86 RPC 41. It is also probably the case that a form of detriment must be shown, although in personal information cases it is sufficient that the individual would rather that the information not be disclosed.

to be that where there is no unfairness to the confider in a possible use of information then there is no breach of confidence, and this is so even when that use is unauthorised. This, however, goes against a number of established principles in this area of law. Existing precedents have made it clear that public interest is the basis of the duty of confidence, and that in large part this also dictates the exceptions to the rule. Normally, information provided in confidence must be treated as such and should not be used for any purpose that transgresses the legitimate boundaries of the consent provided by the confider. And, while a defence in public interest might be available, the onus has been on those who would use the information to demonstrate that the particular use is in a public interest, or otherwise to obtain appropriate consent. However, this decision indicates that the onus has shifted to the confider to show unfairness of use before an action will lie. Moreover, it removes the public interest requirement from the equation, and this is particularly disturbing because it also led the court to ignore the wider and longer term impact of its decision on the public interest in maintaining confidences generally.

An express motive for the court in this regard was the desire to obviate an ever-burgeoning and indistinct public interest defence, but it has succeeded only in replacing the amorphous concept of public interest as a limiting factor on the existence of a duty with the equally unclear concept of fairness as a measure of the scope of the duty. Indeed, if fairness is to become the measure of the scope of the duty of confidence, it is far from clear why, on equitable grounds, the focus should be the good conscience of the party who would disclose information, rather than the conscience of the party whose interests the duty is designed to protect. The answer given by the court, that the sole interest at stake is privacy and that this interest is protected because the patient's identity is protected, is not only to take an exceedingly narrow view of privacy – as the rest of this book would indicate – but it also ignores other perfectly valid claims that individuals might make over their personal information. These might emerge either as part of a richer concept of privacy, or as an aspect of individual autonomy, or indeed as a reflection of a property interest that individuals might have in their own information. But, having delivered a minimalist view of privacy, the court rejected out of hand any prospect that individuals might have a property interest in personal information, or that there might be wider autonomy issues at stake.[145] We shall return to the property issues in chapter 6. As for autonomy claims, Beyleveld and Histed rightly point out that it is easy to offer any number of examples of interests that individuals might have in their own information that are simply not acknowledged by this ruling.[146] They suggest, for example, that 'a patient may object to Source Informatics' scheme because he or she has deep personal ethical concerns about contributing to the profit making of large pharmaceutical manufacturers based on knowledge of those very manufacturers' lack of ethical concerns in other, less advanced, countries'.[147] But, because consent to the use of anonymised data need not now be obtained, a serious question arises over the respect that such a use of information shows for the individuals from whom it was derived.

The ultimate irony of this decision lies in the likely consequences for the individuals who would explicitly object to such uses. On what legal basis might they do so? Arguably, the effect of *Source Informatics* is to reduce the individual's legal interest in her own information to an interest in ensuring that her anonymity is maintained. Once that is assured her legal interests are exhausted. But other fundamental issues are ignored as a result, including the role of consent in legitimising otherwise unacceptable uses of information, the concept of legitimate expectations of use – why would we necessarily expect that information given for a perfectly legitimate health purpose could then be used for an entirely unrelated research or marketing purpose? – and the importance of maintaining a prima facie respect for confidences.

It is unclear how far the authority in *Source Informatics* will extend. On one view, it does not seem to hold that the mere anonymisation of information elides the possibility of a future action for breach of confidence, and the court quoted with approval *X* v. *Y* in this regard.[148] However, at the other extreme, the court seems to have rejected the role of public interest in both founding and potentially overriding a duty of confidence in preference for an assessment of the fairness of *any* particular proposed use, whether of anonymised data or otherwise. For example, when faced with evidence that identifiable patient data are used for research and management purposes, the response

---

[145] *R* v. *Department of Health, ex parte Source Informatics*, p. 797a–d.
[146] D. Beyleveld and E. Histed, 'Betrayal of Confidence in the Court of Appeal' (2000) 4 *Medical Law International* 277.
[147] *Ibid.*, at 295.   [148] *R* v. *Department of Health, ex parte Source Informatics*, at 792j.

of the court was that 'provided ... the use of such identifiable data is very strictly controlled, there appears to be no reason to doubt that it is acceptable – whether because it falls within the public interest defence, or as is perhaps the preferable view, because the scope of the duty of confidentiality is circumscribed to accommodate it'.[149] In other words, the court is prepared to accept that the duty of confidence might not extend to certain 'fair' uses of data at all. But we are left to wonder what the vagaries of judicial activism will make of that parameter, and whose interests will be furthered or compromised in the process.

At the broadest level of abstraction, however, the Court of Appeal has not departed from the starting premise that the question of where the limits of the duty of confidence lie is a matter of balancing interests. And, to the extent that the public interest defence remains in the wake of *Source Informatics* – and this must surely be an arguable case given rulings from the House of Lords that it is the appropriate legal stricture in such cases – it is important to point out that the invocation of the defence is a matter of discretion and not duty. That is, the common law does not require breaches of confidence to further the public interest, although additional statutory measures may do so, for example notifiable diseases legislation and measures to further public interests in research.[150] Similarly, *Source Informatics* merely legitimates certain uses of information, and indeed even facilitates them, but it does not require such uses of otherwise confidential information. But, even if a discretion over disclosure remains, the farthest-reaching effect of this ruling must lie in the fact that it creates an onus for the confider to show unfairness of use *before* a duty will arise in respect of her information.

What are the implications of this in the primary health care context? Well, it further undermines any expectations that patients will have about how health care professionals will treat their confidences. Research and marketing uses of health-related information have now been deemed to be fair uses when that information is anonymised, and patient consent need not be sought. Moreover, the door is left decidedly open for further argument that research or other uses involving

---

[149] *Ibid.*, at 800h–801a.
[150] On this latter point see the provisions of the Health and Social Care Act 2001, s.60, which allow the Secretary of State to make provisions requiring or regulating the processing of patient medical data in their own medical interests or in the public interest.

identifiable information might also qualify as fair uses, with the attendant result that no duty of confidence will arise in respect of such information either. But what does this say of the duties of a health care professional towards her patients? If the prima facie respect for patient confidences is removed, it broadens considerably the scope of the discretion that a health care professional has over any uses of patient information, for now the primary obligation might not even arise so long as the use that is made of patient information is 'fair'. It will be for patients to show that any particular use is unfair. The professional is thus relieved of her secondary obligation to justify departing from a hitherto primary obligation of confidentiality, and the patient is burdened with showing unfairness of use of her own information. But in many cases the patient might find it impossible to do so because consent to a fair use need not be obtained, and so how will a patient know that a use has occurred if her doctor thinks that she herself is acting fairly?

The effects of this legal ruling will be tempered by professional and ethical standards as outlined above, which embody a more respectful model for dealing with patient information and which hopefully will guard against cavalier uses of such information. It should also be remembered that data protection measures will assist in protecting patient privacy, as we shall see presently. None the less, *Source Informatics* might equally signal a cultural and attitudinal shift in the therapeutic relationship, which undoubtedly conceals many unlooked for consequences. It is submitted, however, that by far the better view of the law is that confidentiality is always the right of the patient and the duty of the doctor, and that the onus should fall on the latter to justify departing from this principle. As has been argued above, public and private interests strongly support this position.

Confidentiality and the law

With the exception of *Source Informatics*, then, the above survey of cases reveals the essential features that give rise to a legal duty of confidence and the circumstances in which such a duty can be breached with just cause. Such a duty arises where confidential information is exchanged between parties in circumstances where the parties know or ought to know that the information should remain confidential. In the United Kingdom, this is so even if there is no contractual agreement between the parties or even an express undertaking to maintain confidentiality. On such a view, it is strongly arguable that a duty of confidence is owed by all health care professionals to their patients by virtue of the nature of their relationship and the sensitive nature of information that is exchanged in the course of the relationship. Such a view is supported by both ethical principles and professional guidelines, and the fact that the law departs from this position in the wake of *Source Informatics* is accordingly highly questionable on ethical and professional grounds.

However, to the extent that *Source Informatics* says nothing to modify the legal position once a duty is accepted to exist, the question of when confidential information can be disclosed is dealt with, in the first in-stance, by reference to patient consent. Thus, prima facie, the patient should be consulted about any disclosure of information to others. If consent is forthcoming there can be no question of breach of confidence. If, however, consent is not forthcoming and a health care professional discloses information regardless, this normally constitutes a breach of duty. The only justification then possible is that the disclosure was nec-essary and within the terms of one of the defences to an action for breach of confidence. As we have seen, the most frequently used defence and yet the most difficult to define is that of public interest. In such cases, when faced with a question of justified breach of confidence the courts must balance two public interests: that of maintaining confidentiality and that put forward as a defence for the conduct that would otherwise constitute a breach.

The category of public interests that can qualify for the defence is clearly not closed. It already includes the prevention and detection of crime, the protection of the public from dangerous individuals, and the welfare of children. In certain cases it might be considered that the defence has been stretched to justify a particular outcome, as for example, the decision in *Re C*.[151] In each case, however, the concern of the courts has been to avoid harm to third parties, either as members of a non-specific group such as the general public, or even a single member of a specified group, such as the class of children generally.[152]

---

[151] *Re C (A Minor)(Evidence: Confidential Information)* (1991) 7 BMLR 138, discussed above.

[152] In the employment context, the Public Interest Disclosure Act 1998 protects workers who reveal otherwise sensitive information to further certain designated public ends. For com-ment see Y. Cripps, 'The Public Interest Disclosure Act 1998', in J. Beatson and Y. Cripps, *Freedom of Expression and Freedom of Information* (Oxford, Oxford University Press, 2000), ch. 17.

Thus, the determining factor in recognising third party interests and in balancing these interests with those of the confider has been whether significant harm can be avoided by disclosure of confidential information. In practical terms this places a heavy burden on the shoulders of the health care professional, for neither law, nor ethics, nor professional guidance offers clear direction as to the circumstances in which breach of duty of confidence will be justified, except in the most general of terms. The matter is left to the discretion of the individual health care professional. Although, to the extent that there might be a question over the fairness of use and so the existence of a duty ab initio, that burden may be set to shift in the shadow of *Source Informatics*.

Confidentiality and genetic information

As with the principle of respect for autonomy discussed above, the relevance to genetic information of what has been said about confidentiality should be self-evident. Clearly, although a health care professional owes a duty to respect a patient's genetic information as confidential, conflicts can arise about access to that information and its control, and the problem becomes whether the health care professional would ever be justified legally, ethically or professionally in disclosing such confidential data. So, how do the rules relating to confidentiality apply to genetic information, especially when one considers that third parties such as relatives or the state can claim a significant interest in many forms of this information? If consent to disclosure is not forthcoming, the most likely answer lies once again in the public interest.

The parameters of public interest

Axiomatically, in order to determine which circumstances provide justification for disclosure it is necessary to identify a relevant public interest. Furthermore, it is necessary to demonstrate that the breach of the confidence will de facto further the competing public interest, or at least that there is a reasonable likelihood of this. Thus, for example, the public interests of preventing harm to others and halting the spread of disease are relevant factors when treating patients infected with HIV. These interests might be furthered by informing the sex partner of an intransigent

seropositive patient of the latter's condition.[153] In this way, the sex partner can make future informed decisions, inter alia, about unprotected
sexual relations with the infected person. If the partner chooses to act
responsibly infection will not take place and the public interests that
served as justification for breaching the patient's confidentiality will be
furthered.[154] As a corollary, if a public interest cannot be realised the justification for breaching patient confidentiality is lost. Moreover, it is also
important to weigh in the balance the significant public interest in generally maintaining confidences, and it must be asked whether competing
interests are strong enough to outweigh that interest. Finally, alternative
means of realising the competing public interest should be explored and
if such exist these should be preferred to a breach of confidence.

These factors have clear potential application in the context of genetics, for it might be argued that the prevention of harm to others and the
reduction of the incidence of genetic disease are legitimate public interests that can be furthered through disclosure of genetic information.
This will be explored below. However, to set the scene for this discussion it is important to bear in mind what has been said about the nature
of genetic disease and the relative paucity of cures. These factors have
a direct bearing on any decision concerning the use to which genetic
information is put. Indeed, together with what has been said about the
role of the public interest, they provide a model for determining the legitimate boundaries of the duty of confidentiality with regard to genetic
information.

Confidentiality and informational privacy interests

When a health care professional receives genetic information about a
familial hereditary disease, perhaps through testing of one or more members of that family, what is the scope of her obligations to the persons
to whom that information relates, and most particularly, where are the
beginning and the end of any obligations of confidence?

---

153 For commentary on this see K. M. Boyd, 'HIV Infection and AIDS: The Ethics of Medical
Confidentiality' (1992) 18 *Journal of Medical Ethics* 173, and S. Guttmacher, 'HIV Infection:
Individual Rights v. Disease Control' (1990) 17 *Journal of Law and Society* 66.
154 In a number of US states specific statutory provisions impose a duty of disclosure on HIV
positive persons to disclose their status to their partners: see J. W. Rose, 'To Tell or Not
to Tell: Legislative Imposition of Partner Notification Duties for HIV Patients' (2001) 22
Journal of Legal Medicine 107.

In the first instance the most ethically and legally acceptable course of conduct would be to approach the affected individual to encourage her to inform relatives or to seek permission allowing others to do so. If, however, permission is refused and the health care professional considers that she should nevertheless inform the rest of the family about the condition, the obvious question that arises is whether she can do so without facing a successful action of breach of confidence from her own patient.

One way to consider the public interest defence in this context is to turn it around and ask: which public interests might be jeopardised by non-disclosure of genetic information? Certainly, the interest in preventing harm to others is of paramount importance and is often considered to be of sufficient weight to justify compromising confidentiality. However, can harm be prevented by disclosure in the context of genetics? If a cure for a particular debilitating condition exists it would be foolhardy not to inform relatives of a highly predictive predisposition to such a condition, especially if pre-emptive treatment could prevent the onset of disease.[155] An example is haemochromatosis. This is the most common recessive disorder in the United Kingdom. Around one in every 500 people have the gene (HFE). The condition causes excess accumulation of iron in the body. Where the iron collects fibrosis occurs. Liver cirrhosis, diabetes and heart failure are common related conditions. The symptoms and severity of the condition vary considerably between individuals, but if caught early the condition can be palliated by periodic phlebotomy (blood-letting). The condition is late onset and might not affect women until after the menopause because of menstrual loss of iron which delays onset. Although no cure is available, early phlebotomy can reduce considerably the risk of fibrosis. And because haemochromatosis is a recessive disorder the average chances of relatives in a family being affected range from 25 to 50 per cent in each case. All of this might be taken as the basis of a strong case to justify disclosure to potentially affected individuals.

However, the nature of recessive disease also teaches us that there is a 25–50 per cent chance in each case that relatives might be asymptomatic

[155] However, in circumstances where a cure is available but an individual would not choose to take it – perhaps for religious reasons – it is hard to see how disclosure could be justified because the perceived harm will not be avoided, save for the paternalistic argument that the individual might be persuaded to change her mind.

carriers of the condition, and that there is a 1:4 chance that any particular individual will be unaffected. Indeed, these figures represent the highest possible index of risk and are true only if both parents are at least carriers themselves. If this is not the case, then an individual cannot be personally affected by disease (absent spontaneous mutations), and at worst might be a carrier. It accordingly becomes less clear that disclosure of information about risk that is in breach of another's confidence is justifiable in the public interest. Also, we must consider the harm that is to be avoided. Is it harm to an individual's health – for example, if a person is likely to be affected by disease – or is it harm to lifestyle choice, which arises if the risk is that of carrier status? If the risk is merely harm to choice – such as the choice whether or not to procreate – this weakens considerably the force of a public interest argument, although often the realities of the supposed harms are rarely examined.[156]

One response might be that it is in the public interest to minimise harm generally. This involves the recognition that various forms of harm can arise from disease, and the unrelenting progress of disease itself is but one form of harm. Psychological harm can occur, for example, from the unpreparedness of sufferers faced suddenly with a clinical condition or the knowledge that this could be passed to their progeny. Such harm can, arguably, be minimised by the knowledge that disease will, one day, manifest itself. This allows the individual time to come to terms with her fate and to commence, where possible, early supportive counselling. Yet, as has been argued in chapter 3, if disclosure is made to avoid an ancillary harm such as psychological distress or psychiatric disturbance, then there is less of a guarantee that the harm in question will de facto be avoided. That is, it is not clear that the public interest that one seeks to further by disclosure will actually be achieved. Indeed, the opposite might be true.

The health care professional faced with this dilemma is restricted in at least one further way. Although it is entirely possible to establish statistically the abstract chances of members of a family being affected by a recessive disease, in practice there is no way of knowing which individuals might or might not be affected or have carrier status. To be truly

---

[156] As Ngwena and Chadwick have pointed out, 'It is not clear . . . why choice in this area should be given higher priority than choice over the use of personal information . . . [and] it is not clear that harm to *choice* itself is sufficiently serious to warrant disclosure', Ngwena and Chadwick, 'Genetic Diagnostic Information and the Duty of Confidentiality', 86.

effective disclosure would require to be made to a wide circle of persons with possible diminishing utility. Thus the confidentiality of the original patient who is the source of the familial data would be breached on many occasions with unpredictable, and possibly minimal, results. While this is less true with monogenic conditions such as haemochromatosis, it is certainly true with multifactorial conditions and information about familial susceptibilities.

Might it be argued, however, that disclosure of genetic information to relatives is justifiable on the grounds of halting the spread of genetic disease? Although little or nothing can be done for those already afflicted by genetic disorders, disclosure might prevent the transmission of defective genes to future persons. Is there, then, a public interest in public genetic health?

The public interest in preventing the spread of disease is extremely important, but the point has already been made that in the context of genetic disease the furtherance of this public interest is hindered by one factor – there is no certainty that even if disclosure is made people will no longer reproduce or will only reproduce in a 'responsible' fashion. This, coupled with the fact that the interest can only be furthered through a breach of confidence, casts considerable doubt on the public health justification. Furthermore, potentially more effective means exist by which this public interest can be furthered and which do not involve a breach of confidentiality. These include counselling services, prenatal testing and abortion, and such measures should be preferred to advance any such policy of disease prevention.

Thus, to the extent that these realities about genetic information should call us to question very seriously the admissibility of a public interest defence to the disclosure of confidential genetic information, it can be said that the duty of confidence is perfectly amenable to protect the informational privacy interests of patients as regards their own genetic information.

The role of consent in justifying uses of confidential information

Does confidentiality protect individual informational privacy interests of those suffering from a condition such as alpha$_1$-antitrypsin when employers or insurers seek access to medical records to determine whether someone has this condition or whether they have been tested for it?

Alpha$_1$-antitrypsin is a genetic enzyme deficiency and those with the gene have a high risk of developing adult-onset emphysema. This can be exacerbated by particle-filled living or working environments and is an obvious condition of interest to employers and insurers alike.

In these circumstances it matters very much whether the health care professional from whom information is requested is in the employ of the insurance company or the employer making the request. If this is the case, then she owes a duty of fidelity to her employer and this will require that relevant information be passed on. This is why insurers will frequently require that prospective insured attend the insurers' own clinicians. Similarly, a workplace doctor who is employed to carry out regular examinations of staff is bound by the terms of her contract to deliver information to the employer if this might have a bearing on the employer's business.[157] In such circumstances the legal positions of the doctor and the 'patient' in the United Kingdom are laid out primarily in the Access to Medical Reports Act 1988. This Act establishes a right of patients to have access to reports prepared by a health care professional for employment or insurance purposes.[158] Section 3 of the Act provides that an employer or insurer shall not apply to a medical practitioner for a medical report relating to any individual unless (i) the individual is notified in advance, and (ii) written consent is provided by the individual. In this way the possibility of breach of confidence is avoided because consent is obtained from the subject in question.[159]

However, the most important limitation on the protection afforded by this Act is that it only extends to reports prepared by a health care professional who 'is or has been responsible for the clinical care of the individual'.[160] Thus an insurer or employer can avoid these provisions simply by requiring the individual to see a new doctor, most probably their own. Moreover, before information is revealed to the employer or insurer it will be taken that the patient has tacitly consented to disclosure by virtue of the fact that she has presented herself for examination.

---

[157] *Kapfunde* v. *Abbey National plc and Daniel* (1998) 46 BMLR 176.

[158] Access to Medical Reports Act 1988, s.1.

[159] One could easily mount an argument that consent in such cases will rarely be 'freely' given, in that the individual is in a substantially weaker position compared with the employer or insurer for fear that a refusal would affect employment or insurance chances.

[160] *Ibid.*, s.2(1), referring to Data Protection (Subject Access Modification)(Health) Order 1987, SI 1987/1903. But see now the Data Protection (Subject Access Modification)(Health) Order 2000, SI 2000/413.

However, the question arises whether such consent is properly valid or informed. The element of coercion that is inherent in a request that she see an unfamiliar health care professional calls into question the validity of tacit consent, and indeed of any written consent to disclosure that is obtained. An individual may of course refuse to attend for examination, but the consequence may well be refusal of insurance or employment or adverse consequences for current employment.[161] Fear, rather than a willingness to allow disclosure, might be the motivating factor in such cases.

Thus the present legal view of such medical examinations from the perspective of confidentiality is that communication of personal details to third parties would not be a breach of confidence because some form of consent to disclosure will be in evidence. But the law of confidence is seriously compromised in the context of such requests. In particular, it is questionable whether the law adequately protects the informational privacy interests of individuals from whom the information is sought. Consent may authorise disclosure but at the same time it elides the possibility of protection through the law of confidence.

In contrast, numerous examples of prohibitions on requests for confidential genetic information can be found in the United States. Pritts *et al.* reported on the state of health privacy throughout the fifty US states and the District of Columbia in 1999.[162] They found a number of features to be common to the plethora of statutes that have been enacted to protect the confidentiality of patient information. For example, only three states provided for comprehensive health privacy protection.[163] Rather, states tend to focus their attentions on the entities that use patient information, such as hospitals, schools, insurers, state agencies or physicians themselves, and accordingly state laws regulate activities in a piecemeal fashion. Second, there is often an underlying assumption that health care professionals owe a duty of confidence to their patients, and accordingly such statutes rarely provide for an express duty. However, in terms of protection, a significant number of states have enacted 'condition-specific requirements', that is, greater protection has been accorded to certain kinds of information because of its especially sensitive

---

[161] Subject, of course, to protection measures in employment law.
[162] J. Pritts *et al.*, *The State of Health Privacy: An Uneven Terrain* (Institute for Health Care Research and Policy, Washington DC, Georgetown University, 1999).
[163] Hawaii, Rhode Island and Wisconsin.

nature or the potentially grave impact of its release. So, for example, particular attention has been paid in many states to information relating to mental illness, communicable diseases, cancer and other stigmatising illnesses. Genetic privacy statutes are merely the latest illustration of this sort of response.[164] In some instances, the law completely outlaws access to such information. In Maryland, the law provides that 'an insurer, non-profit health service plan, or health maintenance organization may not . . . request or require a genetic test for the purposes of determining whether or not to issue or renew health benefits coverage'.[165] In New Hampshire, an employer may only use genetic test information 'to investigate a worker's compensation claim, or to determine exposure to toxic substances in the workplace'.[166] While in each case consent to the release of pre-existing data can authorise access, further use of those data to exclude individuals from insurance or employment is prohibited as discriminatory. In the United Kingdom, there is neither a prohibition on requests to generate new (genetic) health information nor any express prohibition on the discriminatory use of (genetic) health data.[167]

Most recently, long-awaited developments in privacy protection have occurred at the federal level in the United States, where before there was no protection whatsoever for patient privacy. Thus, as we saw in chapter 3, President Clinton signed an Executive Order in February 2000 that prohibits federal government agencies from obtaining genetic information from employees or job applicants and from using such information in employment decisions.[168] Finally, on 14 April 2001, the New Rule on Privacy Standards became effective. This obliges providers of health care, health insurers and healthcare clearing houses to adopt standardised levels of protection for patient health records by February 2003. All medical records and other individually identifiable health information held by such entities, in whatever form, are subject to the Rule. Key features include obligations to keep patients informed of the uses to which

---

[164] For an account, see National Human Genome Research Institute, *Health Insurance and Employment Discrimination* (Bethesda, MD, National Institutes of Health, 2001).

[165] Md. Insurance Code Ann. 27–909 (1998).   [166] N.H. Rev. Stat. Ann. 141–H:3.

[167] In this last regard indirect protection might arise from the Disability Discrimination Act 1995 if data were used as a basis to exclude someone from services or employment on the basis that she was 'disabled', but the Act only protects those who are currently disabled and not those who might become so in the future.

[168] President, Executive Order To Prohibit Discrimination in Federal Employment Based on Genetic Information, *Federal Register* 65 (8 February 2000).

their information might be put, patient rights of access to their own information, consent requirements before release of information, and the provision of avenues of recourse if privacy has been violated. Civil and criminal penalties attach to breaches of the Rule. With the exception of psychotherapy data which receive higher standards of protection, all health information is considered to be sensitive and must be treated consistently under the Rule. The Rule sets a base-line of protection which does not supersede state provisions where these confer stronger protection. Inter alia, the law will prevent health care providers and health plans from sharing health data with employers, except for the purposes of providing or paying for health care.

Not all entities or personnel involved in the process of delivering health care are covered by these provisions. For example, regulation of the activities of life insurers, researchers and public health officials do not come within the auspices of the Office of the Secretary of Health and Human Services, by reference to whose authority the Rule was enacted. Moreover, information generated by entities not affected by that authority is also excluded from protection. The general tenor of the Rule is one of balance between individual privacy interests and other public concerns such as research, public health, national defence, quality assurance, law enforcement, and other judicial or administrative proceedings. And, taken in tandem with the limitations on protection imposed by the powers of the Secretary, this broad range of uses in the public interest makes for a patchy quilt of privacy protection, even if that quilt does now extend across the entire country. Furthermore, the implementation process is likely to be slow and costly – the US government itself estimates a compliance expenditure in the region of $18 billion over five years. None the less, to the extent that these measures harmonise for the first time the institutional expectations of confidentiality that normally arise in the health care setting, they are to be welcomed. However, in comparison to many of their state counterparts, the Rule is crude in its conception. Most notably, the conspicuous absence of protection against discriminatory uses of data in turn puts too much emphasis on the role of patient consent to legitimise too many disclosures and uses. To this extent, the same criticism might be made of the US federal provisions as can be made of the British position regarding the protection of patient informational privacy interests through confidentiality.

Confidentiality and spatial privacy interests

While in practice there may be serious limits to the capacity of confidentiality to protect informational privacy, there is no reason in theory why an appeal to confidentiality cannot do so. Entirely the opposite is true, however, in the context of the protection of spatial privacy interests, and an example most clearly illustrates why this is so.

BRCA1 is the gene responsible for between 5 and 10 per cent of female breast cancers. It was discovered in 1994 and is known to be ten times longer than most human genes.[169] This fact means that the likelihood of mutations is increased and this in turn has implications for the efficacy of test kits designed to identify the gene, for they cannot detect all mutations. A high risk of metastasis is associated with the disease, but early detection and radical intervention in the form of mastectomy can virtually eliminate this risk. Preventive measures, also in the form of mastectomies, can reduce the instances of disease,[170] although the psychological effects of this course of action remain very unclear.[171] The condition is also thought to be multifactorial, further complicating matters. Consider, then, the following scenario.

> Nicola is aware of a history of breast cancer in her family. Her mother, her great-grandmother, and one of her aunts died from the disease. Nicola has a sister, Nadia, and three female cousins, Norma, Romana, and Elvira. She does not know the extent to which these relatives are aware of the pattern of disease in the family. Recently, Nicola discovered a lump in her breast which has been diagnosed as malignant. She is concerned that the BRCA1 gene runs in her family and that her sister and cousins are at risk. Nicola's physician has advised a mastectomy and has strongly urged her to contact her relatives to arrange testing. Should she approach her sister and cousins with the news of her own disease and urge them to seek medical advice? She is aware, for example, that Nadia is phobic about operations and that Elvira is prone to bouts of depression.

[169] The gene contains around 100,000 base pairs of nucleotides. It was discovered on 15 September 1994, by a team of researchers at the University of Utah.

[170] Tamoxifen has been used in the treatment of breast cancer for over two decades, but its preventative efficacy remains unknown. See S. Nayfield et al., 'Potential Role of Tamoxifen in Prevention of Breast Cancer' (1991) 83 Journal of the National Cancer Institute 1450.

[171] M. B. Hatcher, L. Fallowfield and R. A'Hern, 'The Psychosocial Impact of Bilateral Mastectomy: Prospective Study Using Questionnaires and Semistructured Interviews' (2001) 322 British Medical Journal 76.

The question at issue here is whether a sister should tell family members that she is affected by breast cancer and that they too might be affected. The spatial privacy interest at stake concerns the possible interest of the relatives in not knowing information about themselves. Can confidentiality protect this interest?

Prima facie, Nicola will be owed a duty of confidence by her health care professional. This entitles her to control the circumstances in which the health care professional can disclose her confidential information to others. She could, for example, object to any proposal by the health care professional to reveal her medical details to her relatives. If, however, Nicola herself decides to disclose these details, then there could be no question of a breach of the doctor/patient duty of confidence. Clearly she herself cannot breach a duty which is owed to her by another. Thus, for Nicola's disclosure to amount to a breach of confidence it must be seen to be an invasion of someone else's right and a breach of Nicola's duty to maintain confidentiality. The problem is essentially two-fold: (i) can a duty of confidence arise as between the relatives? and (ii) can such a duty protect the spatial privacy interest of relatives in not knowing information about themselves?

In the United States it is highly unlikely that a duty of confidence would arise in the familial context absent contractual or other legal impositions,[172] but in the United Kingdom one would ask, first, does the information have the necessary quality of confidence? and second, was the information imparted in circumstances that import an obligation of confidence? Both answers are returned in the affirmative. It is now well settled that personal information that is not of the nature of tittle-tattle and which is not part of the public domain can be protected as confidential information.[173] The second question is, however, less easy to answer. The confidential information must be *imparted* in circumstances that give rise to an obligation of confidence. This would tend to imply that the confider must furnish the confidant with the confidential information, but in our scenario the person to whom a duty

---

[172] In the United States it is not thought that legal duties arise merely by virtue of the fact that an individual comes into possession of personal information about another: see Note, 'Breach of Confidence: An Emerging Tort'. Absent some specific customary or professional, contractual or impliedly contractual relationship a duty to maintain confidences is unlikely to arise: see, for example, *Darnell* v. *Indiana*, 674 N.E. 2d 19 (Ind., 1996); *Evans* v. *Rite Aid Corp.*, 478 S.E. 2d 846 (S.C. 1996); and *Suarez* v. *Pierard*, 663 N.E. 2d. 1039 (Ill. App. 1996).

[173] First confirmed in *Stephens* v. *Avery* [1988] Ch 449 at 454–5.

might be owed, namely the relative, does not even know that the information exists, and therefore certainly could not *impart* it to any other person. This having been said, in the context of medical information one can easily imagine a scenario where information might be known to one party about another who is not aware of its existence, and from which a duty of confidence would arise. Thus a doctor may be in receipt of blood test results and feel that it would not be in a patient's interests to reveal them to the patient, but if the doctor revealed the results to a third party without just cause there can be no doubt that she would be in breach of patient confidentiality. In such a case one would never say that a duty of confidence is not owed. The duty arises here not simply because of the therapeutic relationship but also because of the sensitive nature of the confidential information itself. By extrapolation, Nicola might owe a duty of confidence in respect of her family's genetic information.

Moreover, the law does not necessarily require an original confider since information can assume the necessary quality of confidence even when the person to whom the right is owed does not know of its existence. In *Hellewell* v. *Chief Constable of Derbyshire* it was stated that:

> If someone with a telephoto lens were to take from a distance and with no authority a picture of another engaged in some private act his subsequent disclosure of the photograph would... as surely amount to a breach of confidence as if he had stolen a letter or diary in which the act was recounted and proceeded to publish it.[174]

This implies that there is no need for a pre-existing confidential relationship between any parties before a duty of confidence can arise. In older decisions it was always thought to be the case that such a relationship must exist.[175] Wacks has argued, however, that more recent authority supports the view that a relationship is no longer necessary,[176] and if this is so it is arguable that in our scenario a duty of confidence could be owed between the sister who has been tested for breast cancer and her female relatives also likely to be affected by the disease. However, a related issue concerns the question of the proper person to whom the duty is owed. In the *Hellewell* example the implication is that a duty

[174] *Hellewell* v. *Chief Constable of Derbyshire* [1995] 1 WLR 804 at 807.
[175] With the exception of illegally obtained information.
[176] Wacks, *Privacy and Press Freedom*, pp. 59–71.

of confidence is owed to the person who is the focus of the telephoto lens because the information that is received is about that person. In the context of genetic information the information concerns relatives only in part. It is not, therefore, entirely about them. This might alter the view one takes of the appropriateness of saying that a duty of confidence is owed to relatives.[177] If, however, one accepts the points put in the foregoing paragraphs, it would be sufficient to take a marginally liberal view of the shared nature of the genetic information to hold that a duty could be owed between relatives, but such a duty would probably be modified depending on the nature of the genetic information in question. For example, information about highly penetrant monogenic disorders would be more akin to information *about* a relative than that concerning multifactorial polymorphisms.

Yet, even if one is persuaded that a duty of confidence exists intra-familially, the far more crucial question is whether that duty can be breached by one relative telling the person to whom the duty is owed the information that is the subject of the duty. This must surely be a nonsense. A duty of confidence is breached when confidential information is used or disclosed to those outside the confidential relationship. This is well established.[178] Inherent in the concept of confidentiality is the idea that a breach of duty is constituted by making the information in some way public. Precisely how public the use or disclosure must be is a matter of debate, but it cannot be the case that disclosure of information from one party to a confidential relationship to the other party in any way makes the information public. This then means for our scenario that even if a duty of confidence is owed by Nicola to her female relatives she could not breach that duty by disclosing the information to the women themselves.[179]

---

[177] This is not a merely pedantic point. It matters very much whether or not a duty can be owed to someone simply because the confidential information is about that person. If, on the other hand, the duty is owed to the confider (who herself might be under a duty of confidence) then the person with whom the information is concerned will not be able to avail herself of a remedy using the law of confidence.

[178] See, for example, Gurry, *Breach of Confidence*, ch. 12.

[179] One might argue that for family member A to disclose information to family member C would be a breach of the duty that A owed to family member B, but given that the same information is the source of the same duty to the respective relatives, it is not clear that this argument would succeed, because this would be to argue that A was in fact breaching her duty to B by disclosing information to C which was nevertheless also about C and concerning which A also owed a duty to C.

None the less, such a disclosure might well be seen as a breach in the wall of privacy surrounding the relatives, but the law of confidence cannot help to establish a valid legal basis for a right not to know that will protect them. The consequence of this is that the concept of confidentiality does not accord a right to relatives of a proband to control the flow of familial genetic information towards themselves.

Further limits of the law of confidence

Confidentiality similarly cannot protect individuals from the generation of information about themselves. While requests or requirements from the state, insurers or employers to undergo genetic testing may well give rise to a duty of confidence that would exist between those who receive test results and those who are the subjects of such tests, the law of confidence cannot address all of the interests that arise from these testing practices. Principally, such interests include an interest in not being forced to know information that might be to one's detriment. The interference with spatial privacy interests that is inherent in such practices cannot be prevented by an appeal to the law of confidentiality for the reasons already articulated. This is a serious and further limitation on the law in the realm of genetic information given the not inconsiderable interests that individuals might have in such interests. Nor is consent necessarily a sufficient protection against such requests, once again as has been argued above.

The protection of privacy interests by autonomy and confidentiality

This section draws to a conclusion the second part of this book. We have examined the nature of privacy interests that individuals have in genetic information and identified those as being of two kinds: informational privacy interests which concern issues of security of existing information, and spatial privacy interests which relate to the protection of the self from unwarranted intrusion, including intrusion with information about one's own self. We have seen how the existing concepts of autonomy and confidentiality fare in protecting both of these types of privacy interests. We can conclude easily that the major problem arises in the context of spatial privacy. The law of confidentiality is entirely useless in protecting this interest, and the law that protects personal interests in autonomy does not achieve much more. Both confidentiality and autonomy can, to an extent, help to protect informational privacy but it is submitted that to leave privacy protection to these concepts is a wholly unsatisfactory state of affairs. What is needed is a useful, precise and effective means not only of conceptualising the interests involved, but also of protecting them in an appropriate fashion. The solution that is proposed is that of a robust concept of privacy. In the coming chapters the definition of privacy already argued for is defended further to show how the privacy interests involved can best be protected by an appeal to privacy itself.

5

Privacy and the public interest

Contemporary privacy protection

Not until the closing days of the twentieth century did the English courts eventually recognise a common law right of privacy.[1] Prior to this the judiciary had expressly denied such a right, suggesting that it was for Parliament alone to provide for privacy protection.[2] In ironic and stark contrast, the common law of privacy in the United States enjoyed a rich and productive twentieth century, its creation in turn having been instigated at the end of the previous century by the seminal work of Warren and Brandeis in which the authors relied on English common law actions in copyright, defamation and breach of confidence to argue for the existence of a US right to privacy.[3] We have considered these latter developments in chapter 2.[4] The more recent English volte face represents the culmination of a number of events that demonstrate how conceptually confused thinking continues to beleaguer this field of scholarship, making for ill-conceived and patchy privacy protection. These factors are (i) a failure to distinguish between the concepts of confidentiality and privacy, to the detriment of the legal protection of each; (ii) a lack of theoretical and definitional clarity as to the meaning of privacy more generally; and (iii) the advent of statutory developments that embody equally unclear conceptions of privacy, yet which at the same time have ushered in a new era of sensitivity to individual

---

[1] *Douglas and Others* v. *Hello! Ltd.* [2001] 2 All ER 289.

[2] See *Kaye* v. *Robertson* [1991] FSR 62, in which Leggatt LJ said at 71, '[the] right [of privacy] has so long been disregarded here that it can be recognised now only by the legislature ... it is to be hoped that the making good of this signal shortcoming in our law will not be long delayed'.

[3] S. D. Warren and L. D. Brandeis, 'The Right to Privacy' (1890–91) 4 *Harvard Law Review* 193.

[4] For the most enlightening account of the divisions and development of the US common law privacy right see W. Prosser, 'Privacy: A Legal Analysis' (1960) 48 *California Law Review* 338.

rights, making it politically more expedient to create a new common law right.[5]

Confidentiality and privacy

A frequently advanced option in the debate that has raged for many years both in the United Kingdom and elsewhere about the value of privacy and the proper method of its protection has been the extension of existing legal actions to protect privacy interests.[6] In the health care context and beyond, the most likely candidate has been the action of breach of confidence. Judicial developments in the last few decades have made this option all the more favoured, since they have removed some of the more obvious stumbling blocks to using this action to protect privacy. Thus, for example, the House of Lords in *Spycatcher* finally settled the point that a relationship need not exist between parties in order for a duty of confidence to arise.[7] Similarly, in *Hellewell* v. *Chief Constable of Derbyshire*,[8] the decision of the court that a duty of confidence could arise merely from the circumstances of taking a photograph has led some to argue that the duty can be imposed unilaterally.[9] As Fenwick and Phillipson say, 'It seems that there is only one ingredient which is essential: it must be shown that a reasonable person who acquired the information would have realised that it was confidential.'[10] The authors use this point as part of an argument that the law of confidence can now go a long way in

---

[5] See further B. S. Markesinis, 'Developing an English Law of Privacy', in B. S. Markesinis, *Always on the Same Path: Essays on Foreign Law and Comparative Methodology* (Oxford, Hart Publishing, 2001), II, pp. 321–421.

[6] See, for example, D. J. Seipp, 'English Judicial Recognition of a Right to Privacy' (1983) 3 *Oxford Journal of Legal Studies* 325, P. Prescott, '*Kaye* v. *Robertson* – a reply' (1991) 54 *Modern Law Review* 451. Cf. W. Wilson, 'Privacy, Confidence and Press Freedom: A Study in Judicial Activism' (1990) 53 *Modern Law Review*. Hogg considers a range of cases which can and have protected privacy interests, although ultimately he concludes that these are not adequate to protect the full range of interests subsumed under the privacy rubric: see M. Hogg, 'The Very Private Life of the Right to Privacy', in H. L. MacQueen (ed.), *Privacy and Property* (Edinburgh, Edinburgh University Press, 1994).

[7] *Attorney General* v. *Guardian Newspapers No.2* [1990] 1 AC 109. Arguably, however, this point was already settled in *Stephens* v. *Avery* [1988] Ch. 449, at 482.

[8] *Hellewell* v. *Chief Constable of Derbyshire* [1995] 1 WLR 804.

[9] See, for example, H. Fenwick and G. Phillipson, 'Confidence and Privacy: A Re-examination' (1996) 55 *Cambridge Law Journal* 447, 451–2.

[10] *Ibid.*, 452.

the context of invasions of personal privacy by the press.[11] Similar arguments have been made by Wee Loon, who has submitted that 'judicial activism is ... the answer to the inability of the present law in England to give better protection to an individual's privacy'.[12] This is precisely what happened in December 2000 in the Court of Appeal's decision in *Douglas and Others v. Hello! Ltd.*, in which it recognised for the first time an express common law right to privacy in English law.[13]

That the circumstances of this case were amenable to an action in breach of confidence is not in dispute. Two internationally renowned film stars sought to enter an exclusive agreement with a magazine to produce and publish the photographs of their wedding. Security measures at the event were extremely tight, and all persons in attendance were put on notice of the confidential nature of the proceedings. There is plenty of legal authority to suggest that the photographs in question would have the necessary quality of confidence.[14] However, when nine photographs were taken at the wedding by a party not privy to the agreement, the status of these photographs and the attendant interests surrounding their publication was put more in doubt. Even so, precedent had established that surreptitiously obtained photographs could be the basis for imposing a duty on the taker of those photographs when, objectively assessed, the circumstances would lead a reasonable person to realise that the proceedings, and so information obtained from them, were confidential.[15] But, as Brooke LJ pointed out, 'English law ... has not yet been willing to recognise that an obligation of confidence may be relied upon to preclude such unwanted intrusion into people's privacy when those conditions do not exist.'[16] However, while recognising the obligation of the courts to give effect to privacy protection, inter alia, in the light of the Human Rights Act 1998, his lordship was disinclined to explore the precise nature of the privacy

[11] This argument has been accepted by the European Commission on Human Rights, see *Earl Spencer v. UK* (1998) EHRR CD 105.

[12] N.-L. Wee Loon, 'Emergence of a Right to Privacy from within the Law of Confidence?' [1996] 5 *European Intellectual Property Review* 307, 312.

[13] *Douglas and Others v. Hello! Ltd.* [2001] 2 All ER 289.

[14] See, for example, *Pollard v. Photographic Co.* (1888) 40 Ch. 345 and *Argyll v. Argyll* [1965] 1 All ER 611.

[15] *Shelley Films v. Rex Features Ltd.* [1994] EMLR 134 and *Creation Records Ltd. v. News Group Newspapers Ltd.* [1997] EMLR 444.

[16] *Douglas and Others v. Hello! Ltd.*, 308a.

interests to be protected, it being his view that the criteria for confidentiality had been met and that a privacy argument would not 'add very much'.

Sedley LJ was of an entirely different opinion: 'we have reached a point at which it can be said with confidence that the law recognises and will appropriately protect a right of personal privacy'.[17] This process mirrors the US experience in that the court interpreted a right of privacy out of other actions, principally the action for breach of confidence.[18] But what does this new right look like? Is it purely a form of protection of confidentiality? If so, its scope will be drastically limited by the ruling in *Source Informatics*, as we saw in chapter 4, for this latter decision of the Court of Appeal reduces privacy protection to the mere protection of anonymity, and would allow the use of information so long as this use was deemed to be fair. An argument for the fairness of freedom of expression could certainly be mounted. So, if the clandestine photographer had anonymised the photographs by blanking out the faces of the bride and groom, would this be an end to the privacy protection of the individuals in question, on an application of *Source Informatics*? If it is not, then what is the scope of protection of this right of privacy? While Sedley LJ expressly stated that the right is grounded in confidence,[19] he went on to argue that it is 'a legal principle drawn from the fundamental value of personal autonomy'.[20] So which is it to be, confidentiality or autonomy? This is not to suggest that confidentiality and autonomy need be mutually exclusive, save that the Court of Appeal has more or less expressly stated them to be such in *Source Informatics*. Or at least, it held that so long as privacy is protected – defined along the strictest of terms to mean an interest in maintaining anonymity – then a duty of confidence will not arise in respect of personal information and that there is no further autonomy-based argument that can be mounted to protect a wider set of privacy interests. But from the theoretical standpoint it is entirely meaningful to ground privacy in the same value system as autonomy and, indeed, confidentiality – that is, respect for persons and their dignity. Now, however, there is no clear unifying approach in English law that explains how these principles of law relate to one another while at the same time delineating the appropriate content and parameters of each. If, however, it is the fundamental value of personal autonomy that

---

[17] *Ibid.*, 316h.   [18] *Ibid.*, 320c–d.   [19] *Id.*   [20] *Ibid.*, 320e.

grounds the privacy principle, then privacy is wider than confidentiality, admitting more interests and so offering a broader scope for protection.

Privacy and human rights

There is a further suggestion in *Douglas* v. *Hello!* that the stand-alone privacy right is broader than mere protection of confidentiality. This is because the court takes much of its authority for establishing the privacy principle in English law from the fact that the Human Rights Act 1998 is now in force. That Act embodies Article 8 of the European Convention on Human Rights, which provides that, 'everyone has the right to respect for his private and family life . . .'.[21] 'Private life' includes not merely a right to control personal information,[22] but also protection of privacy interests in physical and moral integrity,[23] the freedom to develop one's personality,[24] and the establishment and maintenance of personal relationships.[25] Moreover, the concept straddles the public/private divide, and it has been held also to protect professional and business activities.[26] Lastly, the right has been affirmed as encompassing both negative and positive obligations, that is, it is not merely a right to be free of interference but, in certain circumstances, it is also a right to have assistance in the fulfilment and enjoyment of one's private life.[27] All of these elements have conspired to make Article 8 one of the most politically useful articles of the Convention.

It remains to be seen what the UK courts will make of this right, but to the extent that it was cited in support of the recognition of a common law privacy right, and given that domestic courts must take into account the jurisprudence of the European Court of Human Rights in giving effect to the Human Rights Act, there is every indication that privacy protection in the United Kingdom is set to enjoy a much richer development than would be suggested by the conflation of privacy and confidentiality.[28]

---

[21] European Convention on Human Rights, Article 8(1).
[22] *Niemietz* v. *Germany* (1992) Series A, vol. 251-B.
[23] *X and Y* v. *Netherlands* (1985) Series A., vol. 91.
[24] *Gaskin* v. *UK* (1989) Series A, vol. 160.
[25] *Beldjoudi* v. *France* (1992) Series A, vol. 234-A.
[26] *Niemietz* v. *Germany* (1992) Series A, vol. 251-B.
[27] *Guerra and Others* v. *Italy* (1998) 26 EHRR 357.
[28] Cf. D. Feldman, 'Information and Privacy', in J. Beatson and Y. Cripps, *Freedom of Expression and Freedom of Information* (Oxford, Oxford University Press, 2000), ch. 19.

Disentangling privacy and confidentiality

While it is undeniable that there is considerable overlap between privacy and confidentiality, there are good theoretical and practical reasons to avoid confusing the two. As MacQueen has rightly pointed out, 'Whatever the merits of the debate, it is clear that confidentiality is not a complete substitute for privacy, and that there may be various problems which the law of confidence cannot reach.'[29] This remains true despite the developments outlined above. As Wacks has said,

> in general terms, the action for breach of confidence is inadequate to deal with the archetypal 'privacy' complaint because the action is largely concerned with: (a) disclosure or use rather than publicity, (b) the source rather than the nature of the information, and (c) the preservation of confidence rather than possible harm to the plaintiff caused by its breach.[30]

Also, as Hogg has noted, there must be use or disclosure of information before an action in confidence can lie, yet with privacy the invasion occurs when the information is obtained. Similarly, only the person to whom the duty is owed can sue for breach of confidence, and not necessarily the persons to whom the information relates.[31] Furthermore, an action of breach of confidence is possible only so long as the confidential information remains confidential. Once it becomes part of the public domain it is no longer protected. In contrast, privacy is concerned with interests in personal information and in the broader concept of personality, and those interests do not necessarily change with circumstances, nor do matters become any less personal simply because more people know about them.

But, within the context of this work, the major shortcoming of the law of confidence is revealed in its failure to take account of spatial privacy interests. The argument for this has been made above, but is repeated here to refute the notion that the law of confidence can dispel effectively our privacy concerns. If privacy is conceived not simply as a desire to control personal information, but rather as a general sphere of separateness from others and so also encompasses notions of spatial

---

[29] *Stair Memorial Encyclopaedia*, vol. 18, para. 1456.
[30] R. Wacks, *Privacy and Press Freedom* (London, Blackstone Press Ltd., 1995), p. 56.
[31] Hogg, 'The Very Private Life', 14–15. Note, however, that Hogg comments that the move towards a reasonable person approach to the establishment of a duty might ease the way for recognition of the fact that the duty should be owed to the person to whom the information relates, and not the person from whom the information has come.

separateness, then it is no answer to say that an action that is concerned solely with information is an acceptable solution to privacy invasions. It may be that such an action can address many of the privacy concerns that arise in the health care context and elsewhere, but to settle for such protection is to adopt an unsophisticated view of the true nature of the problems at hand. For this reason, the piecemeal development and expansion of confidence as a substitute for direct privacy protection must be rejected.[32] Similar limitations arise in respect of the US common law right of privacy.[33]

Data protection as a means of safeguarding informational privacy

The 1995 EC Directive on data protection was a self-avowed attempt to harmonise informational privacy protection throughout Europe.[34] Moreover, this instrument is founded on the broader commitment of EC member states to protect individual privacy, most notably as embodied in Article 8 of the European Convention on Human Rights.[35] Thus, we have the makings of a multi-layered approach to privacy protection, although, as its name suggests, the data protection directive is concerned solely with the protection of information, and so informational privacy interests.[36]

It is not necessary for the purposes of this work to examine the provisions of the Directive in any great depth.[37] It is sufficient simply to note certain key features.[38] The law protects the privacy interests of individuals in respect of their personal data. Personal data are defined as 'any

[32] Other less likely candidates for protecting privacy have also been examined elsewhere, such as trespass and defamation (see Home Office, *Report of the Committee on Privacy and Related Matters* (The Calcutt Report), Cm 1102 (1990)), and intentional infliction of emotional distress (see Wacks, *Privacy and Press Freedom*, pp. 80–9).

[33] G. T. Laurie, 'Challenging Medical–Legal Norms: The Role of Autonomy, Confidentiality and Privacy in Protecting Individual and Familial Group Rights in Genetic Information' (2001) 22 *Journal of Legal Medicine* 1, 37–9.

[34] European Directive 95/46/EC on the Protection of Individuals with Regard to the Processing of Personal Data and on the Free Movement of Such Data (Data Protection Directive).

[35] See, in particular, Recitals 2, 10 and 11 of the Preamble and Article 9 of the Directive.

[36] Moreover, as Birkinshaw points out, the law does not create a privacy right – 'to be left alone' – as such, but rather introduces security safeguards for personal information, see P. Birkinshaw, *Freedom of Expression: The Law, the Practice and the Ideal* (London, Butterworths, 2001), pp. 359–60.

[37] The Directive was implemented in the United Kingdom in the Data Protection Act 1998, which came into force on 1 March 2000.

[38] For a comparative account see J. Klosek, *Data Privacy in the Information Age* (Westport, CT, Quorum Books, 2000).

information relating to an identified or identifiable natural person; an identifiable person is one who can be identified, directly or indirectly, in particular by reference to an identification number or to one or more factors specific to his physical, physiological, mental, economic, cultural or social identity'.[39] The law regulates the processing of such data by reference to a set of eight principles that ensure, inter alia, that data are only processed when it is fair and lawful to do so, that data are processed only so far as is necessary for the purposes for which they were obtained, that the data are accurate and kept up to date, and that they should not be transferred to any jurisdiction where there are inadequate data protection provisions.[40]

The law makes only two attempts to categorise information into distinct groupings. These are (i) sensitive personal data, and (ii) anonymous data. Both are of relevance in the health care setting. Sensitive personal data are defined as data relating to racial or ethnic origin, political opinions, religious or philosophical beliefs, trade union membership, and the processing of data concerning health or sex life.[41] Additional protection is afforded to such data, and once again, the primary point of reference to legitimate dealings with such data is the concept of consent. In most circumstances, the data subject's specific consent to processing must be obtained. However, a wide range of alternative justifications for processing exist, of which the following are most pertinent. For example, it is lawful to process sensitive data to protect the vital interests of the data subject or of another person where the data subject is physically or legally incapable of giving his consent. Also, processing is lawful without specific consent if it is required for the purposes of preventive medicine, medical diagnosis, the provision of care or treatment or the management of health care services, and where those data are processed by a health care professional subject to the obligation of professional secrecy or by another person also subject to an equivalent obligation of secrecy. Overarchingly, member states have the power to create exemptions on the basis of 'substantial public interest'.[42] What those public interests are, or may be, is discernible in large part from the general tenor of the

---

[39] Data Protection Directive, Article 2.

[40] In this latter regard see Commission Decision of 15 June 2001 on standard contractual clauses for the transfer of personal data to third countries, under Directive 95/46/EC (2001/497/EC), OJ L181/19, 4/7/2001.

[41] Data Protection Directive, Article 8.   [42] *Ibid.*, Article 8(4).

Directive, which makes special provisions among others for national security, the investigation and prosecution of crimes, legitimate journalistic activities, and research.[43]

In this last regard, the law creates a number of important protections for scientific researchers using data obtained from individuals. First, there is no requirement to notify a data subject of the identity and purposes of those who will process the data, or of the identity of any further recipients of those data, when the data have not been received directly from the data subject.[44] Normally, this requirement must be met. Moreover, member states have a discretion to waive rights of access for individuals in the context of scientific research.[45] Second, the provisions of the Directive concerning subject access do not apply when data are anonymised, for the law is concerned solely with personal data, that is, those from which an individual can be identified.[46] This having been said, the obligation remains to inform data subjects that processing of data will occur, and the broad purposes of that processing.

An interesting question arises – on which the law is silent – in the context of highly predictive familial genetic data. If 'personal data' include *any* information relating to a natural person who can be identified, directly or indirectly, from those data and/or any other data held by the data processor, then are data about a genetic disorder derived from one member of a family also 'personal data' of *all* members of that family? For example, Dr G might test X for colorectal cancer adenomatous polyposis – a dominant disorder that reveals clear patterns of disease within families. If Dr G is also the family doctor for X's siblings and children, does Dr G now hold 'personal data' on those other family members? If so, he will be *processing* those data whenever they are used in the treatment of X, and this and other uses – such as disclosure of data – might require consent from family members under the data protection legislation.[47] Informal guidance from the Office of the Information Commissioner in

---

[43] In England and Wales this must also be read in conjunction with s.60 of the Health and Social Care Act 2001 which allows the Secretary of State to make regulations allowing or requiring the processing of patient information without patient consent, inter alia, 'in the public interest'. On this see D. Beyleveld, 'How Not to Regulate in the Public Interest' (2001) 2(1) *Genetics Law Monitor* 5.

[44] *Ibid.*, Article 11(2).   [45] *Ibid.*, Article 13(2).

[46] *Ibid.*, Recital 26. It has been argued, however, that the law applies to the anonymisation process itself; see A. Grubb, 'Breach of Confidence: Anonymised Information' (2000) 8 *Medical Law Review* 115, 118.

[47] Although see now in England and Wales s.60 of the Health and Social Care Act 2001.

the United Kingdom concedes that this scenario is possible under the current provisions of the law, although whether or not processing of a relative's data was occurring would depend on whether she or he was *identifiable* from the genetic data and any other data held by the data processor.[48] Raw genetic data alone would not qualify as a relative's personal data. However, where such processing does occur, it potentially poses considerable difficulties for the protection of a proband's privacy, as well as for her treatment.

A number of points emerge from this brief analysis. Clearly, no special case is made of genetic information. It is caught by the broad concept of personal information, and will be treated as sensitive personal information as part of the genus of health information. The provisions are all-embracing regarding identifiable personal information, and to that extent are to be welcomed, although possible issues might arise from processing certain kinds of familial genetic data that would remain to be resolved.[49]

Consent has a role to play in the process of data protection, but it does not emerge as a trump card. Indeed the broad and indistinct categories of justifications for processing without consent potentially weaken the protection that is afforded to informational privacy interests, although the model is, as always, a search for a balance, and few could deny that privacy protection should sometimes bow to other interests. But the devil is in the detail of determining which interests should be weighed in the balance and how far privacy should be compromised in any given case. The example of research is particularly apt. Is it meaningful, for example, to say from the theoretical standpoint that anonymisation of data is sufficient to address privacy concerns? This is subject to the same challenge as was mounted to the Court of Appeal's decision in *Source Informatics*, namely, that it makes for a very thin and weak conception of privacy. Now, this is not to say that in most circumstances such a measure will not perfectly adequately accommodate privacy interests, but it does indicate that even within the limited scope of a data protection

---

[48] Personal Communication from Iain Bourne, Compliance Manager (Health), Office of the Information Commissioner, 4 December 2000.

[49] In May 2001 the Information Commissioner issued a Draft Guidance on Use and Disclosure of Medical Data as part of a consultation process to examine the particular data protection issues that arise in the health sphere. A similar exercise was undertaken in Scotland in July 2001 by the Confidentiality and Security Advisory Group for Scotland, Protecting Patient Confidentiality: A Consultation Paper (Scottish Executive, Edinburgh, 2001).

law – which is solely to cater for informational privacy – there is a woeful absence of a more robust view of the meaning and content of privacy. Anonymisation is purely a mechanism to avoid or minimise harm, and that is of course a perfectly legitimate goal. Indeed, we shall return to the role of anonymity in due course. But the avoidance of harm is not the only reason that we respect individual privacy. We also respect privacy in order to respect individuals themselves. It is not clear, however, that this particular goal is currently being met. It indicates that something is missing from our perspective on privacy.

Informational and spatial privacy

If we were to attempt to accommodate the recent legal developments in the protection of privacy within the rubric of privacy offered in this work, it could be done as follows. The remit of data protection legislation is clearly the protection of informational privacy interests, and it is not suggested here that it be made to do more. The common law protection of confidences is similarly concerned with informational privacy, and, as has been shown, it cannot do more. It remains to be seen, however, if the same is true of the common law privacy protection so recently created. It is certainly not true of the protection afforded by the European Court of Human Rights, which has developed an amorphous concept of privacy in its interpretation of Article 8 that goes far beyond the simple right to control personal information. This last example is the only one to accord to any extent with the concept of spatial privacy advocated in this work. But even then, the privacy right developed by the court is ineffective because of its indistinctiveness and the need to rely on further judicial fancy for its development. Nevertheless, the English Court of Appeal has shown openness to the view that its function is to be activist in this regard, without committing itself to a position on the role of the courts in giving effect to European human rights in a domestic context.[50] But mere *volonté* is not enough in the absence of an underlying and unifying theoretical framework for conceiving of personal privacy and so protecting it coherently.[51] It is this that has been missing from our efforts to date.

[50] *Douglas and Others* v. *Hello! Ltd.*, 320–1.
[51] There is also the additional problem that European human rights do not necessarily have horizontal effect, that is, prima facie they are rights against the state and public authorities and not rights against other persons or private institutions: cf. *X and Y* v. *The Netherlands*, 1985, Series A, vol. 91.

The inadequacies of the current approach are neatly encompassed in a decision from the European Court of Justice.[52] In 1989 a candidate for a temporary position in the European Commission underwent a pre-employment medical examination. He declined the invitation to be tested for HIV. None the less, the medical examiner ordered tests relating to immune deficiency, and, on receiving the results, advised the Commission that the applicant was unsuitable for employment. He further contacted the applicant's doctor indicating that his patient was suffering from a condition consistent with 'full blown AIDS'. The applicant contested the decision of the Commission not to employ him. The European Court of Justice held that the right to respect for private life embodied in Article 8 of the European Convention on Human Rights is a fundamental right also protected by the legal order of the European Community.[53] And, while it is permissible to impose restrictions on that right to further a general public interest – such as the interest of the Community institutions in having a healthy workforce – this does not extend to carrying out medical tests against a person's will. The privacy right therefore includes the right to keep one's state of health secret. Crucially, however, that right does not protect an individual from requests to know his health status, and in the face of a refusal the Commission could not be obliged to take the risk of recruiting the applicant. Thus, while the privacy of the individual entitled him to an absolute right to refuse, he was nevertheless left without a remedy because an adverse inference could be drawn when that right was exercised. This is an entirely hollow view of privacy, lacking in substance and bereft of conceptual rigour. We are entitled to expect more.

Building a case for privacy using the example of genetics

Using genetics as an exemplar provides an excellent mechanism for discerning the problems and solutions in the search for a unifying concept of privacy. It should be stressed, however, that much of what is said here about privacy is of potentially much broader application, as the above example demonstrates.[54] None the less, the use of genetics as an

---

[52] Case C-404/92P *X v. Commission* [1994] ECR I-4737.

[53] Case C-62/90 *Commission v. Germany* [1992] ECR I-2575, para. 23.

[54] See further M. Temmerman *et al.*, 'The Right Not to Know HIV Test Results' (1995) 345 *Lancet* 969.

illustrative tool focuses the discussion and allows more detailed analysis of the specifics of privacy protection. Thus, the arguments have been made above that the attendant concepts of autonomy and confidentiality fail at a fundamental level to protect certain interests surrounding genetic data, and most particularly regarding the right not to know.[55] Where lacunae emerge they must be closed. A robust view of genetic privacy can serve this purpose.

Genetic privacy

A spatial privacy analysis underscores a right not to know information. If, in the context of a dilemma about whether someone should be told, the individual has no knowledge at all that familial information exists, then the spatial privacy interest stands as a prima facie bar to the person being approached and told the information. Spatial privacy requires that, before such an approach is made, we consider how the individual might be harmed by disclosure and what good, if any, might come from disclosure. It requires that we reflect on the act of disclosure and places the onus on those who would disclose not to do so unless faced with compelling reasons. Finally, it goes some way to ensuring that the decision-maker does 'not rest content with assumptions that flow from preconceived value preferences'.[56] That is, a privacy analysis reveals the broader and more complex reality of scenarios involving genetic information. This does not happen when we analyse the problem from the perspectives of autonomy or confidentiality. As we have seen, autonomy is susceptible to argument for autonomy enhancement through disclosure of information. On the other hand, confidentiality permits wide exceptions – such as the broad-ranging public interest – whereby disclosure can easily be justified at the discretion of those in possession of confidential information and when the value judgements of those persons dictate when information is so disclosed.[57]

[55] Cf. J. Taupitz, 'The Right Not to Know in German Legislation' (1998) 8/9 *Law and the Human Genome Review* 163.

[56] R. Macklin, 'Privacy and Control of Genetic Information', in G. J. Annas and S. Elias (eds.), *Gene Mapping: Using Ethics and Law as Guides* (New York, Oxford University Press, 1992).

[57] P. Lombardo, 'Genetic Confidentiality: What's the Big Secret?' (1996) 3 *University of Chicago Law School Roundtable* 589, 593 (suggesting that so many exceptions have been made to confidentiality over the years that it has now been rendered meaningless and outlived its usefulness).

A spatial privacy analysis offers a more sophisticated model than is currently available with which to determine how to proceed in dealings with genetic information. It is undeniable that this is a paternalistic stance.[58] It cannot be otherwise in the absence of more information about what individuals would want.[59] However, such an approach must be accepted for what it is and should not be eschewed out of hand in favour of disclosure in the name of autonomy enhancement.[60] While autonomy-based arguments tend to create an imperative to let the individual make *a personal choice*, too frequently this amounts to an abrogation of responsibility on the part of the discloser of the information; for, with the passing of the information goes too the responsibility for assisting in how the information should be used. But the transference of the burden of decision does not in itself absolve the first party of her moral obligations to the recipient of the information. And, because of the susceptibility of autonomy to value-laden enhancement or facilitation arguments, it is often overlooked that decisions to enhance the autonomy of another are just as paternalistic as decisions not to disclose information at all.[61] As Pellegrino has said, 'To thrust the truth or the decision on a patient who expects to be buffered against news of impending death is a gratuitous and harmful misinterpretation of the moral foundations for respect for autonomy.'[62]

What should happen, then, in the case of a refusal based on limited knowledge? For example, if a thirty-eight-year-old woman whose

[58] T. Austad, 'The Right Not to Know: Worthy of Preservation Any Longer – An Ethical Perspective' (1996) 50 *Clinical Genetics* 85.

[59] The results of recent surveys show that a majority of family members (83 per cent) would not want an elderly relative to be informed of a diagnosis of Alzheimer's disease, although this could be explicable either as a desire to protect their relative or as an unwillingness to deal with a relative's distress and grief. In contrast, 71 per cent of family members expressed a desire to know of their own diagnosis should this ever be determined: see C. P. Maguire *et al.*, 'Family Members' Attitudes Towards Telling the Patient with Alzheimer's Disease their Diagnosis' (1996) 313 *British Medical Journal* 529.

[60] M. Zwitter *et al.*, 'Professional and Public Attitudes Towards Unsolicited Medical Intervention' (1999) 318 *British Medical Journal* 251.

[61] See G. T. Laurie, 'Protecting and Promoting Privacy in an Uncertain World: Further Defences of Ignorance and the Right Not to Know' (2000) 7 *European Journal of Health Law* 185 in response to M. Canellopoulou Bottis, 'Comment on a View Favouring Ignorance of Genetic Information: Confidentiality, Autonomy, Beneficence and the Right Not to Know' (2000) 7 *European Journal of Health Law* 173, commenting on G. T. Laurie, 'In Defence of Ignorance: Genetic Information and the Right Not to Know' (1999) 6 *European Journal of Health Law* 119.

[62] E. D. Pellegrino, 'Is Truth Telling to the Patient a Cultural Artefact?' (1992) 268 *Journal of the American Medical Association* 1734, 1735.

father died from Huntington's disease has expressed a disinclination to know her own health status, should she nevertheless be told if her own twenty-year-old daughter tests positive for the disease? This puts the mother's status beyond doubt. But should she be informed? In these circumstances we have an indication that an individual might not wish to know information. Autonomy indicates that we should respect such a wish and a spatial privacy analysis gives us another good reason to do so. It is accepted that a privacy analysis does not necessarily make it easier for us to respect a wish not to know if that wish seems irrational (for example, if a cure for the condition is available and yet refusal is still made), but it does give us all the more cause to reflect that the refusal should be respected none the less. In addition, while autonomy-based arguments can be undermined because the subject is not in full possession of all material facts to enable her to make a truly autonomous decision, a privacy paradigm offers a prima facie starting point of non-interference, which places the onus of justifying disclosure firmly on the shoulders of those who would do so.

None of the above should be taken as suggesting that disclosure should never be made. Rather, it is offered as a model for re-evaluating the information disclosure decision-making process, and for considering the weight and merit of a range of factors in deciding if, when and in what circumstances, disclosure should occur. Furthermore, it should not be forgotten that hypotheticals rarely translate easily into real-life situations. It is acknowledged that it is very difficult to keep matters secret or private within a family. Also, faced with the prospect of death, many would consider that everyone would wish to know of a predisposition to disease, no matter how upsetting the knowledge. But the point to be made is that the privacy analysis advanced here can be seen as a reflection of a wider trend in medicine and the care of others. The principle of sanctity of life is no longer seen to be the governing value in health care. Quality of life has taken over that role. And acceptance of this requires many paradigm shifts. If it were thought that the supreme value were to save life at all cost (vitalism), then subtle privacy issues such as those advanced here would not arise. If, however, one values quality of life and accepts that we might prefer quality to the mere continuation of life, then this requires us to acknowledge that individuals might have an interest in preserving their current quality of life, even if that comes at the ultimate cost of life itself. The privacy model suggested here provides us with one way of seeking to respect such an interest.

Further use for this model is found when claims to have access to familial genetic information come from outside the family context. The requests of employers or insurers that individuals undergo genetic testing can be seen as an invasion of privacy, given that these individuals are required to know information about themselves that they might not otherwise discover or seek out. In the balance of interests that could be undertaken, it would be hard to justify the promotion of the interests of employers and insurers – being primarily financial – over the significant personal spatial privacy interests of individuals that might be compromised by such requests. This demonstrates the potential extension of our privacy model to other areas. It is a sphere that requires considerably closer examination.

At the present time, at least in the United Kingdom, there is no real evidence that employers or insurers are requesting genetic testing. Indeed, the Association of British Insurers has expressly committed its members not to do so,[63] and the only employer to request testing is the Ministry of Defence, which has traditionally tested applicants for air-crew training for sickle-cell disease.[64] However, this should not detract from the fact that if such testing were requested there is no means in law to prevent its being carried out or to protect aggrieved individuals from such intrusions into their private sphere. And to say that individuals can simply refuse is an inadequate response. Anti-discrimination and privacy legislation in the United States prevents such requests in a number of states, providing individuals with a civil remedy in damages for equitable relief if the law is breached.[65] This is the sort of protection that should flow from a clear commitment to privacy. The imperative to provide adequate privacy protection led the House of Commons Science and Technology

---

[63] Association of British Insurers, *Genetic Testing: ABI Code of Practice* (ABI, London, 1999).

[64] See Human Genetics Commission, *Whose Hands on Your Genes?* (HGC, London, 2000), p. 38. It would appear that the Ministry of Defence is reviewing this policy of testing.

[65] See, for example, Maine (Me. Rev. Stat. Tit. 5, 19302 and Me. Rev. Stat. Tit. 24-A, 2159-C), Nevada (Nev. Rev. Stat. 689, 417, 689B.069, 689C.198, 695B.317 and 695C.207). In New Hampshire employment testing is only permissible to investigate a worker's compensation claim or to determine exposure to toxic substances in the workplace (N.H. Rev. Stat. 141-H:2). In 2000, Massachusetts passed a law prohibiting both disclosure of test results and the requirement of genetic testing as a condition of employment or insurance; see An Act Relative to Insurance and Genetic Testing and Privacy Protection, Chapter 254 of the Acts of 2000.

Committee to conclude that 'misuse of genetic information should be both a criminal and a civil offence'.[66]

Striking the correct balance

In addition to the above, there are several factors that must be considered when trying to resolve complex issues surrounding genetic information. These are not only highly relevant but context specific, and can be invoked – alone or in combination – in particular situations to assist in making the strongest argument for the most appropriate outcome. These factors are listed below.

The availability of a therapy or cure

If death or disease can be avoided incontrovertibly or if the effects of disease can be substantially diminished, then it is trite to state that the onus of justifying disclosure is easily discharged and, indeed, very strong arguments should be advanced if disclosure to those affected is not to take place. If, however, nothing can be done to prevent the onset of genetic disease or to alleviate suffering then the argument for disclosure is accordingly weakened. Moreover, in the absence of effective therapeutic intervention, arguments that favour disclosure to facilitate choice or engender preparedness are suspect for the simple fact that it is far from clear that these ends are achievable,[67] and indeed disclosure in such cases might lead to additional harms.

The severity of the condition and likelihood of onset

The instinctive response to a potentially fatal condition is that action should be taken so that death can be prevented. In contrast, a mild condition for which nothing can be done makes it more difficult to argue for disclosure. In like manner, a 50 per cent risk of developing a genetic condition which lies with a first-degree relative is more compelling than a 1 per cent or 2 per cent risk to unidentified third cousins.

[66] House of Commons Science and Technology Committee, *Human Genetics: The Science and its Consequences*, Third Report (London, HMSO, 6 July 1995), para. 225.
[67] T. M. Marteau and C. Lerman, 'Genetic Risk and Behavioural Change' (2001) 322 *British Medical Journal* 1056.

The nature of genetic disease

The affliction of one individual with genetic disease does not pose any
direct threat to any other living human being. In this respect, genetic
disease is very different to many other diseases. Also, with recessive disorders that render people asymptomatic carriers, there is additionally no
threat to the health of the carrier. Only future progeny might be affected.
Facts such as this can have a bearing on how one views particular complex scenarios. For example, the United Kingdom Advisory Committee
on Genetic Testing (ACGT) issued a Code of Practice that recommends
strongly that over the counter test kits should only be made available
in respect of carrier status, and not for more severe conditions such as
late-onset Huntington's disease or X-linked disorders. The rationale is
that while the discovery of carrier status has no direct implications for
a proband's health, the discovery of a fatal condition such as Huntington's disease should not occur outside the clinical setting, where full
and appropriate counselling can be provided.[68] Moreover, if the only
persons likely to be affected directly by genetic disease are 'future persons', the recognition of their interests depends entirely on the view that
is taken by society of those yet-to-be born. In most Western legal systems – with the notable exceptions of Germany[69] and Éire[70] – foetuses
and future generations are not accorded recognised legal status. Accordingly, the overall balance of legal interests is not tipped in their favour,
and this would also be true in the present context.[71] In moral terms, of
course, matters might be entirely different. An appeal to the principle of

---

[68] ACGT, *Code of Practice for Genetic Testing Offered Commercially Direct to the Public* (London,
Department of Health, 1997).
[69] The German Constitution (Grundgesetz) states in Article 1(1): 'The dignity of the human
person is inviolable. To respect it shall be the duty of all public authority', and in Article
2(2)(1): 'Everybody has the right to life and bodily integrity'. Both of these provisions were
held to extend to the unborn by Federal Constitutional Court (Bundesverfassungsgericht)
in its *First Abortion Decision* (25 February 1975, BVerfGE 39, 1). The Court held that the
right to life also protects developing life in the womb as an 'independent legal value'.
[70] The Irish Constitution (Bunreacht na hÉireann) provides in Article 40.3.3 that 'The State
acknowledges the right to life of the unborn and, with due regard to the equal right to life of
the mother, guarantees in its laws to respect, and, as far as practicable, by its laws to defend
and vindicate that right.'
[71] Note, however, that in *LCB* v. *UK* (1999) 27 EHRR 212 the European Court of Human Rights
purported to impose an obligation on the state under Article 2 (right to life) to protect not
just the yet-to-be-born, but also the yet-to-be conceived. The case failed, however, for
insufficiency of evidence that the state knew or could have known of the risk.

intergenerational justice, for example, might serve the interests of future persons well.[72]

The nature of genetic testing

The point has already been made that predictive genetic testing (and family history) are imprecise tools for assessing future risk. Thus it is important to appreciate that any trade in information is trade in further uncertainty. People may be alerted to a possibility, but they cannot be apprised of a medical certainty in respect of their own health without undertaking further steps, such as additional testing. If there is good reason to suspect that such further steps will not be taken, then there is good reason to reflect seriously on any decision to disclose information at all.

The nature of the information to be disclosed

Different forms of genetic information reveal different facts about risk, certainty, probability, harm, and the future. Accordingly, different considerations must be brought to bear, depending on what the disclosee is to be told. The significance of being told that one is likely to be suffering from a highly penetrant monogenic condition is clearly of a different order to being told that population studies have revealed that schizophrenia might be influenced by susceptibility genes. Individualised risk assessment is not possible for neurological disorders. At best, estimates of risk can only reflect results gleaned from family studies, which in themselves are currently very inconclusive. Thus, while 1 in 100 persons in the general population will develop schizophrenia, we know that there is a tenfold higher risk if a first-degree relative is also affected. Within a particular family, however, this reveals nothing of further significance to members of that family. Nor will the detection of a susceptibility gene necessarily furnish individuals with more detail about their own particular risk of becoming ill. In the abstract, therefore, one can only meaningfully talk about risk within the population as a whole, while on the individual level it is unclear what benefit information of this kind brings.

---

[72] S. A. M. McLean, 'Intergenerational Justice: A Brave New World or a Leap in the Dark?' (2000) 1(1) *Genetics Law Monitor* 1.

The nature of the request

If individuals are asked to disclose or receive genetic information, then the specific nature of the request might have an influence on the outcome one would recommend. For example, if an individual is asked simply to take part in linkage tests to determine a relative's particular risk – say, for procreative purposes – and the tested individual receives guarantees that she will not be given the test results, then such an altruistic gesture is unlikely to conflict in any way with that individual's interests. Compare this with an unexpected approach from a health care professional or relative to disclose a 50 per cent chance of developing a late-onset condition in the future. In the former example, the individual is not being asked to take on board any information about herself, while in the latter she is placed in a position where she has no other option but to do so.

The views and likely reaction of the disclosee

Evidence of how individuals might react to information about their genetic make-up can be of considerable assistance in determining whether a disclosure should be made. Clearly, of most value is evidence that the individual has specifically requested to know or not to know the information in question.

A right not to know

A well-defined spatial privacy right could embody a clear account of the kind of factors that would make disclosure in different circumstances acceptable or unacceptable. An obvious problem with this approach, however, is that the existence of a right not to know implies that a duty not to disclose information should exist in certain cases. However, an important factor in determining whether such a duty exists is the question of how the individual to whom the information is to be disclosed might react. This is a subjective matter that can be especially difficult for any third party to assess. It leads to the possibility that individual A might determine that individual B should not be informed of information, when in fact individual B actually would want to know, were she given the opportunity. As we have seen, the privacy argument in favour of non-disclosure is based primarily on a desire to respect and not to harm the individual, but in such a case the very fact of non-disclosure might cause harm and might be an act of disrespect in itself. In recognition of this, a number of additional factors could be brought to bear on the problem.

First, an objective assessment of circumstances could serve to delimit the parameters of any duty not to disclose. That is, the person in possession of the information would assess factors such as likelihood of onset and availability of cure, together with an objective consideration of what a person in the subject's position would or would not wish to know. Such a 'reasonable subject' could assume the particular characteristics of the actual subject. Ultimately, provided that the assessment of what should be done is reasonable, no legal redress should lie against someone who had decided (not) to disclose information. The relevance of any views of the subject clearly would be significant in the assessment of reasonableness, as would the extent of the effort made by the duty-holder to seek out evidence of those views.

None of this is to ignore the reality that the assessment of these factors is a difficult exercise in itself. On the one hand, clinical data concerning the extent of risk or the likely success of therapy or cure are best assessed by health care professionals, while the question of which characteristics should be taken into account to determine if this subject should be told is better determined by those close to the person, such as her relatives or a significant other. And, while a health care professional might be in a position to gather a range of data to assist in the assessment of the situation, it is far less clear whether family members are in a position to make meaningful assessments, let alone whether they should be the subject of a legal action if they disclose information in unjustified circumstances. It is therefore submitted that it is more permissible to impose a duty to respect the right not to know on parties outside the family milieu. Primarily, this would affect employers, insurers and the state.[73] Thus, for example, requests for genetic testing from these parties would be seen to be a clear invasion of spatial privacy.

To exclude family members from this duty is simply an admission that the law does not always have a role to play in determining what should be done with genetic information. It does not follow, however,

---

[73] K. D. Weaver, 'Genetic Screening and the Right Not to Know' (1997) 13 *Issues in Law and Medicine* 243.

that the range or importance of the interests under consideration should not be discussed with individuals who seek genetic testing and who might contemplate disclosure to their relatives. Indeed, it could become a duty for health care professionals to discuss such matters with probands.

An additional defining factor for a duty not to disclose could be the need to show the reasonable prospect that a tangible benefit would come to the person to whom disclosure is to be made. The benefit should be more than the facilitation of preparedness or the promotion of autonomy, and should represent some clinical benefit to the subject. Thus, for example, employers and insurers would not be able to rely on the argument that individuals can choose whether or not to undergo testing at their behest, but rather would have to show some real medical benefit to those persons to justify their requests for testing and/or access to genetic data. State screening initiatives would also only be justified if such a benefit could be shown.[74] Health care professionals similarly could be obliged to discuss with probands the likely real benefits of disclosure to relatives.

Third, even if all of the above is accepted, a concern may remain: is this approach not simply a paternalistic assessment of spatial privacy interests? To an extent it is, but perhaps this can never be avoided in circumstances where individuals cannot be approached directly to determine how to proceed. But the worth of this approach is found in its responsiveness to broader, less atomistic interests. It is a paradigm that does not view the beginning and the end of ethical discourse as lying with the autonomy of individuals, but rather responds to the wide range of interests from the perspective of an ethic of care, wherein respect for autonomy has a significant role to play, but where protection of privacy is also required to complete the model.

What kind of genetic privacy right should there be?

If dominant theories of privacy are deficient, and if current legal protection is inadequate, then what kind of privacy right should there be? This question can be approached in one of two ways, (i) by refusing to

---

[74] H. Malm, 'Medical Screening and the Value of Early Detection: When Unwarranted Faith Leads to Unethical Recommendations' (1999) 21 *Hastings Center Report* 26.

impose any duty to disclose through the law of negligence;[75] or (ii) by recognising a duty *not* to disclose, either in the existing common law or through statutory intervention.

No duty to inform

The negligence action has been used widely in tort law to delimit the duty of care that a health care professional owes to patients. Occasionally, however, a duty is deemed to be owed to persons outside the therapeutic relationship,[76] and, in such circumstances, the courts rely heavily on policy arguments to shape and temper such extensions of the law. The beginnings of a trend to extend the duty of care to relatives of persons diagnosed with genetic disease can be discerned in a number of US states.[77] Thus in *Pate v. Threlkel*,[78] the Florida Supreme Court specifically addressed the question: 'Does a physician owe a duty of care to the children of a patient to warn the patient of the genetically transferable nature of the condition for which the physician is treating the patient?' In answering this question in the affirmative, the court concluded that 'when the prevailing standard of care creates a duty that is obviously for the benefit of certain identified third parties and the physician knows of the existence of those third parties, then the physician's duty runs to those third parties ... a patient's children fall within the zone of foreseeable risk'.[79] It was at pains to stress, however, that the duty did not

---

[75] See R. Macklin, 'Privacy and Control of Genetic Information' in Annas and Elias, *Mapping the Human Genome*, pp. 162–3, and also J. Husted, 'Autonomy and A Right Not to Know', in R. Chadwick, M. Levitt and D. Shickle (eds.), *The Right to Know and the Right Not to Know* (Aldershot, Avebury, 1997), pp. 64–5.

[76] This has occurred primarily in the United States. See, for example, *Bradshaw v. Daniel*, 854 S.W.2d 865 (Tenn. 1993); *DiMarco v. Lynch Homes-Chester County*, 559 A.2d 530, aff'd 583 A.2d 422 (Pa. 1990); *Shepard v. Redford Comm. Hosp.*, 390 N.W.2d 239 (Mich. 1986); *Gooden v. Tips*, 651 S.W.2d 364 (Tex. 1983); *Bradley Ctr. v. Wessner*, 287 S.E.2d 716 (Ga. 1982); *McIntosh v. Milano*, 403 A.2d 500 (N.J. 1979); *Renslow v. Mennonite Hosp.*, 367 N. E. 2d 1250 (Ill. 1977); *Tarasoff v. Regents of University of California*, 551 P.2d 334 (Cal. 1976); *Hofmann v. Blackmon*, 241 So. 2d 752 (Fla. 1970).

[77] C. M. Parker, 'Camping Trips and Family Trees: Must Tennessee Physicians Warn Their Patients' Relatives of Genetic Risks?' (1998) 65 *Tennessee Law Review* 585.

[78] *Pate v. Threlkel* 661 So. 2d 278 (Fla. 1995).

[79] In *Schroeder v. Perkel*, 432 A. 2d. 834 (NJ 1981) the court recognised a duty of a physician to the parents of a child whose cystic fibrosis had not been correctly diagnosed to inform the parents of the child's condition. The court said: 'The foreseeability of injury to members of a family other than one immediately injured by the wrongdoing of another must be viewed in light of the legal relationships among family members. A family is woven of the fibers of

require that relatives be approached directly by the physician: 'the duty will be satisfied by warning the patient'.[80]

This view is unsatisfactory as a matter of policy for two reasons. First, it says nothing about the nature of the physician's duty if the patient refuses to disclose to relatives. Second, it assumes that the interests of patient and relatives necessarily coincide. But one can foresee circumstances, for example, in which it might not be in a patient's interests to be told that she is dying of a genetic condition, yet a failure to do so would potentially be a breach of the physician's duty to the patient's relatives. The two duties of care are not, therefore, always reconcilable.

A 1996 decision of the Superior Court of New Jersey has addressed at least the first of these problems. In *Safer* v. *Estate of Pack* the court refused to follow the Florida court's restriction of the duty, and 'decline[d] to hold . . . that, in all circumstances, the duty to warn will be satisfied by informing the patient'.[81] The court continued: 'It may be necessary, at some stage, to resolve a conflict between the physician's broader duty to warn and his fidelity to an expressed preference of the patient that nothing be said to family members about the details of the disease.'[82] Here the court contemplates preferring a physician's duty of care to third parties to the patient's right to confidentiality. That it does so at least recognises that the physician's duty of care to those parties is separate from the relationship she has with the patient (albeit that it might have its origins in that relationship). Furthermore, it recognises that the requisite standard of care should be judged on the conduct of the physician and should not be discharged merely by telling the patient about her condition and its likely implications for her family.

But, even if this line of authority is thought to be persuasive,[83] the fundamental premise for extensions of this sort in tort law should not be forgotten, namely, that public policy must dictate the future course of the negligence action. It is for the courts to decide this matter, and a number of factors have a direct bearing on whether such an extension should be

---

life; if one strand is damaged, the whole structure may suffer. The filaments of family life, although individually spun, create a web of interconnected legal interests', at 839.

[80] *Pate*, 661 So. 2d, at 282. An analogous decision in the context of HIV infection is *Reisner* v. *The Regents of the University of California*, 37 Cal. Rptr. 2d 518 (Cal. 1995).

[81] *Safer* v. *Estate of Pack* 677 A.2d 1188 (N.J. 1996) at 1192–3.   [82] *Id.*

[83] It is by no means certain that it will be followed. See, for example, *Olson* v. *Children's Home Soc'y of California*, 252 Cal. Rptr. 11 (Cal. 1988); *Ellis* v. *Peter*, 627 N.Y.S.2d 707 (N.Y. App. 1995); *Conboy* v. *Mogeloff*, 78 N.Y. 2d. 862 (N.Y. App. 1991); *Sorgente* v. *Richmond Mem. Hosp.*, 539 N.Y.S.2d 269 (N.Y. Supreme 1989).

made. Several considerations should be immediately apparent, including the burden that such a duty would place on health care professionals,[84] the difficulty in knowing who should be contacted and how,[85] and the possible detrimental effect that such a duty would have on the physician–patient relationship if confidentiality can be disregarded in favour of the duty to disclose.[86]

Other, more specific, points can be made. First and foremost, it must be remembered that genetic information only allows an uncertain prediction of risk concerning the relatives of a proband. With dominant disorders there can be a one in two chance that first-degree relatives will be affected, but with multifactorial conditions this probability drops considerably. It might therefore be very difficult to predict the likelihood of harm to relatives. Second, we must ask what kind of harm merits the imposition of a duty of care. If the harm in question is death or physical injury and something can be done to avoid this, then the case for disclosure is strong. But what of carrier status or information about genetic susceptibilities? Is this threat of harm enough to impose a duty of care on the health care professional? Could it ever be argued that a duty is owed to future persons, and so information should be disclosed to facilitate informed reproductive choices? Disclosure can only be justified if it furthers the public interest that it is designed to address. While this is likely when physical harm can be avoided through cure or therapy, it is less so when the harm is lack of psychological preparedness or harm to reproductive choice. A final point to note concerns the cause of harm. If a duty to warn were imposed which did not take account of the particular facts of each condition and primarily whether or not a cure existed, then, as Nys has said, 'a duty to warn ... would not only conflict with the right of confidentiality of the patient but also with the right not to know of the relatives'.[87]

---

[84] For an interesting attitudinal survey about the responsibility of patients and genetic services providers to remain in contact, see J. Fitzpatrick *et al.*, 'The Duty to Recontact: Attitudes of Genetics Service Providers' (1999) 64 *American Journal of Human Genetics* 852.

[85] L. Andrews, 'Torts and the Double Helix: Malpractice Liability for Failure to Warn of Genetic Risks' (1992) 29 *Houston Law Review* 149, 181 (recognition of a duty of disclosure to relatives with whom a physician has no direct professional relationship should, logically, also give rise to a duty for physicians to tell strangers of the health risks that they run).

[86] See also G. T. Laurie, 'Obligations Arising from Genetic Information – Negligence and the Protection of Familial Interests' (1999) 11 *Child and Family Law Quarterly* 109.

[87] H. Nys, 'Genetics and the Rights of the Patient: Informed Consent and Confidentiality Revisited in Light of Reproductive Freedom', in L. Westerhall and C. Phillips (eds.), *Patients' Rights – Informed Consent, Access and Equality* (Stockholm, Nerenius and Santerus Publishers, 1994), pp. 137–54, especially p. 153.

The courts should not rely unquestioningly on an assumption that non-disclosure is necessarily a (legal) harm. Legal precedents to date ignore the possible significance of the interest in not knowing and certainly it will not be served by imposing a duty on health care professionals to make disclosures without first considering the consequences for those to whom disclosure will be made. One way, therefore, to recognise and protect the interest in not knowing would be refuse to endorse the extension of tort law to impose a duty to disclose. The problem with such an approach is that it leaves the matter of the recognition of spatial privacy interests to the judiciary, which can only act when relevant disputes come to court. Also, and more importantly from the individual's perspective, such an approach does not accord any right of compensation to those who have suffered invasions of privacy. It merely pays abstract lip-service to the interests in question.

This having been said, the likelihood of a duty of disclosure being imposed in the United Kingdom is currently slight. As Norrie has correctly stated, 'There is no Good Samaritan principle in our law. The law only requires positive preventative action when there is a special relationship between the parties, or when the danger is caused by one of them.'[88] Thus, only if a third party were a patient of the same health care professional would a duty of care be imposed. However, if this is the case, then both proband and relative are owed duties of confidentiality *and* duties of care and there is accordingly a real possibility of conflict for the clinician. Consider the following example. If a health care professional is aware of a genetic disorder in a family through tests on patient A, yet does not wish to offer a pre-natal test to pregnant patient B, a relative of A, for fear of alerting her to A's afflicted status, if no test is done and a baby is born with a debilitating condition, might an action lie in negligence?

A strong case for liability might arise from the general failure to inform of a risk of genetic disease.[89] Indeed, there is no difference between disclosure of a known risk of genetic disease and the disclosure of any other kind of known risk. Thus, in *Gregory* v. *Pembrokeshire Health Authority* the failure of a doctor to inform of a failed amniocentesis test

---

[88] See K. McK. Norrie, 'Medical Confidence: Conflicts of Duties' (1984) 24 *Medicine, Science and the Law* 26, 29.

[89] For recent developments in Israel, see R. Hakimian, 'Caveat Doctor: Medical Negligence and Genetic Testing' (2001) 2(1) *Genetics Law Monitor* 7.

was held to be negligent.[90] Does it matter, then, by what means the information becomes known? Surely the duty arises when the health care professional is in a position to act and a failure to do so would be a failure to show reasonable care. What is reasonable depends on all facts and circumstances, but in the straightforward case of a highly penetrant monogenic disorder it is strongly arguable that a health care professional would owe a duty to a pregnant patient if he were to come into knowledge about genetic risk from testing a member of the patient's family.[91]

While there is an ethical dilemma in such circumstances, there need not be a legal conflict. This is because the harm that can be avoided by disclosure will be enough to justify breaching A's confidentiality in the public interest. Thus no action would lie in breach of confidence. This having been said, the longer-term impact of such an outcome is less clear. At the micro-level the imposition of such duties of disclosure might damage irreversibly the particular therapeutic relationship, and at the macro-level there is always the risk that patients will lose trust generally in the medical profession if confidences cannot reasonably be relied upon.[92]

Such cases aside, if no special relationship exists between the third party and the practitioner, the only way sensitivity can be shown to all interests concerned is if no duty to disclose is imposed. At best, health care professionals should have a discretion to disclose confidential information.[93] The limits within which such discretion should operate would be subject to the factors outlined above regarding the nature of genetic disease and the nature of the information to be disclosed. Moreover, practical guidance has come from the US Institute of Medicine Committee on Assessing Genetics Risks for resolving the ethical dilemma: 'confidentiality [should] be breached and relatives informed about genetic risks only when (1) attempts to elicit voluntary disclosure fail, (2) there is a high probability of irreversible or fatal harm to the relative, (3) the disclosure of the information will prevent harm,

---

[90] *Gregory* v. *Pembrokeshire Health Authority* [1989] 1 Med LR 81. The case failed, however, on the point of causation: the plaintiff failed to show that if she had known of the result of the first test she would have had an abortion.

[91] This is subject to the application of a calculation of risk test. That is, an assessment of likelihood of disease, severity of injury likely to be sustained, the availability of precautions etc.

[92] *X* v. *Y* [1988] 2 All ER 648, at 653.

[93] This view is supported by the Nuffield Council on Bioethics, *Genetics Screening: Ethical Issues* (London, Nuffield Council on Bioethics, 1993), para. 5.29.

(4) the disclosure is limited to the information necessary for diagnosis or treatment of the relative, and (5) there is no other reasonable way to avert the harm'.[94]

A duty not to inform

An alternative means to enshrine a right not to know in law would be to make an unauthorised disclosure a cause of action leading to the payment of damages, either for consequential harm or, simply, because the privacy of the individual had not been respected. There is authority in German and South African law to the effect that legal liability on the part of a health care professional can attach for 'over-information' (*Übermassaufklärung*).[95] Physical or psychological harm that results from excessive information disclosure to a patient can therefore result in a successful action for damages.

The Anglo-American position is less clear. The common law position on privacy protection in the United Kingdom is currently in a nascent state as we have seen above, and there is precious little evidence of how it might develop. A far more sophisticated model is found in the United States, where a common law privacy right has existed for almost a century. As a right *in rem*, this privacy right is good against the world at large, and so is unlike the US right of confidentiality, which must be owed specifically and voluntarily to one individual or group of individuals.[96] Famously, the privacy tort was categorised by Dean Prosser into four discrete actions that continue to reflect its core of protection.[97] The four privacy rights of action are (i) appropriation of an individual's name or likeness; (ii) unreasonable intrusion upon the seclusion of another; (iii) public disclosure of private facts, and (iv) subjecting an individual to publicity that casts them in a false light in the public's eye.

Of these, the most appropriate to protect genetic privacy might be public disclosure of private facts or unreasonable intrusion upon the

---

[94] L. B. Andrews, J. E. Fullarton, N. A. Holtzman and A. G. Motulsky (eds.), *Assessing Genetic Risks: Implications for Health and Social Policy* (Washington, DC, National Academic Press, 1994), pp. 264–73, 278.

[95] F. F. W. Van Oosten, 'The Doctor's Duty of Disclosure and Excessive Information Liability' (1992) 11 *Medicine and Law* 633.

[96] See, for example, *Darnell* v. *Indiana* 674 N.E. 2d 19 (Ind. 1996) and *Suarez* v. *Pierard* 663 N.E.2d. 1039 (Ill. App. 1996).

[97] Prosser, 'Privacy: A Legal Analysis'.

seclusion of another. However, the first of these would only assist if the information were revealed – as with confidentiality – to parties other than the person to whom the information relates, and no interest would be infringed if individuals are told information about themselves.[98] With respect to unreasonable intrusion, it might be thought that the offensive intrusion could be the receipt of burdensome information, but a perusal of the case law does not bear this out as a means of constituting the tort. Rather, an element of intentional invasion of private space is required, which is bound up with the possibility that personal information will be acquired or removed from that space by unacceptable means, rather than, as with our concern, that personal information will be added to that personal space.[99] Thus, the tort is constituted when an illegal search of property is carried out,[100] or when one's home is physically invaded,[101] or when eavesdropping or spying occurs,[102] or even when an individual is the subject of harassing telephone calls.[103] There is no authority to suggest that an actionable tort is committed by adding private information to the private sphere. It would seem that the conceptual underpinnings of the tort do not encompass such an invasion.

Thus, the US common law right of privacy cannot help to establish a valid legal basis for a right not to know information. The focus of the tort on the need to extract information from the private sphere (usually with a view to placing it in the public sphere[104]) renders it ill-equipped to protect against such intrusions into the private sphere as occur when an interest in not knowing is compromised. The parallel that might be drawn, then, is that the common law tort is more akin to an informational privacy right, and not a spatial privacy right.

In contrast to the common law, statutory intervention could provide a right to compensation for invasion of genetic privacy. However, no such

[98] Laurie, 'Challenging Medical–Legal Norms', 38.
[99] See *Doe* v. *Mills*, 536 N.W. 2d. 824 (1995) in which the Michigan Court of Appeals made it clear that the tort is constituted when secret and private subject matter is obtained by means that would be objectionable to a reasonable person.
[100] *Sutherland* v. *Kroger Co.*, 110 S. E. 2d 716 (W. Va. 1959).
[101] *Ford Motor Co.* v. *Williams*, 134 S. E. 2d 483 (Ga. 1963).
[102] *Rhodes* v. *Graham*, 37 S.W. 2d 46 (Ky. 1931); *McDaniel* v. *Atlanta Coca-Cola Bottling Co.*, 2 S.E. 2d 810 (Ga. 1939).
[103] *Carey* v. *Statewide Finance Co.*, 223 A. 2d 405 (Conn. Cir. 1966).
[104] Public disclosure is not, however, a prerequisite. See *Cort* v. *Bristol-Myers Co.*, 431 N.E. 2d. 908 (Mass. 1982); *Themo* v. *New England Newspaper Publishing Co.*, 27 N.E. 2d. 753 (Mass. 1940).

measure has been proposed in the United Kingdom to date.[105] By contrast, 110 bills seeking to protect genetic privacy were introduced in the
105th session of the US Congress, although none was debated beyond the
subcommittee stage.[106] Similar measures are before the current session,
although no federal initiative on genetic privacy has ever been successful. The Rule on Privacy Standards adopted in April 2001 relates broadly
to health information, makes no special case of genetic data, and is solely
concerned with informational privacy. It is more apposite, therefore, to
consider a model law designed to address the specific problems that are
thought to surround genetic information and which has been proposed
as a national solution to the problem of genetic privacy.[107]

The Genetic Privacy Act

The Genetic Privacy Act (GPA) was produced for the Human Genome
Project's Ethical, Legal and Social Issues division by George Annas,
Leonard Glantz and Patricia Roche of Boston University's School of Pub-
lic Health. This draft model law is in the format of a federal statute and
has already been a source of inspiration for several state legislatures.[108]
The introduction to the Act states,

> the overarching premise of the Act is that no stranger should have or con-
> trol identifiable DNA samples or genetic information about an individual
> unless that individual specifically authorizes the collection of DNA sam-
> ples for the purpose of genetic analysis, authorizes the creation of that
> private information, and has access to and control over the dissemination
> of that information.

Thus, the GPA envisages a highly individualistic approach. This having
been said, the Act defines the term 'private genetic information' to mean

---

[105] For a comparative analysis see P. M. Schwartz, 'European Data Protection Law and Medical
Privacy', in M. A. Rothstein (ed.), *Genetic Secrets: Protecting Privacy and Confidentiality in
the Genetic Era* (New Haven, CT, Yale University Press, 1997).

[106] See J. Colby, 'An Analysis of Genetic Discrimination Legislation Proposed by the 105th
Congress' (1998) 24 *American Journal of Law and Medicine* 443.

[107] Cf. T. McGleenan, 'Rights to Know and Not to Know: Is There a Need for a Genetic Privacy
Act?' in Chadwick, Levitt and Shickle, *The Right to Know and the Right Not to Know.*

[108] The Genetic Privacy Act and Commentary (1995) is available on request from the
Health Law Department, Boston University School of Public Health, 715 Albany Street,
Boston, MA 02118 and also on the Department's web site at: http://www.bumc.bu.edu/
www/sph/lw/pvl/act.html

'any information about an identifiable individual that is derived from
the presence, absence, alteration, or mutation of a gene or genes, or the
presence or absence of a specific DNA marker or markers, and which
has been obtained: (1) from an analysis of the individual's DNA; or,
(2) from an analysis of the DNA of a person to whom the individual is
related'.[109] This clearly seeks to take account of the interests that relatives
of a sample source can have in genetic information. As a corollary, the
GPA gives a property right in a DNA sample to its source.[110] However,
it is not clear how well the distinction is drawn between a DNA sample
and private genetic information derived from a sample.[111] Axiomatically, the first is unique and personal to the individual from whom the
sample was taken. The same is not necessarily true of the information,
but the GPA nevertheless provides that the exclusive right over such
information (as with samples) is retained by the sample source.[112] The
provisions of §101(b)(8) stipulate, however, that prior to the collection
of a DNA sample from individuals they should be informed, among
other things, that 'the genetic analysis may result in information about
the sample source's genetic relatives which may not be known to such
relatives but could be important, and if so the sample source will have
to decide whether or not to share that information with relatives'.[113] We
shall return to the property issue in chapter 6. The acknowledgement of
familial interests in genetic information is an important step forward in
responding to the possible peculiarities of some forms of genetic data
and merits further attention.

It is fortunate that the text of the GPA is accompanied by a commentary prepared by its authors in which they seek to clarify their general
aims and to expand upon the specific terms contained in the Act. Of the
above familial provision they state:

> Creating either a contractual or statutory obligation for individuals to
> share [genetic] information with their family members would not only be
> unprecedented, but inadvisable. The creation of new substantive rights or

[109] Genetic Privacy Act (GPA), s.3.
[110] GPA §104(a). For comment see M. Lin, 'Conferring a Federal Property Right in Genetic
Material: Stepping into the Future with the Genetic Privacy Act' (1996) 22 *American Journal
of Law and Medicine* 109.
[111] Part A of the Act deals with collection and analysis of DNA samples; Part B concerns
disclosure of private genetic information.
[112] See Part B of the Act, which is concerned with matters of consent and disclosure.
[113] GPA §101(b)(8).

duties of family members is not our intention and is beyond the scope of this Act. However, because the Act creates rules that govern the use and disclosure of information, it is imperative that individuals be informed of the fact that by seeking genetic information about themselves through genetic analysis, they may also become privy to information about other family members who would also want and/or need such information . . . While it will be an individual choice as to whether or not to share that information with others, this disclosure should instigate discussion between the sample source and the collector of the sample.[114]

Thus the GPA allows sample sources to decide for themselves whether to disclose genetic information to relatives. Many would argue that this is not necessarily a bad thing, because often such a person will be better (or even best) placed to establish how relatives might feel about receiving such information. However, the GPA does not give any guidance to a sample source on how to decide whether or not disclosure should be made, nor does it guide health care professionals in their dealings with such persons. In particular, there is no recognition of the possible spatial privacy interests that relatives might have in not knowing. If it is accepted that individuals can have such interests and that these are valid, then an act that purports to deal with genetic privacy should include provisions aimed at recognising and protecting such interests.

In fact, the GPA achieves this in part in respect of the rights of minors. Section 141 of the Act provides:

(a) INDIVIDUALS UNDER 16 – . . . the individually identifiable DNA sample of a sample source who is under 16 years of age shall not be collected or analyzed to determine the existence of a gene that does not in reasonable medical judgment produce signs or symptoms of disease before the age of 16, unless :
(1) there is an effective intervention that will prevent or delay the onset or ameliorate the severity of the disease; and
(2) the intervention must be initiated before the age of 16 to be effective; and

[114] See also G. J. Annas, L. H. Glantz and P. W. Roche, 'Drafting the Genetic Privacy Act: Science, Policy, and Practical Considerations' (1995) 23 *Journal of Law, Medicine and Ethics* 360, and P. W. Roche, L. H. Glantz and G. J. Annas, 'The Genetic Privacy Act: A Proposal for Legislation' (1996) 37 *Jurimetrics* 1. For a critique of the Act see E. Troy, 'The Genetic Privacy Act: An Analysis of Privacy and Research Concerns' (1997) 25 *Journal of Law, Medicine and Ethics* 256.

(3) the sample source's representative has received the disclosures required by section 101 of this Act and has executed a written authorization which meets the requirements of section 103 of this Act and which also limits the uses of such analysis to those permitted by this section.

The authors justify these provisions as follows.

> There are two reasons for this prohibition on the exercise of parental discretion. First, if someone learns that the child is a carrier of a gene that disposes the child to some condition later in life, this finding may subject the child to discrimination and stigmatization by both the parents and others who may learn of this fact. Second, a child's genetic status is the child's private genetic information and should not be determined or disclosed unless there is some compelling reason to do so.[115]

This mirrors arguments that have been made above concerning the spatial privacy interests of individuals. The GPA here acknowledges the spatial privacy interests of children and, further, it recognises that these should not be invaded without due cause.[116] The GPA is remiss, however, in not recognising the spatial privacy interests of all persons about whom genetic information is known but who have not sought it out themselves.

The situation of the minor is not in all respects the same as that of the adult relative of a proband. One clear point of difference concerns the initial generation of information. In the case of the minor, the legal prohibition concerns the initial collection or analysis of genetic material. In the case of an adult relative of a proband, this is not the point at issue because no one can (or should) prevent others from having their own genetic material analysed. However, this is a distinction without a difference for present purposes. For the essential issue in both cases is the same, namely, the unwarranted intrusion of personal genetic information into the private sphere of the individual in question. Thus, the interest of the adult relative is not in seeking to control the proband's access to the information, but rather it is in having her own spatial privacy interests of non-intrusion respected. For the minor, precisely the

---

[115] Commentary on the GPA, p. 79.
[116] The GPA does not go so far as to recognise any spatial privacy interests for foetuses. Sections 151 and 152 provide that a competent pregnant woman has the sole right to determine both when DNA samples shall be taken from her foetus and how genetic information about the foetus shall be used.

same interest is at stake. The means to protect the child's interest may lie in securing control over the minor's own sample, but simply because the same means are not available to relatives of a proband should not lead to the conclusion that the spatial privacy interests of those relatives are any less deserving of protection.

In relation to this, because the minor is the proband in such cases, the minor has the primary right to decide what happens to her genetic sample and, accordingly, to any genetic information derived from that sample. Given this, it might be argued that the above provisions simply ensure that the decision to access genetic information be left until the child is capable of making independent choices. And so it might be concluded that no specific provision is necessary in the case of an adult because it is axiomatic that the adult may choose to know or not to know her own information. However, the question here is not simply one of access, but also one of non-access. The interest is not merely one of control but of maintaining a state of ignorance: a state of non-access to the person. However, the focus of the GPA on control of samples (and so on autonomy and choice) means that the minor is only protected from attempts to gain specific access to personal genetic information. She is not protected from unwarranted disclosure of genetic information from relatives. Adults are in an equally vulnerable position. In fact, a clear parallel can be drawn between the child and the unknowing adult in that, in many senses, they are both incapax with respect to the genetic information. While the child is generally incapax, the adult can certainly make a choice to know, in that she has the capacity to choose to know. But to offer the individual the opportunity to choose might be to offend the very interests with which we are concerned. Thus it is meaningful in the case of genetic information to adopt the position that both adult and child are incapax. The consequence of this is in each case the same, namely, that neither should be approached with unsolicited disclosures of genetic information without due cause and justification.

The conclusion to be drawn is that it would not be inappropriate to extend the form of protection offered by the GPA to relatives of a proband. The prohibition on disclosure could not only cover requests for direct testing, but also could extend to unwarranted approaches to family members with genetic information of which they are unaware. The determination of a warrantable approach would need to be settled by more debate on the legitimate nature of competing interests and a proper assessment of genetic risks and consequences within the family and the wider community setting. In this way a spatial privacy right could be established that would require proper justification before a legally acceptable approach to a person could be made.

In many other respects the GPA is an admirable piece of work that represents a genuine attempt to respond to the subtleties of genetic information and also to strike an equitable balance between the various interests that are at stake.[117] Matters of consent predominate, but control of private data also gives way in the face of stronger interests such as law enforcement, court-ordered analysis or scientifically valid research, provided that adequate safeguards remain in place. This is an entirely correct approach, for in no way can it be argued that privacy is the ultimate trump in all circumstances. And, as the next section demonstrates, nor is there any reason to imagine that privacy interests need necessarily be set up in opposition to other (public) interests.

Privacy and the public interest

Powers has rightly pointed out that 'a commitment to privacy rights does not entail a commitment to absolute rights'.[118] Indeed, in the context of genetic privacy there are many reasons why this cannot be so, not least of which is the fact that we are dealing with a plethora of interests stemming from the familial nature of much of the information in question. What, then, might the limits and exceptions to privacy protection be? It is difficult to reject the argument that public interest is a valid exception to such a right, just as it is a determining factor in the law of confidentiality. The classic tension is that between the public interest in protecting private interests such as privacy and confidentiality, and the promotion of other public interests that protect the community from harm and further its collective interests. However, the devil is in the detail of determining what is meant by *public interest* in each case.

---

[117] For further discussion on the key elements required of a Genetic Privacy Act, see R. S. Fedder, 'To Know or Not to Know: Legal Perspectives on Genetic Privacy and Disclosure of an Individual's Genetic Profile' (2000) 21 *Journal of Legal Medicine* 557.

[118] M. Powers, 'Privacy and the Control of Genetic Information' in M. Frankel and A. Teich (eds.), *The Genetic Frontier: Ethics, Law and Policy* (Washington, DC, Directorate for Science Policy Programs, American Association for the Advancement of Science, 1994), p. 82.

A number of well-accepted public interests are self-evident and certainly would be included in any genetic privacy legislation. These include the prevention and detection of crime, scientifically valid and ethically justified research, and court-ordered disclosures.[119] Public health initiatives aimed at particular populations similarly might be justified where, for example, tangible harm can be avoided by effective screening and treatment. Screening of newly born babies for phenylketonuria and hypothyroidism is acceptable on such grounds.[120] In each of these examples the public in question is the community at large. But does this definition of 'public' necessarily exhaust the concept? More specifically in the context of genetics, when we ask who is the public in the public interest exception should this include the family of persons who have been tested for genetic conditions?

The family as community in microcosm

A public is a collective defined – like society – by reference to the individual. Relatively speaking, the collection of individuals in a family unit might constitute a public by virtue of the fact that, as a collective with a common interest in familial information, they have claim to the information in question. However, this is not to suggest that a familial public necessarily has the same common interest in the information,[121] for, as we have seen, a number of potentially competing interests may be in play. Nor is it to propose that a familial public should have an automatic or

---

[119] The US Secretary of Health and Human Services recommended five guidelines in 1997 to shape the future of health privacy laws. Among these was the principle of 'public responsibility' which states that 'individuals' claims to privacy must be balanced by their public responsibility to contribute to the public good through use of their information for important socially useful purposes, with the understanding that their information will be used with respect and care and will be legally protected': see Department of Health and Human Services, *Confidentiality of Individually-identifiable Health Information: Recommendation of the Secretary of Health and Human Services, Pursuant to Section 264 of the Health Insurance Portability and Accountability Act 1996* (Washington, DC, DHHS, 1997).

[120] But the security of the samples taken from such infants deserve no less stringent security measures for having been the source of valuable medical interventions; see generally R. Weir (ed.), *Stored Tissue Samples: Ethical, Legal and Public Policy Implications* (Iowa City, University of Iowa Press, 1998), especially ch. 1.

[121] Note, however, that Ruth Chadwick has pointed out that the concept of solidarity can be invoked to justify a claim that families do have a collective claim concerning the use and control of their genetic information. See R. Chadwick, 'The Philosophy of the Right to Know and the Right Not to Know', in Chadwick, Levitt and Shickle, *The Right to Know and the Right Not to Know*, p. 20.

strong(er) claim to the information by virtue of its strength of numbers alone. The balance, were there to be one, would need to be between the familial public interest weighed against another public interest, such as the interest in respecting individual privacy, or the public interest in protecting individuals from potentially harmful uses of their own personal information.

While such a communitarian approach to privacy and genetic information scarcely has been contemplated,[122] it is a self-evident and natural corollary to the recognition of the range of claims surrounding this sort of information. If the family is to come to be seen as community in microcosm, then the collective claims and interests of that community also must be determined and weighed in the balance of values when assessing the appropriateness of any dealings with familial genetic data. If the main thrust of this work, which is to suggest the need for a paradigm shift in ethical and legal responses to genetic advances, is accepted then this might necessitate refocusing attention more generally away from purely individualistic, autonomy-based concerns. If this is the case, then the relevance of other similar claims, such as group claims, also falls to be considered.[123]

So, then, can we and should we ever set the individual against the group? In other words, should we recognise group rights in respect of familial genetic information? If so, this presupposes that such a familial interest could be coherently formulated. This is by no means an easy task. While we have already seen some evidence of the law giving effect to familial group interests in the context of exceptions to the duty of confidence, and while similar exercises of discretion might also feature in any specific genetic privacy protection, it is another matter entirely to consider whether the family as a distinct group should be granted rights of its own. Such a process would face numerous difficult questions and problems: (i) who is the 'family' in this context? does it, for example, include non-blood relatives who have married into the genetic family and who have an interest in their own reproductive choices? (ii) which

---

[122] Cf. A. Etzioni, *The Limits of Privacy* (Basic Books, NY, 1999), M. Foster *et al.* 'The Role of Community Review in Evaluating the Risks of Human Genetic Variation Research' (1999) 64 *American Journal of Human Genetics* 1719, and H. Rubinstein, 'If I Am Only for Myself, What Am I? A Communitarian Look at the Privacy Stalemate' (1999) 25 *American Journal of Law and Medicine* 203.

[123] M. Parker, 'Public Deliberation and Private Choice in Genetics and Reproduction' (2000) 26 *Journal of Medical Ethics* 160.

rights could the family claim? how could the family as a unitary entity simultaneously claim rights to know and rights not to know when, in essence, these are matters for the individuals within the group? (iii) how are these rights to be established or exercised in the absence of consensus among family members? (iv) how strong or weak would family rights be in the light of the different kinds of knowledge that different forms of genetic information give us? (v) who would speak for the interests of the family? (vi) how should family interests be set up against individual interests? and (vii) how would conflict be resolved?

Community consent

The focus of modern autonomy discourse on individual choice tends to ignore the fact that individual choices cannot be taken in isolation. The impact of personal decisions on a wider community must also be examined, and this is self-evidently the case in the context of genetics, when uses or misuses of genetic information can have repercussions within families or indeed entire communities. The communitarian nature of many forms of genetic information has certainly been recognised. There is a wealth of literature on familial rights and responsibilities and the collective claims of groups such as indigenous peoples to their genetic heritage.[124] But one avenue of research to emerge from this is that of community consent. In most cases, this has been typified by the attempt to force the essentially individualistic paradigm of consent into a communitarian model, with considerable lack of success, not least because the power of the community can be usurped by the actions of the individual, for example by the individual who consents to provide samples when the community has refused to do so.[125] More fundamentally, however, this approach is misguided because it is blinkered to the more important issue of respect.[126] Consent is not the only means of offering respect to human beings, either as individuals or as a collective. Thus,

---

[124] For an informative and unique perspective see D. Posey and G. Dutfield, *Beyond Intellectual Property: Towards Traditional Resource Rights for Indigenous Peoples and Local Communities* (Ottawa, International Development Research Centre, 1996).

[125] As an example of an attempt at guidelines see North American Regional Committee of the Human Genome Diversity Project, 'Proposed Model Ethical Protocol for Collecting DNA Samples' (1997) 33 *Houston Law Review* 1431.

[126] For this and other reasons Annas prefers to seek community consultation rather than community consent; see G. J. Annas, 'Rules for Research on Human Genetic Variation – Lessons from Iceland' (2000) 342 *New England Journal of Medicine* 1830.

respect for familial interests in genetic information need not be accorded only by obtaining consent from the family. Indeed, this might prove to be impossible. Respect, however, might be achieved in a number of alternative ways, for example by placing clear limits on what individuals can expect of, or do with, their own genetic data.[127] Furthermore, we are not required to grant families rights over genetic data in order to respect their interests in those data. A rights-based discourse polarises the parties who might have competing claims, and offers us little means to differentiate between those claims. This approach also obscures the possibility that we might owe *duties* to others in respect of the claims that they might make of us, and that such duties can in turn temper the legitimacy of any rights that we might claim.[128] This is a far less individualistic view of the problem and takes us some way towards a communitarian perspective on the interests and roles that each of us might have.[129] It also raises the spectre of cultural relativism.[130]

Communitarianism and social paternalism

This work is written from within a highly individualistic culture, where the cult of the individual holds strong sway both in ethics and in law. Despite this, it is not difficult to find examples of less individualistic, more communitarian ethical approaches and legal provisions that regulate the medical sphere and those in it. A good example is Israel's Patients' Rights Act 1996, which attempts to integrate an autonomy perspective into a tradition that is strongly paternalistic and communitarian. Inter alia, this law permits patients a right to informed consent but denies a right to informed refusal. Refusals are considered by committees who have the power to override the patient's wishes and order treatment if this is thought to be in the patient's own interests. For example, in one case the refusal by a parent was overridden in respect of extraordinary treatment

[127] L. Skene, 'Patients' Rights or Family Responsibilities? Two Approaches to Genetic Testing' (1998) 6 *Medical Law Review* 1.
[128] C. Kutz, *Complicity: Ethics and Law for a Collective Age* (Cambridge, Cambridge University Press, 2000).
[129] J. A. K. Kegley, 'Using Genetic Information: The Individual and the Community' (1996) 15 *Medicine and Law* 377.
[130] F. Maekawa and D. Macer, 'The Japanese Concept of Familial Privacy and Genetic Information' (1999) 9 *Eubios Journal of Asian and International Bioethics* 66, and Y. K. Chan, 'Privacy in the Family: Its Hierarchical and Asymmetric Nature' (2000) 31 *Journal of Comparative Family Studies* 1.

for his child who was suffering from Tay-Sachs disease.[131] Decision by committee is, therefore, not alien to this society.[132] Nor, in fact, is the determination of the optimal outcome by reference to the interests at stake. One rationale behind this regulation is a philosophy of *social paternalism* which reflects interdependence, a desire to harmonise individual and social good, and a belief that the individual will subdue selfish interests and actions for the greater good of the collective. This is not to say, however, that social paternalism ignores individual autonomy: 'Social paternalism repersonalizes amorphous individuals by making them the object of intense concern by members of the community. Regard for the individual reaffirms the individual's self-esteem and individuality'.[133] Social paternalism provides a 'moral voice' to guide the individual in making the 'right moral decision'. Listening only to one's 'inner voice', as Etzioni suggests, 'renders one's moral deliberations "defective"'.[134]

More recently, Israel has passed the Genetic Information Act 2000 which guarantees protection for genetic privacy while at the same time setting limits on that protection in the name of communitarian interests.[135] Thus, for example, the legislation permits disclosure of personal genetic data to relatives when this is necessary to preserve the relatives' health or to improve it, or to avoid death, disease or disability in a relative, including the unborn.[136] This recognition of the interests of the yet-to-be-born goes beyond any guidance that has been issued in states such as the United Kingdom or the United States. It also admits the reproductive choice interests of relatives as a justification for compromising a proband's privacy. Moreover, the Act acknowledges the interest in not knowing, for it leaves the decision whether to disclose genetic test results to the discretion of the health care professional if it is thought that this will cause serious physical or mental harm to the disclosee. If

---

[131] For comment generally, see M. Gross, 'Autonomy and Paternalism in Communitarian Society: Patient Rights in Israel' (1999) July–August *Hastings Center Report* 13.

[132] For a similar proposal see J. Gunter Bruns and M. Wolman, 'Morality of the Privacy of Genetic Information: Possible Improvements of Procedures' (2000) 19 *Medicine and Law* 127.

[133] Gross, 'Autonomy and Paternalism', 17.

[134] A. Etzioni, 'On Restoring the Moral Voice', in A. Etzioni (ed.), *Rights and the Common Good: The Communitarian Perspective* (New York, St. Martin's Press, 1995), pp. 271–6 at p. 273.

[135] I am grateful to Roy Gilbar for providing me with a translation of this Act.

[136] Genetic Information Act 2000, s.20. The Act goes on to provide that disclosure must be the sole means to achieve this aim and that the benefit to the relative must outweigh any harm to the person from whom the information is initially derived.

the health care professional decides not to disclose, this must be communicated to the relevant ethics committee, which can take evidence
and confirm or overturn the decision.[137]

To Western eyes these measures are strongly paternalistic – probably
unacceptably so – but according to another view it is an approach that
is invitingly non-confrontational. It seeks to imbue the community and
its members with a collective consciousness that places others, and not
oneself, as the paramount consideration in a decision-making process.
Perhaps within such a belief system familial group rights will one day
be realisable. Certainly, as an approach that seeks harmony, it stands in
stark contrast with the more autonomy-driven view that is represented
by Anglo-American legal systems, where conflict is the order of the day
and competing 'rights' are in constant tension.

But how does one change an entire culture and its beliefs? This work
clearly cannot answer that question, but it is worth reflecting none the
less on the possibilities that are open to us. Is this a classic example of
the search for the original progenitor: should we seek to reform beliefs
through law, or should law respond to cultural beliefs? If advances in
genetics teach us anything, they teach that even with a system of ethics
and law that has been many hundreds of years in the making, we should
still be receptive to the need to reflect and possibly change our approach
as to how we organise our society.

Legal policy and political will

At no point should we dismiss the possibility that the role of the law
might, in fact, be limited in a complex domain such as this. For one
thing, it would prove very difficult in practice to control the free flow of
information within families. To attempt to police something as intangible as information within the family unit might prove to be foolhardy.
Indeed, it is hard to get away from the conclusion that in many circumstances families are best left alone to deal with familial issues in their
own way. But this still leaves considerable scope and need for privacy
protection against parties outside the family, such as employers, insurers, health care professionals and the state. Certainly, in many cases the
most serious of threats will come from such quarters.

---

[137] *Ibid.*, s.14.

A communitarian perspective for group claims might carry considerable moral and political weight even if it does little to advance legal policy. Two examples illustrate this point. In the United States, families affected by pseudoxanthoma elasticum (PXE) – a rare genetic disorder that causes tissues in the skin, eyes and arteries to calcify – set a new precedent in 2000 by entering an agreement with scientists to cooperate in research in return for being named as joint-applicants in any subsequent patent filing arising from the studies. The patients' advocacy group, PXE International, established its own blood and tissues bank and was thereby able to control access to samples. Scientists were required to sign an agreement prior to gaining access.[138] The group hopes to exert its influence to ensure free licensing access and low cost tests and treatments.[139] That the group was able to reach this stage is a testament to its cooperation and initiative, but from the legal perspective a serious question mark hangs over the success of the project. Absent an action for breach of contract, it is not at all clear where a remedy for PXE International would lie if further patent applications were filed by the researchers without its involvement. In particular, it is very doubtful whether a claim to ownership of samples, the contents of the gene banks or any information derived from them would stand, although this would be the most amenable remedy to address the issues at hand. We shall return to this matter in chapter 6. The point to note for present purposes is that a role for the law might nevertheless remain in this new age of commercialisation.

The prospect of community-wide benefit from genetic and other health research has been offered in support of the establishment of the Icelandic Health Sector Database. Controversially, however, the collective interests of the Icelandic people have been held out as justification for a regime that seems to go against individual interests in that it requires no active giving of informed consent to participate in the database. It might be thought, therefore, that these two examples pull in different directions. The families affected by PXE have staked a claim to their own condition and have thereby been able to exercise continuing control over the uses of their genetic information, while the Icelandic example appears to thwart individual interests at the expense of public

---

[138] P. Smaglik, 'Tissue Donors Use their Influence in Deal Over Gene Patent Terms' (2000) 407 *Nature* 821.

[139] See http://www.pxe.org

benefit. However, seen from another perspective these two examples are not as inconsistent as they might first appear.

Public and private interests in research

A strong commitment to the concept of privacy could assist in further-ing public health interests that might otherwise be compromised by an overly zealous adherence to traditional ethical paradigms. The Icelandic Health Sector Database is an example of this.[140] It was established after the Icelandic parliament, the Althing, adopted a law of 17 December 1998 permitting a private company, DeCode Genetics, to establish and maintain a database of the population's health records. One of the ul-timate aims of this project is to tap the rich genetic resources of the Icelandic people as a uniquely genetically homogeneous population. But in order to provide the best epidemiological and statistical data, a high proportion of the population must participate. To facilitate this, the Icelandic law adopted an opt-out scheme for participation in the database. In addition to the obvious utilitarian public interest that this serves, the ethical justification relies upon the stringent privacy protec-tion measures that are embodied in the law.[141] In other words, strong privacy protection of individual personal information is a justification for the use of that information in the public interest. The alternative, and more traditional, approach of an opt-in scheme pays requisite lip-service to the principle of respect for individual autonomy, but runs the risk of inadequate participation in the project. That the Icelanders have departed from this latter principle is of considerable interest. While it is by no means uncontroversial,[142] it does signal a shift in the percep-tion of the relative values of public and private interests when valuable

[140] O. M. Arnardóttir, D. T. Björgvinsson and V. M. Matthíasson, 'The Icelandic Health Sector Database' (1999) 6 *European Journal of Health Law* 307, and H. Jónatansson, 'Iceland's Health Sector Database: A Significant Head Start in the Search for the Biological Grail or an Irreversible Error?' (2000) 26 *American Journal of Law and Medicine* 31.

[141] Inter alia, privacy is protected by the Act on a Health Sector Database no. 139/1998, Act on Biobanks no. 110/2000, Government Regulation no. 32/2000 on a Health Sector Database, Act on the Protection of Individuals with regard to Processing of Personal Data no. 77/2000, and Regulations on the Keeping and Utilisation of Biological Samples in Biobanks no. 134/2001.

[142] See, for example, R. Chadwick, 'The Icelandic Database – Do Modern Times Need Modern Sagas?' (1999) 319 *British Medical Journal* 441, and H. Roscam Abbing, 'Central Health Database in Iceland and Patients' Rights' (1999) 6 *European Journal of Health Law* 363.

research is at stake.[143] Arguably, it is an approach that remains ethically justifiable and which challenges established ethical parameters by showing a renewed faith in privacy as a principle that can serve both public *and* private interests. Estonia has also started work on plans to create a similar database of its 1.4 million population,[144] which would be the largest such resource in the world.[145]

Iceland, for its part, has more recently extended its model to biological samples. Regulations on the keeping and utilisation of biological samples in biobanks emerged in 2001, making it lawful to use samples gathered for the purposes of clinical tests or treatment with the proviso that presumed consent could only be assumed after patients had been furnished with relevant information concerning this possible use.[146] In like manner, the advent of the Health Sector Database saw a nationwide publicity campaign designed to inform every citizen of the proposed scheme and offering them the opportunity to opt out. Almost 20,000 Icelanders had done so by May 2001, representing some 7 per cent of the population. Mannvernd, the Association of Icelanders for Ethics in Science and Medicine, has mounted a lawsuit challenging the constitutionality of the law creating the database.[147]

An analysis of the Icelandic experience should proceed along two lines of inquiry, that into principles and that into practicalities. It is submitted that there is nothing in principle that is wrong with the model of presumed consent adopted by the Icelanders. There is a strong public interest that can be best furthered by the model that has been instituted, and there is nothing to indicate that that model is prima facie disrespectful of the Icelandic people. An opt-out system is entirely commensurate with respect for individual autonomy because individuals have the option to choose not to participate.[148] It is true that once data are entered

---

[143] R. Chadwick and K. Berg, 'Solidarity and Equity: New Ethical Frameworks for Genetic Databases' (2001) 2(4) *Nature Reviews* 318.

[144] Human Genes Research Act 2000.

[145] On the inestimable value of creating a database using information from the NHS in the United Kingdom, see R. Fears and G. Poste, 'Building Population Genetics Resources Using the UK NHS' (1999) 284 *Science* 267.

[146] Regulations on the Keeping and Utilisation of Biological Samples in Biobanks no.134/2001, Article 8.

[147] The law suit was launched on 4 February 2000: see Mannvernd (Human Protection): http://www.mannvernd.is/english/home.html

[148] Other examples of opt-out systems in the public good already exist in countries such as Belgium and Austria concerning organ removal on death. This is not an exact analogy, however, given that the individuals are deceased when the public good is to be furthered, thereby restricting, although not entirely eliminating, any impact on their interests.

into the database it can become difficult or impossible for them to be removed, but so long as people are aware of this and are given the opportunity to opt out in time, then there is no first-order objection. The obligation to ensure that the people are informed should, of course, fall to the government as the progenitor of the database, and the standard should be one of informed dissent. More fundamentally, while the interests of those who are willing to participate should always be protected, the public good of research is a strong reason not to place all of our eggs in the consent basket. As Harris has said:

> in the case of research on the human tissue archive, that is research on samples that have already been taken for some other purpose, there is no risk whatsoever – or rather there is no risk save that which might flow from any breach of confidentiality or anonymity. If there were no strong reasons to pursue such research we would have no reason to think about whether or not there might be an obligation to participate. But, this is emphatically not the case with research on human tissue.
>
> Of course contributions to this archive must be made with scrupulous ethical and legal safeguards and the respect for human individuals and human rights that these safeguards represent.[149]

According to such a view there is not only a strong public interest in research but there is a societal and individual obligation to participate, even if this occurs in some circumstances without informed consent.[150] Moreover, the ethical appropriateness of such a scheme derives from the fact that individual interests and rights are protected under a privacy model, and privacy therefore becomes the paramount ethical imperative.

The proper concerns about the Icelandic experience should lie with the practicalities and not the principle of what has or has not been done. Practically there is much wrong with this scheme.[151] For example, there is evidence that the public was insufficiently informed about the database, thereby undermining the principle of informed dissent. Moreover, the law simply requires that 'The Director General of Public Health shall ensure that information on the health-sector database and on the rights of patients shall be accessible to the public. Health institutions and self-employed health workers shall have this information available

---

[149] J. Harris, 'Ethics and Research on Human Genetic Material' (2001) 1(4) *Genetics Law Monitor* 1, 2.

[150] *Id.*

[151] For a history and review of the system see H. Rose, *The Commodification of Bioinformation: The Icelandic Health Sector Database* (London, The Wellcome Trust, 2001).

to patients on their premises.'[152] This falls far short of ensuring an adequate standard of public awareness, knowledge and understanding.[153]

In other respects there has been insufficient discussion of the harder cases. What should happen to children's information or that of incapacitated persons? It has been assumed that families will act in the interests of such persons, but this cannot be guaranteed nor will a consensus necessarily emerge among family members. Also, it is not clear whether data can be withdrawn as a matter of right once it has been entered into the database.

From the privacy perspective there have been concerns over the security provisions of information on the database.[154] Personal data are stripped of personal identifiers and the exclusive licensee has no opportunity to match data it receives with actual individuals. None the less, a report commissioned by the Icelandic Medical Association was critical of this approach as 'insufficient', arguing that in such a small population a very few fragments of information could lead to identification and that the technical security measures that were envisaged were lacking.[155] Since then the Icelandic Data Protection Commission has issued tighter guidelines on the general security terms under which data are to be kept.[156]

Perhaps most controversially, the Icelandic model has been criticised over its for-profit approach in granting a monopoly licence to a commercial organisation to create, maintain and ultimately exploit the database. Inter alia, this has led to accusations that the Icelandic government has 'sold the genes of its people', for undoubtedly patents and other property rights will emerge from the work of DeCode and its partners.[157] Certainly, the private enterprise aspect of the project has tainted its

---

[152] Act on a Health Sector Database no. 139/1998, Article 8.

[153] For a critique of the presumed consent approach, see D. E. Winickoff, 'Biosamples, Genomics and Human Rights: Context and Content of Iceland's Biobanks Act' (2000) 4 *Journal of BioLaw and Business* 11.

[154] See generally J. G. Anderson and C. E. Aydin, 'Evaluating Medical Information Systems: Social Contexts and Ethical Challenges', in K.W. Goodman (ed.), *Ethics, Computing, and Medicine* (Cambridge, Cambridge University Press, 1998).

[155] R. Anderson, 'Iceland's Medical Database is Insecure' (1999) 319 *British Medical Journal* 59, and R. Anderson,'The DeCODE proposal for an Icelandic health database' (1998) 84 *Icelandic Medical Journal* 874.

[156] Icelandic Data Protection Commission, General Security Terms of the Icelandic Data Protection Commission, January 2000.

[157] See H. T. Greely, 'Iceland's Plan for Genomics Research: Facts and Implications' (2000) 40 *Jurimetrics* 153.

credibility and the prospect of property rights has sullied its reputation even further. But this debate is riddled with misconceptions and inaccuracies that ignore the realities of contemporary scientific culture whereby little in the way of population-wide research can be done exclusively in the public sector.[158] Public/private partnership is often inevitable. This controversy will be examined more closely in chapter 6. Estonia has avoided this level of criticism by ensuring that its population health database will be managed by a non-profit organisation.[159] The Estonian legislation also does not envisage control by an exclusive licensee, thereby also eliding the criticism of the Icelandic system that its operation will give too great a monopoly to one enterprise, thereby hindering, rather than promoting, research.

All of these observations are well made. None, however, undermines the point of principle that an opt-out system that is designed to further research in the public good, and which does so within a regime of stringent privacy protection, is, in and of itself, an ethically justifiable public good. But this is not to suggest either that problems of principle do not arise. For example, while it might be possible to opt out of the system at any time with respect to future data, it might not be practically possible to withdraw existing data from the database. Thus, I might be happy to participate when the government is running the database, but I might not wish to continue if the government sells out to private enterprise.[160] But if I cannot claw back data that have already been supplied this might be seen as a limitation on my autonomy. This point could, however, be addressed through the mechanism of informed dissent, that is, that part of the information people should be given should make provision for the fact that data, once entered, cannot be retrieved. The decision then not to opt out is taken in the light of these realities. Moreover, even if there is a recognised limitation on the autonomy of those who later opt out, it might be justified or outweighed by the greater public interest in

---

[158] Cf. J. B. Martin and D. L. Kasper, 'In Whose Best Interest? Breaching the Academic–Industrial Wall' (2000) 343 *New England Journal of Medicine* 1646.

[159] Human Genes Research Act 2000, §3.

[160] The impact of the political unacceptability of such a reversal of fortune should also not be underestimated. In January 2001 a Massachusetts company was disbanded after it proposed to turn a non-profit fifty-year-old heart study project in Framingham, MA, into a for-profit venture. This research has been highly significant in the understanding of heart disease, and the proposal to privatise it met with such a storm of protest that the plans were quickly scrapped; see K. Philipkoski, 'Framingham Gene Project Killed' *Wired News*, 2 January 2001: http://www.wired.com/news/medtech/

population-based research. The following analogy is helpful. If I create an artistic work in the course of employment any intellectual property rights over it will go to my employer, even though the work is an expression of my personality. When I leave that employment I will control any future artistic works that I create, but I cannot retrospectively stake a claim to past creations, even if in moral terms I retain a relationship with them. I will, none the less, retain legally recognised *moral rights* in respect of those works,[161] which means, inter alia, that the intellectual property holder cannot treat the works in a manner that is disrespectful to my personality. In like manner, while it may not be feasible or acceptable to expect extraction of personal data from a database on withdrawal, that does not mean that those data are then freed from constraints ensuring adequate security and respect for them.

Children will automatically be entered on the Icelandic database unless their parents express a contrary wish. How, then, does this respect the interests of the child who ultimately might object to the fact that eighteen years of data have been collected and used for research? How, though, is this different to the current practice of taking Guthrie blood spots from every newborn child for the purposes of testing and research? As an adult I might object to the fact that it was done, but because it was done it has served both my own and other public interests. Certainly, it might be argued that the Icelandic Health Sector Database will contain much more information about me than could be derived from a Guthrie spot – although a spot could reveal my entire genetic make-up – but this is a difference of degree and not of kind. The justification for both practices is the same.

Finally, if the major point of principled objection is the failure to obtain informed consent, those who advocate this approach must address the fundamental flaw in their position; namely, how can meaningful informed consent be obtained to future, yet-to-be-determined research? Realistically and logically this is simply not possible, unless the consent to be obtained is blanket consent for all time coming.[162] If so, then the ethical credentials of this approach are seriously in doubt, for how can

---

[161] Certainly this is true in Europe.

[162] In *Norman-Bloodshaw* v. *Lawrence Berkeley Laboratory*, 135 F 3d 1260 (9th Cir. 1998) the Court of Appeals for the 9th US Circuit held that when samples that had been provided for one set of genetic tests were then tested for others without express consent this constituted 'a separate and more invasive intrusion into privacy', 1275.

I give valid consent to something I do not know about? Do consent advocates seriously contend that consent should be obtained for each and every future use? This, of course, would be practically impossible and in some cases unethical.[163] What, then, is the value of informed consent to such a project beyond paying mere lip-service to the principle of respect for autonomy? As an alternative, Roche *et al.* have argued that research would be permissible and that new consent would not be required provided that DNA is stripped of all of its identifiers.[164]

Knoppers has rightly pointed out that our ethical normative frameworks to date have largely focused on the protection of the individual, and that we are ill-equipped at the present time to accommodate the ethical issues surrounding any dealings with 'collectivities' such as heterogeneous populations.[165] While in no way should it be suggested that protection of individual rights is not important, there are more imaginative ways in which this can be achieved without rigid adherence to a consent model, and which can at the same time further collective interests such as those relating to valuable genetic research. Robust protection of privacy is one such alternative model that can achieve this while maintaining ethical credibility and offering some basis for more appropriate legal protection.

Research and anonymity

Ellis and Mannion have argued that 'The key to solving this dilemma of using unconsented samples has to be in anonymising the samples.'[166] This view accords with the English Court of Appeal which held in *Source Informatics* that so long as the privacy interests of patients were protected by anonymity no action for breach of confidence could lie if data were subsequently used for research purposes.[167] Indeed, to the extent that this decision now represents the legal position in the United Kingdom,

[163] Royal College of Pathologists, Guidelines for the Retention of Tissues and Organs at Postmortem Examination (Royal College of Pathologists, London, 2000), and Royal College of Pathologists, Submission to the Chief Medical Officer's National Summit on the Retention of Organs and Tissues (RCP, London, 11 January 2001).
[164] Roche *et al.*, 'The Genetic Privacy Act', and the GPA itself, §105(c).
[165] B. M. Knoppers, 'Of Populations, Genetics and Banks' (2001) 1(4) *Genetics Law Monitor* 3.
[166] I. Ellis and G. Mannion, 'Humanity versus Utility in the Ethics of Research on Human Genetic Material' (2001) 1(5) *Genetics Law Monitor* 1.
[167] *R v. Department of Health, ex parte Source Informatics Ltd.* [2000] 1 All ER 786.

that position is arguably more detrimental to the interests of citizens than the regime in operation in Iceland. This is because the law in the United Kingdom does not require any consent from patients for such uses of anonymised data, nor does it provide for any means to object provided that the uses are 'fair'.[168] The Icelandic model does at least allow citizens to exercise their autonomy to opt out of the scheme. Moreover, the terms of the Data Protection Act 1998 do not apply to protect UK citizens in this context because its provisions only extend to data from which individuals can be identified. Indeed, the EC Directive on Data Protection expressly excludes anonymised data from the remit of the law.[169] Furthermore, it ensures that in some circumstances data can be processed without consent, provided that to do so is justifiable by reference to a valid public interest, such as scientific research.[170]

But anonymisation is not the complete answer. For one thing, it is not clear that it is an adequate means in and of itself to protect privacy. Certainly, anonymisation of data or samples can go far in protecting the interests of the persons to whom they relate, and it can influence the ethical appropriateness of gathering and using samples or data, because the risk of harm through misuse is greatly reduced. When anonymisation occurs, the quality of the relationship that an individual has with her sample or her information is reduced, and this permits other interests to weigh more heavily in the balance. At no point, however, does that relationship cease to exist, for anonymisation is merely a process to ensure security. And, because no process is infallible, there always remains the possibility that anonymity can be breached and that significant harm to individuals will result. The fundamental interest that individuals have in their genetic samples and information must never be forgotten, for genomic data can serve as a marker unique to the individual from whom they were derived. Such data cannot, therefore, be completely anonymised. This is not to say that the information cannot be used in anonymised programmes of research, it is simply to state that the risk is increased of non-person-specific information becoming person-specific. The problem then distils, initially at least, into one of ensuring adequate protection of the informational privacy interests of those who provide sensitive genetic data. The imperative to protect arises in respect of all anonymised information, but, as Gostin has said,

---

[168] See further ch. 4.   [169] Data Protection Directive, Recital 26.
[170] *Ibid.*, Recitals 30–36.

although the ability to identify a named individual in a large population simply from genetic material is unlikely, the capacity of computers to search multiple data bases provides a potential for linking genomic information to that person. It follows that non linked genomic data do not assure anonymity and that privacy and security safeguards must attach to any form of genetic material.[171]

Two forms of anonymity exist. Absolute anonymity is achieved when no means are available to link data to an identifiable individual. Proportional or reasonable anonymity exists when no reasonable means of identification of specific individuals is possible. In this latter respect, the use of linked or linkable coded information is a common means of achieving anonymity, when access to the link is restricted appropriately. It is generally accepted that proportional anonymity of samples or personal data is sufficient to comply with international standards of anonymisation, as laid down, inter alia, in the EC Directive on Data Protection.[172] However, as a less secure method of protection, proportional anonymisation alone does not necessarily meet the ethical requirements of respect for individuals. That is, mere compliance with legal standards of anonymity may not be enough, if, for example, anonymisation procedures are inadequate, without review, or otherwise defective in their protection of individual interests.[173]

Anonymisation should be seen simply as part of the process of respect for individuals and the interests that they have in their own genetic samples and information. As the World Health Organisation Working Group on Genetic Databases has recommended,

> While the use of anonymisation can lead to a re-assessment of the balance between the protection of individual interests on the one hand, and the legitimate pursuit of public interests on the other, it is recommended that any anonymisation process be overseen by an independent body that would have the following obligations:

---

[171] L. Gostin, 'Genetic Privacy' (1995) 23 *Journal of Law, Medicine and Ethics* 320, 322. For comment on US legal attempts and proposals to protect patient interests while allowing access to genetic information, see E. W. Clayton, 'Panel Comment: Why the Use of Anonymous Samples for Research Matters' (1995) 23 *Journal of Law, Medicine and Ethics* 375.

[172] See also the Council of Europe's Recommendation on Regulations for Automated Medical Databanks (No. R (81)1) and Council of Europe Recommendation on the Protection of Medical Data (1997, No. R (97)5).

[173] For practical advice see P. Furness, *The Data Protection Act and Human Tissue* (Royal College of Pathologists, London, 2001).

(1) To scrutinise and ensure the legitimacy of requests to the database;
(2) To act, where possible, as an intermediary between the creators and the users of the database, in respect of decoding apparatus used to anonymise and/or link data held on the database;
(3) To maintain standards and keep anonymisation processes under review.[174]

Tension and trust

The irony is that we have at the same time too much and too little privacy.[175] The dearth of privacy protection has already been well documented. The excess of protection stems from the fact that autonomy interests have been taken to be synonymous with those of privacy, when the reality is that the two interrelate but also have separate existences. However, the focus on protection of autonomy has led to an atomistic view of the ethical and legal appropriateness of public interest measures such as genetic research, with the result that the attempt to further those interests has led to a serious tension between individual rights and public goods.[176] For example, the House of Lords has recommended – 'as a matter of urgency' – that the General Medical Council advise its members that they are not required to obtain signed consent from patients before personal data are passed to disease registries. Ambiguous guidance on this matter was roundly condemned in evidence to the Select Committee as being an unwarranted threat to the public value of such registers.[177]

But it is not at all clear that tension is an inevitable given.[178] Thurston *et al.* have argued that ethically valid research can be carried out in certain circumstances without consent, but that 'research curiosity and the

---

[174] World Health Organisation European Partnership on Patients' Rights and Citizens' Empowerment, *Genetic Databases: Assessing the Benefits and the Impact on Patients and Human Rights* (WHO, Copenhagen, 2001), para. 4.2.

[175] See generally Etzioni, *The Limits of Privacy*.

[176] On the problems of requiring consent from family members to conduct genetic research, see American Society of Human Genetics, 'Should Family Members About Whom You Collect Only Medical History Information for Your Research Be Considered "Research Subjects"?' (March 2000, http://www.ashg.org/genetics/ashg/policy/pol-38.htm), responding to B. M. Knoppers *et al.*, 'Professional Disclosure of Familial Genetic Information' (1998) 62 *American Journal of Human Genetics* 474.

[177] House of Lords Select Committee on Science and Technology, *Human Genetic Databases: Challenges and Opportunities* (2001 HL 57), paras. 7.29–7.33 and 7.55.

[178] J. Harris, 'Ethical Genetic Research on Human Subjects' (1999) 40 *Jurimetrics* 77.

convenience of database research cannot justify the suspension of moral concerns about privacy and confidentiality'.[179] This is entirely correct. Sound ethical review of all such proposed research is axiomatic.[180] Adequate privacy protection of subjects must always follow. Beyond this, however, the consent imperative should not be imbued with an importance that tips the balance of interests too far in its own favour. The Medical Research Council (MRC) has recommended that

> If individual written consent cannot be obtained, research using samples of material surplus to clinical requirements is only acceptable if the results cannot affect the patient's or their family's interests. The patient must also have been informed at the time the sample was taken that their material might be used for research, for example by clearly displaying notices, by distribution of leaflets, or on the clinical consent form itself.[181]

A proposal under the joint auspices of the Wellcome Trust and the MRC has been made to establish a Population Biomedical Collection in the United Kingdom involving up to 500,000 participants.[182] The study would follow subjects through various stages of their lives and through periods of good and ill health,[183] examining genotypic and phenotypic data together with environmental factors to establish the relationships between diseases and genes and the interaction between genes and environment.[184] While informed consent would form an essential feature of the study, and rightly so in such circumstances, the study is currently on hold while wider issues are addressed, among which are questions of security of data and privacy protection. It is entirely fit and proper that a study of this magnitude and potential importance have

---

[179] W. E. Thurston et al., 'Ethical Issues in the Use of Computerized Databases for Epidemiological and Other Health Research' (1999) 20 *Chronic Diseases in Canada* 127, citing Medical Research Council of Canada, Natural Sciences and Engineering Research Council of Canada, Social Sciences and Humanity Research Council of Canada, *Tri-council Policy Statement: Ethical Conduct for Research Involving Humans* (Public Works and Government Services Canada, Ottawa, 1998).

[180] R. J. R. Blatt, 'Banking Biological Collections: Data Warehousing, Data Mining, and Data Dilemmas in Genomics and Global Health Policy' (2000) 3 *Community Genetics* 204.

[181] Medical Research Council, *Human Tissue and Biological Samples for Use in Research* (MRC, London, 2001), para. 3.5. See too MRC, *Personal Information in Medical Research* (MRC, London, 2000).

[182] For a comparison of the UK proposal with the Icelandic experience, see J. Kaye and P. Martin, 'Safeguards for Research Using Large Scale DNA Collections' (2000) 321 *British Medical Journal* 1146.

[183] The cohort of volunteers would be aged between 45 and 64 years.

[184] The Wellcome Trust: http://www.wellcome.ac.uk/en/1/awtpubnwswnoi24ana2.html

the healthiest of ethical credentials.[185] But of equal importance is the need for the support of the public in such a venture. As the next chapter will explore, this aspect of 'ethicising' research has for too long received short shrift, with the result that a crisis of confidence is now a serious hurdle to the success of such a project.

---

[185] For an indication of the kind of issues that must be addressed see House of Lords, *Human Genetic Databases*.

6

Privacy *and* property?

Privacy, property and the personality

Privacy issues in the field of genetics have been addressed by a number of international bodies in a variety of instruments. For example, the Bilbao Declaration highlights the main problem areas that are likely to arise from the work of the Human Genome Project, and pinpoints matters considered to be worthy of immediate attention by the legal systems of the world. The Declaration includes, 'protection of the personal privacy or confidentiality of genetic information, and determination of cases in which it could feasibly be altered or overstepped'.[1] Moreover, the interest in not knowing – a central focus of this work – has also been recognised. The Council of Europe states in Article 10(2) of its Convention on Human Rights and Biomedicine: 'Everyone is entitled to know any information collected about his or her health. However, the wishes of individuals not to be so informed shall be observed'.[2] Similarly, the UNESCO Universal Declaration on the Human Genome and Human Rights states in Article 5c: 'The right of every individual to decide whether or not to be informed of the results of genetic examination and the resulting consequences should be respected'.[3] These instruments embody the best and the worst features of the dilemma that we currently face. They recognise the value of an interest which has hitherto received short shrift, but offer aspirational means of protection that, in the absence of specific national interventions, have no substance. Furthermore, while these instruments endorse the value of

---

[1] The Bilbao Declaration on the Human Genome was drafted in May 1993 at the International Workshop on Legal Aspects of the Human Genome Project, which took place in Bilbao, Spain.

[2] Council of Europe, *Convention for the Protection of Human Rights and Dignity of the Human Being with Regard to the Application of Biology and Medicine: Convention on Human Rights and Biomedicine* (Oviedo, 1997).

[3] UNESCO, *Universal Declaration on the Human Genome and Human Rights*, adopted unanimously on 11 November 1997 in Paris at the Organisation's 29th General Conference.

a rights discourse, they subsume the protection of the interest in not knowing within a rubric of rights of autonomy and choice. These constructs are ill-suited to the task at hand. Thus, while these international texts offer us a new way of looking at genetic information, they provide only one means of addressing the problem – one that is typical of the focus on the autonomy-based argument that is so much a cornerstone of current medical law and bioethics.

This work has argued for an original concept of privacy that would recognise and protect the interest that individuals might have in being unaware of their genetic constitution, and it has offered a view of how such an interest could be protected by legal means within a domestic system. More broadly, however, the thesis that has been put forward challenges the role and the validity of many of the existing medico-legal norms that have to date shaped our responses to medical and scientific advances. Genetics have been singled out in order to illustrate the problems that the standard current approach leaves unsolved, but the value of the privacy concept reaches far beyond the boundaries of genetic knowledge. The argument has been as much about identifying the problems and the most appropriate tools to solve them as it has been about offering concrete means to address all of the nuanced issues that arise. It is as much an appeal to view the matter from an alternative perspective, as it is an offer of a solution to the dilemmas at hand. And, just as the solution offered is not without its problems, so the reader is invited to reflect that the current approach yields little by way of solution.

A serious limitation on any concept of privacy is the fact that, as a right, it is negative in nature. That is, a privacy right – however conceived – is always a right of non-interference. It never constitutes a right of positive entitlement. To this extent, privacy suffers from limitations similar to those that afflict the principle of respect for autonomy; namely, it does not provide for any continuing control over personal matters once they enter the public sphere. Autonomy in the guise of consent reduces control to the giving or withholding of that consent, after which an individual is largely powerless to dictate what happens. Thus, for example, while an individual might consent to make private information public, she will have no continuing control over what is then done with the data. Similarly, if an individual consents to provide tissue samples for research purposes she loses personal control of those samples for all time coming. She is not in a position to control the fate of the samples by exercising her right to privacy. And, while her privacy regarding any information derived from those samples may continue to be protected, any residual authority depends on the nature of her original consent and, more importantly, on the assumption that its terms will not be violated.

Thus, it is not to be denied that privacy and autonomy offer a measure of control over our lives, but we must recognise that the power of control operates within relatively narrow limits. The interrelated concepts of privacy and autonomy are unified at the fundamental level by the fact that each reflects a valued aspect of the human personality.[4] If, however, we find them inadequate guardians of 'self', we should explore other options – as yet largely uncharted – that may give fuller protection to interests in the persona. German law, for example, protects the body as an aspect of the right to personality. So, if interference occurs with samples removed from the body – such as the unauthorised destruction of sperm – the law will provide a remedy for a breach of the *Persönlichkeitsrecht*.[5] Anglo-American law is less sophisticated in this regard. As a complement, then, to privacy and autonomy this chapter considers property rights in the self as the ultimate expression of respect and control over one's own existence.

Information as property

An important primary distinction to be made in any discussion of the attribution of a property model to the person is that between samples that are taken from individuals, such as blood or saliva, and information derived from these samples, such as genetic information. While samples are more easily recognisable as physical entities to which a property model might be applied, they are also potentially an exhaustible resource requiring careful management and control lest their existence or value be extinguished. The same is not true of abstract information. Information is a unique entity whose intangible character renders it a potentially

---

[4] The European Group on Ethics in Science and New Technologies to the European Commission recognises the same connection between personal health data and personality; see Opinion of the EGE, Ethical Issues of Healthcare in the Information Society (Opinion No.13, July 1999), para. 2.2.

[5] Bundesgerichtshof, 9 November 1993, BGHZ, 124, 52. Removed body parts that are not intended for another (such as transplant organs) or for return to the individual (such as stored sperm) are subject to the normal rules of personal property, *ibid.*

inexhaustible resource but at the same time leaves it less amenable to protection as property. If I have possession, and therefore control, over your genetic sample this necessarily and automatically deprives you of a significant interest in that sample, in that you are no longer in a position to use it directly. Yet, if we share information – be it genetic or of any other kind – my use or control of the information does not immediately threaten your enjoyment of it. Indeed, a particular use by one person or group of persons does not preclude others from engaging in other uses of the information, for no two uses are mutually exclusive. Moreover, the essential character of that information may remain unchanged. And, while the information might be put to uses which result in undesirable consequences for you, it is not immediately apparent that I have interfered in any meaningful sense with a property interest that you might claim in the information.[6]

This is reflected in the law more generally, and certainly in the United Kingdom, where information is not normally regarded as something that can be owned. Information cannot be stolen, for example, because it is deemed not to have the necessary character of property, and theft requires the taking of the property of another.[7] But it is here that we encounter the first of many paradoxes that beleaguer this field, for at the practical level many kinds of information are bought and sold every day, and so-called 'know-how agreements' are the staple of many hi-tech companies. However, in legal terms, it is normally only in the area of intellectual property that a form of property right emerges to protect information, and even here very specific rules apply which restrict such protection as there is to clearly defined forms of information. Thus patent or copyright protection is only afforded to information that reveals, respectively, a new *invention* or an original creative *work*. More commonly, information is protected by an array of actions that promote

---

[6] A. D. Moore, 'Intangible Property: Privacy, Power, and Information Control' (1998) 35 *American Philosophical Quarterly* 365.

[7] See, in Scotland, *Grant* v. *Allan* 1988 SCCR 402, in which it was held that 'no crime known to the law of Scotland' arose when an employee made copies of his employer's computer printouts and offered to sell these to rivals. Theft of the physical documents would certainly disclose a crime, but the mere making of copies was not contrary to the criminal law. Similarly, in England in *Oxford* v. *Moss* [1979] Crim. LR 119 it was held not to be a contravention of the Theft Act 1968 for a student to remove an examination paper, read its contents, and then return the paper. Confidential information was not 'property' within the meaning of s.4(1) of the Act. For discussion, see R.G. Hammond, 'Theft of Information' (1984) 100 *Law Quarterly Review* 252.

ancillary interests. For example, an action for breach of confidence protects information that is not part of the public domain, although historically the action was concerned as much with protecting confidential
relationships as with protecting confidential information as such.[8]

British patients enjoy rights of access to their medical records both
under statute,[9] and at common law,[10] but this in no way accords a right
of property in the information they contain. Indeed, the Court of Appeal
has expressly ruled that property in records is held by the local authority, although this is property in the physical records rather than in the
information.[11] Contrary authority can be found in the United States,
however, where it has been held that while a hospital might own the
physical records held on patients, patients themselves have a property
right in their own information.[12]

The English Court of Appeal has expressly denied that any such right
exists in England and Wales – a proprietary interest in abstract information cannot vest in an individual even when she was the source of that
information.[13] The law will, however, step in to protect that individual's
personal privacy if it is improperly placed at risk, and there is evidence
that it will do so increasingly as opportunity arises.[14]

All of which goes to show that the protection of privacy and of property have thus far been treated as mutually exclusive legal commitments,
at least in the United Kingdom.[15] This – and particularly the isolation
of property from other interests – is reflected at the international level
in the special context of genetic and other human material. Article 4 of
the Universal Declaration on the Human Genome and Human Rights
provides that 'the human genome in its natural state shall not give rise to

---

[8] See F. Gurry, *Breach of Confidence* (Oxford, Clarendon Press, 1984).

[9] See, in the UK, the Access to Medical Reports Act 1988, Data Protection Act 1998, Part II,
and the Access to Health Records Act 1990 as it relates to deceased persons (after amendment
by the 1998 Act).

[10] *R v. Mid Glamorgan Family Health Services Authority & Another, ex parte Martin* [1995] 1
WLR 110.

[11] *Ibid.*

[12] *Pyramid Life Insurance Co. v. Masonic Hospital Association of Payne County Oklahoma* 119
F. Supp. 51 (Okl. 1961), *Striegel v. Tofano* 399 N.Y.S. 2d. 584 (1977), and *Gerkin v. Werner*
434 N.Y.S. 2d. 607 (1980).

[13] *R v. Department of Health, ex parte Source Informatics Ltd.* [2000] 1 All ER 786.

[14] *Douglas and Others v. Hello! Ltd.* [2001] 2 All ER 289.

[15] For an American perspective see National Bioethics Advisory Committee, *Research Involving Human Biological Materials: Ethical Issues and Policy Guidance, Vol. I: Report and
Recommendations of the National Bioethics Advisory Committee* (NBAC, Rockville, MD,
1999), ch. 4.

financial gains', while Article 21 of the Council of Europe Convention on Human Rights and Biomedicine states: 'The human body and its parts shall not, as such, give rise to financial gain.' Similarly, the so-called Bermuda Statement of 1996 is founded on the rhetoric that the human genome is the heritage of humanity, and stipulates that 'all human genome sequence information from a publicly funded project should be freely available in the public domain', and that 'finished sequences should be submitted immediately to public databases'.[16]

These positions are in no way mirrored by the practice on the ground. In fact, the human body, its parts and information about them have become extremely valuable commodities in recent years. This is seen most particularly in developments in the fields of biotechnology and intellectual property, as the next section demonstrates. However, the irony is that while property rights are routinely granted in respect of human material, this is usually done to the exclusion of the one person who is central to the entire enterprise, namely, the individual from whom the material has been taken. Objections to this are now being raised from those who advocate a more consistent application of the property model to human matter.[17] This in turn is part of a wider movement that involves a re-assessment of the relationship that individuals enjoy with their own bodies and the legal rights that can be claimed in respect of that relationship. It is against this background that we shall examine the exclusion of property rights over personal bodily material, including genetic samples and genetic information.[18]

Intellectual property and genetic material

The continued use of the highly inappropriate and inaccurate term 'patenting life' encapsulates the problems that beleaguer the biotechnology industry in seeking intellectual property protection for its innovations. Many misconceptions surround the patenting of biotechnological

[16] Human Genome Organisation, *Summary of Principles Agreed at the International Strategy Meeting on Human Genome Sequencing – Bermuda, 25–28 February 1996* (Wellcome Trust, London, 1996).

[17] See, for example, D. Beyleveld and R. Brownsword, 'My Body, My Body Parts, My Property?' (2000) 8 *Health Care Analysis* 87, J. W. Harris, *Property and Justice* (Oxford, Clarendon Press, 1996), and D. Morgan, *Issues in Medical Law and Ethics* (Cavendish, London, 2001), ch. 6.

[18] See further J. I. de Witte and H. ten Have, 'Ownership of Genetic Material and Information' (1997) 45 *Social Science and Medicine* 51.

inventions, although there are also many valid concerns as to patenting practices and the uses and abuses of patent monopoly protection.

A common theme to emerge is that of differing understandings of key concepts in patent law. While patent lawyers might have a clear idea of the difference between 'invention' and 'discovery', the application of property rights to naturally occurring entities such as human gene sequences or cell-lines is nothing short of anathema to those outside the closed circle of intellectual property law. Nowhere is this more clearly seen than in the context of the invention/discovery dichotomy. How can the removal of an entity from its natural environment and its study be described as anything other than a discovery? How can it be meaningful to call such an entity an invention, and so make it the subject of patent law?

The answer lies in how these terms are defined. Certainly, a scientific or lay conception of a discovery would encompass much of the work of the Human Genome Project and other genetic research, but matters are less simplistic in practice. Within the law, the terms *discovery* and *invention* have particular technical meanings that reflect fundamental policy objectives of patent law, such as encouraging innovation and rewarding endeavour. In particular, while both discoveries and inventions contribute new additions to the sum total of human understanding, an invention does so through the application of human endeavour to produce a technical solution to a previously unresolved technical problem. According to this view, it becomes entirely meaningful to reward the efforts of innovators who contribute worthwhile knowledge to our experience of the world through study and manipulation of organisms at the cellular and sub-cellular level. Why should this area of science and not any other be excluded from protection?

The stock response to this last question is usually that patents over such work are tantamount to patenting life and that to do so is an immoral activity. This argument is flawed in a number of respects, not least because it hijacks the emotive term 'life' and applies it in a context where it is largely devoid of meaning. Whatever life may be, it is not just a string of DNA. Human beings are much more than the sum of their genetic parts, and patent law does not permit the patenting of the human body as such.[19]

---

[19] In Europe see Directive 98/44/EC of the European Parliament and of the Council of 6 July 1998 on the Legal Protection of Biotechnological Inventions, Article 5.1.

The term 'patenting life' also betrays a fundamental misconception of the effect of patent grant. A patent is not a right of positive entitlement. A patent merely allows the patent holder to prevent competitors from using her invention in direct commercial competition. There is no corresponding right to exploit the invention. Thus, if the invention is a drug, it must still pass many rigorous safety procedures before it can be marketed. Moreover, a patent is simply a right to stop a competitor using information that is the subject of the patent. This is information about the essence of the invention – whether it be the chemical composition of a drug, or the technical workings of a new engine, or the genetic make-up of a genetically modified animal – but fundamentally, a patent is simply a right to control the use of such information in the market. Understood in this way, the expression 'patenting life' is stripped of much of its emotive appeal.

This having been said, excessively restrictive uses of patents can mean that products or processes embodying the information that is the subject of the patent are kept out of the marketplace, and so denied to the public. The consequences of this in the health care setting are self-evident, and the recent example of South Africa's challenge to the pharmaceutical patents cartel in respect of AIDS drugs stands as testament to the political unacceptability of overly aggressive use of patents. The fact that this was still *legally* permissible leads us to question the morality of granting monopolies over inventions as a whole.[20]

European patent law contains a morality provision which can prevent the grant of a patent if the exploitation of the invention is likely to cause immoral or publicly offensive behaviour.[21] US patent law contains no such provision. This disparity of approach has a number of consequences. First, the search for a meaning of immorality in Europe has been time-consuming and costly and remains unsatisfactorily resolved.[22] Second, there are serious concerns that it will disadvantage European economic interests. This, in turn, has meant that Europe's morality

---

[20] M. A. Heller and R. S. Eisenberg, 'Can Patents Deter Innovation? The Anticommons in Biomedical Research' (1998) 280 *Science* 698.

[21] European Patent Convention (Munich, 1973), Article 53, and EC Directive on the Legal Protection of Biotechnological Inventions, Article 6.

[22] See, for example, *HARVARD/ONCO-mouse* [1991] EPOR 525, *HOWARD FLOREY/Relaxin* [1995] EPOR 541, and *PLANT GENETIC SYSTEMS/Glutamine Synthetase Inhibitors* [1995] EPOR 357.

provisions have been interpreted very narrowly to avoid dissuading investors and innovators from locating elsewhere. The result is an extremely skewed view of morality.[23]

But again, a serious misconception as to the role of morality in patent law lies at the heart of the debate. It is often argued that biotechnological patents should be denied protection because it is immoral to grant protection for such work. But the irony of this approach is revealed if we stop to consider the effect of such a prohibition. It does not mean that the work will not be done. By contrast, it means that *anyone* can do the work, for the effect of the patent is to restrict control of the technology to the patentee. Thus, if the concern is about the act of invention the denial of a patent cannot address that concern. The patent system is not a regulatory mechanism for science, nor should it be. Indeed, any attempt to use patent law to control the inventive process is futile, for the invention has already taken place by the time the patent is sought. The genie cannot be put back in the bottle.

The only appropriate use of the morality provision is in respect of the question of whether a monopoly right should be granted for the particular invention under consideration. It might be entirely defensible, for example, to deny protection because the public good that can come from free access to the technology is to be preferred to the granting of a private right over its commercial exploitation. But if that is so, this argument can be mounted in respect of any area of science or technology – and most particularly of the pharmaceutical industry.

None the less, it is undeniable that there is considerable concern on the part of the public and the research community about the granting of patents for biotechnological inventions. The adoption of a European Directive in July 1998 designed to harmonise the law throughout Europe is unlikely to allay fears.[24] While the Directive attempts to put the patentability of biotechnological inventions beyond doubt, only two member states have fully implemented its terms so far. Many others remain in confusion as to what the Directive actually means, and two

---

[23] For comment, see G. T. Laurie, 'Biotechnology: Facing the Problems of Patent Law', in H. L. MacQueen and B. G. M. Main (eds), *Innovation, Incentive and Reward: Intellectual Property, Law and Policy*, Hume Papers on Public Policy 5 (Edinburgh, Edinburgh University Press, 1997), pp. 46–63.

[24] EC Directive 98/44/EC.

have challenged the law before the European Court of Justice.[25] The way forward, it seems, does not lie with law alone.[26]

A number of options are open.[27] There is, of course, the prospect of abandoning altogether intellectual property protection for the biotechnology industry. But quite apart from assurances from venture capitalists that biotechnology research will effectively cease in any territory where this occurs, grounds for making a special case for excluding biotechnology from protection simply do not exist. Realistically, there is much that can be done to improve the current patent system. For example, standards of drafting patent applications should be strengthened to ensure that inventions are properly described and that unsustainable claims to protection are not made. This, in turn, would facilitate a more rigorous examination process that should ensure that protection is granted only to innovations that are truly inventive and which have never been made available to the public. Ultimately, patent offices and courts must work together more closely so as to limit the effects of overly broad patents, by restricting protection to the precise contribution that an invention makes to human knowledge and no further.

Most radically, however, the grant of a patent could be made conditional on the assumption of certain attendant responsibilities to the community. For example, the Human Genome Organisation's Ethics Committee recommended in April 2000 that, 'profit-making entities dedicate a percentage (e.g. 1–3 per cent) of their annual net profit to healthcare infrastructure and/or to humanitarian efforts'.[28] There is no reason why this quid pro quo should not become part of patent law, provided that there is sufficient political will to make it so. It is a form of benefit-sharing that could go a long way to restoring public trust in privately funded research, and it might give a more acceptable face to the prospect of patenting the human genome.

---

[25] *Case C-377/98 Netherlands* v. *Council of the European Union and the European Parliament* [1998] OJ C378/13, pending. The Netherlands (supported by Italy) failed to elide its responsibility to implement the Directive by the deadline of 30 July 2000 and to have the Directive suspended until a full hearing of the court – *Order of the President of the Court of 25 July 2000,* [2000] ECR I–6229. The Opinion of the Advocate General (Jacobs) rejected each ground of challenge mounted by the Netherlands – Opinion of 14 June 2001. This does not augur well for the case before the European Court of Justice.

[26] G. T. Laurie, 'Owning the Genome?' (2001) June *Science and Public Affairs* 14.

[27] See J. H. Barton, 'Intellectual Property Rights: Reforming the Patent System' (2000) 287 *Science* 1933, and M. Bobrow and S. Thomas, 'Patent in a Genetic Age' (2001) 409 *Nature* 763.

[28] HUGO Ethics Committee, *Statement on Benefit-Sharing* (Vancouver, 9 April 2000).

Crisis of confidence

There is an undeniable public crisis of confidence in genetic research, even though the promise of great benefits is well recognised. This is borne out by the UK Medical Research Council's survey into public perceptions of the collection of human biological samples – published in October 2000 and discussed in chapter 3.[29] The same is true of the MORI poll conducted by the British Human Genetics Commission.[30] This general atmosphere of mistrust is compounded in large part by the increased role that the private sector has assumed in undertaking, financing and staking a claim to research involving human genetic material. The granting of intellectual property rights over the products of this research has served only to alienate the public even further. But, as has been discussed above, these issues will not be addressed adequately just by the simple removal of intellectual property protection from the equation. Pragmatically, this is not even a viable option, but more importantly the very strong public interest in encouraging innovation would be lost to any state or geographical area that attempted to use it; the research and innovation that biotechnology attracts would simply move elsewhere. The real problem is twofold. First, where should the proper focus lie in addressing this crisis of confidence? Second, what role, if any, should law play in that process?

The truth is that those who participate as subjects and who provide vital genetic research material are the key components of the genetic research machine and are crucial to its continued success. Whether they are represented by individuals or by communities, they are currently undervalued, under-respected and undermined. The way forward is to empower these parties to take a more equal role in the partnership that is formed when they participate in research.[31] The starting point is to break free of current institutional constraints that stand in the way of this progress and to explore more imaginative ways by which we can establish, and perhaps protect, the role of those who further the *public* interest in genetic research. The Council of Europe, for example, has

[29] Medical Research Council, *Public Perceptions of the Collection of Human Biological Samples* (London, MRC, 2000).

[30] Human Genetics Commission, *Public Attitudes to Human Genetic Information* (HGC, London, 2001), pp. 20–2.

[31] H. T. Greely, 'The Control of Genetic Research: Involving the "Groups Between"' (1998) 33 *Houston Law Review* 1397.

recommended the establishment of national and international fora to monitor the ethical dilemmas thrown up by genetic research, and to encourage the 'widest possible participation by citizens in the discussion on the human genome'.[32]

Further limits on autonomy and consent

The conflation of autonomy with consent that is typical of current approaches to medico-legal dilemmas reduces the means of respecting individuals to one solitary event – the obtaining of informed consent. And, while numerous ways of maintaining respect for individuals are available when they remain passive in the process,[33] the equiparation of autonomy with consent means that informed consent has come to be the primary, and arguably the only, legitimate way of *empowering* individuals in their dealings with health care professionals and researchers. This is also true in the spheres of intellectual property and biotechnology. But this need not and should not be so. Two examples illustrate the current approach.

When the European Patent Office's Opposition Division was called upon in 1994 to examine the morality of Howard Florey's patent over the H2-Relaxin – a protein secreted by pregnant woman that eases the process of childbirth – it did so in large part by reference to the principle of informed consent.[34] It had been objected, inter alia, that the granting of the patent offended morality because it required the removal of tissue from pregnant women; this was said to be an affront to human dignity because it used a particular female condition (pregnancy) for a technical process oriented towards profit. The answer of the Opposition Division, however, was that the tissue had been freely donated by the women in question, and that, therefore, the manipulation of genetic material from those samples was not immoral.[35]

Second, Recital 26 of the European Directive on the legal protection of biotechnological inventions provides that

---

[32] Council of Europe, Recommendation on the Protection of the Human Genome by the Council of Europe, No. 1512 (2001).

[33] Examples include doing no harm and respecting individual privacy.

[34] *HOWARD FLOREY/Relaxin* [1995] EPOR 541.

[35] *Ibid.*, at 550. It was left open, however, whether the research in se was immoral, but this was not addressed by the Division as it is a question outside its remit (the remit being to determine whether the granting of a patent would be immoral).

Whereas if an invention is based on biological material of human origin or if it uses such material, where a patent application is filed, the
person from whose body the material is taken must have had an opportunity of expressing free and informed consent thereto, in accordance with
national law.[36]

This ethical stance is supplemented by other recitals, such as Recital 43,
which emphasises the commitment of the European Community to respect human rights, and Recital 16, which provides that patent law must
respect 'the dignity and integrity of the person'. Indeed, the terms of
Recital 26 were originally intended for inclusion as an Article of the
Directive, with clear binding force on member states, but heavy lobbying by representatives of the biotechnology and patent industries meant
that it was ultimately relegated to the Preamble to the Directive, where
its legal status and its effect on member states is far less certain.[37] Indeed,
the UK has opted not to include the requirement in its implementing
provisions.[38]

Such formulations of consent certainly provide adequate protection
for the researchers. They also represents one means of respecting individuals. Indeed, they are highly desirable safeguards and the UK government's rejection of Recital 26 should accordingly be subject to serious
objection. However, they are considerably less successful as a means
of empowering individuals. But, it might be asked, why would we be
concerned to empower individuals anyway? Well, it is precisely because
people feel disenfranchised from, and disempowered by, the modern machinery of research that we face the current public crisis of confidence in
research in general and genetic research in particular. Individuals who
provide samples for research purposes are not, and do not feel like, stake-
holders in the enterprise. The continued participation and support of
the public in research activity can only be ensured by a fundamental
reappraisal of the relationships with the subjects that have traditionally
been accepted.

---

[36] Directive 98/44/EC.

[37] For a trenchant critique see D. Beyleveld, 'Why Recital 26 of the E.C. Directive on the Legal
Protection of Biotechnological Inventions Should Be Implemented in National Law' (2000)
4 *Intellectual Property Quarterly* 1.

[38] *Patents Regulations* 2000. For comment, see M. Llewelyn, 'The UK Patents Regulations 2000:
A Hostage to Fortune' (2000) 1(3) *Genetics Law Monitor* 5.

Consent as disempowerment

The imperative to seek and obtain consent from research subjects gives them an illusion of power and control. In reality, it delegates extremely limited control to individuals. The sole power that is afforded is that to withhold consent – that is, to refuse. Moreover, there is no residual power once consent has been given unless further consent is required at some future point. This is demonstrated particularly well in the context of the donation of samples for research. While no individual will be forced to give samples – and in most cases the only ethically and legally appropriate approach is to seek informed consent to the provision of a sample – the individual retains no continued relationship with the sample in either a factual or a legal sense once consent has been obtained and the sample surrendered. Thus, the focus on consent renders the participatory process disempowering in at least two senses.

First, for those who genuinely wish to participate in research the availability of a 'right to refuse' is useless. They will not exercise this right and so are left with no power in the relationship that is forged with the researcher who takes and uses their samples. Second, the one-off event of consent is disempowering because it fails to recognise the individual subject – or indeed, the community of research subjects – as a party with an interest in the overall endeavour. In sum, the fundamental problem with the consent model is that it does not provide a means by which the subject can exercise *continuing control* of her materials.[39]

Revisiting the gift model

This problem is compounded by the continuing use of the gift model that has traditionally served to govern the researcher–subject relationship. The notion of gift has a strong normative appeal in lay terms, not least because it is seen to be a laudable act, demonstrating the virtues of altruism and beneficence, and untainted by the twin evils of self-interest or exploitation. In practice, it has considerable utility for the recipient, in that gifts for research purposes are treated as unconditional. This provides broad scope for the future use or disposal of the gift. As to public

---

[39] For a defence of the role of autonomy and consent as a counter to property claims, see L. Skene, 'Proprietary Rights in Human Bodies, Body Parts and Tissue: Regulatory Climates and Proposals for New Laws' (2002) *Legal Studies,* forthcoming.

interest, unconditional gifting can serve a number of valuable social ends, including advances in medical research and the development of therapeutic agents or cures. This particular consideration weighs heavily as an unquestionable given, to which we shall return presently. But such a concept of gift is seriously incongruous in legal terms. In English law 'gift' is defined as follows.

> A gift . . . may be defined shortly as the transfer of any *property* from one person to another gratuitously . . . It is an act whereby something is voluntarily transferred from the true owner in possession to another person with the full intention that the thing shall not be returned to the donor.[40] (emphasis added)

Gift in Scots law is more correctly termed *donation*, and is similarly defined as 'a gratuitous transfer of *property*'.[41] Strong evidence is required that a gifting has taken place or is intended. Indeed, in Scots law there is a presumption against donation in all cases. As the Stair Memorial Encyclopaedia on the Laws of Scotland states, this is based 'on the jaundiced but, perhaps, realistic view that generosity is not to be expected'.[42] To rebut this presumption there must be convincing evidence of proof of an intention to donate. Implied consent is not enough.[43]

Thus, in legal terms the invocation of *gift* presupposes underlying property rights or interests in the subject matter that constitutes the gift. As a result, the legal position in respect of ownership of donated human body parts is in disarray in most Western legal systems.[44] A fair summation is that while there is no clear prohibition on ownership of body parts – and indeed, one can find many examples of a property model being applied to human tissues – the one player who is routinely excluded from the property model is the source of the property itself.[45] Beyond this, however, body parts can form the essence of patentable inventions,[46] can become the property of those who do work

---

[40] Halsbury's *Laws of England*, Fourth Edition, Vol. XX: Gifts, para. 1.

[41] Stair Memorial Encyclopaedia, *The Laws of Scotland*, Vol. VIII: Donation, para. 601.

[42] *Ibid.*, para. 620.

[43] Stair, *Institutions*, I, 8, 2; IV, 45, 17; XIV: *donatio non praesumitur* (donation is not presumed).

[44] For a discussion see J. K. Mason and R. A. McCall-Smith, *Law and Medical Ethics*, 5th edn (Edinburgh, Butterworths, 1999), ch. 20.

[45] See J. K. Mason and G. T. Laurie, 'Consent or Property? Dealing with the Body and its Parts in the Shadow of Bristol and Alder Hey' (2001) 64 *Modern Law Review* 710.

[46] EC Directive 98/44/EC. In the United States see the classic formulation by the Supreme Court in *Diamond* v. *Chakrabarty* 447 US 303 (1980), 309: 'Congress intended statutory subject matter to include anything under the sun that is made by man'.

on them,[47] and can even be stolen and so subject to the criminal law.[48] The classic policy decision on self ownership is to be found in the decision of the Supreme Court of California in *Moore* v. *Regents of the University of California.*[49]

John Moore suffered from hairy cell leukaemia, and his spleen was removed at the Medical School of the University of California at Los Angeles. His doctor, Dr Golde, discovered that cells from the spleen had unusual and potentially beneficial properties, and he developed an immortal cell-line without his patient's knowledge or consent. Moreover, Dr Golde sought and obtained a patent over the cell-line which he subsequently sold to the drug company Sandoz for $15 million. It has been reported that the drugs and therapies which were developed from the patented product are worth in excess of $3 billion.[50] When Moore discovered what had happened to his cells he brought an action against the researchers, the university and the drug company. Thirteen causes of action were filed by Moore in total, but those of most direct interest concerned the questions of property and consent. In particular, Moore alleged *conversion*: that as the 'owner' of the cells his property right had been compromised by the unauthorised work carried out by the defendants. Inter alia, he also alleged breach of fiduciary duty and lack of informed consent because he had never been told of the potential commercial use of his cells, and consequently he had never given his full and informed agreement to the initial operation. The Californian Supreme Court upheld these latter two claims, but rejected the argument in conversion.

The court held that because no precedent could be found on which to ground Moore's property claim, and because of the utilitarian consideration that a finding for the plaintiff would be a hindrance to medical research 'by restricting access to the necessary raw materials',[51] it was inappropriate to recognise individual property rights in the body. Moreover, the Court was concerned that a contrary decision would '[threaten] to destroy the economic incentive to conduct important medical research' because 'If the use of cells in research is a conversion, then

---

[47] *Doodeward* v. *Spence* (1908) 6 CLR 406.

[48] *R* v. *Kelly* [1998] 3 All ER 741. For general commentary see A. Grubb, ' "I, me, mine": Bodies, Parts and Property' (1998) 3 *Medical Law International* 299.

[49] *Moore* v. *Regents of the University of California* 793 P.2d 479 (Cal. 1990), 271 Cal. Rep. 146. See too *Brotherton* v. *Cleveland* 923 F.2d 661 (6th Cir. 1991).

[50] B. Merz, 'Biotechnology: Spleen-Rights' *The Economist*, 11 August 1990, 30.

[51] *Moore*, Cal. Rep. at 161.

with every cell sample a researcher purchases a ticket in a litigation lottery.'[52] The paradox in this decision was highlighted by the dissent of Broussard J, wherein he stated:

> the majority's analysis cannot rest on the broad proposition that a removed part is not property, but rather rests on the proposition that a *patient* retains no ownership interest in a body part once the body part has been removed from his or her body.[53]

A similar position would undoubtedly prevail in the United Kingdom.[54] Thus, while each of us is denied recognition of a property interest in excised parts of our bodies, other parties may not only gain such an interest but can go on to protect it, as in *Moore*, by forms of property law such as the law of patents. But is it reasonable or defensible to exclude completely from the equation the one person who can make everything possible?

More particularly, it is interesting to note how the court in *Moore* seemed entirely satisfied that its adoption of the consent model was sufficient to provide respect for, and to empower, the plaintiff (for Moore won in respect of lack of informed consent). The consent model and the property model were treated as though they were mutually exclusive, a phenomenon that has also been noted above in respect of property and privacy. There is, however, no sound reason why this should be so.

A property paradigm

It is undeniable that an attitudinal shift is occurring in respect of the way we regard our bodies and any parts removed from them. The recent MRC survey on the perceptions of the public on the collection and use of human biological samples found that younger people tended to view payment for excised bodily tissues as a matter of right or at least as a logical and acceptable option.[55] This was especially so when research was undertaken for profit by private enterprises. In corroboration, the Human Genetic Commission's poll found considerable antipathy to the idea of

---

[52] *Ibid.*, at 162–3.

[53] *Ibid.*, at 168. For comment on *Moore* see B. Hoffmaster, 'Between the Sacred and the Profane: Bodies, Property, and Patents in the *Moore* Case' (1992) 7 *Intellectual Property Journal* 115.

[54] Nuffield Council on Bioethics, *Human Tissue: Ethical and Legal Issues* (London, NCB, 1995).

[55] Medical Research Council, *Public Perceptions of the Collection of Human Biological Samples* (London, MRC, October 2000).

exclusive ownership of genetic information by research organisations.[56] Contrariwise, members of the older generation found more comfort in the classic gift paradigm, expecting nothing in return for altruistic and public spirited donations.[57] And yet, many general practitioners and nurses who took part in the survey also supported the view that volunteers should retain a degree of ownership in donated samples.[58] Indeed, the MRC Working Group on Human Tissue and Biological Samples for Use in Research opined that, 'it was more practical and more attractive from a moral and ethical standpoint to adopt the position that, if a tissue sample could be property, the original owner was the individual from whom it was taken'.[59]

It is submitted that there is nothing in principle to prevent recognition of property interests in aspects of the self, subject to limitations against self-harm. A personal property paradigm could, in fact, serve an all-important role in completing the picture of adequate protection for the personality in tandem with other protections such as autonomy, confidentiality and privacy.[60] However, the added value of a property model lies in its ability to empower individuals and communities and to provide the crucial continuing control over samples or information through which ongoing moral and legal influence may be exerted.

Property implies many things, including ownership and control. A generic definition of the meaning of property can be found in the work of George Joseph Bell, a Scottish Institutional Writer:

> Ownership in moveables is a right of exclusive and absolute use and enjoyment, with uncontrolled powers of disposal, provided no use be made of the subject and no alienation attempted, which, for purposes of public policy, convenience, or justice, are, by the general disposition of the common law, or by special enactments of the Legislature, forbidden; or from which, by obligation or contract, the owner has bound himself to abstain.[61]

---

[56] Human Genetics Commission, *Public Attitudes to Human Genetic Information*, pp. 27–8.
[57] *Ibid.*, para. 6.12.   [58] *Ibid.*, para. 17.
[59] Medical Research Council, *Working Group on Human Tissue and Biological Samples for Use in Research: Report of the Medical Research Council Working Group to Develop Operational and Ethical Guidelines* (London, MRC, 1999), para. 2.2.1.
[60] A. D. Moore, 'Owning Genetic Information and Gene Enhancement Techniques: Why Privacy and Property Rights May Undermine Social Control of the Human Genome' (2000) 14 *Bioethics* 97.
[61] G. J. Bell, *Principles of the Law of Scotland* (1829), s. 1284.

Ownership, therefore, is a strong and significant means by which to control and to protect our interests. Property protection is, however, by no means an absolute, and as with all of our other legal rights, property rights can be tempered in our own interests or in those of others. Exercises of self-ownership therefore need not be recognised if these conflict with an individual's best interests. Examples include attempts to dispose of vital organs or tissues that would be detrimental to health. Nor should the law ever condone ownership of entire living, breathing human beings, as this would be a fortiori impermissible as slavery. The recognition of property rights in body parts or samples does not carry any of these risks.

The exclusion of the individual from the property model has been widely advocated up until now,[62] but nevertheless such a recommendation usually reveals an ambiguousness about the true status of body parts, and betrays underlying conflicting notions about the nature of any claims that we might have to control our selves.[63] In particular, the reliance on the language of 'gift' implies property and ownership, but the way in which the concept of gift has been used in research culture presumes surrender of all residual interests in donated samples. It has been our tendency to date to focus on this latter aspect of gift rather than the former. However, not only does this lack support in law but it has also prompted the dual disservices of justifying a distorted gift paradigm while fuelling inconsistencies that ultimately undermine public confidence in research.[64]

It is no longer clear that the model of gifting currently employed in the modern research environment remains appropriate. It is not true, for example, that individuals retain no interest in materials surrendered for research. The moral significance of body parts remains even when they are separated from their original source. The MRC has found, for example, that, 'Virtually everyone said that if they donated a sample they would appreciate feedback on what the research using their samples had discovered or achieved'.[65] Moreover, the reaction of parents in the United Kingdom to the practice of removing and retaining children's tissues and organs at post-mortem examination stands in testament to

---

[62] But cf. The Health Council of the Netherlands, which has suggested that every individual owns his or her genetic material: Health Council of the Netherlands, *Heredity, Science and Society: On the Possibility and Limits of Genetic Testing and Gene Therapy* (The Hague, HCN, 1989).

[63] See, for example, Nuffield Council on Bioethics, *Human Tissue: Ethical and Legal Issues*.

[64] Mason and Laurie, 'Consent or Property?'   [65] MRC, *Public Perceptions*, para. 6.9.

the continuing moral relationship between individuality, personhood and body parts.[66]

Nor should we ignore the fact that the commercial value that human material might represent to researchers also represents a potential value in those terms to the sample sources themselves. Not everyone agrees with the Supreme Court of California in *Moore*.[67] Numerous commentators point to principles of fundamental equity, the redress of unjust enrichment and the protection of personal interests that can be furthered through property rights.[68]

The recognition of this kind of interest in personal samples would provide the continuing control that is so lacking under the consent model alone.[69] Meaningful, legally relevant and enforceable conditions could be placed on any transfer of the property and so ensure that a research participant or indeed a community retains a vested interest in samples and in the goals and outcomes of any research for which those samples are provided. By the same token, restrictions on the inclusion of undesirable clauses by either side could easily be imposed by law.[70] It might be objected, for example, that property rights could easily be waived under pressure. The obvious retort to this is that no such assignation of rights should be legally permissible. Thus, while individuals or communities might choose not to exercise their rights, they cannot give them away.

---

[66] See the Bristol Royal Infirmary Inquiry, *Interim Report: Removal and Retention of Human Material* (May 2000); the *Report of the Royal Liverpool Children's Inquiry* (London, House of Commons, January 2001); Advice from the Chief Medical Officer, *The Removal, Retention and Use of Human Organs and Tissue from Post-mortem Examination* (London, Department of Health, 2001); Chief Medical Officer, *Report of a Census of Organs and Tissues Retained by Pathology Services in England* (London, Department of Health, 2001); Health Services Directorate, *Report of Content Analysis of NHS Trust Policies and Protocols on Consent to Organ and Tissue Retention at Post-mortem Examination and Disposal of Human Materials in the Chief Medical Officer's Census of NHS Pathology Services* (London, Department of Health, 2000). For Scotland, see *Report of the Independent Review Group on the Retention of Organs at Post-mortem* (January 2001).

[67] M. M. J. Lin, 'Conferring a Federal Property Right in Genetic Material: Stepping into the Future with the Genetic Privacy Act' (1996) 22 *American Journal of Law and Medicine* 109.

[68] See, for example, Beyleveld and Brownsword, 'My Body, My Body Parts, My Property?'; W. Boulier, 'Sperm, Spleens and Other Valuables: The Need to Recognize Property Rights in Human Body Parts' (1995) 23 *Hofstra Law Review* 693, and C. M. Valerio Barrad, 'Genetic Information and Property Theory' (1993) 87 *Northwestern University Law Review* 1037.

[69] E. B. Seeney, '*Moore* 10 Years Later – Still Trying to Fill the Gap: Creating a Personal Property Right in Genetic Material' (1998) 32 *New England Law Review* 1131.

[70] On experiences to date of applying contract law to reproductive materials, see D. M. Vukadinovich, 'Assisted Reproductive Technology Law: Obtaining Informed Consent for the Commercial Cryopreservation of Embryos' (2000) 21 *Journal of Legal Medicine* 67.

Current movements towards a property model

A number of examples illustrate that a serious attitudinal shift is indeed under way that requires us to revisit the prospect of applying a property model to ourselves.

Indigenous peoples

Many examples can be found of indigenous peoples working together in an attempt to protect their interests in their genetic heritage and natural environments.[71] The 1993 Mataatua Declaration on the Cultural and Intellectual Property Rights of Indigenous Peoples states that 'indigenous flora and fauna are inextricably bound to the territories of indigenous communities and any property right claims must recognise their traditional guardianship. Commercialisation of any traditional plants and medicines of indigenous peoples must be managed by the indigenous peoples who have inherited such knowledge.'[72]

The work of Posey and Dutfield on the concept of Traditional Resource Rights (TRRs) is an original, imaginative and potentially fruitful means of recognising and protecting such interests. TRRs respect the right to self-determination enjoyed by indigenous peoples as well as the essential relationship between the people and their resources that are so keenly sought by others. TRRs amass a 'bundle of rights' already widely recognised by international agreements. Reference to these rights establishes a solid base on which to build more equitable and appropriate forms of protection and benefit sharing of resources. These include human rights, self-determination and collective rights, land and territory rights, rights to privacy, the right to development, informed consent, farmers' rights, folklore, cultural property and environmental integrity. Those who advocate this approach hail it more as 'a process than a product'.[73] That

---

[71] See generally M. Blakeney (ed.), *Intellectual Property Aspects of Ethnobiology* (London, Sweet & Maxwell, 1999).

[72] The Declaration, signed in New Zealand, has not been formally adopted in any legal sense but acts as a benchmark. See too the Bellagio Declaration resulting from the 1993 Rockefeller Conference 'Cultural Agency/Cultural Authority: Politics and Poetics of Intellectual Property in the Post-Colonial Era' held in Bellagio, Italy, 7–10 June 1993, and the Final Statement of the Regional Consultation on Indigenous Peoples' Knowledge and Intellectual Property Rights, Suva, Fiji, 1995.

[73] D. A. Posey, 'Indigenous Peoples and Traditional Resource Rights: A Basis for Equitable Relationships?', paper prepared for a workshop on traditional resource rights and indigenous peoples, Oxford, 28 June 1995, p. 18.

is, TRRs are a starting point from which to move towards a better and more accurate understanding of the true rights of indigenous peoples. It is also a basis from which to argue for a better balance between potentially competing interests, and, possibly, for a reform of intellectual property rights themselves.[74]

Examples from non-Western societies of social ownership of information include concepts of *rights* and *ownership* from which Western cultures can learn much.[75] Moreover, they demonstrate that it is not the case that the only ethical and equitable answer lies in banning research and denying all parties any form of property claim.[76] The World Intellectual Property Organisation, for its part, has carried out a global assessment of the intellectual property needs and expectations of traditional knowledge holders, including indigenous peoples.[77] The ultimate aim is to strike a more acceptable balance between the interests of the various parties – all within a property-based approach – albeit one that might require considerable revision in the longer term. An Intergovernmental Committee on Intellectual Property and Genetic Resources, Traditional Knowledge and Folklore has been established to further this objective.

Community solidarity

Examples of communities working together are also found in North America, where families have used their genetic uniqueness as a bargaining tool. As we saw in chapter 5, those suffering from the rare genetic disorder pseudoxanthoma elasticum (PXE) have reached agreement with researchers to provide samples only on the condition that they are named as joint patentees in any subsequent patent applications, with

---

[74] Cf. government initiatives to encourage peoples to offer genetic samples for research purposes; see L. Skene, 'Sale of DNA of People of Tonga' (2001) 1(5) *Genetics Law Monitor* 7.

[75] J. Frow, 'Public Domain and Collective Rights in Culture' (1998) 13 *Intellectual Property Journal* 39.

[76] Cf. United Nations Economic and Social Council, Working Group on Indigenous Populations, Standard Setting Activities: Evolution of Standards Concerning the Rights of Indigenous Peoples – Human Genome Diversity Research and Indigenous Peoples (July 1998, E/CN.4/Sub.2/AC.4/1998/4).

[77] World Intellectual Property Organization (WIPO), *Protection of Traditional Knowledge: A Global Intellectual Property Issue*, No. WIPO/IPTK/RT/99/2 (Geneva, WIPO, 1999); WIPO, *Matters Concerning Intellectual Property and Genetic Resources, Traditional Knowledge and Folklore*, No. WO/GA/26/6 (Geneva, WIPO, 2000), and WIPO, *Draft Report on Fact-finding Missions on Intellectual Property and Traditional Knowledge* (1998–99) (Geneva, WIPO, 2000).

a right to 50 per cent of any proceeds.[78] This is an interesting reversal of fortune, for historically researchers would not take samples unless the consent included a grant of full title, even if this was meaningless in law. That such a bargain has been struck signals an important change in research culture, although the point remains that the property interests claimed by the families and their representatives may be unfounded in law. Fundamental principles of justice certainly support this approach,[79] but whether it could withstand serious legal analysis is open to debate.[80] Nevertheless, more such arrangements will undoubtedly be made.

The history of the discipline of medical law is punctuated by events that have significantly influenced its future course. These include the successful challenge to the all-pervasive authority of the medical profession, the recognition of legally enforceable patients' rights, and the triumph of the doctrine of informed consent. The next milestone will be the legal recognition of rights of self-ownership. But, for now, the particular direction of the path remains open to influence and it is therefore imperative that we put our best foot forward.

The reader should not take away from this discussion an impression that the property model being advocated amounts only to some crude instrument requiring that research subjects be paid for their trouble. Rather, it is offered as a vehicle for further discussion and analysis of certain crucial elements that must be strengthened in order to advance the public interest in genetic research. A cultural shift in attitude must occur, as must a reassessment of the nature of the relationship between researchers and subjects. These can be achieved in part through the discourse of property.

The language that we use predisposes us to certain attitudes towards each other and serves to establish the nature and the limits of any claims that we might make on each other. The law has the power to legitimise some of these claims by giving them the status of enforceable rights. We ought, then, to consider what it would mean to talk in terms of property rights in ourselves and how that language might be translated into law.

At the time of writing a seminal case is proceeding through the US courts brought by parents of children affected by Canavan disease against

[78] http://www.pxe.org/
[79] HUGO Ethics Committee, 'HUGO Urges Genetic Benefit-Sharing' (2000) 3 *Community Genetics* 88.
[80] B. M. Knoppers, 'Population Genetics and Benefit Sharing' (2000) 3 *Community Genetics* 212.

researchers who developed and patented a test for the disorder using samples donated by the families.[81] The defendants had worked closely with afflicted families, receiving samples and gaining access to registers containing details of other affected groups around the world. However, when the Canavan gene was eventually identified the researchers sought a patent over it and a related test and proceeded to restrict access to the latter save through tightly controlled exclusive licences. The plaintiffs objected strongly and have mounted an action on a number of grounds. These include: (i) lack of informed consent; (ii) breach of fiduciary duty; (iii) unjust enrichment – inter alia, that benefits were conferred in the guise of the donated samples, the genetic information derived from them, and monetary support from the families to the researchers; (iv) fraudulent concealment of the researchers' true intentions; (v) breach of the joint venture agreement; (vi) misappropriation of trade secrets – these being lodged in the Canavan Register that the plaintiffs had constructed for the research; and (vii) conversion. In this last respect, the plaintiffs claim a property interest in their samples, the genetic information therein and information contained in the Canavan Register.

Paradoxically, this case stands in stark contrast to *Moore*, for here policy favours the plaintiffs. The families want information about the disease and the test to be freely available while it is the patent holders who wish to restrict access and so potentially hinder research. The *Moore* decision merely stands as a solitary precedent in the state of California. The current action is brought in the federal courts of Illinois and it is entirely open to those courts to plough their own furrow. Authority supporting the proposition for property rights is cited in the pleadings of the case including reference to *Pioneer Hi-Bred Int'l. v. Holden Foundation Seeds Inc.*, in which an Iowa court accepted that property could exist in genetic information to the extent that it could be subject to an action in conversion at common law.[82] Neither the facts that the information was intangible,[83] nor that the tangible entities embodying the information were not themselves converted, stood in the way of the ruling. In like manner, it could be argued that the genetic data derived

---

[81] *Greenberg et al. v. Miami Children's Hospital Research Institute Inc. et al.*, (2001), pending. I am grateful to my colleague Winnie Roche of Boston University for bringing this case to my attention.

[82] *Pioneer Hi-Bred Int'l. v. Holden Foundation Seeds Inc.*, No. 81–60-E, 1987 U.S. Dist. LEXIS 18286 (S.D. Iowa, Oct 29 1987), aff'd 35 F.3d 1226 (8th Cir, 1994).

[83] *United States v. May*, 625 F.2d 186 (8th Cir., 1980).

from the samples surrendered by the Canavan families and contained in the Canavan Register could be the subject of a successful conversion action. It remains to be seen how such arguments will fare. Policy will undoubtedly have a significant role to play in the outcome, but the policy arguments are strong on both sides,[84] and attitudes have moved on since *Moore* was decided in 1990.[85] If this current case fails, another will surely arise to take its place.[86]

Examples of attempts to recognise self-ownership rights can also be found in statutes of both Commonwealth countries and of the United States. A bill currently before the Australian Parliament provides that consent to the collection, storage and analysis of DNA samples must include a waiver of, or provision for, economic benefit to the sample source, implying a property interest in the samples themselves.[87] In 1995 the US state of Oregon took the step of embodying a personal property right in genetic information and DNA samples when used for anonymous research, with the result that unauthorised interference with either constituted a tort actionable at law.[88] However, after several years of lobbying by the pharmaceutical industry and research institutes, a new bill was passed in the Oregon legislature in June 2001 that removed this right and replaced it with more stringent privacy protection.[89] The claim is that Oregon will now have the most far-reaching privacy legislation of its kind in the United States.[90] The reality is that, once again, these two concepts are treated as 'either/or' options when there is no sound reason to do so. The Oregon experiment was not given sufficient

---

[84] Cf. A. Ryan, 'Self-Ownership, Autonomy and Property Rights' (1994) 11 *Social Philosophy and Policy* 241, and S. R. Munzer, 'An Uneasy Case Against Property Rights in Body Parts' (1994) 11 *Social Philosophy and Policy* 259.

[85] In *Hecht* v. *Superior Court* 20 Cal. Rptr. 2d 275 (1993), quoting *Davis* v. *Davis* 842 SW 2d 588 (1992), the California Court of Appeals held that stored sperm 'occupies an interim category that entitles them to special respect because of their potential for human life', but that none the less a deceased donor had an interest 'in the nature of ownership, to the extent that he had a decision making authority as to the sperm ... which falls within the broad definition of property in the Probate Code', *ibid.*, at 281.

[86] There is tentative Australian authority that stored human tissue can be the property of those from whom it was taken and their heirs: see *Roche* v. *Douglas* [2000] WASC 146.

[87] Genetic Privacy and Non-Discrimination Bill 1998, clause 16.

[88] ORS 659.700–720.

[89] Senate Bill 114 was before the 71st Oregon Legislative Assembly (8 January – 7 July 2001).

[90] At the time of writing it remained for the bill to be signed by the State Governor, and it was uncertain that he would do so, see S. Mayes, 'Legislators Strengthen State's Genetic Privacy Law: The Governor Now Will Consider a Bill that Would Give Patients Greater Say About How Their Genetic Material Is Used', *The Oregonian*, 12 June 2001, p. B04.

time for the promise and the pitfalls of a property paradigm to be explored and addressed. Certainly, a flaw in the legislation lay in the fact that an individual would simultaneously sign away her privacy rights with any property rights in a genetic sample,[91] but a simple amendment could have remedied this anomaly. It is to be regretted that the legislature bowed to pressure to change the law so as to exclude the property clause altogether, for the voices in support of property in the person are becoming louder and the ears on which they fall will not always be deaf.

Defending a property model

A number of counter-arguments can, however, be mounted. The concern that property rights in the self will hinder research held sway in *Moore* and lies at the core of the amendments to the Oregon law. However, it is far from an established fact that research will be obstructed by furnishing sample sources with some small measure of bargaining power. Indeed, in the scheme of relative powers, those who provide the samples are at by far the greatest disadvantage. In most cases individuals would find that their property was of very little economic significance to researchers. But more positively, it has been suggested that research might be furthered rather than hindered by the recognition of property rights, because those previously reluctant to come forward now have an incentive to do so.[92] Furthermore, the mere recognition of property does not preclude altruistic gifting.

The second major counter-argument is that commercialisation of body parts leads to the prospect of exploitation. This is undoubtedly true. But merely because we face that prospect is no reason in itself to refuse to recognise property rights as a matter of principle. Exploitation can be guarded against. Indeed, it is naive to imagine that a black market in body parts does not already exist. It most certainly does.[93] To ignore the reality does not make it go away. Moreover, this argument is open to significant challenge as an example of undue paternalism. As Andrews

---

[91] Genetic Research Advisory Committee, *Assuring Genetic Privacy in Oregon* (Portland, GRAC, 2000), p. 13.

[92] M. M. J. Lin, 'Conferring a Federal Property Right in Genetic Material: Stepping into the Future with the Genetic Privacy Act' (1996) 22 *American Journal of Law and Medicine* 109.

[93] For an indication of the scale of the problem visit the following site run by the University of Berkeley – Organs Watch – http://sunsite.berkeley.edu/biotech/organswatch/

has argued in the context of surrogacy, it may be more devaluing to persons not to recognise their worth in monetary terms for the contributions they can make to society from the use of their bodies than it is to protect them from potential predators – provided, always, that the value that they represent is not entirely reducible to those terms.[94]

The exploitation argument also provides an example of an overly pessimistic view of the utility of self-ownership rights. Rather than prejudicing individual interests, the recognition of property rights can bolster the respect that individuals deserve and at the same time can provide a crucial means of ensuring that that respect endures. The wholesale application of a traditional property model to the human body and its parts is not, however, envisioned. This would be inappropriate and unacceptable in many respects. However, to the extent that a body property model reflects a desire and need to protect the human personality, certain key features of the language and operation of property rights could serve this end very well.[95] An apt analogy is found in intellectual property law, as we saw in chapter 5.

The creator of an aesthetic work is entitled to copyright protection of that work in the first instance. She may none the less assign her intellectual property right to another and thereby abandon any future claim to control unauthorised copying of the work. However, in Europe at least, aesthetic works also attract moral rights, being rights that protect the element of the creator's personality embodied in her work. Inter alia, they protect against derogatory treatment of the work if this will adversely affect the reputation of the creator, and they ensure due recognition of the creator's identity whenever the work is placed in the public domain. In many continental European countries moral rights are inalienable and cannot be assigned. In like manner, a property right in one's own genetic material might be deemed to be inalienable, and even if control of physical samples is lost, the right would ensure proper recognition of the continuing relationship between individuals and their samples.

Researchers might object, however, that it would be impossible to monitor individuals' samples, for these would invariably become mixed

---

[94] L. B. Andrews, 'Beyond Doctrinal Boundaries: A Legal Framework for Surrogate Motherhood' (1995) 81 *Virginia Law Review* 2343.

[95] See, for example, M. B. Bray, 'Personalizing Personalty: Toward a Property Right in Human Bodies' (1990) 69 *Texas Law Review* 209, and M. J. Radin, 'Property and Personhood' (1982) 34 *Stanford Law Review* 957.

with others during the research process. But this is not problematic in property terms. The concepts of *commixtion* and *confusion* are well established in property law.[96] Where two separate entities are mixed together and cannot be separated, property in each element ceases and is replaced by common property in the resulting mixture. The new property is owned by each of the interested parties and must be held in trust for the benefit of all. So, if two piles of corn (solids are governed by *commixtion*) or two bottles of wine (liquids are examples of *confusion*) are merged, the resulting property is owned in common by the owners of the original elements. So too could genetic samples. Indeed, the notion that property is to be held in trust is entirely apposite in this modern context. The benefits to be derived from the new property should accrue to all of those who have contributed. Alternatively, specification might occur when a new entity has been created without the knowledge or consent of the original owners, for example where A builds a new house using B's bricks. B cannot claim the return of her bricks in such a case but she is nevertheless entitled to compensation for her loss. So too, once again, it might be with genetic samples. Matters may be more problematic, however, in the context of the ownership of information derived from samples. As has been stated, information is a difficult concept to fit into the property paradigm, but it is by no means impossible to do so.[97] Collective claims to property in information – such as familial genetic information – might therefore also arise.

Proprietary rights in information are granted in the realm of intellectual property. However, the right arises in that sphere because new information has been contributed to the sum total of human knowledge, and it acts both as a reward and an incentive to others to do the same. But the prospect of establishing yet more property rights over the fundamental constituents of genetic research has led bodies such as the Medical Research Council to endorse the position under the Council of Europe Convention on Human Rights and Biomedicine that 'The human body and its parts shall not, as such, give rise to financial gain.'[98] The MRC

---

[96] This terminology is drawn from Scots law which is, in turn, derived in large part from Roman law. However, the concepts are well recognised in the laws of most Western legal systems.

[97] For an argument in support of this, see Valerio Barrad, 'Genetic Information and Property Theory'.

[98] Medical Research Council, *Human Tissue and Biological Samples for Use in Research*, para. 2.5

has further opined that 'the sale of human biological samples for research is not ethically acceptable ... researchers may not sell for profit (in cash or in kind) samples they have collected with MRC funding'.[99] However, it would seem that 'A clear distinction can be drawn between samples of human material and intellectual property rights arising from research making use of such samples. Such intellectual property may be sold or licensed in the usual way.'[100] How convenient. And yet how unprincipled.[101] Certainly it is true that the respective property rights are different in kind – at least in their origins – but that is no reason in itself to recognise the reality of intellectual property and not that of property in the person. This is particularly so when the base material of any future intellectual property right cannot be assembled without the contribution of research subjects. Genetic samples are the sine qua non of genetic inventions, and so of genetic patents. To acknowledge this is not to denigrate the extensive labours of researchers that turn raw samples into patentable inventions. Rather, it is a plea to give proper recognition to the interests of the non-scientific partners who are so crucial to the success of the research. It is unprincipled and inconsistent to do otherwise.[102]

Conclusion

Within a framework of disputed value – namely privacy – this book has considered the delicate problems of access to, and control of, genetic information and genetic material. We have examined the special problems that arise from the fact that many instances of genetic information relate both to the individual from whom the information was derived and to the relatives of that individual. The concepts of informational and spatial privacy have been distilled from an examination of the nature of the interests that a number of parties might have in genetic samples or information; it has been argued that current laws and practices do not

[99] *Ibid.* [100] *Id.*
[101] This distinction is perpetuated in the recommendations of the House of Lords on genetic databases: see House of Lords Select Committee on Science and Technology, *Human Genetic Databases: Challenges and Opportunities* (2001 HL 57), paras. 8.27–8.31.
[102] On the continuing uncertainty on this position see European Society of Human Genetics Public and Professional Policy Committee, *DNA Storage and DNA Banking for Biomedical Research: Informed Consent, Confidentiality, Quality Issues, Ownership, Return of Benefits: A Professional Perspective* (Birmingham, ESHG, 2000), para. 3.3.

provide us with appropriate means either to recognise all such interests or to protect them adequately. A strong case has been made that a useful and valuable alternative construct of genetic privacy can be established which is amenable to legal protection. At the same time, the limits of other interest-based approaches have been examined, most notably that of the consent model. The overarching theme to emerge from this discussion has been the need for a multi-layered protection of interests in genetic information and material under the broader rubric of protection of the personality. This final chapter has added another layer in the form of a property paradigm. This is offered as a complement, not an alternative, to the consent and privacy models that are explored elsewhere in the book.[103] Ultimately, a uniform and formalistic framework on which to build the optimal approach to dealings in genetic information is required – one that takes account of the wide range of interests at stake and which shows due deference to the special role for privacy, even if this cannot always be achieved by legal means. As Schoeman has said, 'It is possible to act insensitively to the privacy interests of another even though one does not actually violate his privacy rights, and indeed even if he has no privacy rights. A person may be skeptical about recommending a legal right to privacy without having any doubts about the importance of privacy.'[104]

---

[103] See also R. Rao, 'Property, Privacy and the Human Body' (2000) 80 *Boston University Law Review* 359.

[104] F. D. Schoeman (ed.), *Philosophical Dimensions of Privacy: An Anthology* (Cambridge, Cambridge University Press, 1984), p. 4.

INDEX